THAT TIME I GOT REINCARNATED AS

SLIME

2

Author: FUSE

Artist: TAIKI KAWAKAMI

Character design: MITZ VAH

CONTENTS

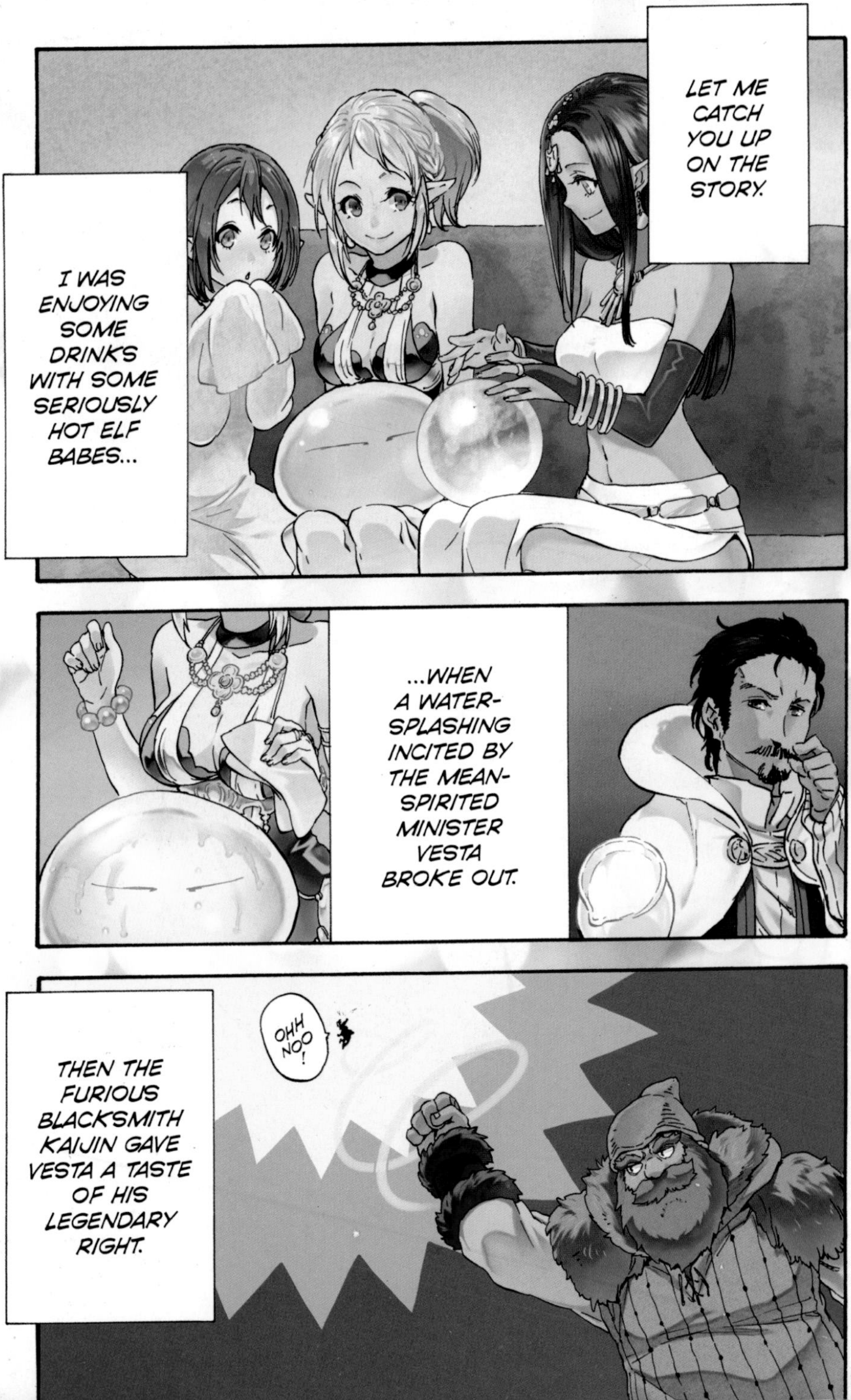
LET ME CATCH YOU UP ON THE STORY.
I WAS ENJOYING SOME DRINKS WITH SOME SERIOUSLY HOT ELF BABES...
...WHEN A WATER-SPLASHING INCITED BY THE MEAN-SPIRITED MINISTER VESTA BROKE OUT.
OHH NOO!
THEN THE FURIOUS BLACKSMITH KAIJIN GAVE VESTA A TASTE OF HIS LEGENDARY RIGHT.

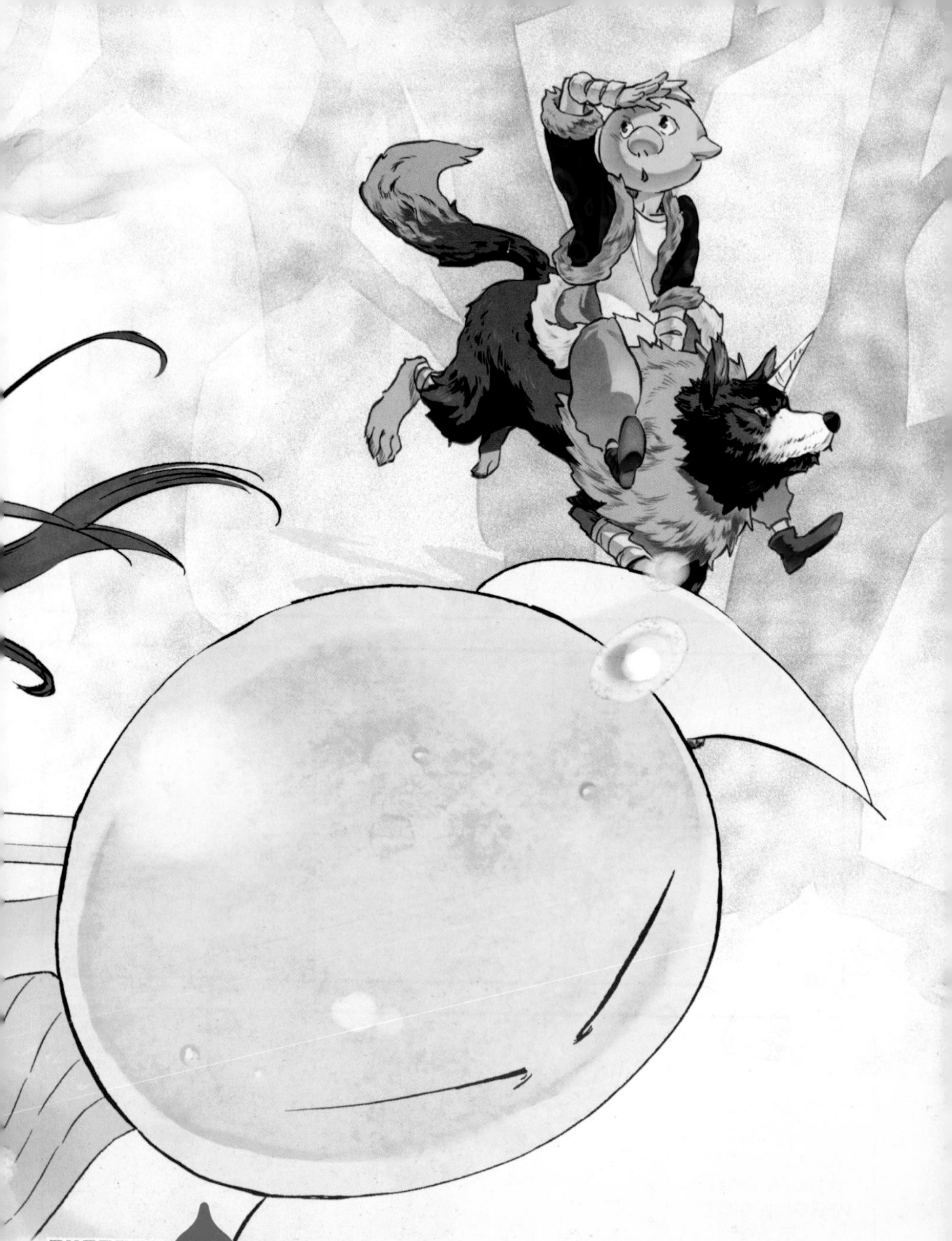

CHAPTER 7 The Hero-King's Judgment

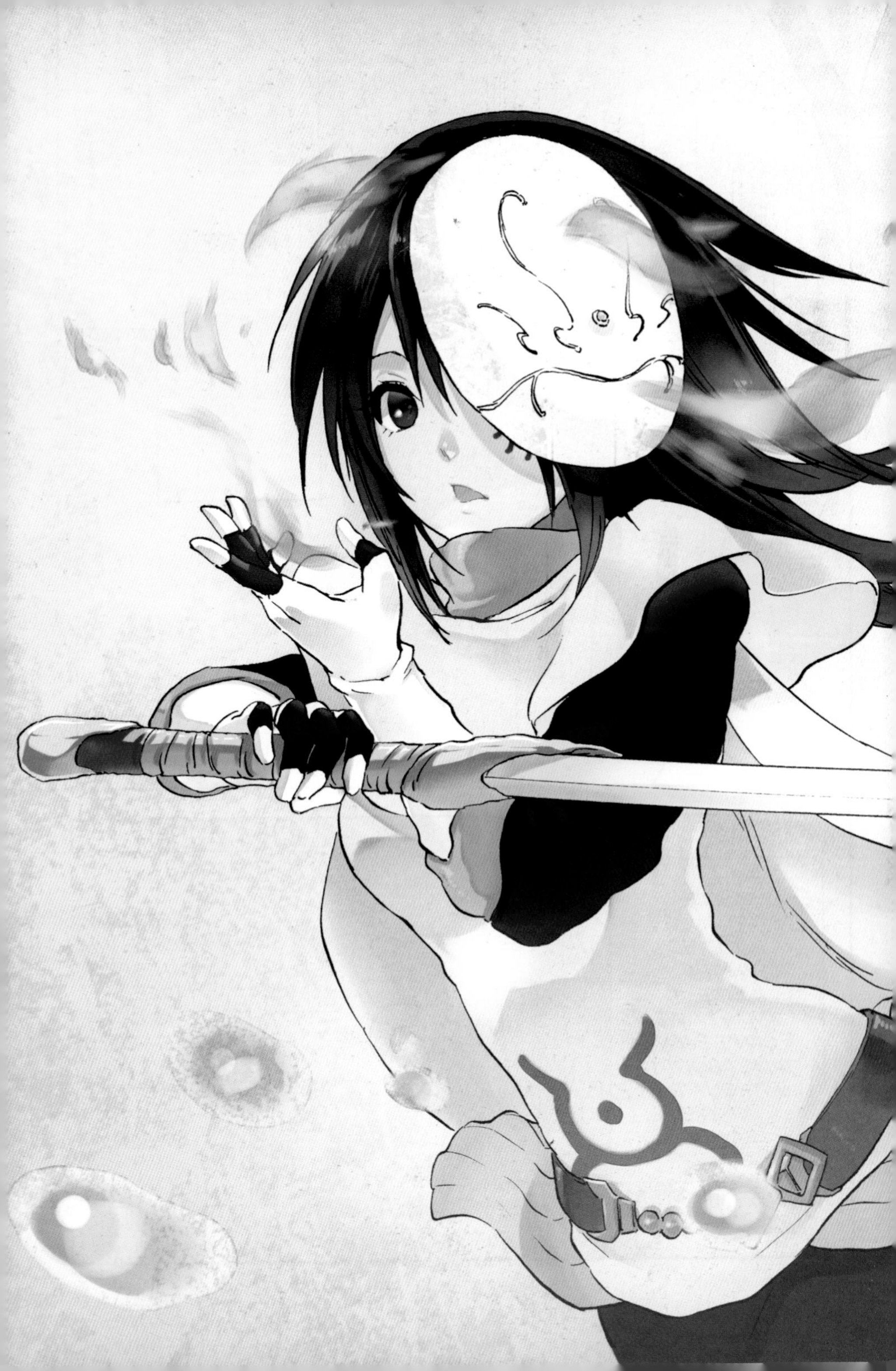

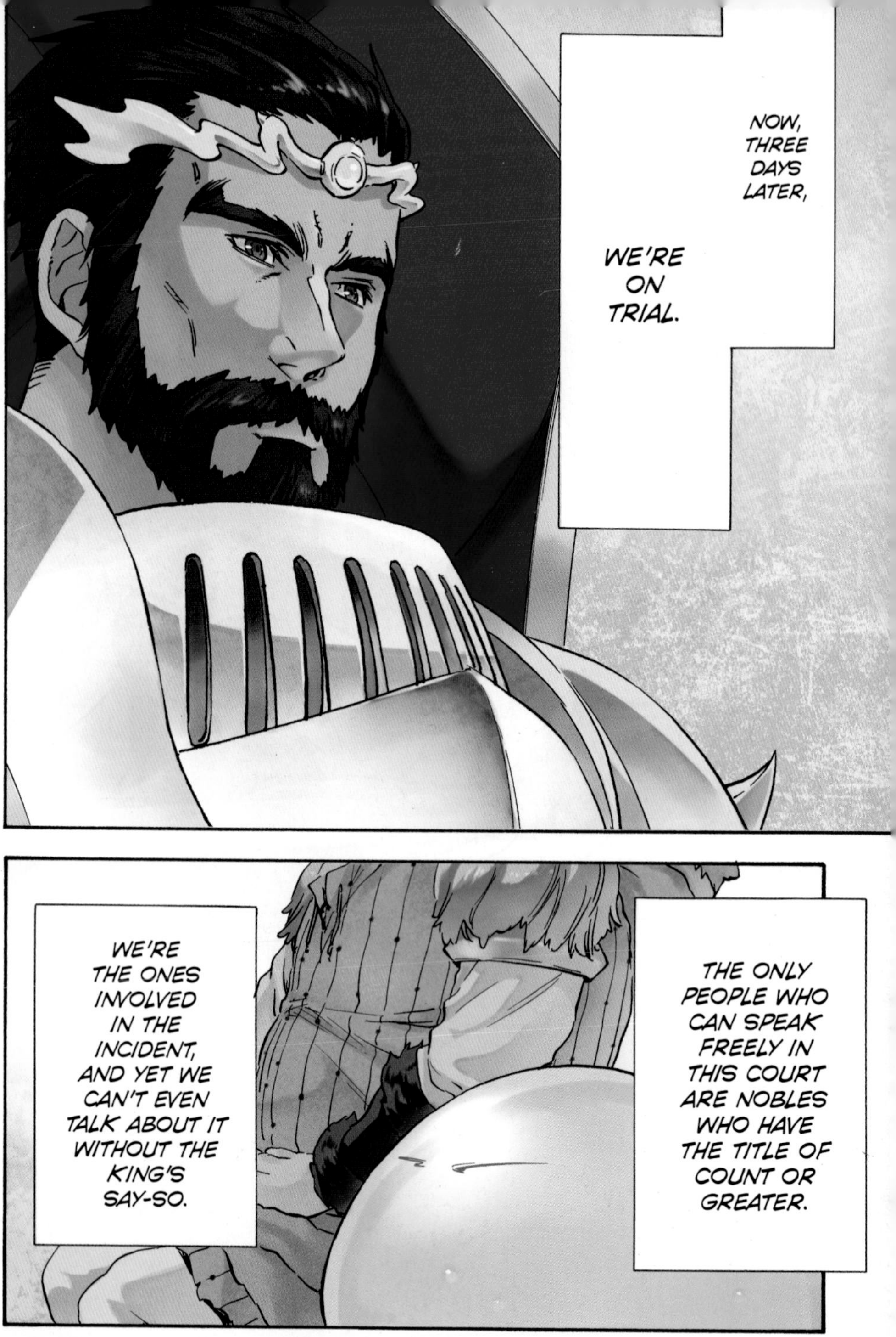
NOW, THREE DAYS LATER,
WE'RE ON TRIAL.
THE ONLY PEOPLE WHO CAN SPEAK FREELY IN THIS COURT ARE NOBLES WHO HAVE THE TITLE OF COUNT OR GREATER.
WE'RE THE ONES INVOLVED IN THE INCIDENT, AND YET WE CAN'T EVEN TALK ABOUT IT WITHOUT THE KING'S SAY-SO.

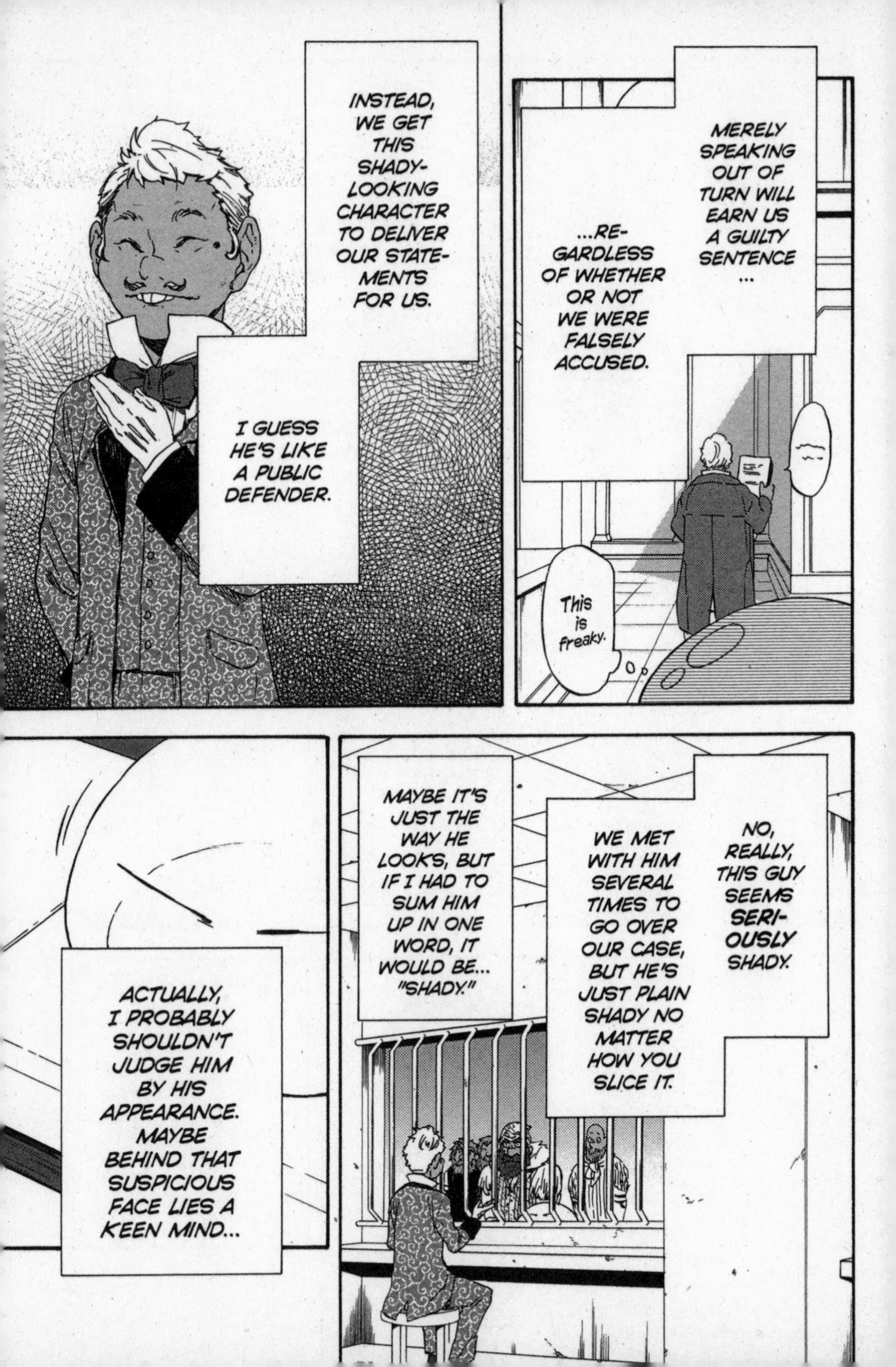
MERELY SPEAKING OUT OF TURN WILL EARN US A GUILTY SENTENCE ...
...REGARDLESS OF WHETHER OR NOT WE WERE FALSELY ACCUSED.
This is freaky.
INSTEAD, WE GET THIS SHADY-LOOKING CHARACTER TO DELIVER OUR STATEMENTS FOR US.
I GUESS HE'S LIKE A PUBLIC DEFENDER.
NO, REALLY, THIS GUY SEEMS SERIOUSLY SHADY.
WE MET WITH HIM SEVERAL TIMES TO GO OVER OUR CASE, BUT HE'S JUST PLAIN SHADY NO MATTER HOW YOU SLICE IT.
MAYBE IT'S JUST THE WAY HE LOOKS, BUT IF I HAD TO SUM HIM UP IN ONE WORD, IT WOULD BE... "SHADY."
ACTUALLY, I PROBABLY SHOULDN'T JUDGE HIM BY HIS APPEARANCE. MAYBE BEHIND THAT SUSPICIOUS FACE LIES A KEEN MIND...

...AND IT WAS AT THAT POINT THAT MINISTER VESTA, WHO WAS ENJOYING HIMSELF AND POSING NO TROUBLE TO ANYONE AT ALL...

...WAS SET UPON BY KAIJIN AND HIS COHORTS AND SUBJECTED TO MULTIPLE PHYSICAL INJURIES.

ARE YOU FREAKING KIDDING ME?!

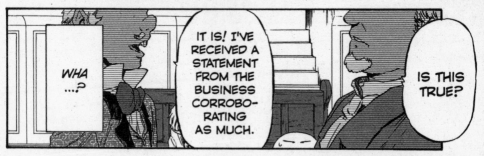

WHA ...?

IT IS! I'VE RECEIVED A STATEMENT FROM THE BUSINESS CORROBO-RATING AS MUCH.

IS THIS TRUE?

THAT CRAFTY GOON BOUGHT THEM OFF...

And you weren't hurt that bad!

peek

8

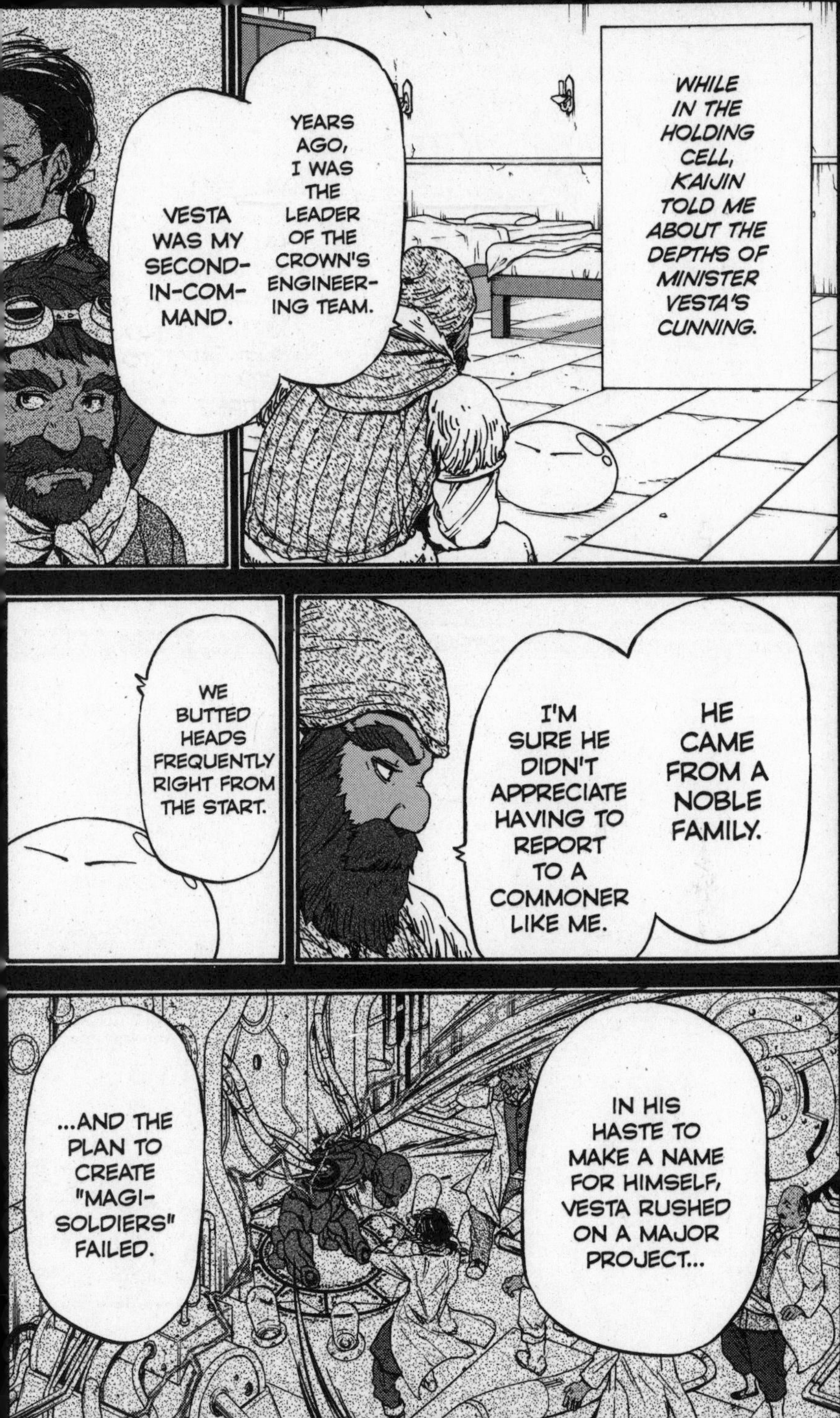
WHILE IN THE HOLDING CELL, KAIJIN TOLD ME ABOUT THE DEPTHS OF MINISTER VESTA'S CUNNING.
YEARS AGO, I WAS THE LEADER OF THE CROWN'S ENGINEER-ING TEAM.
VESTA WAS MY SECOND-IN-COM-MAND.
HE CAME FROM A NOBLE FAMILY.
I'M SURE HE DIDN'T APPRECIATE HAVING TO REPORT TO A COMMONER LIKE ME.
WE BUTTED HEADS FREQUENTLY RIGHT FROM THE START.
IN HIS HASTE TO MAKE A NAME FOR HIMSELF, VESTA RUSHED ON A MAJOR PROJECT...
...AND THE PLAN TO CREATE "MAGI-SOLDIERS" FAILED.

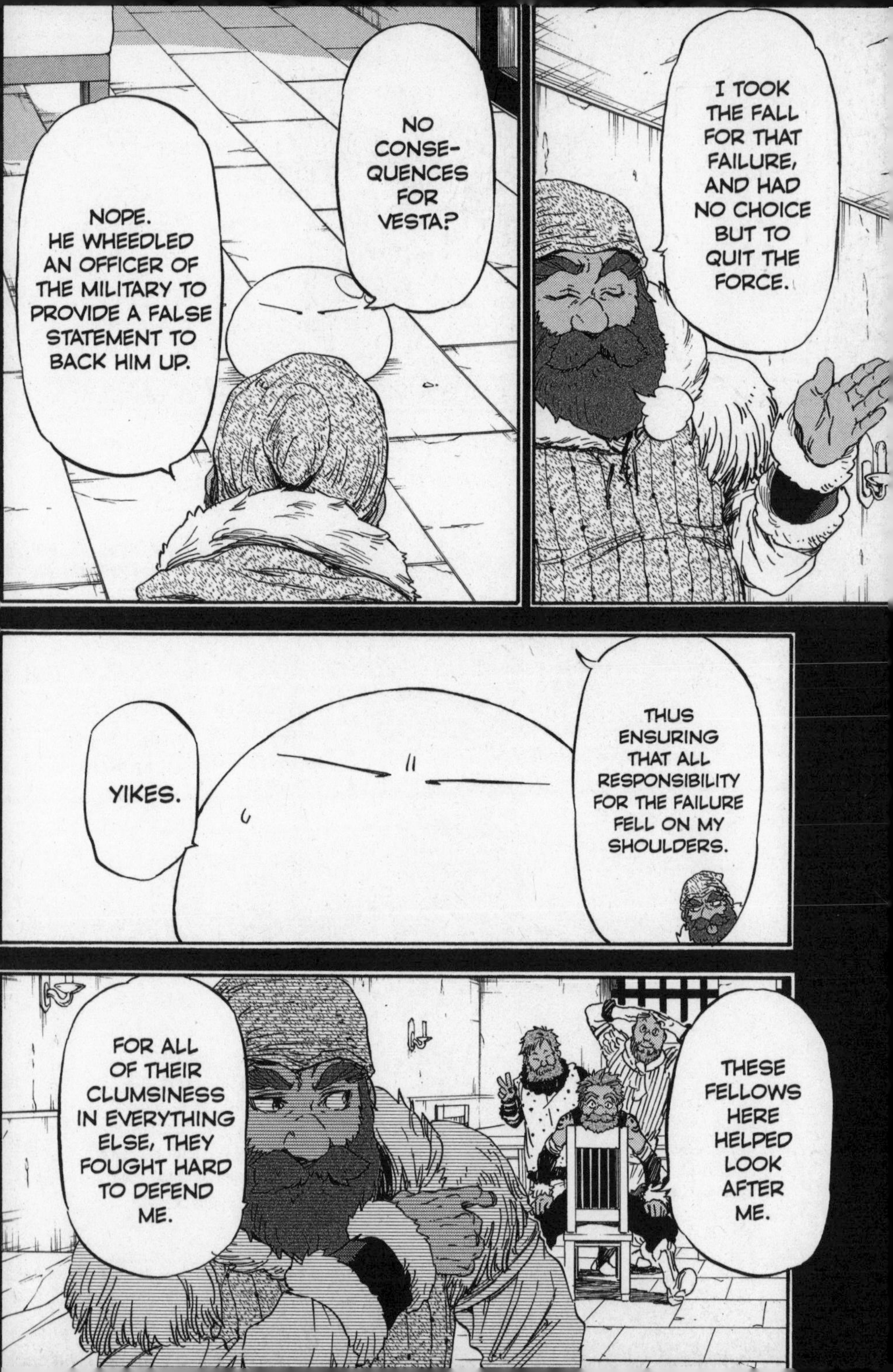
I TOOK THE FALL FOR THAT FAILURE, AND HAD NO CHOICE BUT TO QUIT THE FORCE.
NO CONSE-QUENCES FOR VESTA?
NOPE. HE WHEEDLED AN OFFICER OF THE MILITARY TO PROVIDE A FALSE STATEMENT TO BACK HIM UP.
THUS ENSURING THAT ALL RESPONSIBILITY FOR THE FAILURE FELL ON MY SHOULDERS.
YIKES.
THESE FELLOWS HERE HELPED LOOK AFTER ME.
FOR ALL OF THEIR CLUMSINESS IN EVERYTHING ELSE, THEY FOUGHT HARD TO DEFEND ME.

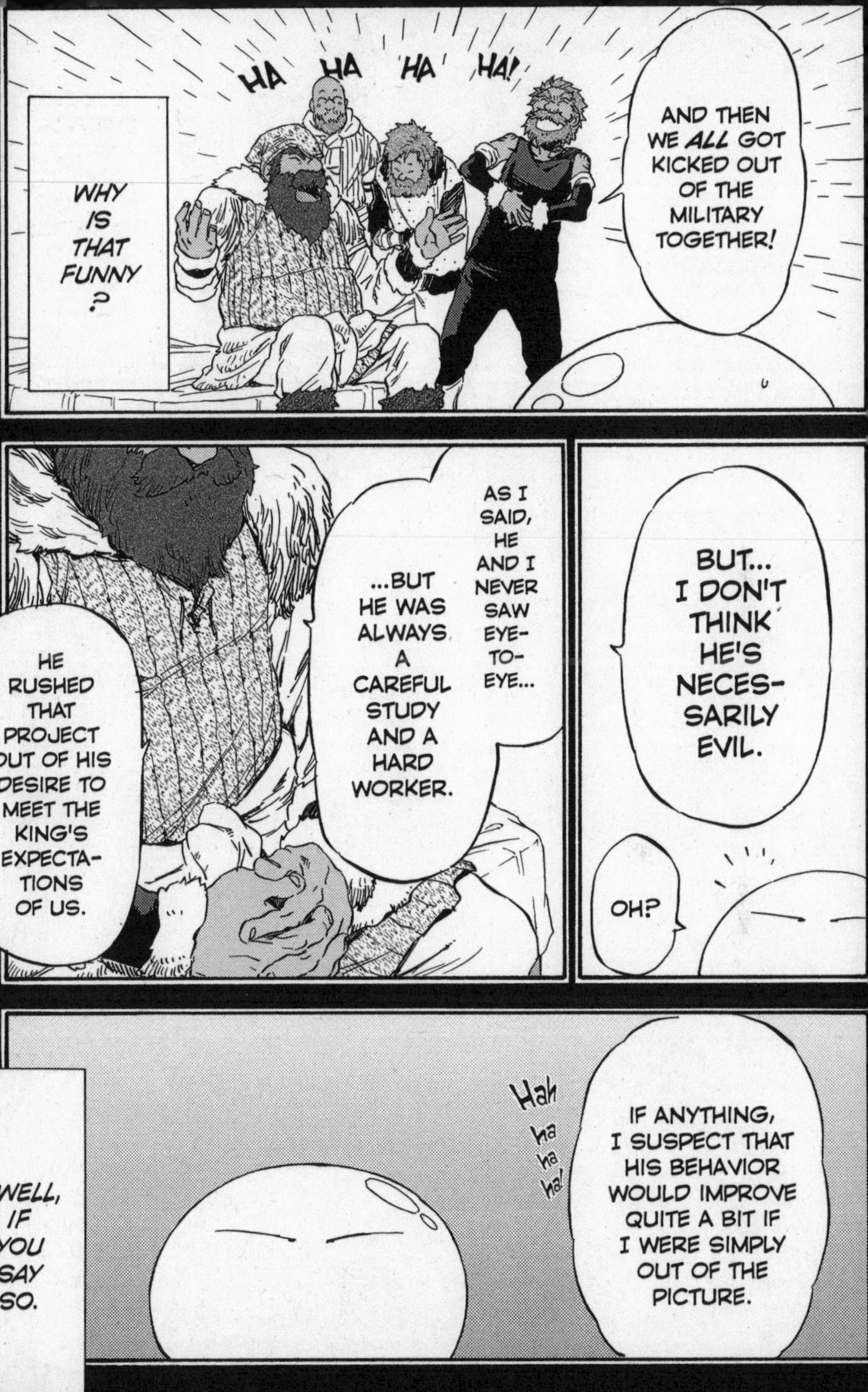
AND THEN WE ALL GOT KICKED OUT OF THE MILITARY TOGETHER!
HA HA HA HA!
WHY IS THAT FUNNY?
BUT... I DON'T THINK HE'S NECES-SARILY EVIL.
OH?
AS I SAID, HE AND I NEVER SAW EYE-TO-EYE...
...BUT HE WAS ALWAYS A CAREFUL STUDY AND A HARD WORKER.
HE RUSHED THAT PROJECT OUT OF HIS DESIRE TO MEET THE KING'S EXPECTA-TIONS OF US.
IF ANYTHING, I SUSPECT THAT HIS BEHAVIOR WOULD IMPROVE QUITE A BIT IF I WERE SIMPLY OUT OF THE PICTURE.
Hah ha ha ha!
...WELL, IF YOU SAY SO.

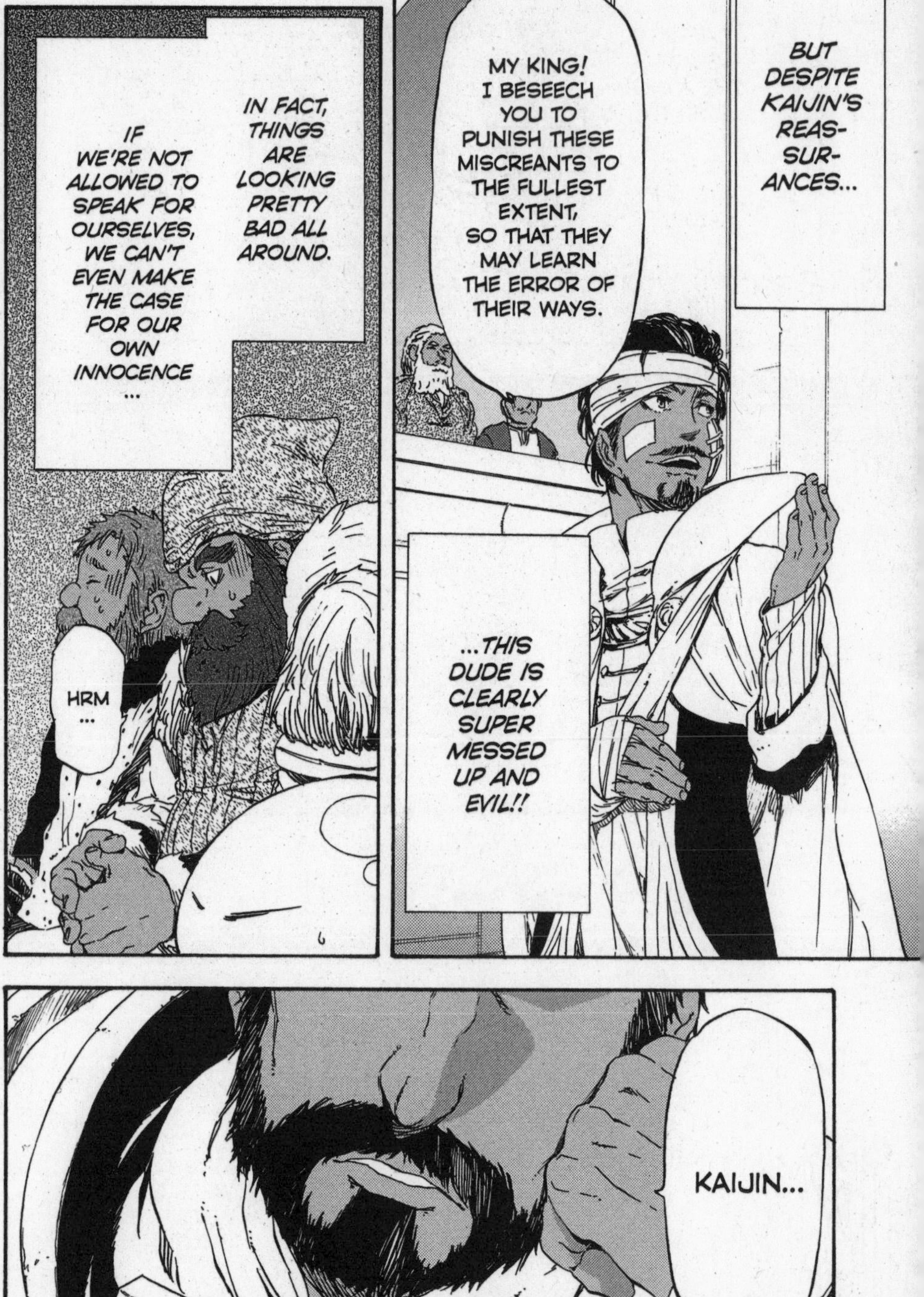
BUT DESPITE KAIJIN'S REAS-SUR-ANCES...
MY KING! I BESEECH YOU TO PUNISH THESE MISCREANTS TO THE FULLEST EXTENT, SO THAT THEY MAY LEARN THE ERROR OF THEIR WAYS.
...THIS DUDE IS CLEARLY SUPER MESSED UP AND EVIL!!
IN FACT, THINGS ARE LOOKING PRETTY BAD ALL AROUND.
IF WE'RE NOT ALLOWED TO SPEAK FOR OURSELVES, WE CAN'T EVEN MAKE THE CASE FOR OUR OWN INNOCENCE ...
HRM ...
KAIJIN...

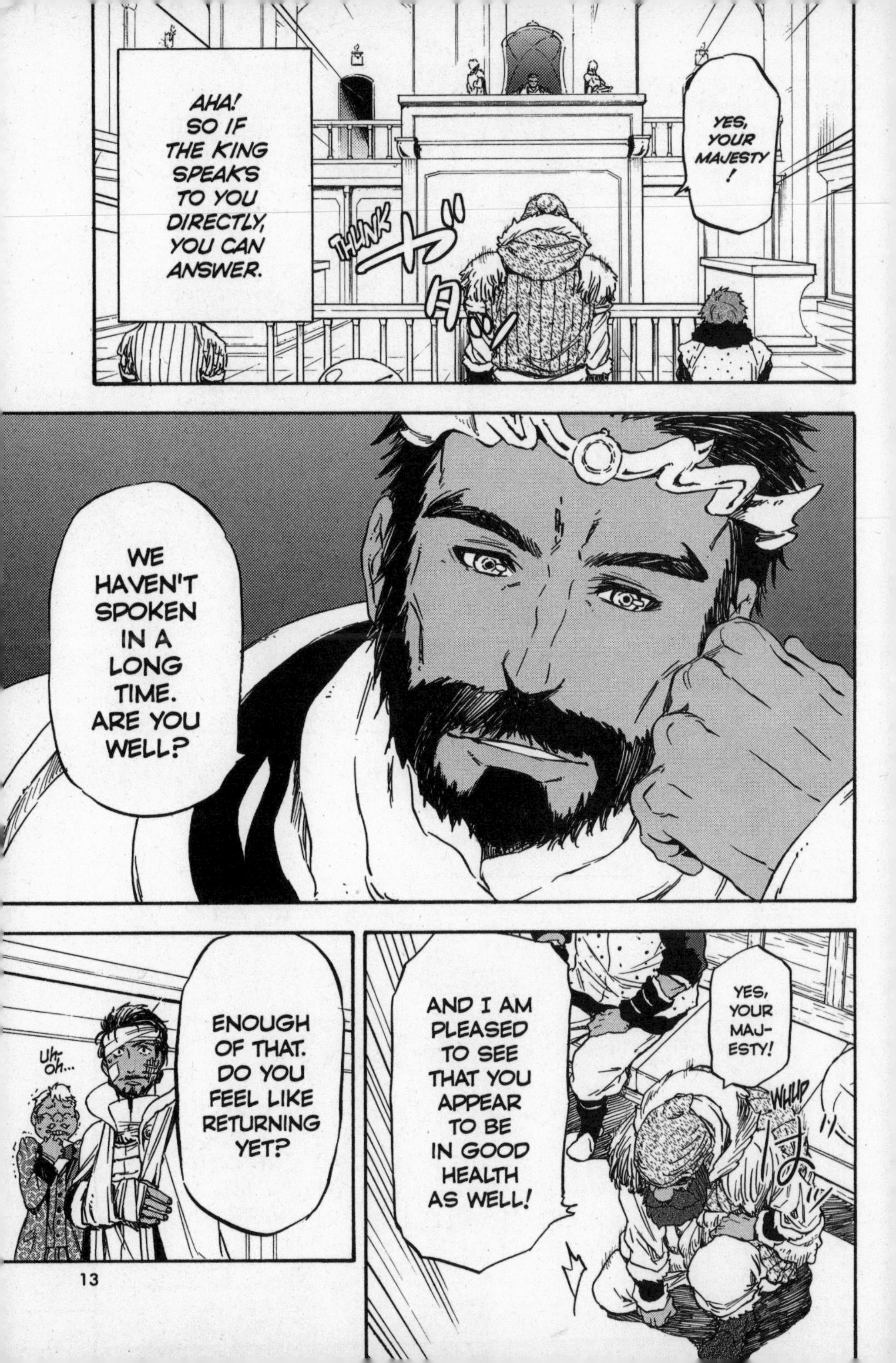
YES, YOUR MAJESTY!
THUNK
AHA! SO IF THE KING SPEAKS TO YOU DIRECTLY, YOU CAN ANSWER.
WE HAVEN'T SPOKEN IN A LONG TIME. ARE YOU WELL?
YES, YOUR MAJ-ESTY!
WHUP
AND I AM PLEASED TO SEE THAT YOU APPEAR TO BE IN GOOD HEALTH AS WELL!
ENOUGH OF THAT. DO YOU FEEL LIKE RETURNING YET?
Uh-oh...

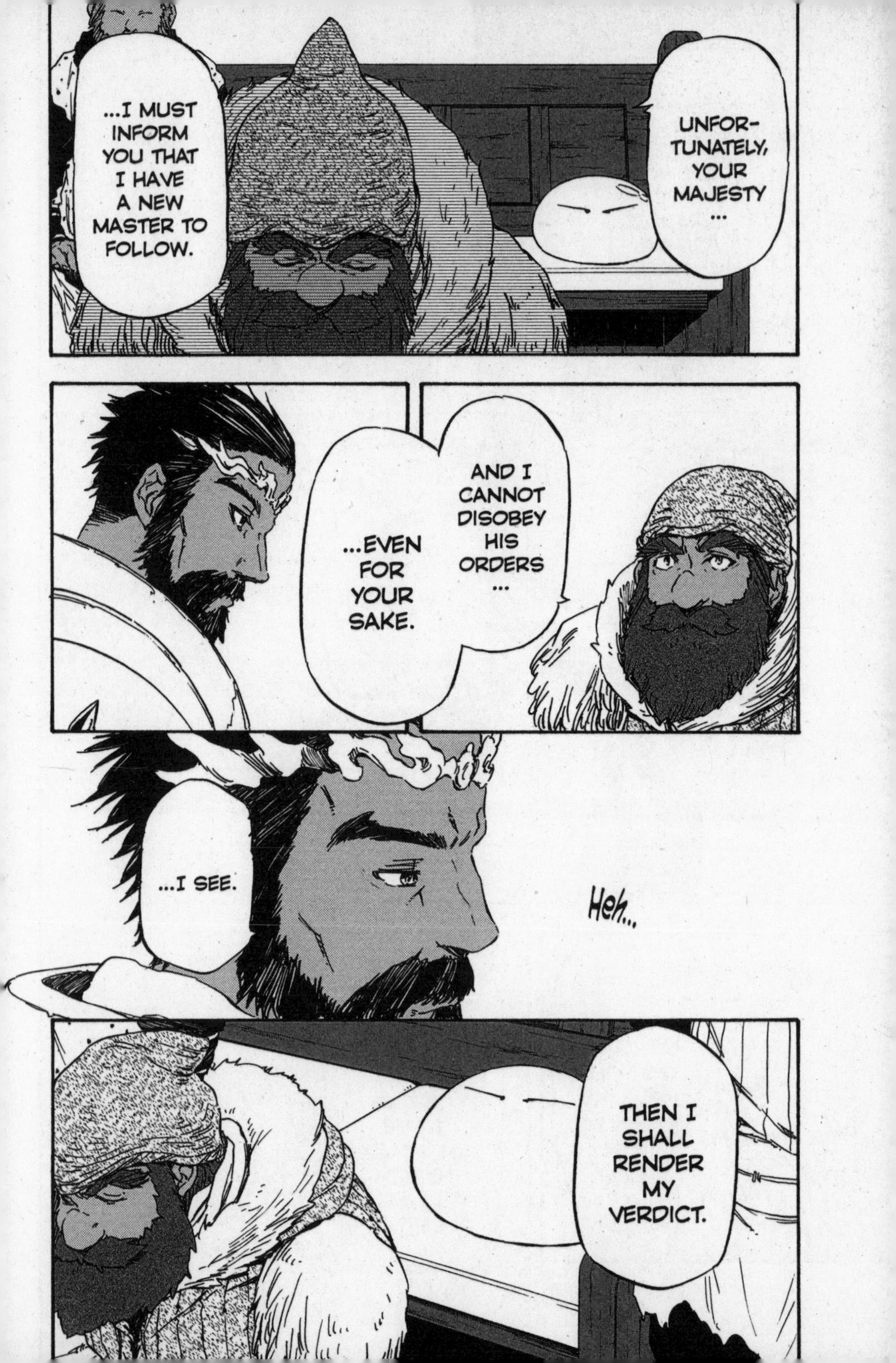
UNFORTUNATELY, YOUR MAJESTY...
...I MUST INFORM YOU THAT I HAVE A NEW MASTER TO FOLLOW.
AND I CANNOT DISOBEY HIS ORDERS...
...EVEN FOR YOUR SAKE.
Heh...
...I SEE.
THEN I SHALL RENDER MY VERDICT.

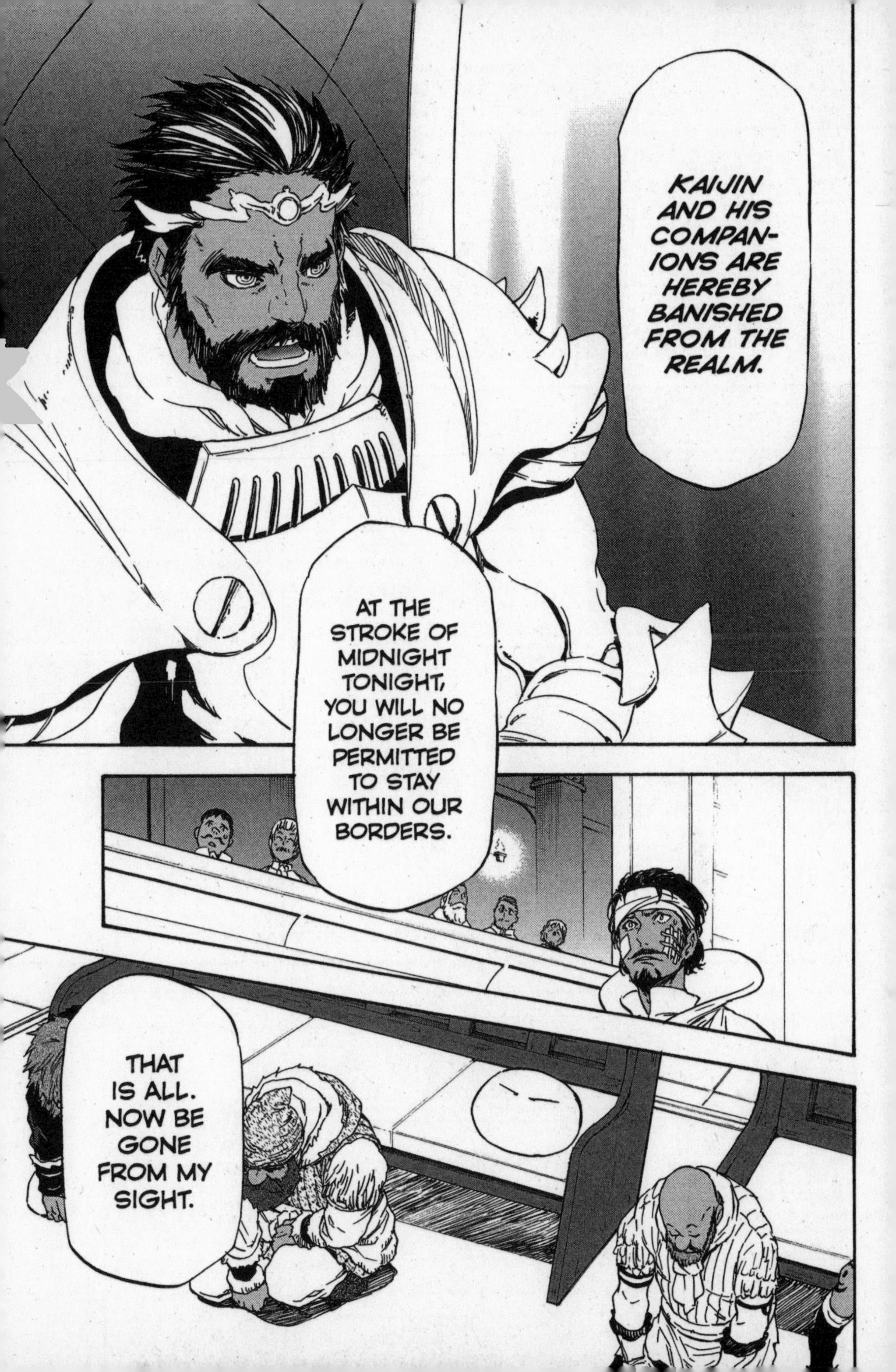
KAIJIN AND HIS COMPANIONS ARE HEREBY BANISHED FROM THE REALM.
AT THE STROKE OF MIDNIGHT TONIGHT, YOU WILL NO LONGER BE PERMITTED TO STAY WITHIN OUR BORDERS.
THAT IS ALL. NOW BE GONE FROM MY SIGHT.

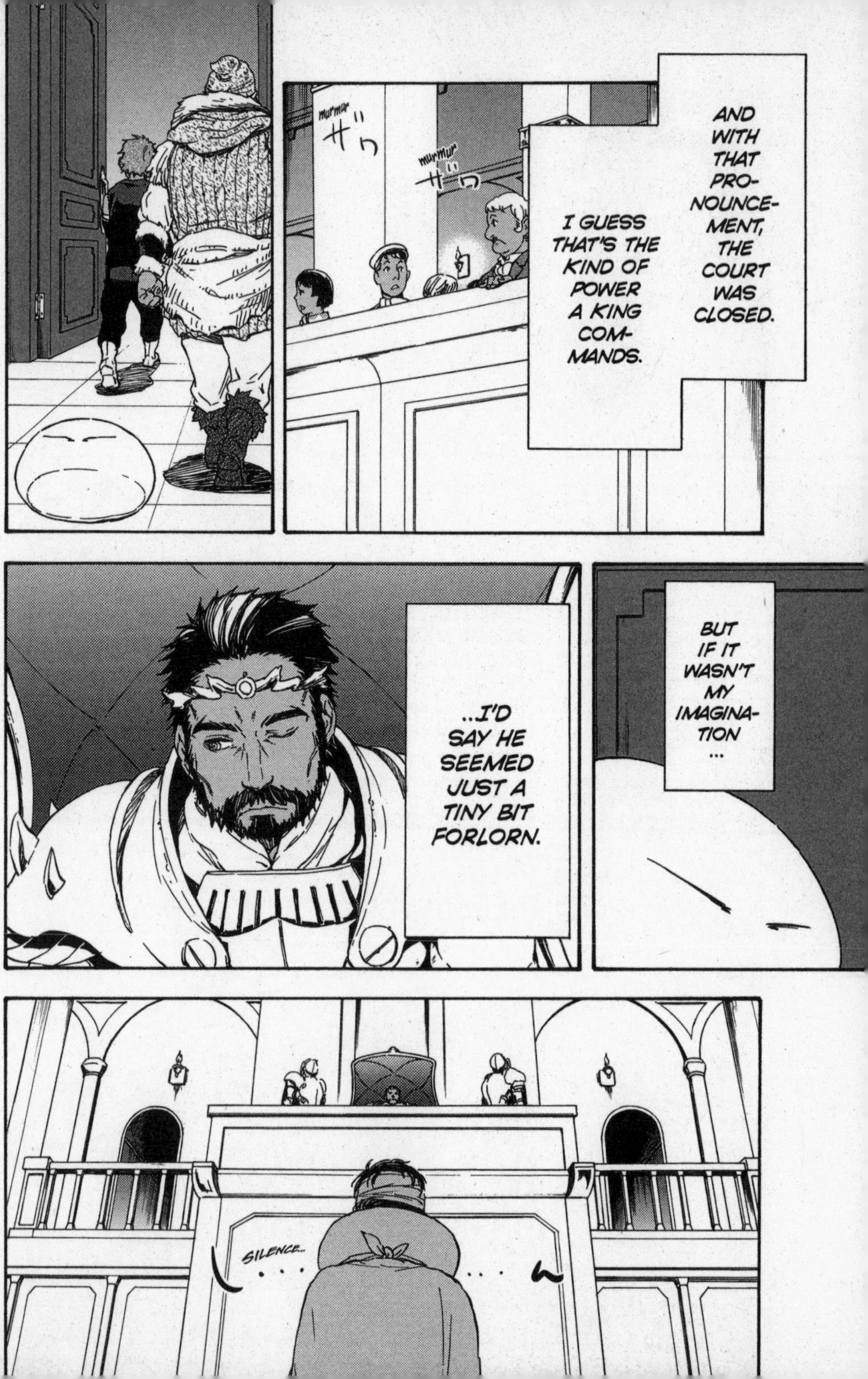
AND WITH THAT PRONOUNCEMENT, THE COURT WAS CLOSED.
I GUESS THAT'S THE KIND OF POWER A KING COMMANDS.
murmur
murmur
BUT IF IT WASN'T MY IMAGINATION...
...I'D SAY HE SEEMED JUST A TINY BIT FORLORN.
SILENCE...

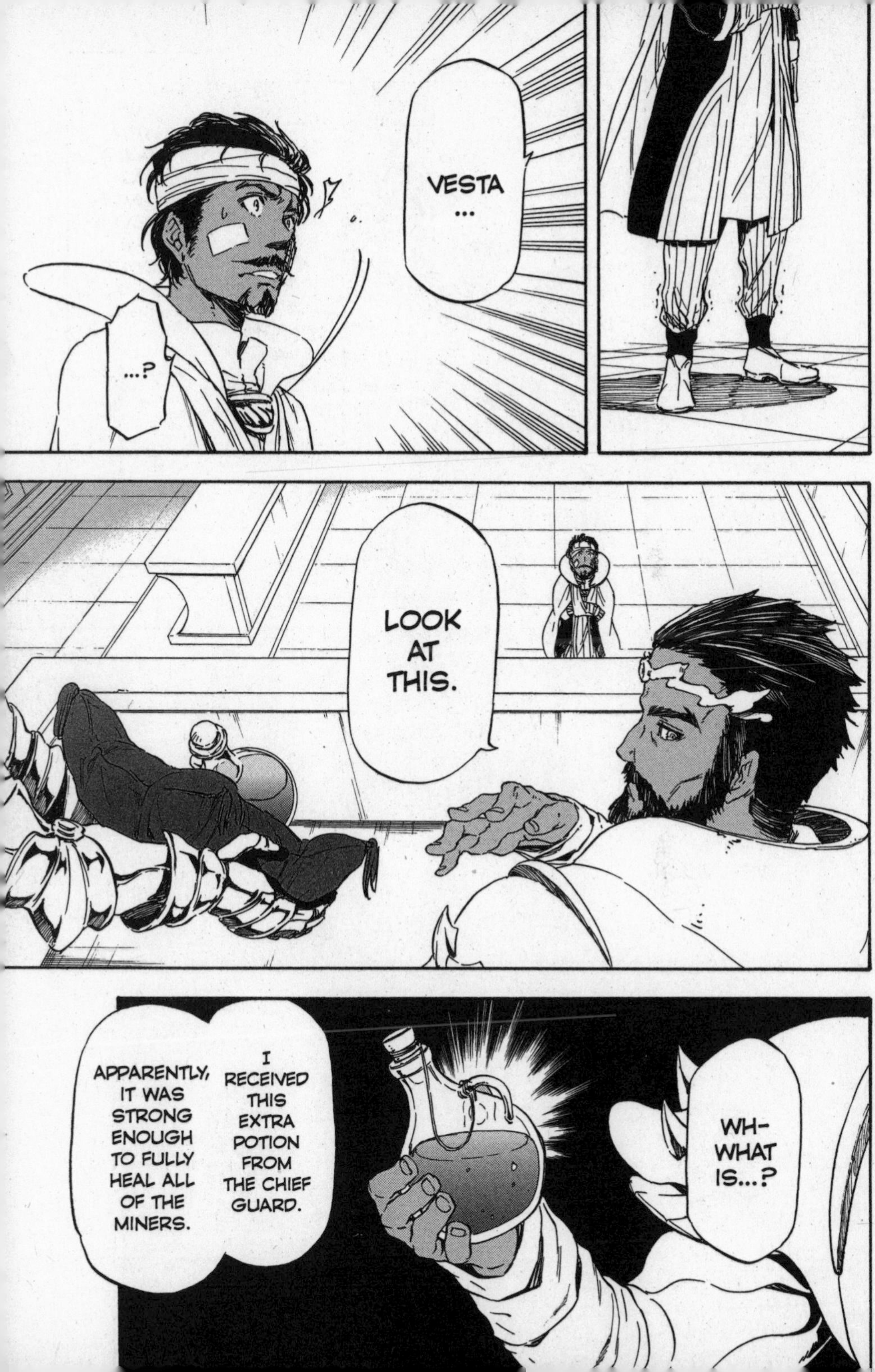
VESTA ...
...?
LOOK AT THIS.
WH-WHAT IS...?
I RECEIVED THIS EXTRA POTION FROM THE CHIEF GUARD.
APPARENTLY, IT WAS STRONG ENOUGH TO FULLY HEAL ALL OF THE MINERS.

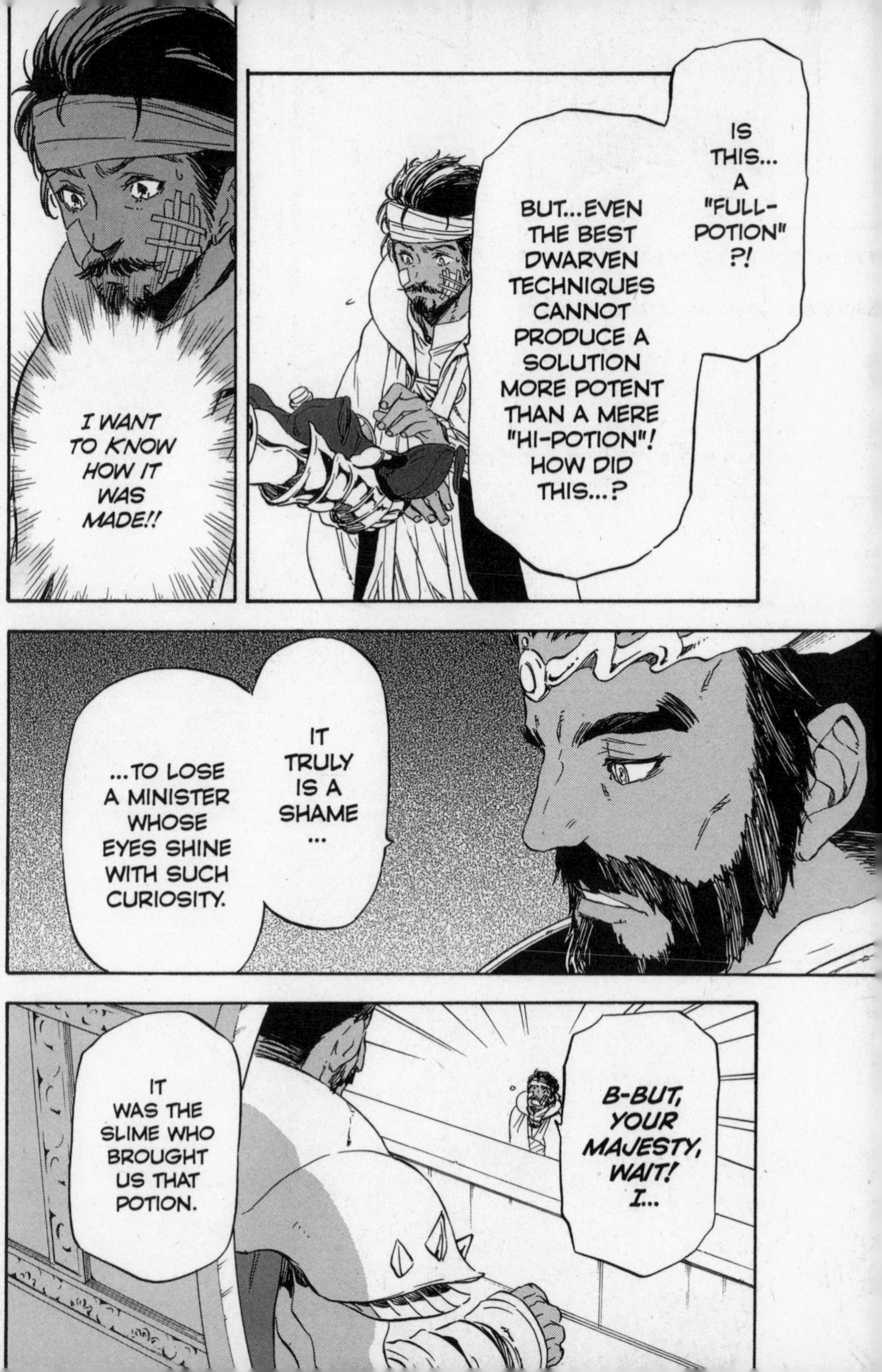
IS THIS... A "FULL-POTION"?!
BUT...EVEN THE BEST DWARVEN TECHNIQUES CANNOT PRODUCE A SOLUTION MORE POTENT THAN A MERE "HI-POTION"! HOW DID THIS...?
I WANT TO KNOW HOW IT WAS MADE!!
IT TRULY IS A SHAME...
...TO LOSE A MINISTER WHOSE EYES SHINE WITH SUCH CURIOSITY.
B-BUT, YOUR MAJESTY, WAIT! I...
IT WAS THE SLIME WHO BROUGHT US THAT POTION.

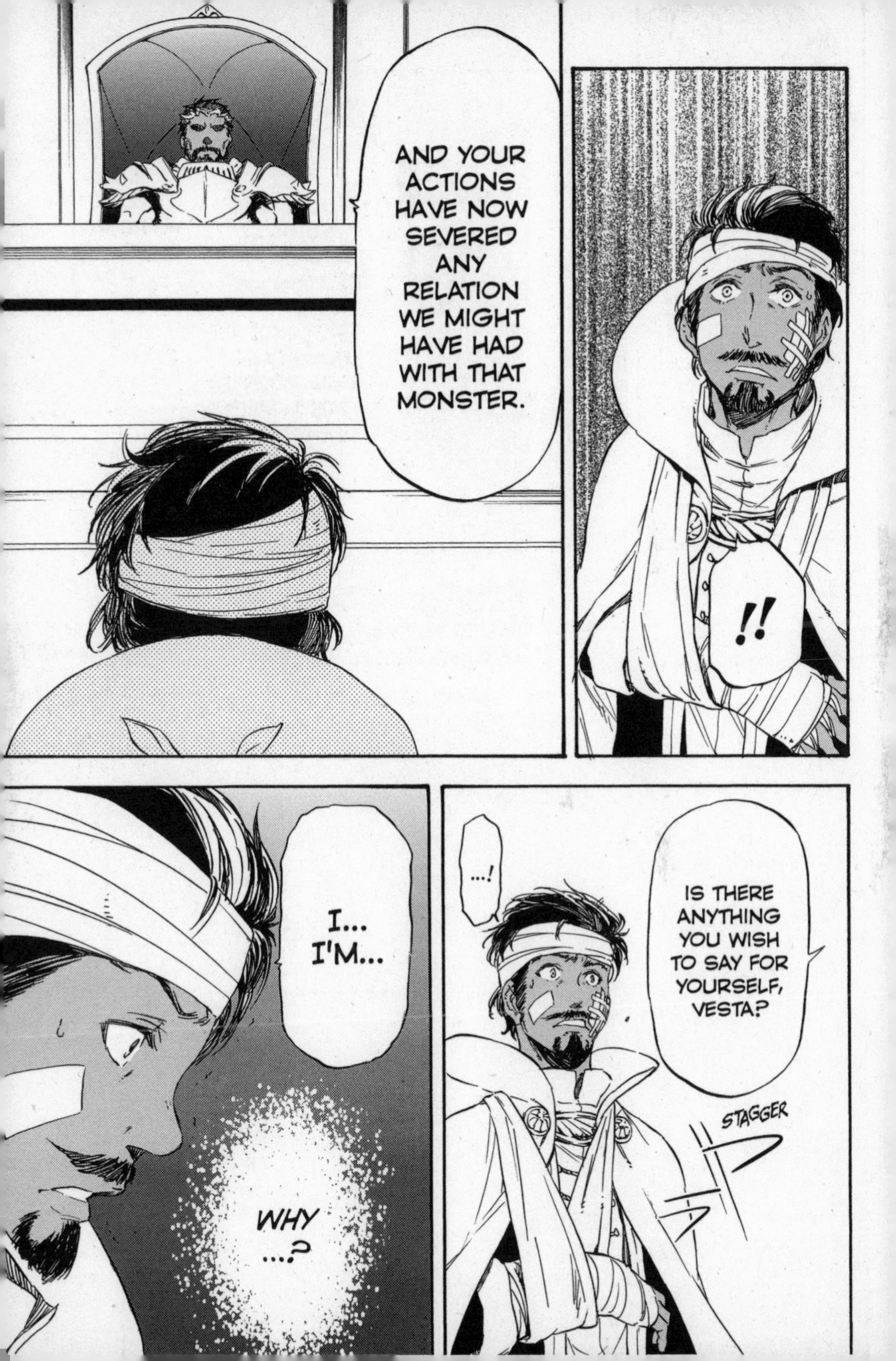
AND YOUR ACTIONS HAVE NOW SEVERED ANY RELATION WE MIGHT HAVE HAD WITH THAT MONSTER.
!!
IS THERE ANYTHING YOU WISH TO SAY FOR YOURSELF, VESTA?
...!
STAGGER
I... I'M...
WHY ...?

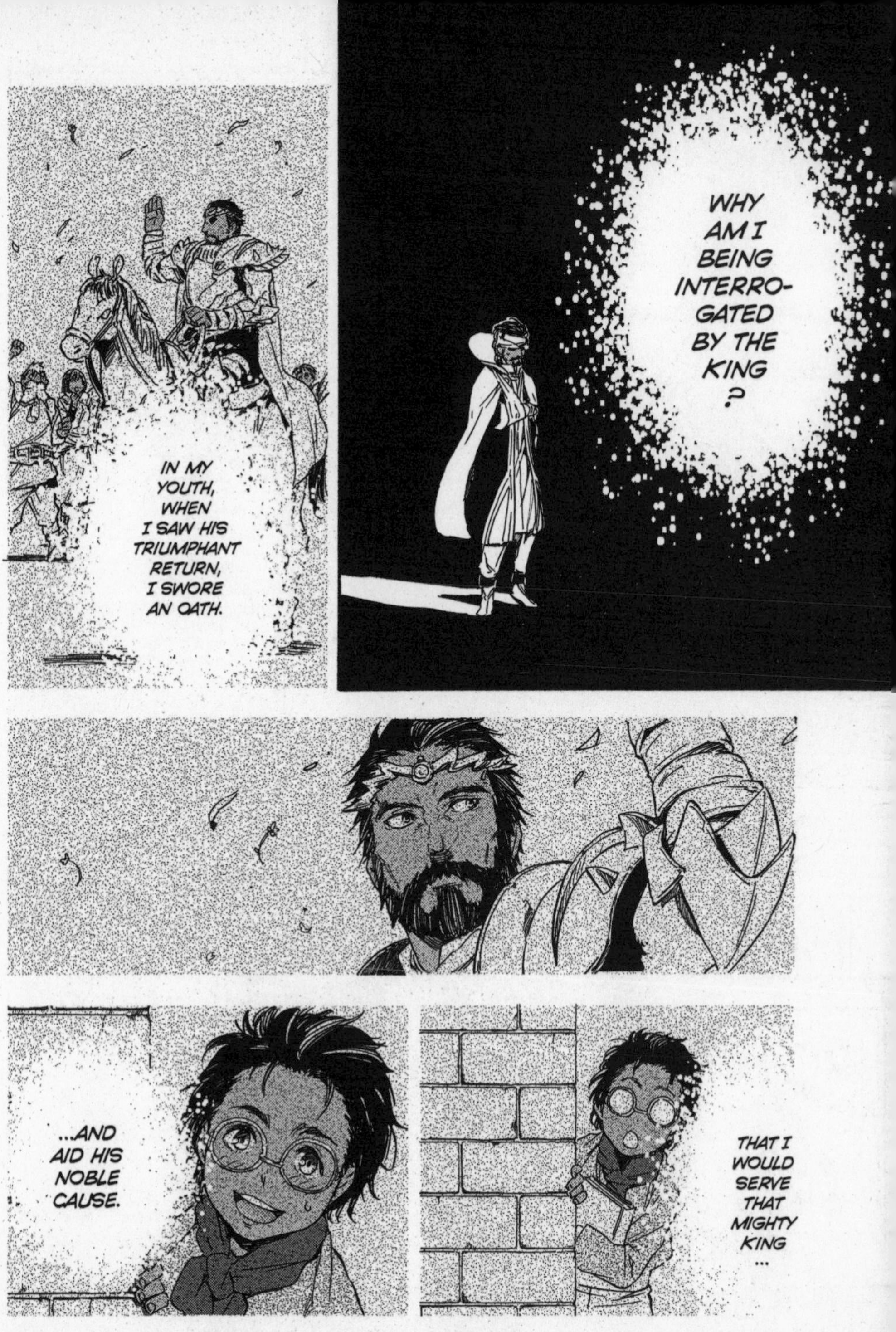
WHY AM I BEING INTERRO-GATED BY THE KING ?
IN MY YOUTH, WHEN I SAW HIS TRIUMPHANT RETURN, I SWORE AN OATH.
THAT I WOULD SERVE THAT MIGHTY KING ...
...AND AID HIS NOBLE CAUSE.

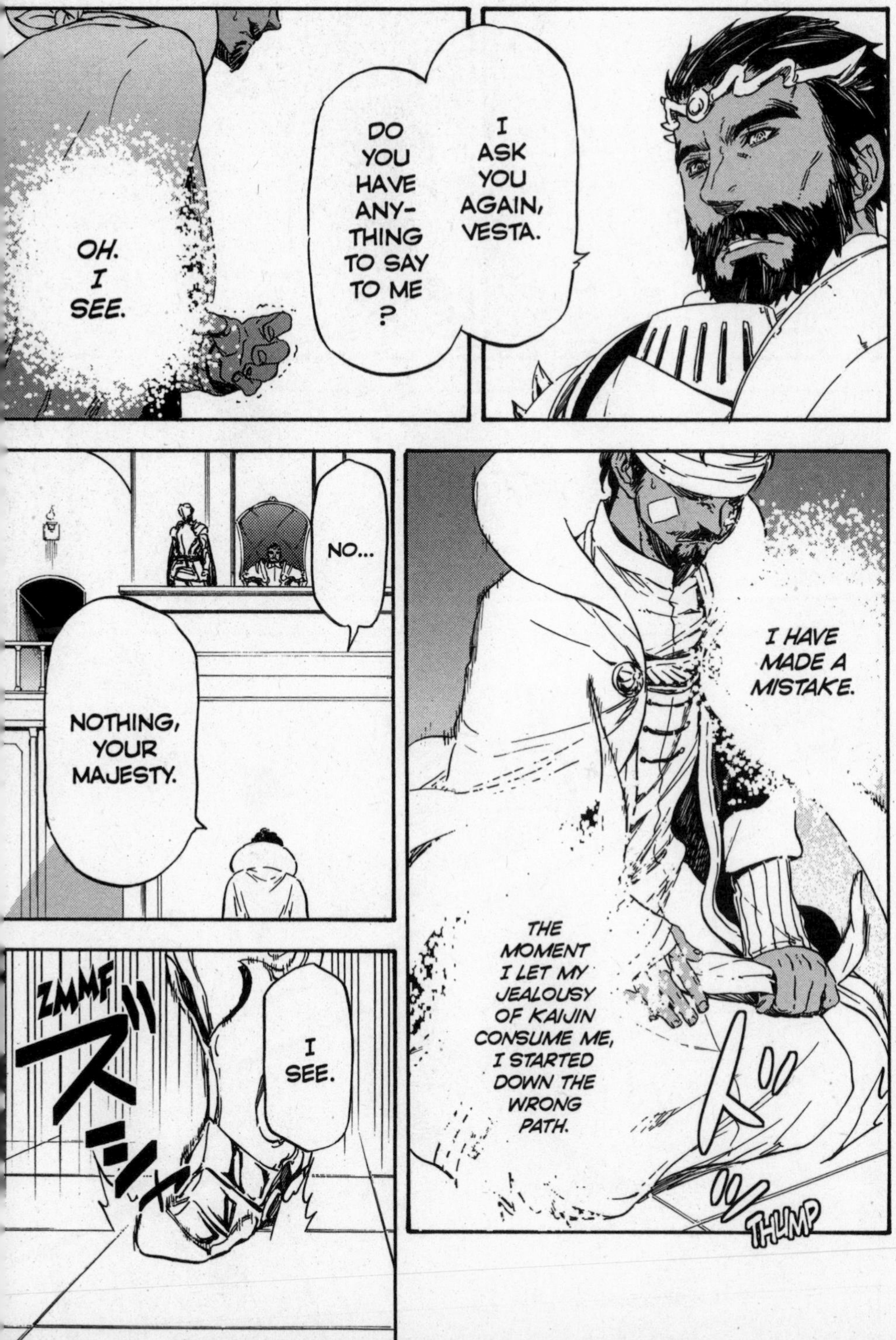

I ASK YOU AGAIN, VESTA.
DO YOU HAVE ANYTHING TO SAY TO ME?
OH. I SEE.
I HAVE MADE A MISTAKE.
THE MOMENT I LET MY JEALOUSY OF KAIJIN CONSUME ME, I STARTED DOWN THE WRONG PATH.
THUMP
NO...
NOTHING, YOUR MAJESTY.
ZMMF
I SEE.

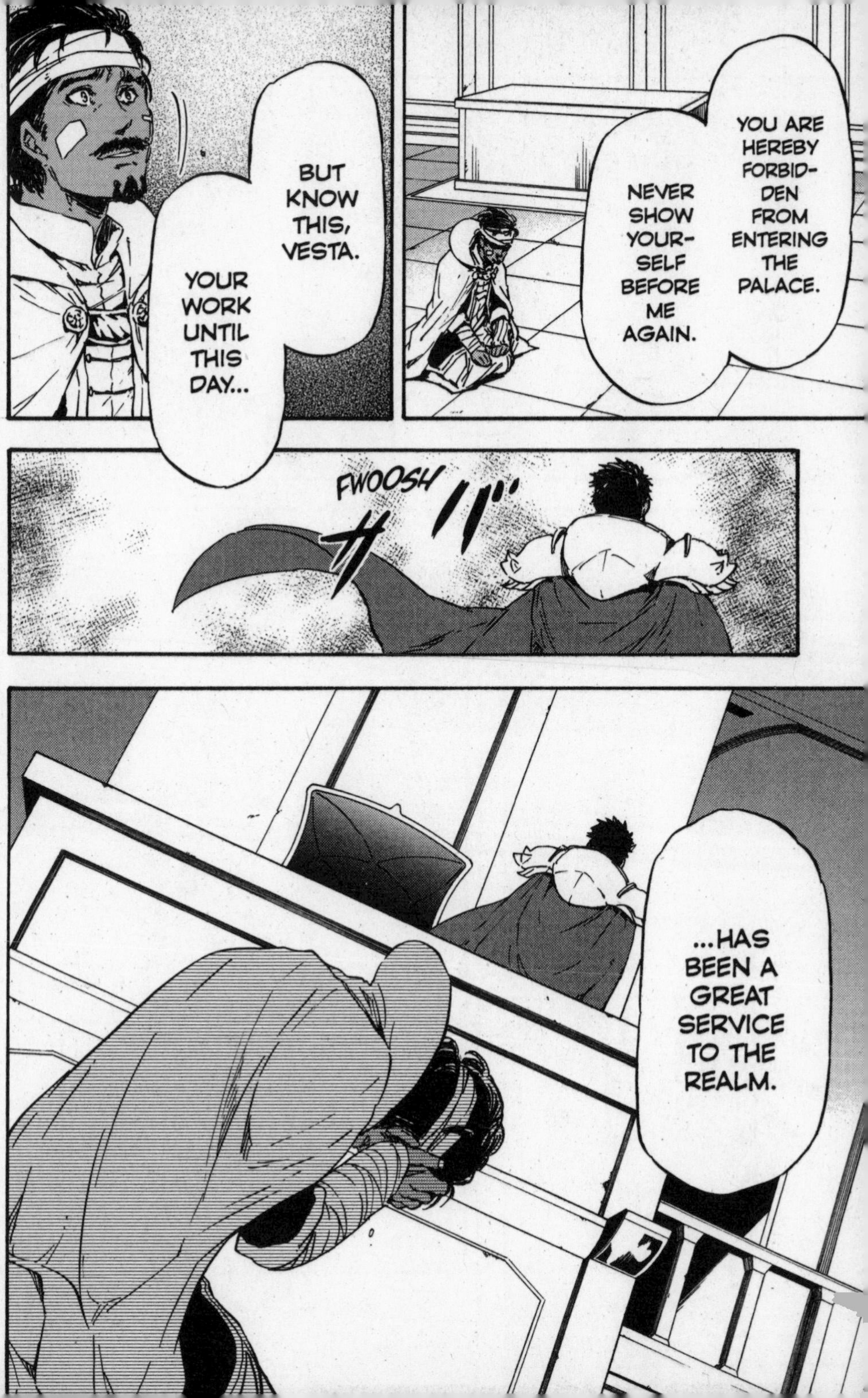
YOU ARE HEREBY FORBIDDEN FROM ENTERING THE PALACE.
NEVER SHOW YOURSELF BEFORE ME AGAIN.
BUT KNOW THIS, VESTA.
YOUR WORK UNTIL THIS DAY...
FWOOSH
...HAS BEEN A GREAT SERVICE TO THE REALM.

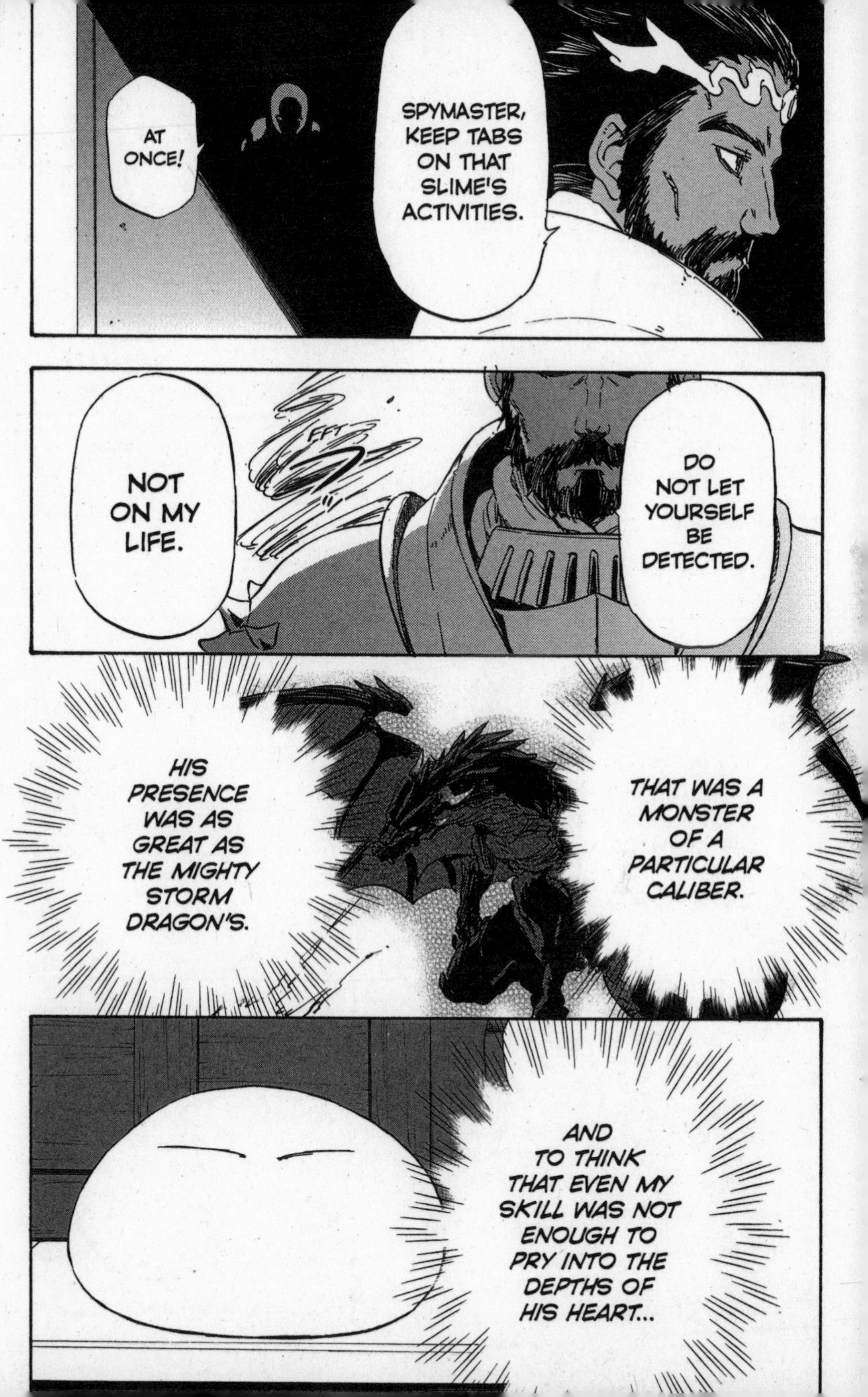
SPYMASTER, KEEP TABS ON THAT SLIME'S ACTIVITIES.
AT ONCE!
DO NOT LET YOURSELF BE DETECTED.
FFT
NOT ON MY LIFE.
THAT WAS A MONSTER OF A PARTICULAR CALIBER.
HIS PRESENCE WAS AS GREAT AS THE MIGHTY STORM DRAGON'S.
AND TO THINK THAT EVEN MY SKILL WAS NOT ENOUGH TO PRY INTO THE DEPTHS OF HIS HEART...

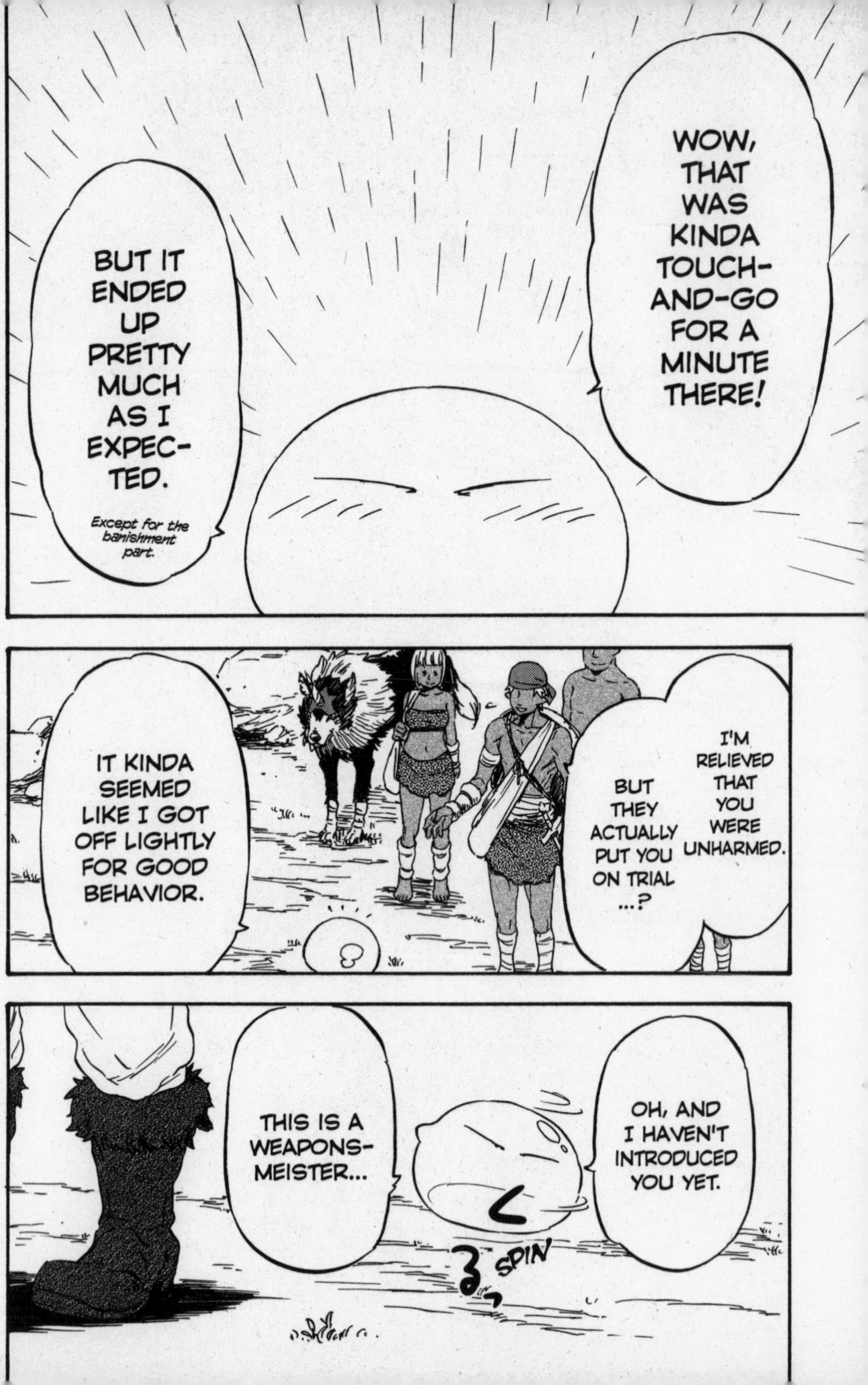
WOW, THAT WAS KINDA TOUCH-AND-GO FOR A MINUTE THERE!
BUT IT ENDED UP PRETTY MUCH AS I EXPECTED.
Except for the banishment part.
I'M RELIEVED THAT YOU WERE UNHARMED.
BUT THEY ACTUALLY PUT YOU ON TRIAL ...?
IT KINDA SEEMED LIKE I GOT OFF LIGHTLY FOR GOOD BEHAVIOR.
OH, AND I HAVEN'T INTRODUCED YOU YET.
SPIN
THIS IS A WEAPONS-MEISTER...

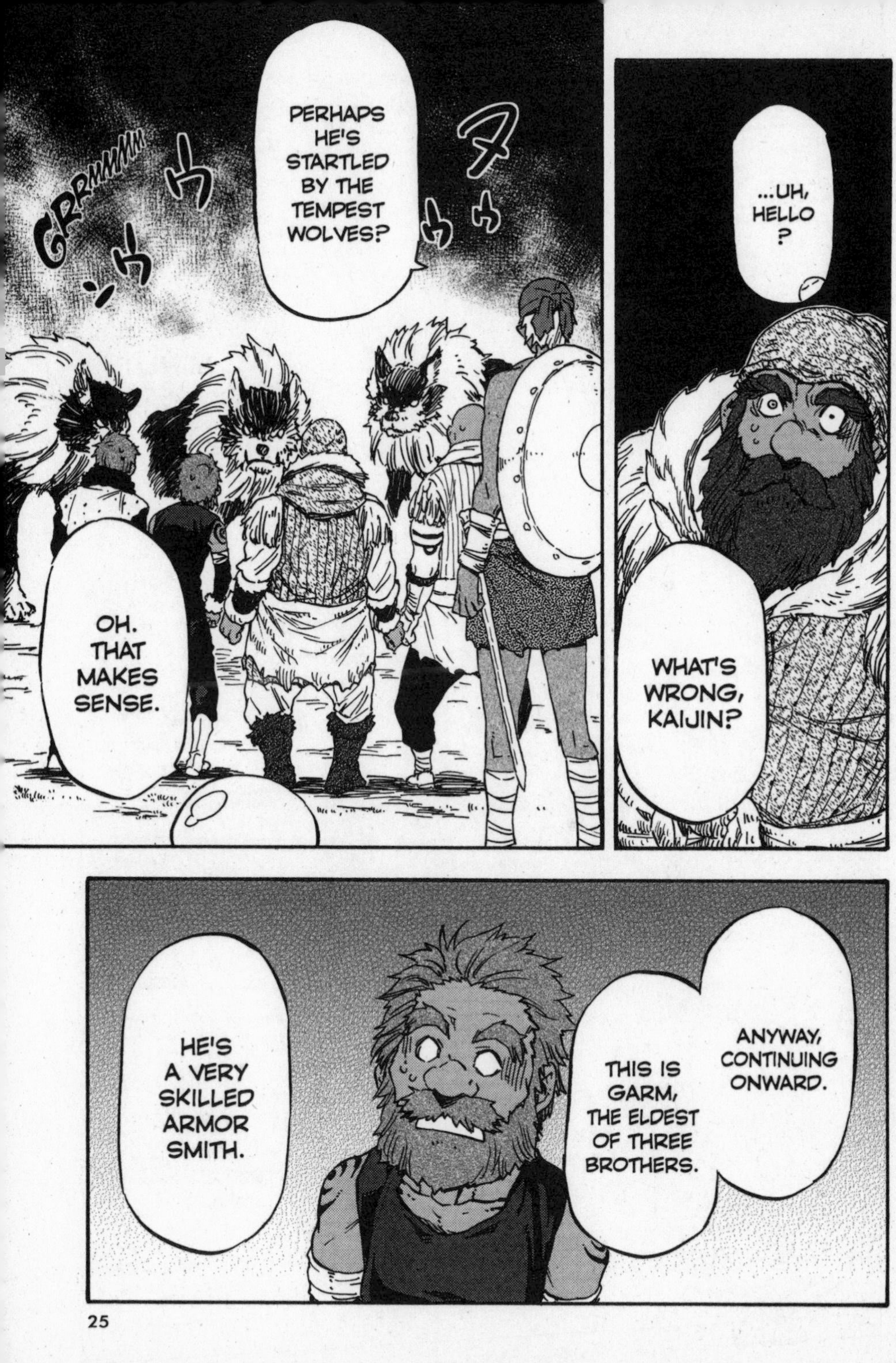
...UH, HELLO?
WHAT'S WRONG, KAIJIN?
PERHAPS HE'S STARTLED BY THE TEMPEST WOLVES?
OH. THAT MAKES SENSE.
ANYWAY, CONTINUING ONWARD.
THIS IS GARM, THE ELDEST OF THREE BROTHERS.
HE'S A VERY SKILLED ARMOR SMITH.

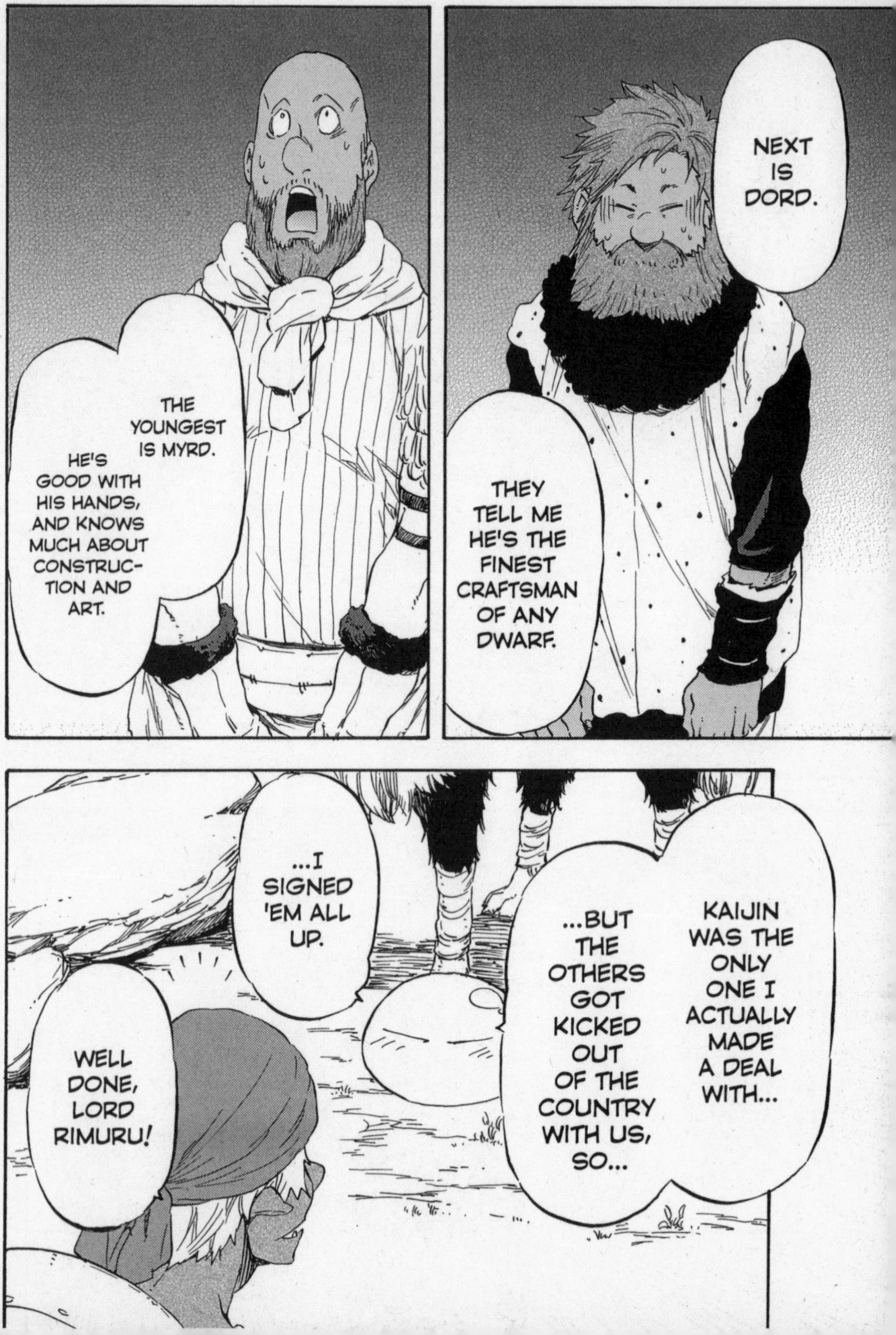
NEXT IS DORD.
THEY TELL ME HE'S THE FINEST CRAFTSMAN OF ANY DWARF.
THE YOUNGEST IS MYRD.
HE'S GOOD WITH HIS HANDS, AND KNOWS MUCH ABOUT CONSTRUCTION AND ART.
KAIJIN WAS THE ONLY ONE I ACTUALLY MADE A DEAL WITH...
...BUT THE OTHERS GOT KICKED OUT OF THE COUNTRY WITH US, SO...
...I SIGNED 'EM ALL UP.
WELL DONE, LORD RIMURU!

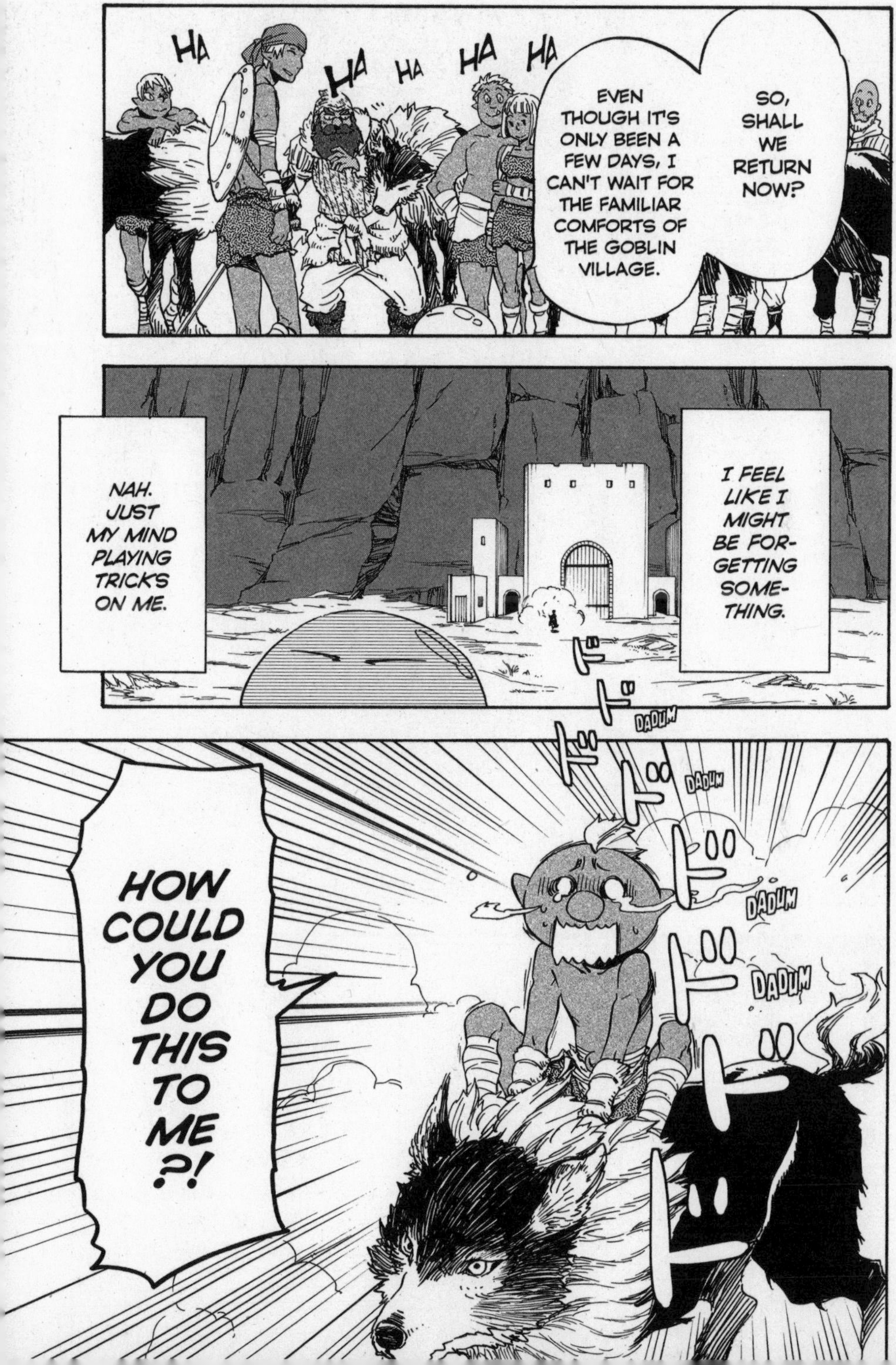
SO, SHALL WE RETURN NOW?
EVEN THOUGH IT'S ONLY BEEN A FEW DAYS, I CAN'T WAIT FOR THE FAMILIAR COMFORTS OF THE GOBLIN VILLAGE.
HA
HA
HA
HA
HA
I FEEL LIKE I MIGHT BE FOR-GETTING SOME-THING.
NAH. JUST MY MIND PLAYING TRICKS ON ME.
DADUM
DADUM
DADUM
DADUM
HOW COULD YOU DO THIS TO ME?!

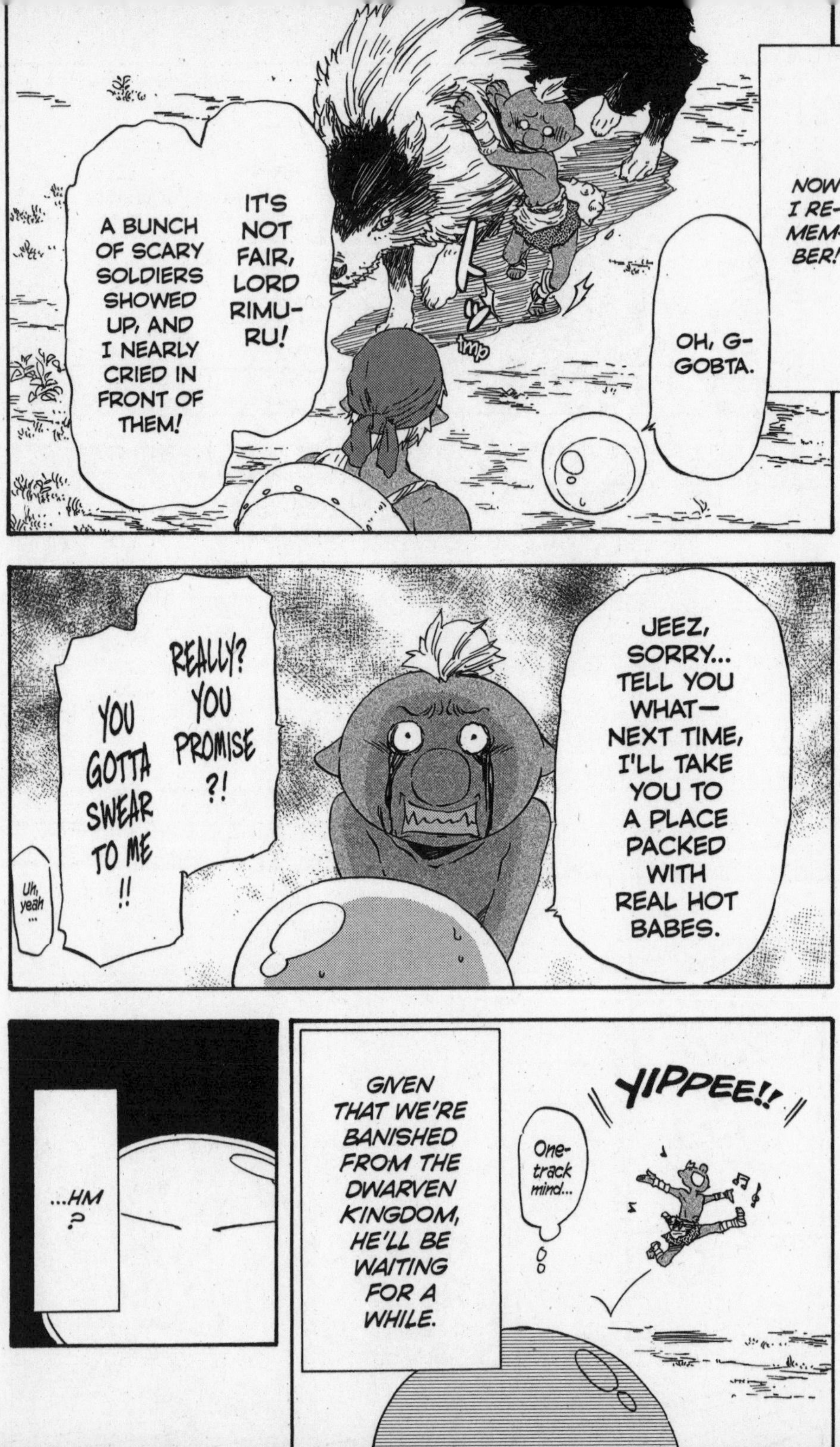
NOW I RE-MEM-BER!
OH, G-GOBTA.
tmp
IT'S NOT FAIR, LORD RIMU-RU!
A BUNCH OF SCARY SOLDIERS SHOWED UP, AND I NEARLY CRIED IN FRONT OF THEM!
JEEZ, SORRY... TELL YOU WHAT— NEXT TIME, I'LL TAKE YOU TO A PLACE PACKED WITH REAL HOT BABES.
REALLY? YOU PROMISE ?!
YOU GOTTA SWEAR TO ME !!
Uh, yeah ...
YIPPEE!!
One-track mind...
GIVEN THAT WE'RE BANISHED FROM THE DWARVEN KINGDOM, HE'LL BE WAITING FOR A WHILE.
...HM ?

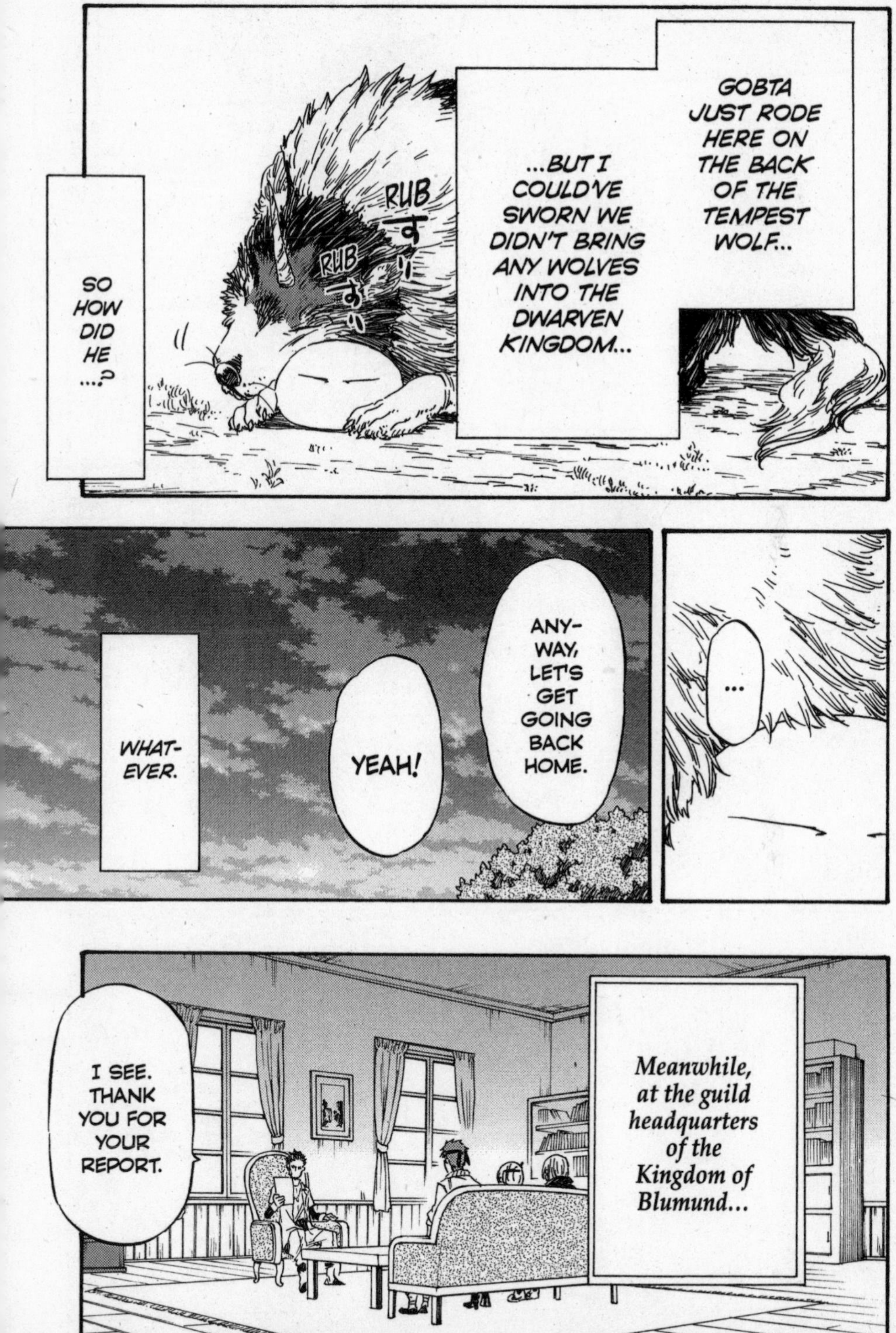
GOBTA JUST RODE HERE ON THE BACK OF THE TEMPEST WOLF...
...BUT I COULD'VE SWORN WE DIDN'T BRING ANY WOLVES INTO THE DWARVEN KINGDOM...
RUB
RUB
SO HOW DID HE ...?
...
ANY-WAY, LET'S GET GOING BACK HOME.
YEAH!
WHAT-EVER.
Meanwhile, at the guild headquarters of the Kingdom of Blumund...
I SEE. THANK YOU FOR YOUR REPORT.

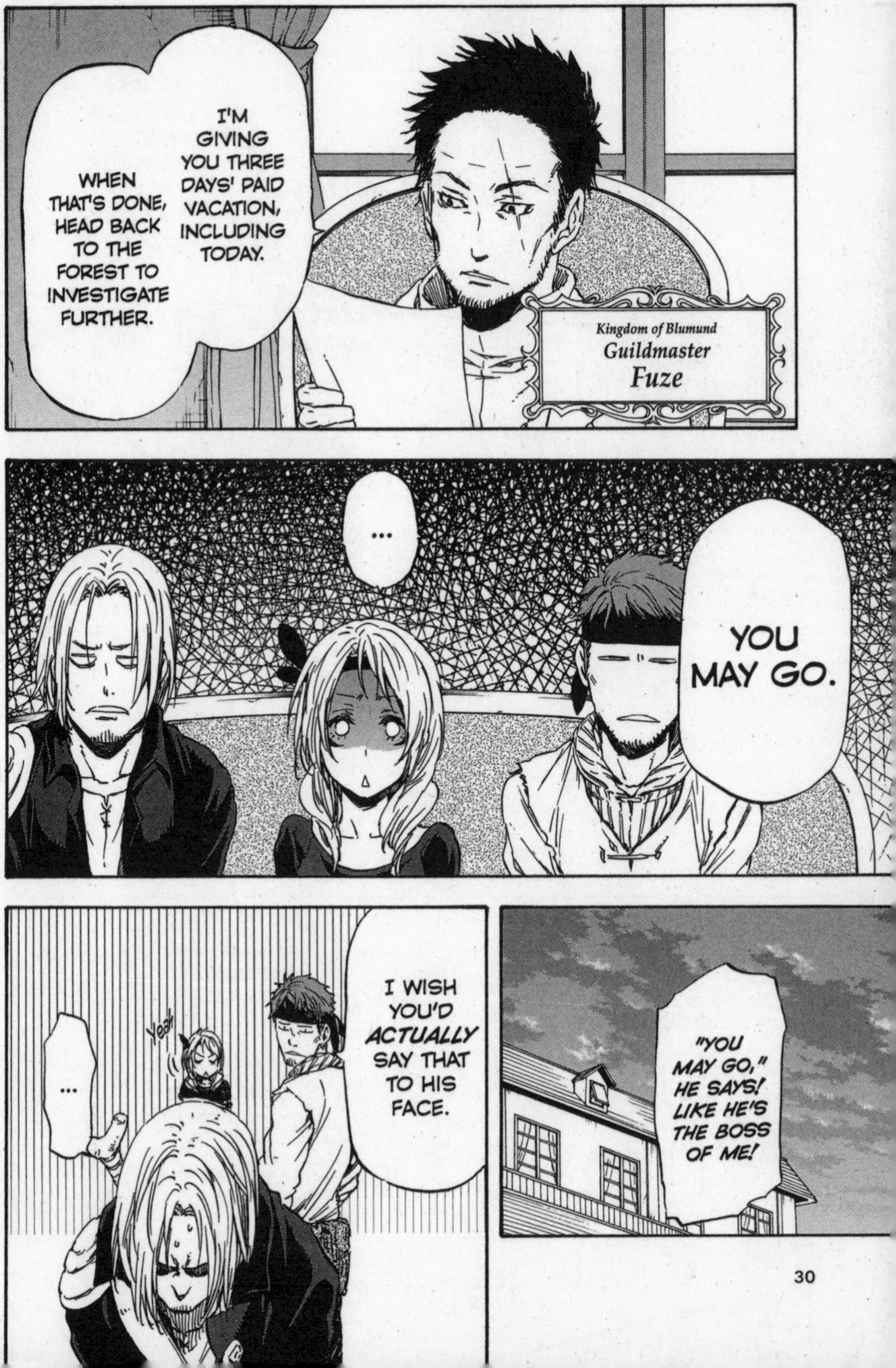

Kingdom of Blumund Guildmaster Fuze
I'M GIVING YOU THREE DAYS' PAID VACATION, INCLUDING TODAY.
WHEN THAT'S DONE, HEAD BACK TO THE FOREST TO INVESTIGATE FURTHER.
YOU MAY GO.
...
"YOU MAY GO," HE SAYS! LIKE HE'S THE BOSS OF ME!
I WISH YOU'D *ACTUALLY* SAY THAT TO HIS FACE.
Yeah
...

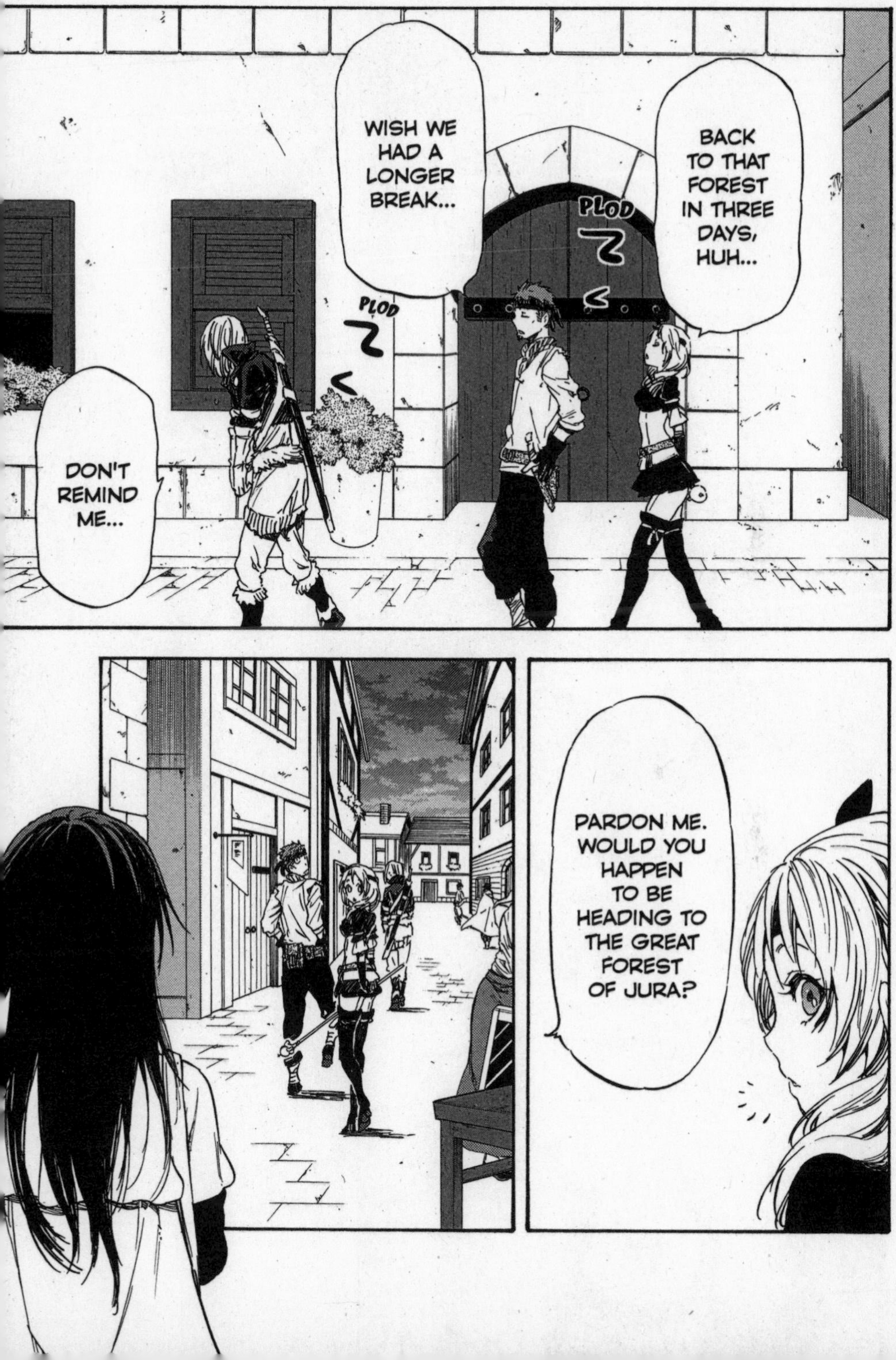
BACK TO THAT FOREST IN THREE DAYS, HUH...
PLOD
WISH WE HAD A LONGER BREAK...
PLOD
DON'T REMIND ME...
PARDON ME. WOULD YOU HAPPEN TO BE HEADING TO THE GREAT FOREST OF JURA?

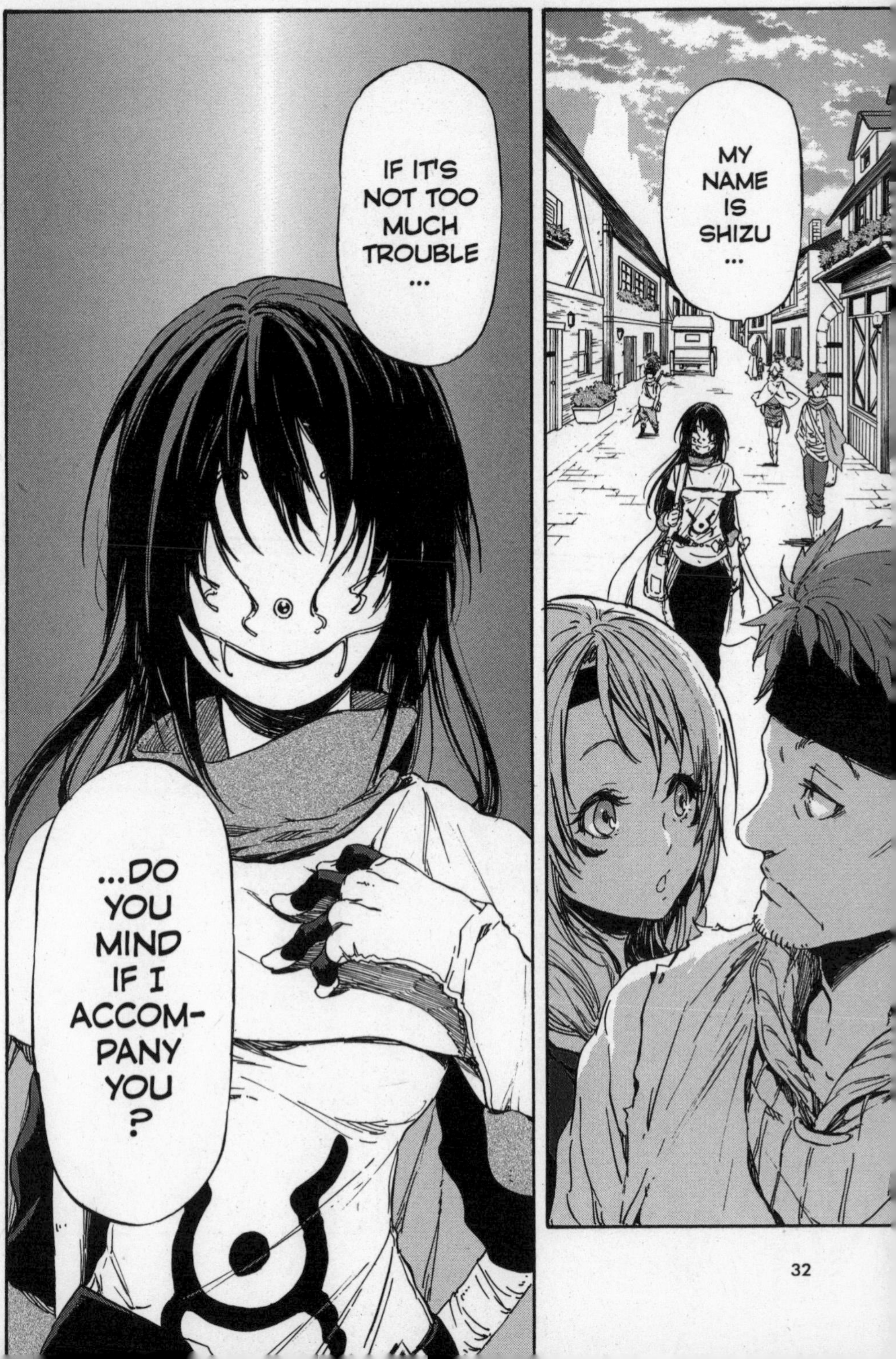
MY NAME IS SHIZU ...
IF IT'S NOT TOO MUCH TROUBLE ...
...DO YOU MIND IF I ACCOMPANY YOU ?

YOUNG VESTA
WAS MORE OF A
BABYFACE THAN
EXPECTED

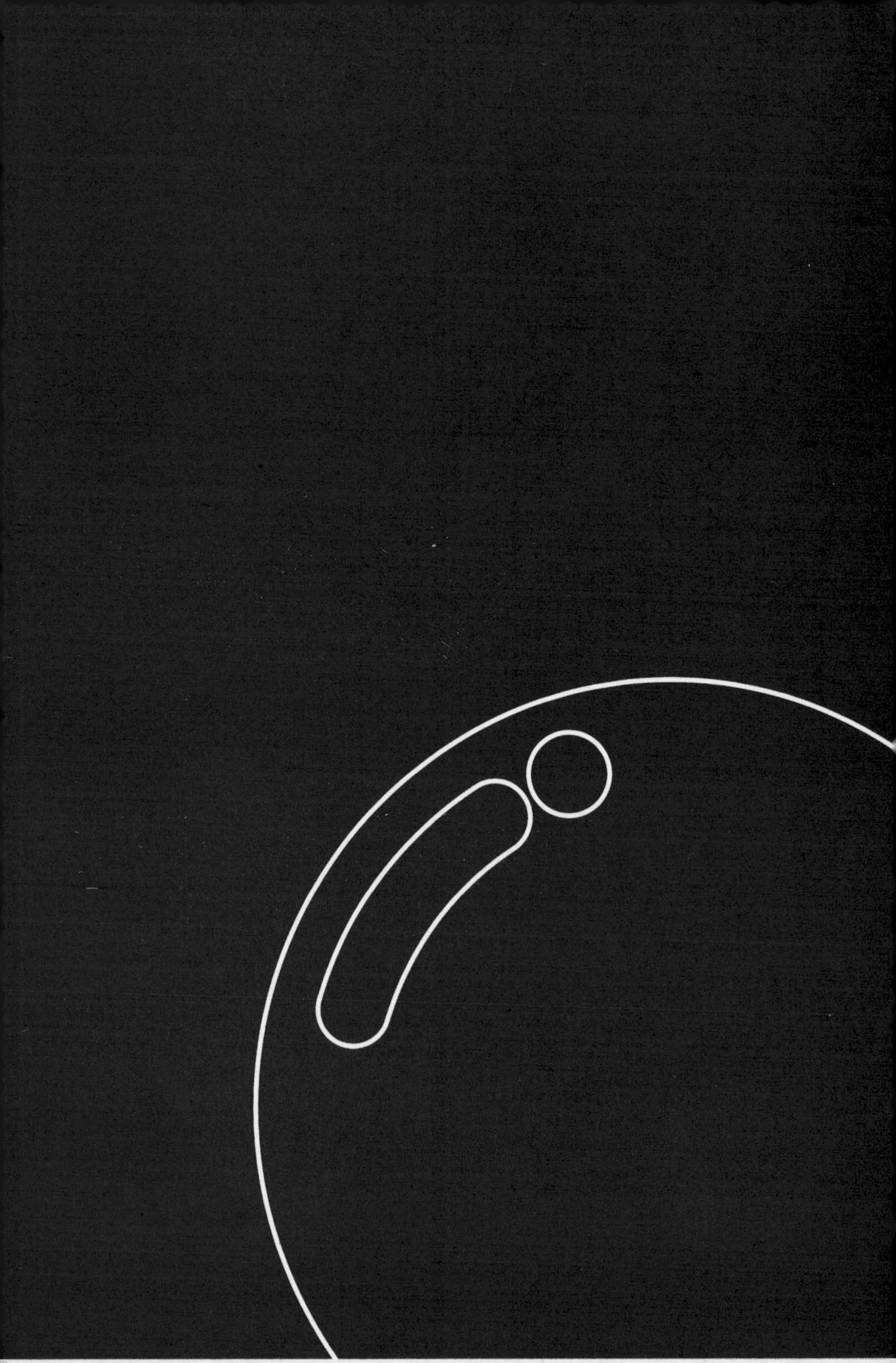

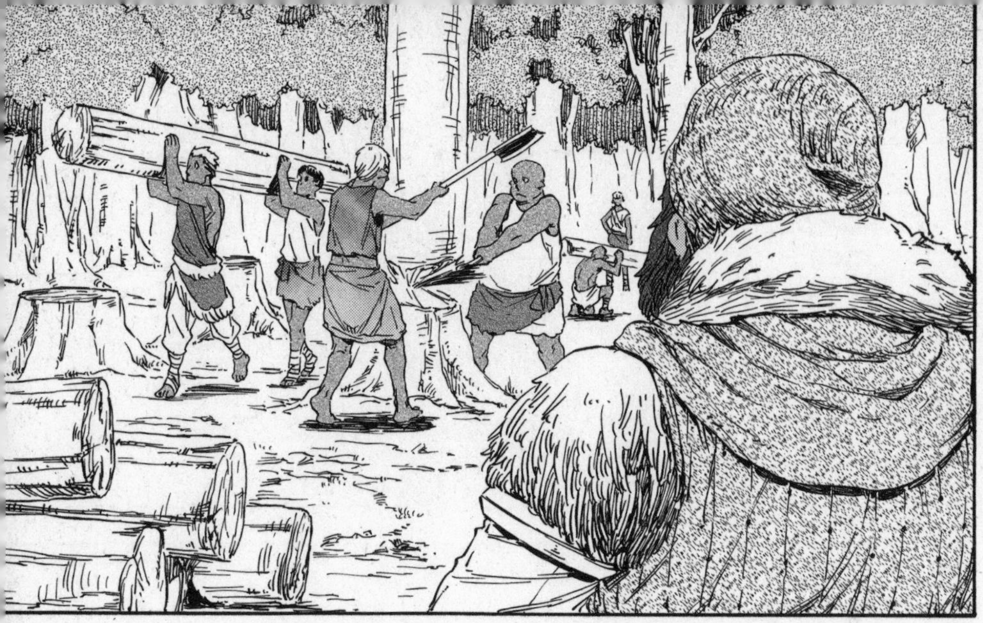

CHAPTER 8 A Familiar Scent

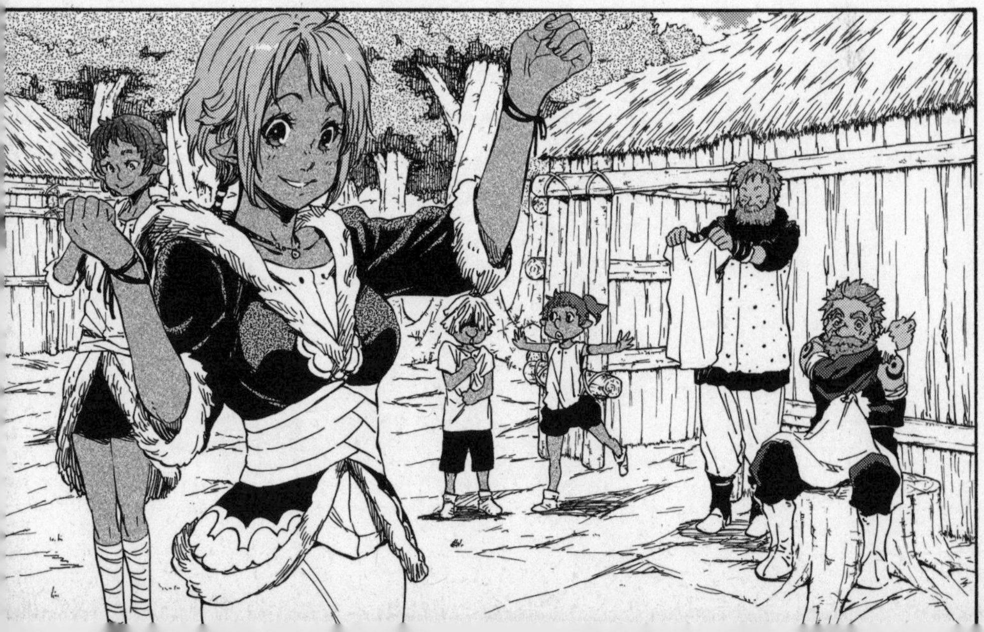

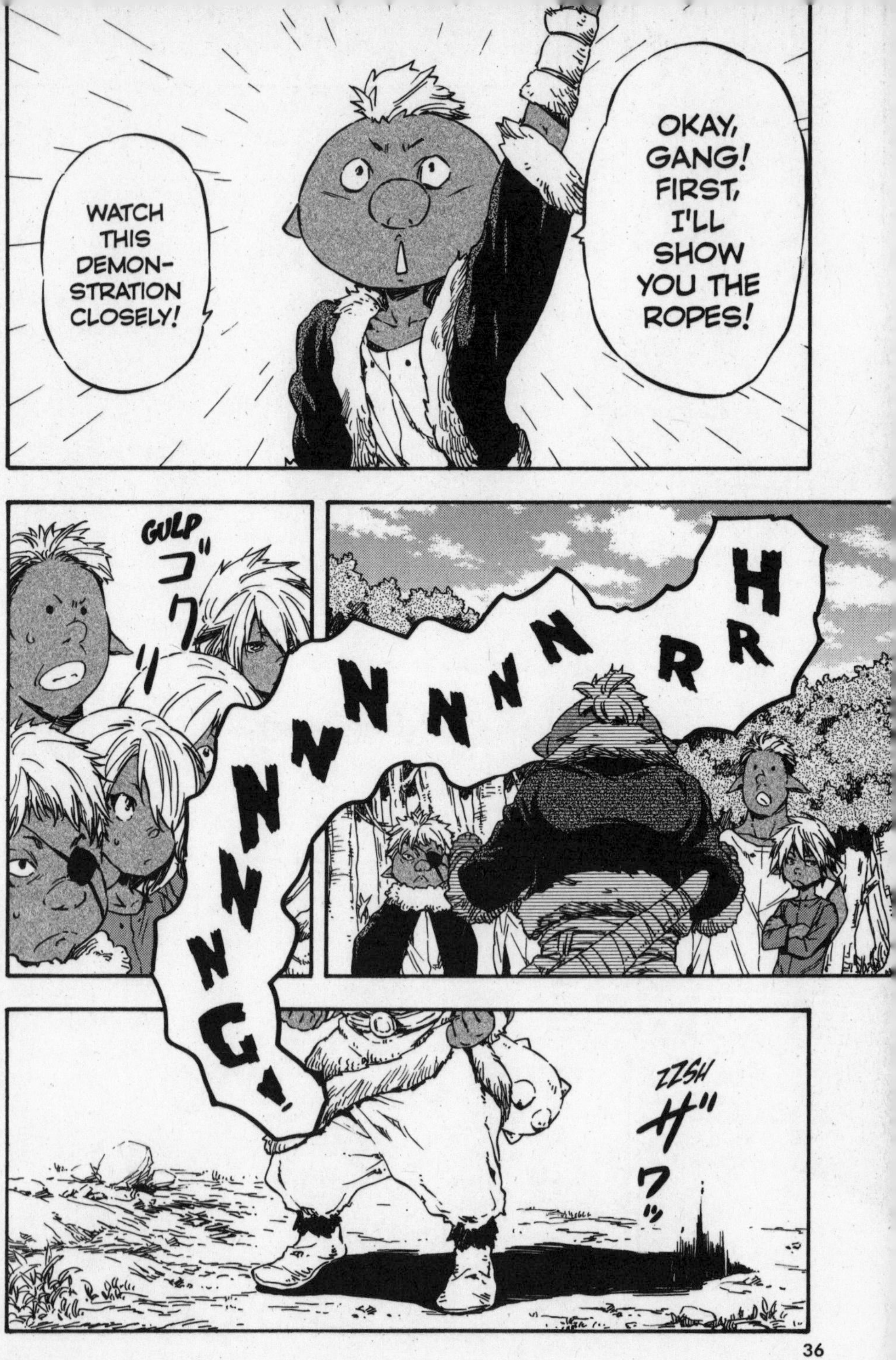
OKAY, GANG! FIRST, I'LL SHOW YOU THE ROPES!
WATCH THIS DEMON-STRATION CLOSELY!
HRRNNNNNNNNG!
GULP
ゴクリ
ZZSH
ザワッ

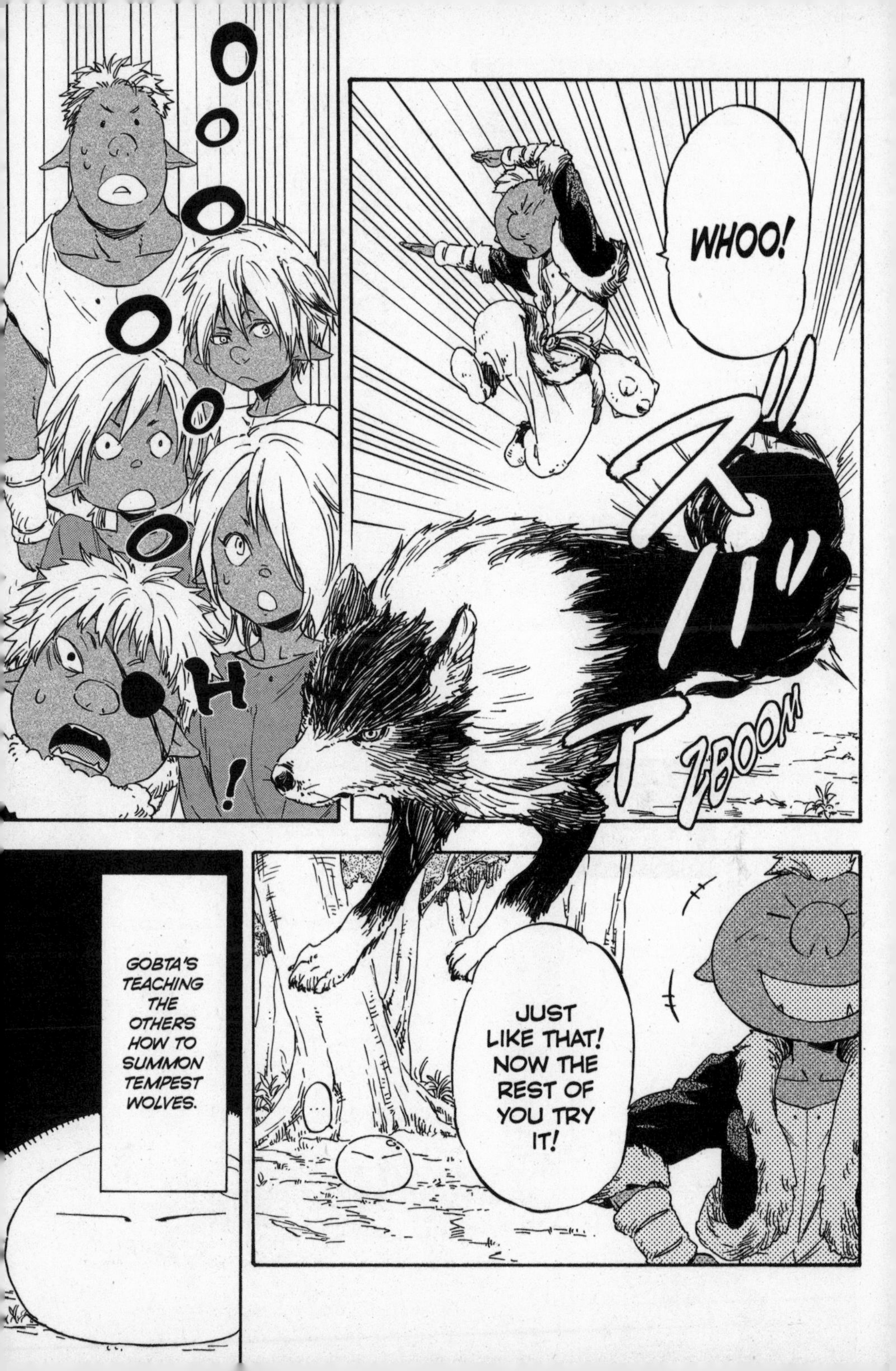
WHOO!
ZBOOM
OOOOOOOH!
JUST LIKE THAT! NOW THE REST OF YOU TRY IT!
...
GOBTA'S TEACHING THE OTHERS HOW TO SUMMON TEMPEST WOLVES.

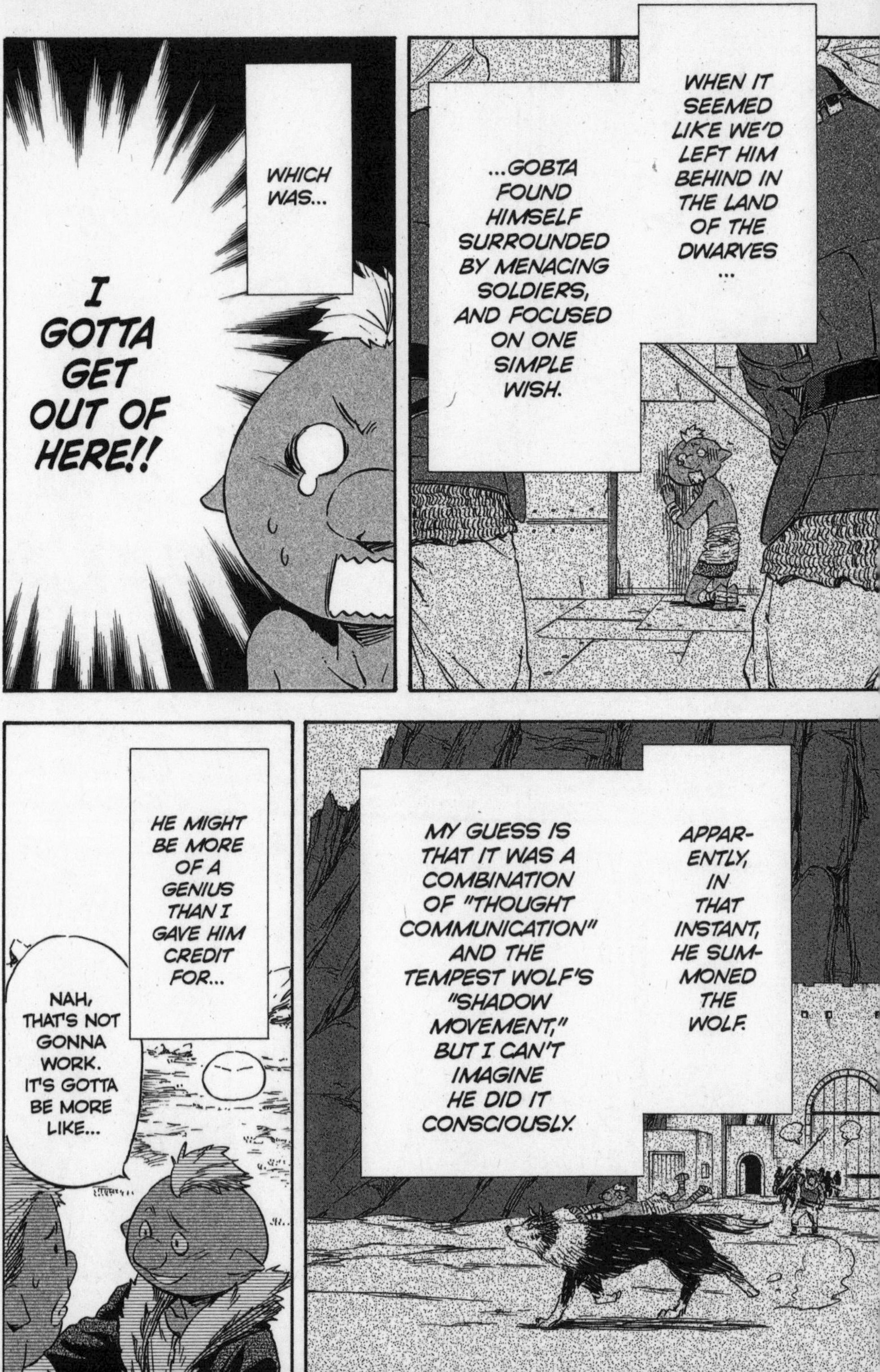
WHEN IT SEEMED LIKE WE'D LEFT HIM BEHIND IN THE LAND OF THE DWARVES ...
...GOBTA FOUND HIMSELF SURROUNDED BY MENACING SOLDIERS, AND FOCUSED ON ONE SIMPLE WISH.
WHICH WAS...
I GOTTA GET OUT OF HERE!!
APPARENTLY, IN THAT INSTANT, HE SUMMONED THE WOLF.
MY GUESS IS THAT IT WAS A COMBINATION OF "THOUGHT COMMUNICATION" AND THE TEMPEST WOLF'S "SHADOW MOVEMENT," BUT I CAN'T IMAGINE HE DID IT CONSCIOUSLY.
HE MIGHT BE MORE OF A GENIUS THAN I GAVE HIM CREDIT FOR...
NAH, THAT'S NOT GONNA WORK. IT'S GOTTA BE MORE LIKE...

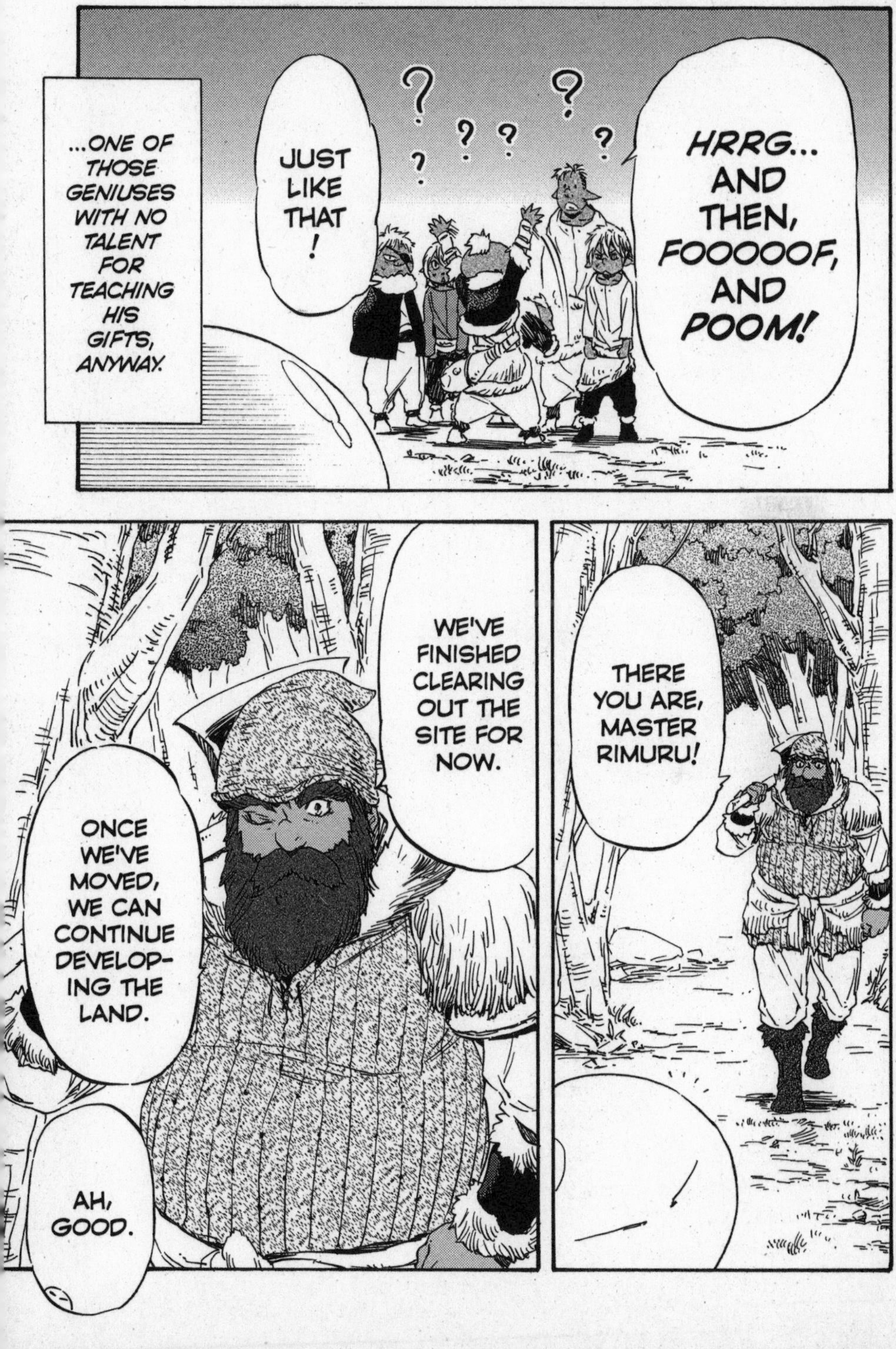
HRRG... AND THEN, FOOOOOF, AND POOM!
JUST LIKE THAT!
...ONE OF THOSE GENIUSES WITH NO TALENT FOR TEACHING HIS GIFTS, ANYWAY.
THERE YOU ARE, MASTER RIMURU!
WE'VE FINISHED CLEARING OUT THE SITE FOR NOW.
ONCE WE'VE MOVED, WE CAN CONTINUE DEVELOPING THE LAND.
AH, GOOD.

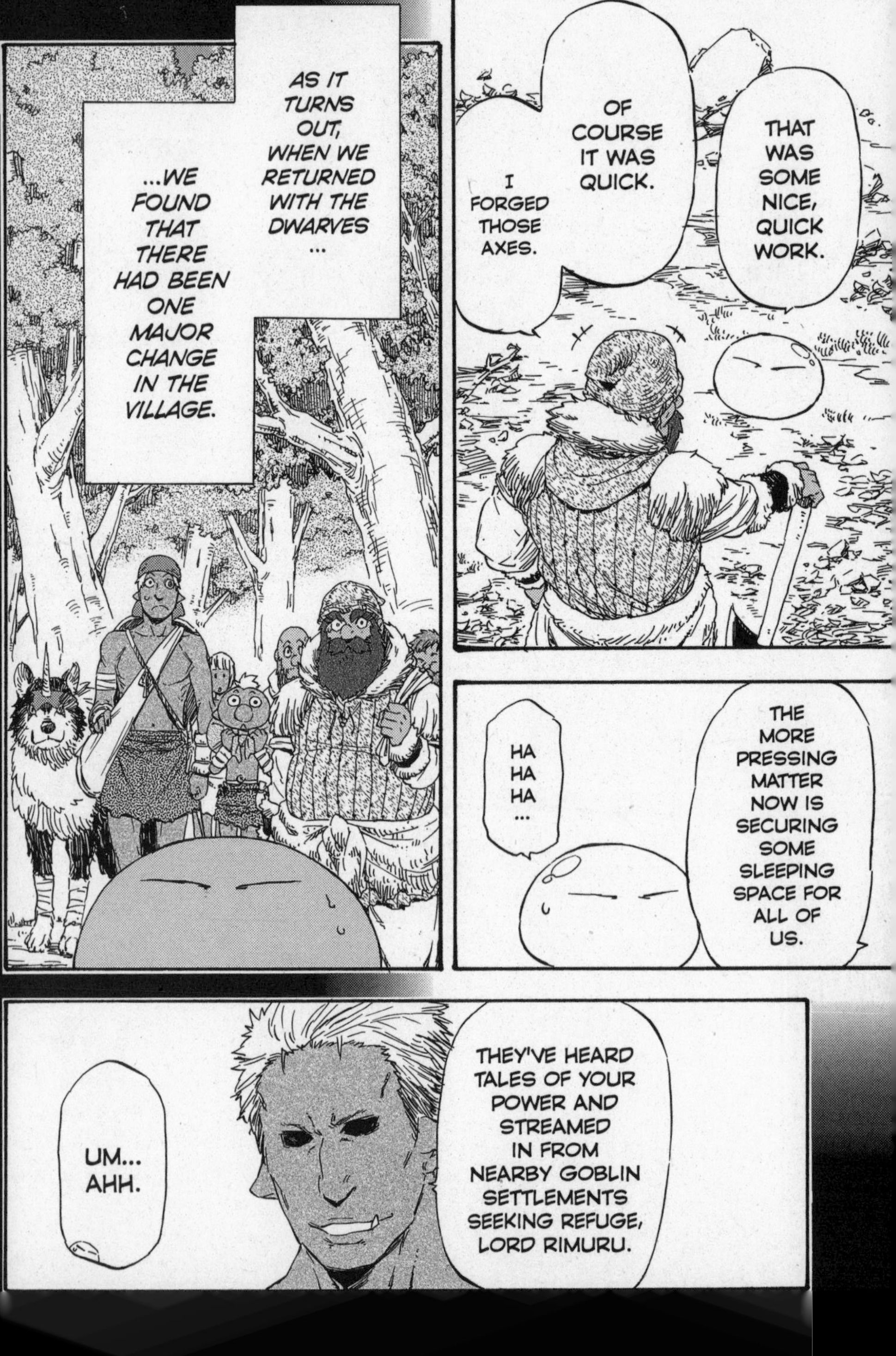
THAT WAS SOME NICE, QUICK WORK.
OF COURSE IT WAS QUICK.
I FORGED THOSE AXES.
THE MORE PRESSING MATTER NOW IS SECURING SOME SLEEPING SPACE FOR ALL OF US.
HA HA HA ...
AS IT TURNS OUT, WHEN WE RETURNED WITH THE DWARVES ...
...WE FOUND THAT THERE HAD BEEN ONE MAJOR CHANGE IN THE VILLAGE.
THEY'VE HEARD TALES OF YOUR POWER AND STREAMED IN FROM NEARBY GOBLIN SETTLEMENTS SEEKING REFUGE, LORD RIMURU.
UM... AHH.

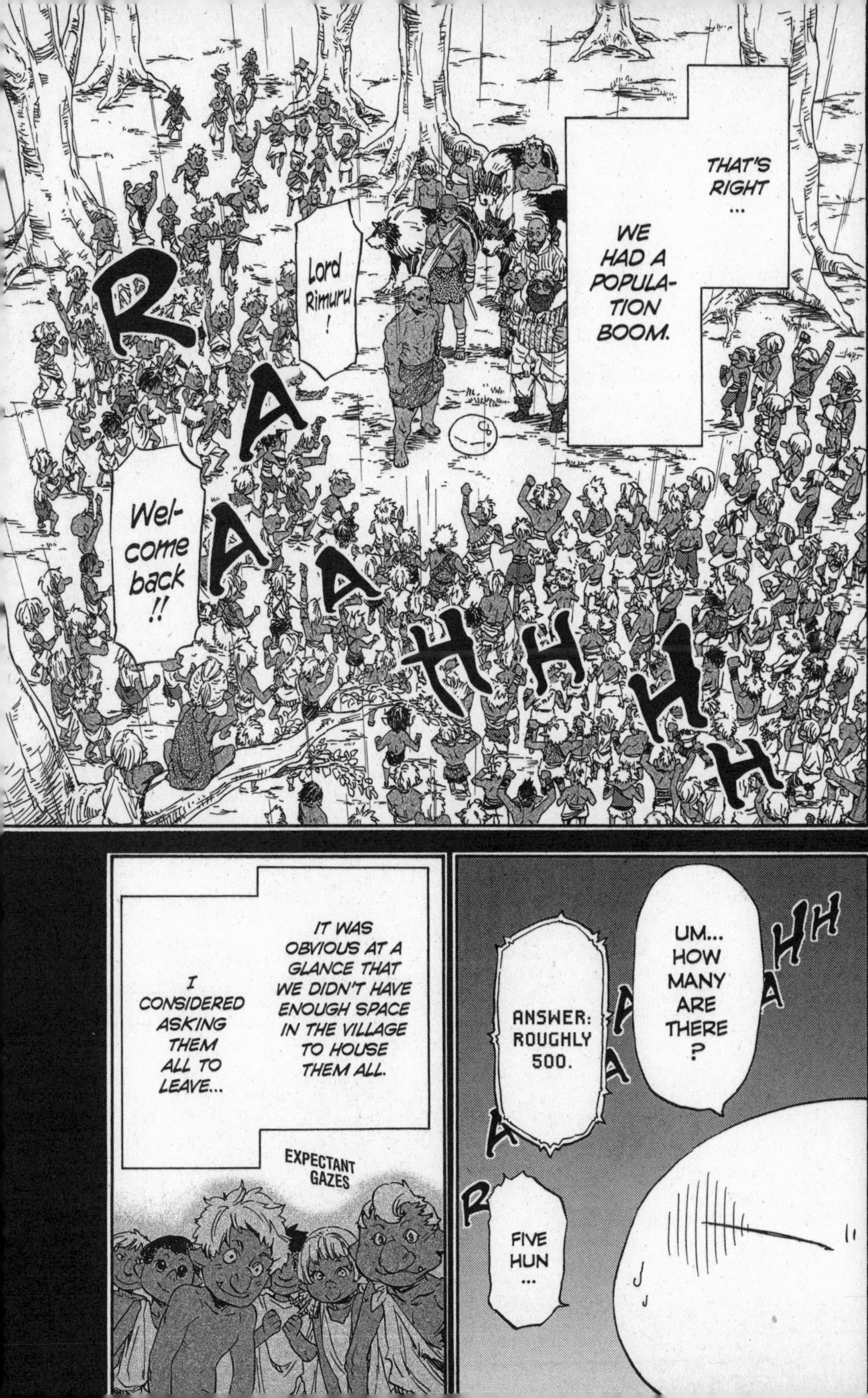
THAT'S RIGHT...
WE HAD A POPULATION BOOM.
Lord Rimuru!
Welcome back!!
RAAAHHHH
UM... HOW MANY ARE THERE?
ANSWER: ROUGHLY 500.
RAAAAHH
FIVE HUN...
IT WAS OBVIOUS AT A GLANCE THAT WE DIDN'T HAVE ENOUGH SPACE IN THE VILLAGE TO HOUSE THEM ALL.
I CONSIDERED ASKING THEM ALL TO LEAVE...
EXPECTANT GAZES

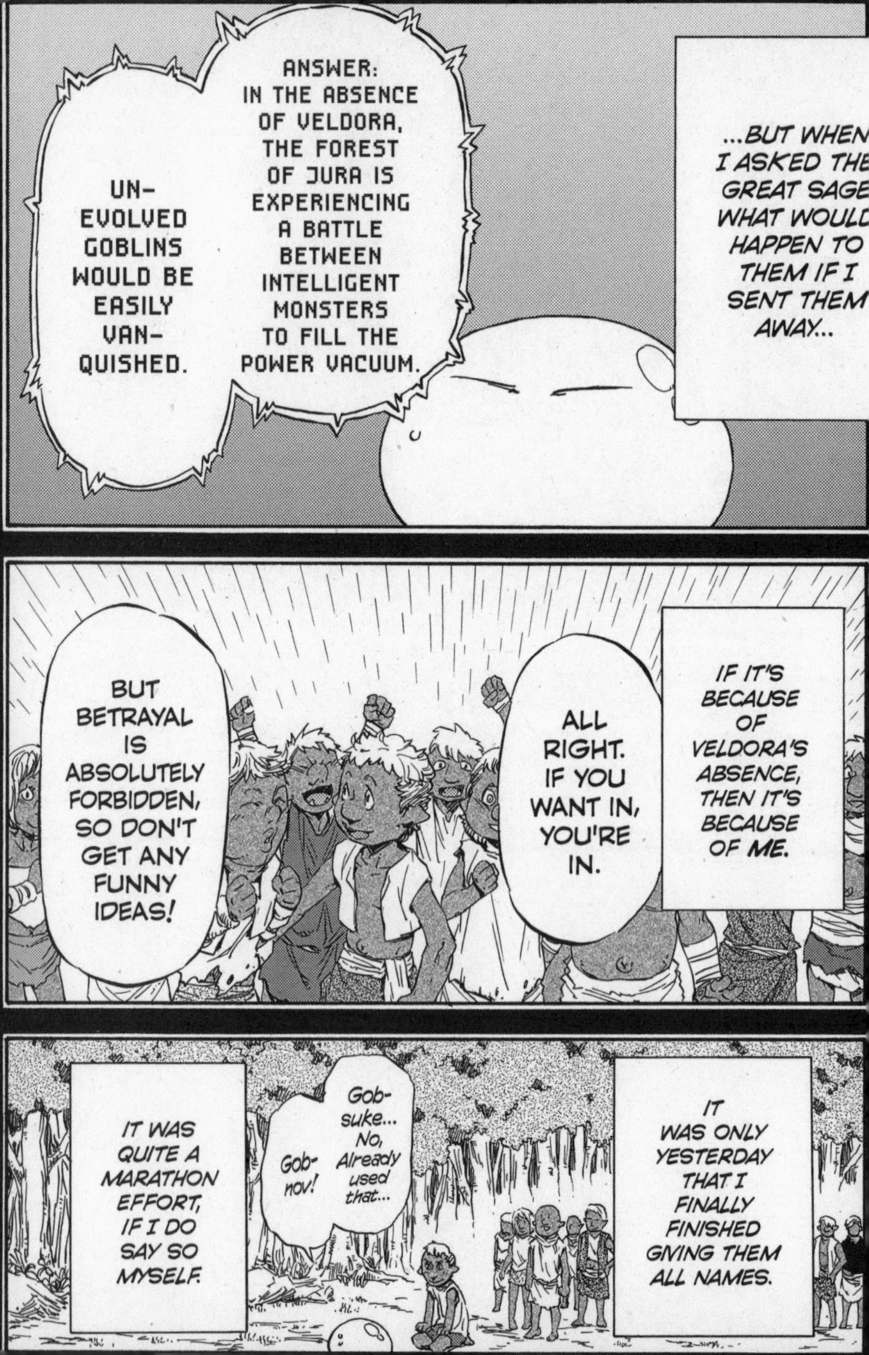
...BUT WHEN I ASKED THE GREAT SAGE WHAT WOULD HAPPEN TO THEM IF I SENT THEM AWAY...
ANSWER: IN THE ABSENCE OF VELDORA, THE FOREST OF JURA IS EXPERIENCING A BATTLE BETWEEN INTELLIGENT MONSTERS TO FILL THE POWER VACUUM.
UN-EVOLVED GOBLINS WOULD BE EASILY VAN-QUISHED.
IF IT'S BECAUSE OF VELDORA'S ABSENCE, THEN IT'S BECAUSE OF ME.
ALL RIGHT. IF YOU WANT IN, YOU'RE IN.
BUT BETRAYAL IS ABSOLUTELY FORBIDDEN, SO DON'T GET ANY FUNNY IDEAS!
IT WAS ONLY YESTERDAY THAT I FINALLY FINISHED GIVING THEM ALL NAMES.
Gob-suke... No, Already used that...
Gob-nov!
IT WAS QUITE A MARATHON EFFORT, IF I DO SAY SO MYSELF.

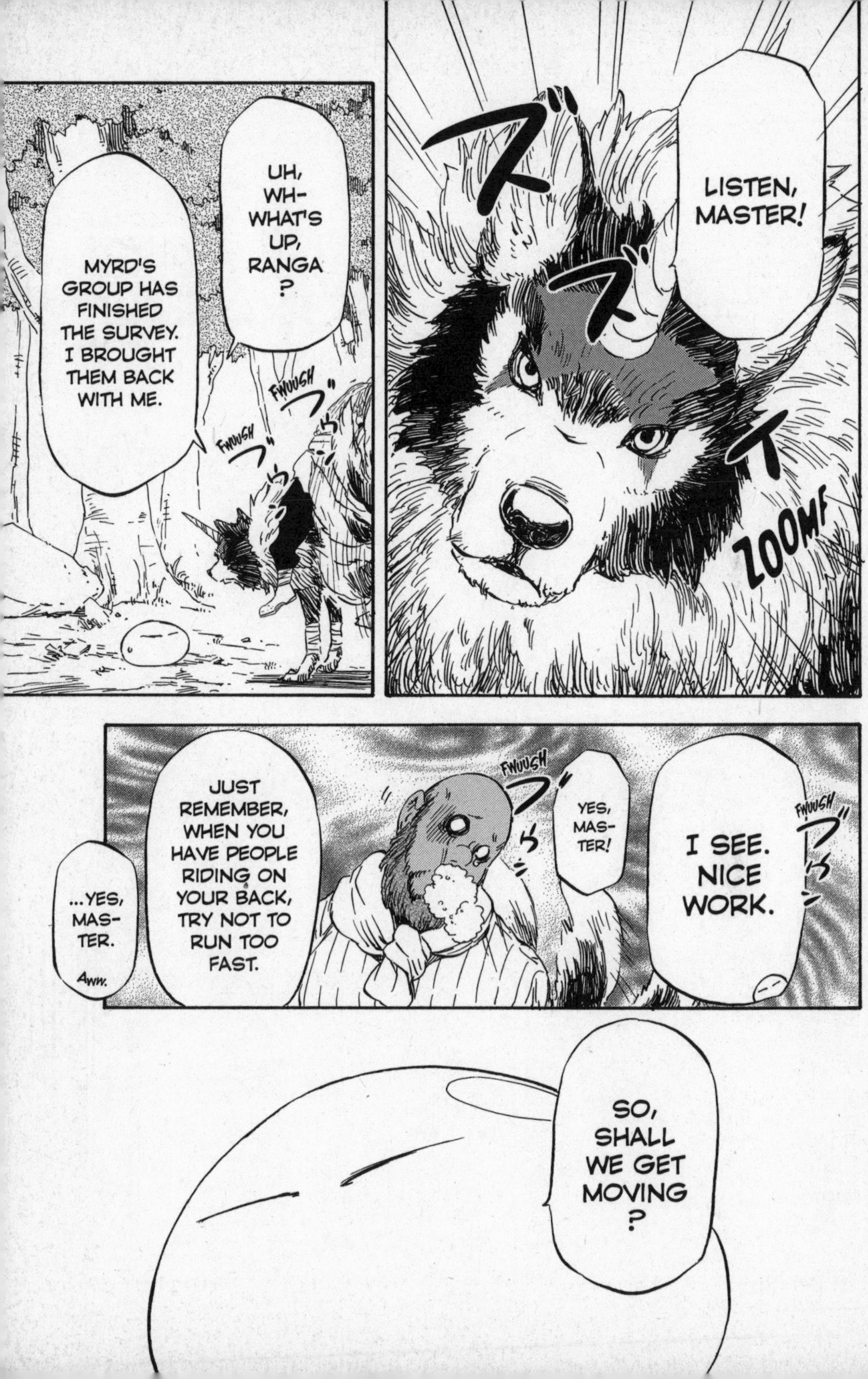
LISTEN, MASTER!
ZOOMF
UH, WH-WHAT'S UP, RANGA?
MYRD'S GROUP HAS FINISHED THE SURVEY. I BROUGHT THEM BACK WITH ME.
FWUUSH
FWUUSH
FWUUSH
I SEE. NICE WORK.
YES, MASTER!
FWUUSH
JUST REMEMBER, WHEN YOU HAVE PEOPLE RIDING ON YOUR BACK, TRY NOT TO RUN TOO FAST.
...YES, MASTER.
Aww.
SO, SHALL WE GET MOVING?

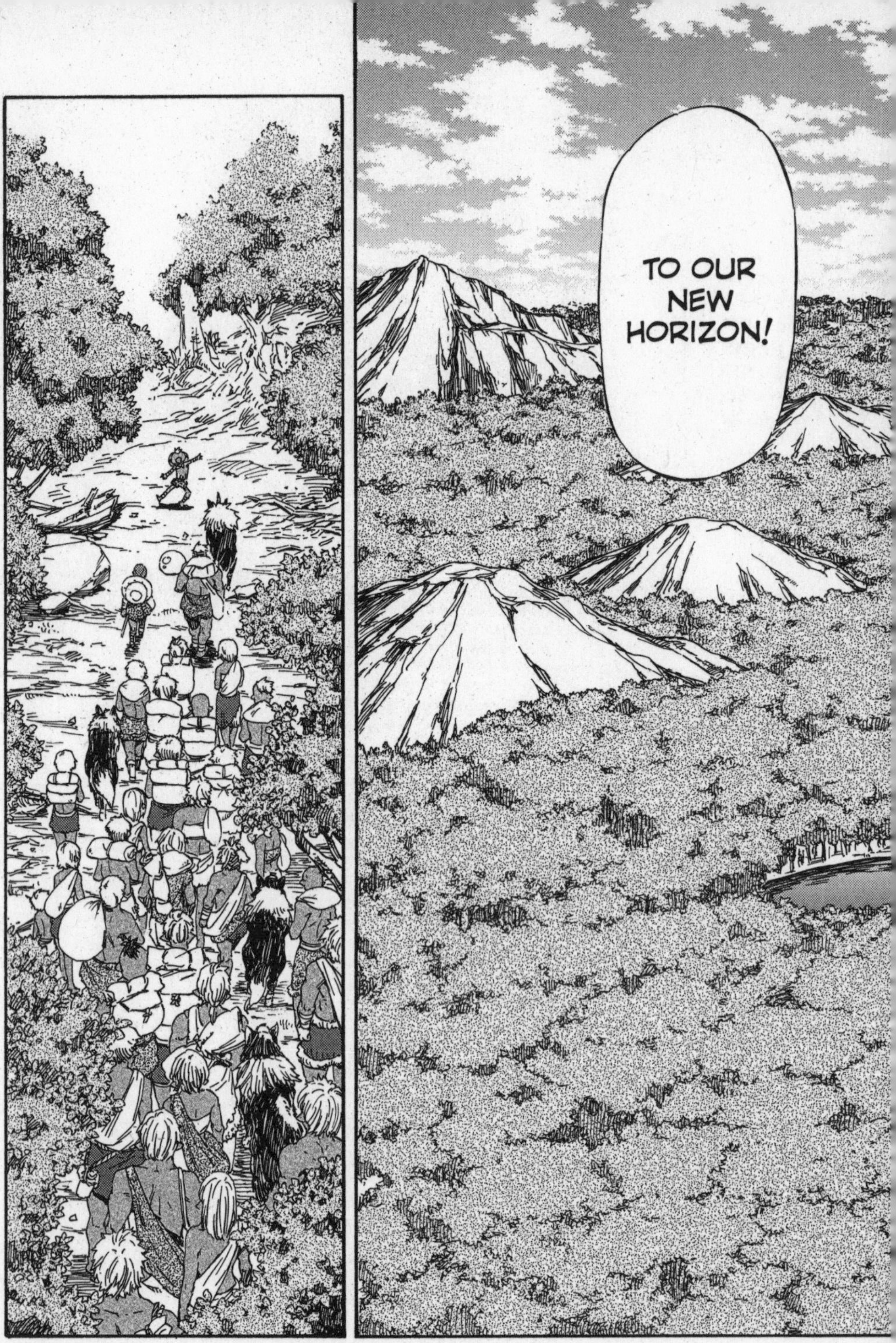
TO OUR NEW HORIZON!

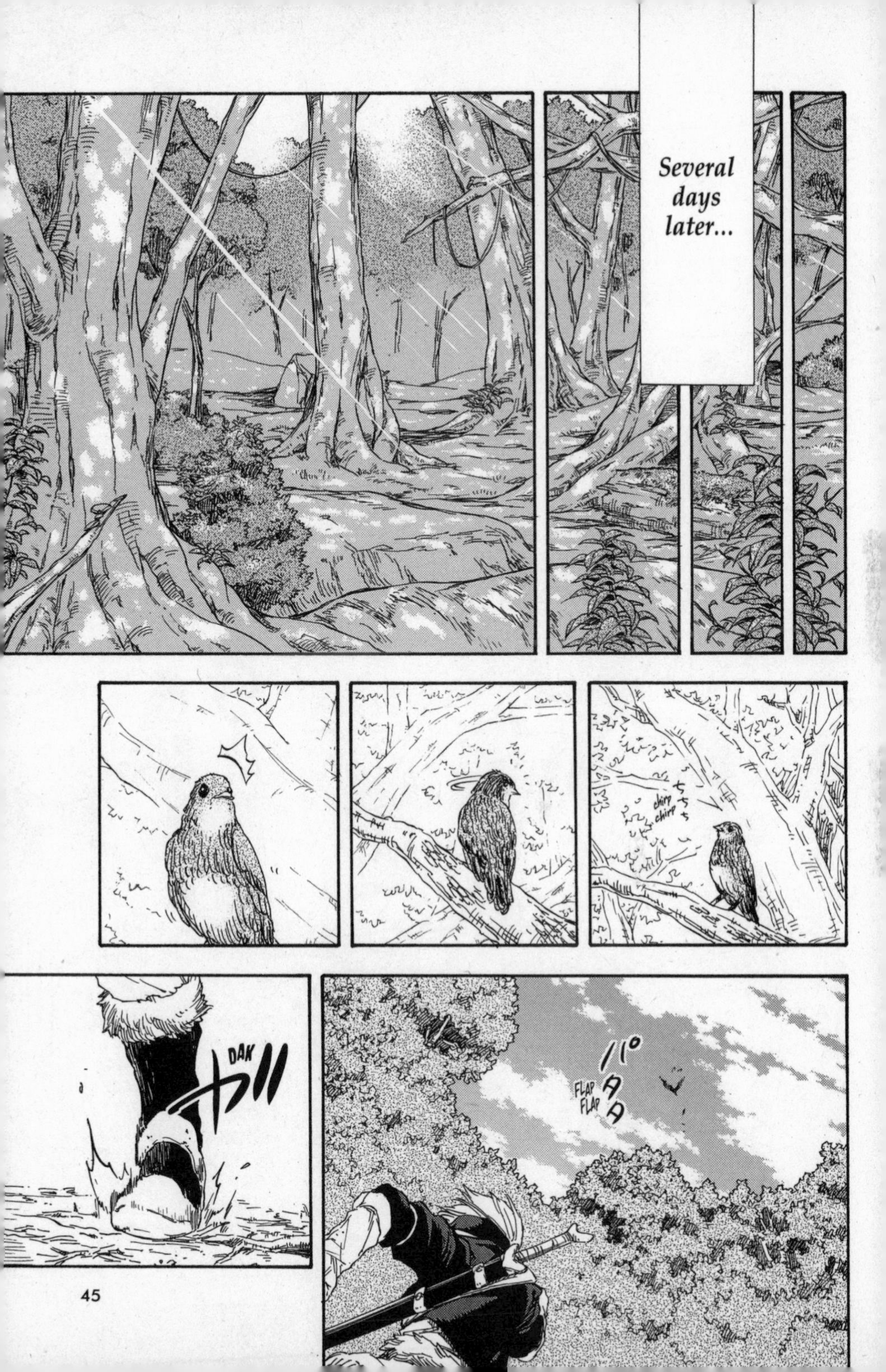
Several days later...
chirp chirp
FLAP FLAP
DAK

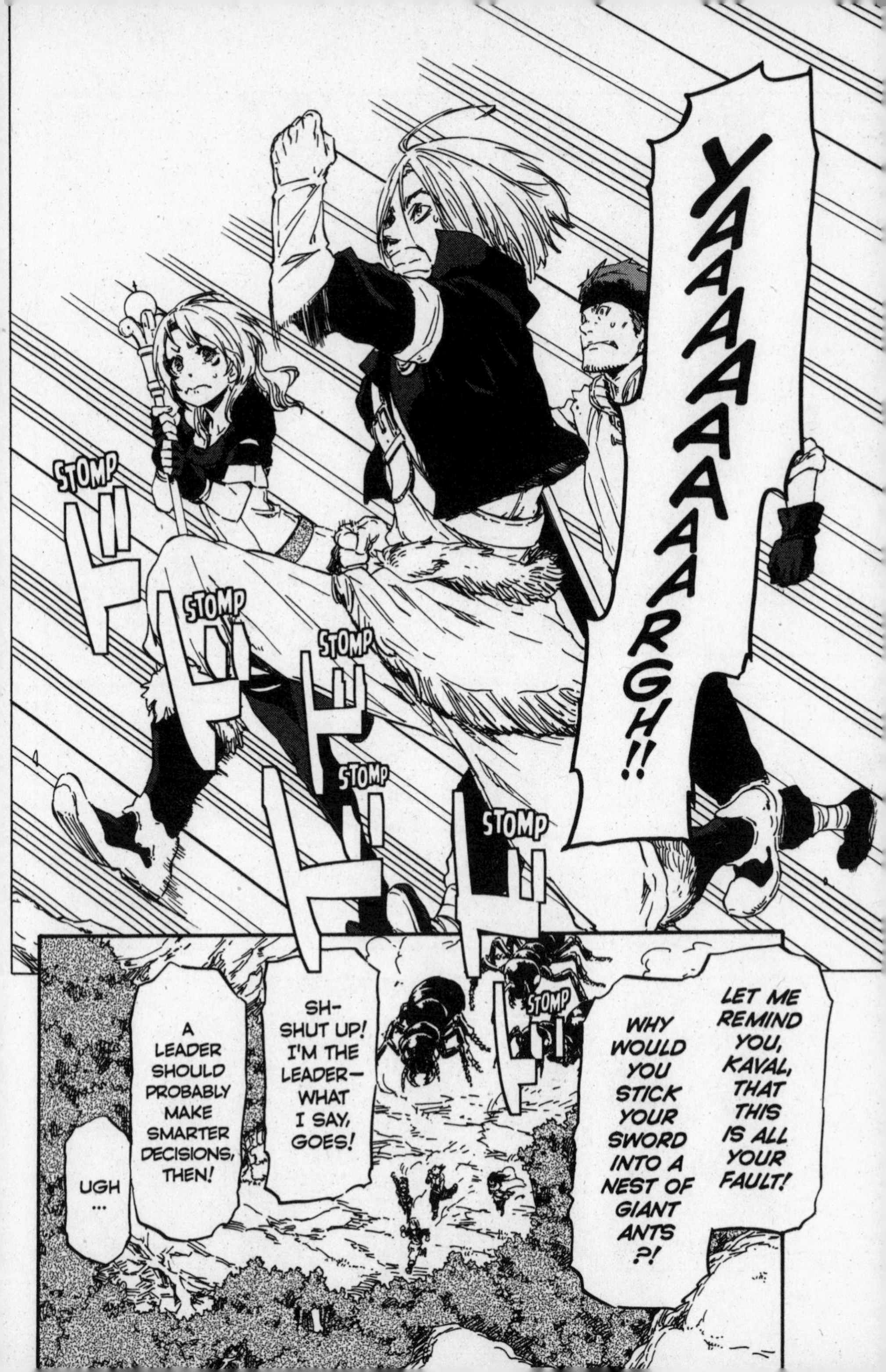
YAAAAAAARGH!!
STOMP
STOMP
STOMP
STOMP
STOMP
STOMP
LET ME REMIND YOU, KAVAL, THAT THIS IS ALL YOUR FAULT!
WHY WOULD YOU STICK YOUR SWORD INTO A NEST OF GIANT ANTS?!
SH-SHUT UP! I'M THE LEADER—WHAT I SAY, GOES!
A LEADER SHOULD PROBABLY MAKE SMARTER DECISIONS, THEN!
UGH...

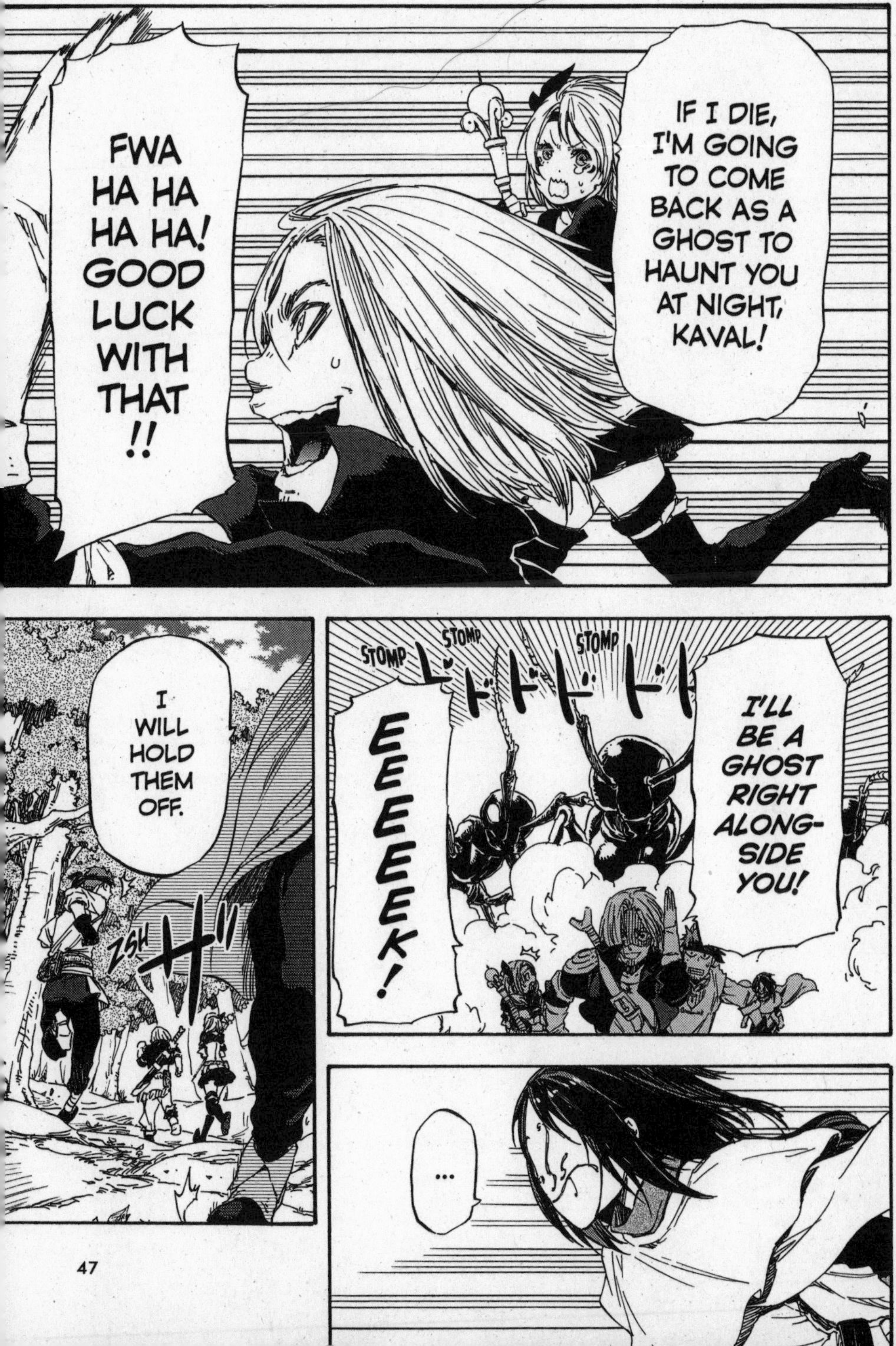
IF I DIE, I'M GOING TO COME BACK AS A GHOST TO HAUNT YOU AT NIGHT, KAVAL!
FWA HA HA HA HA! GOOD LUCK WITH THAT!!
STOMP STOMP STOMP
I'LL BE A GHOST RIGHT ALONG-SIDE YOU!
EEEEEEK!
...
I WILL HOLD THEM OFF.
ZSH

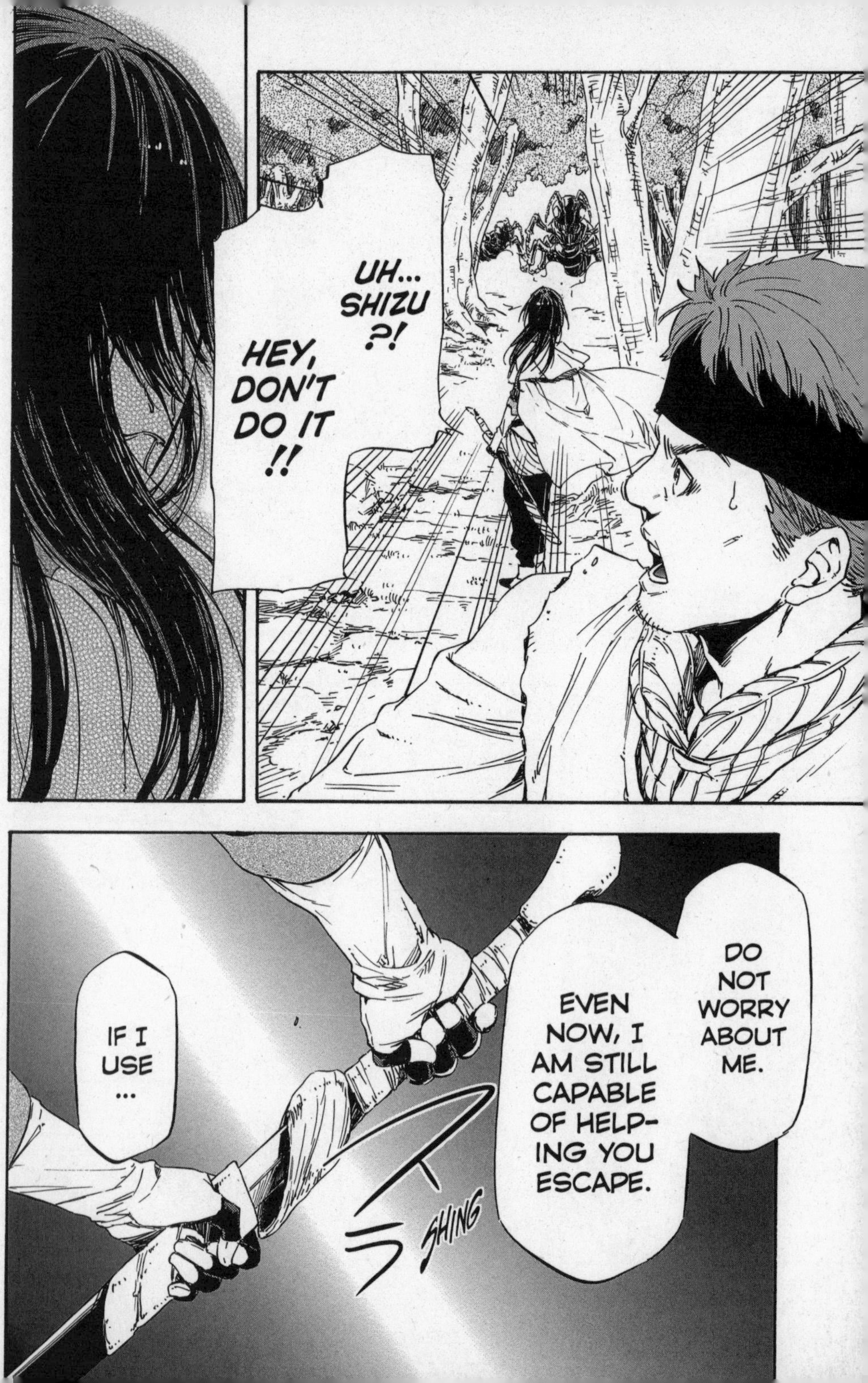
UH... SHIZU?!
HEY, DON'T DO IT!!
DO NOT WORRY ABOUT ME.
EVEN NOW, I AM STILL CAPABLE OF HELPING YOU ESCAPE.
SHING
IF I USE ...

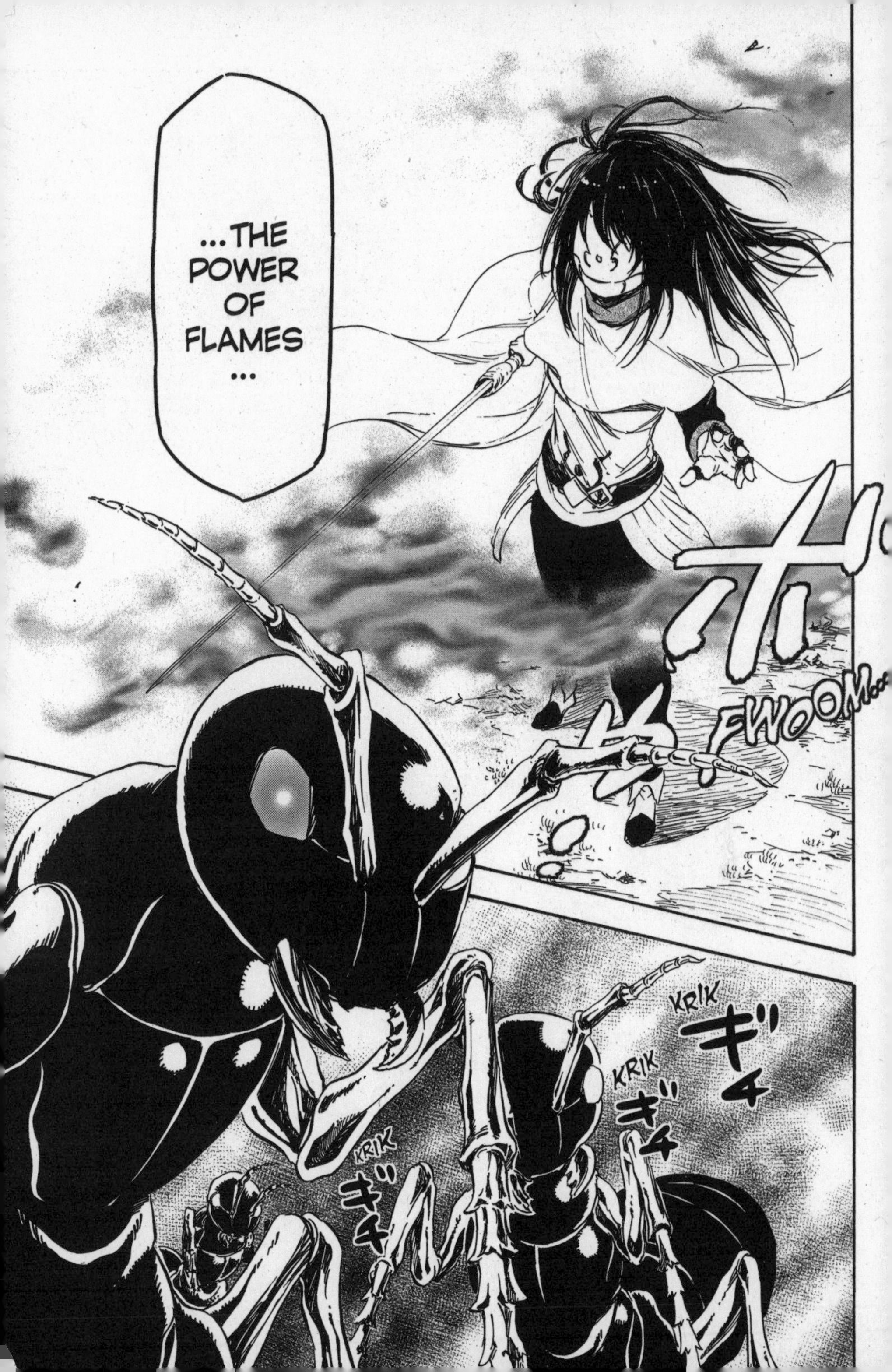
...THE POWER OF FLAMES ...
FWOOM...
KRIK
KRIK
KRIK

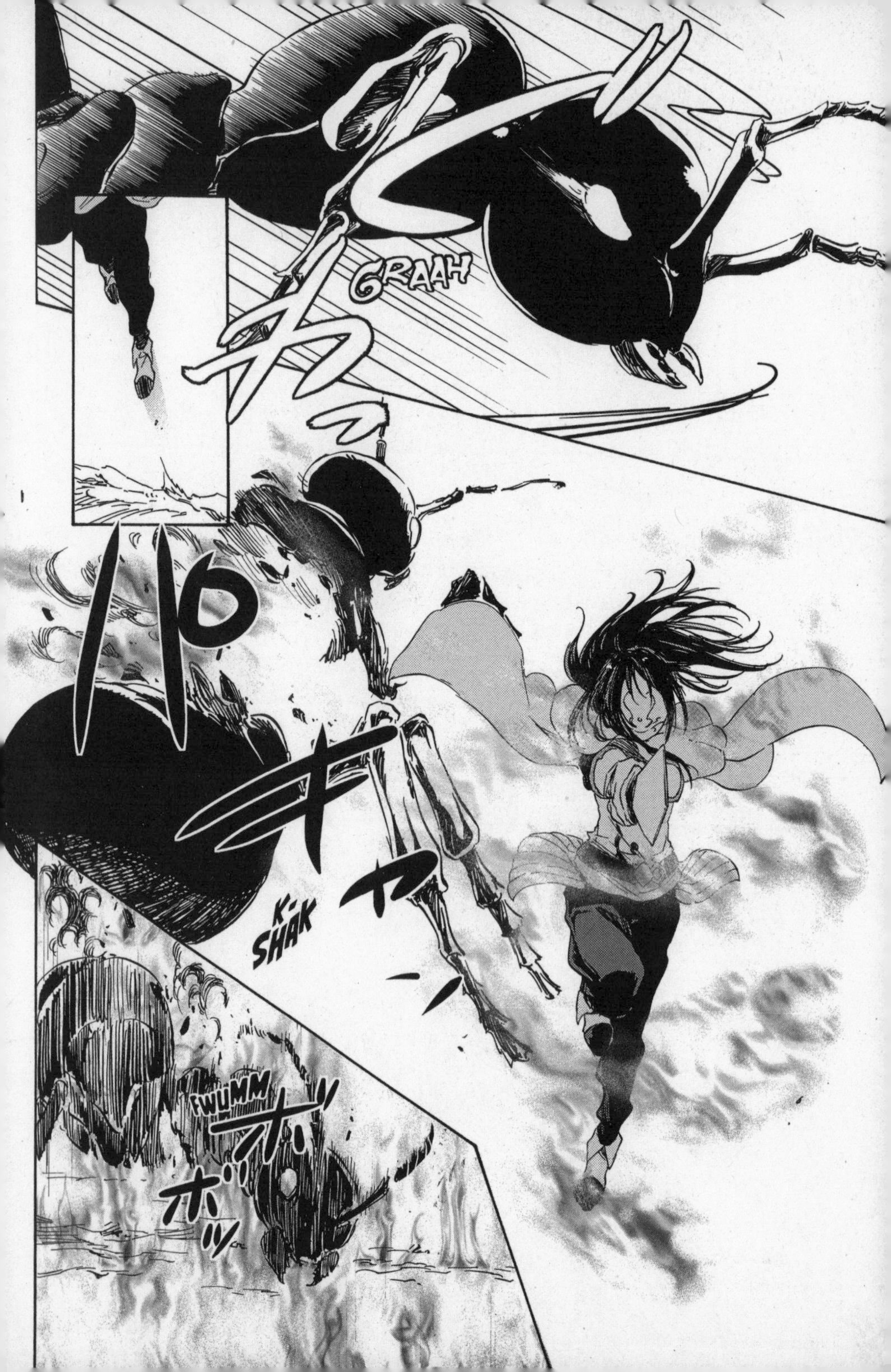
GRAAH
K-SHAK
FWUMM

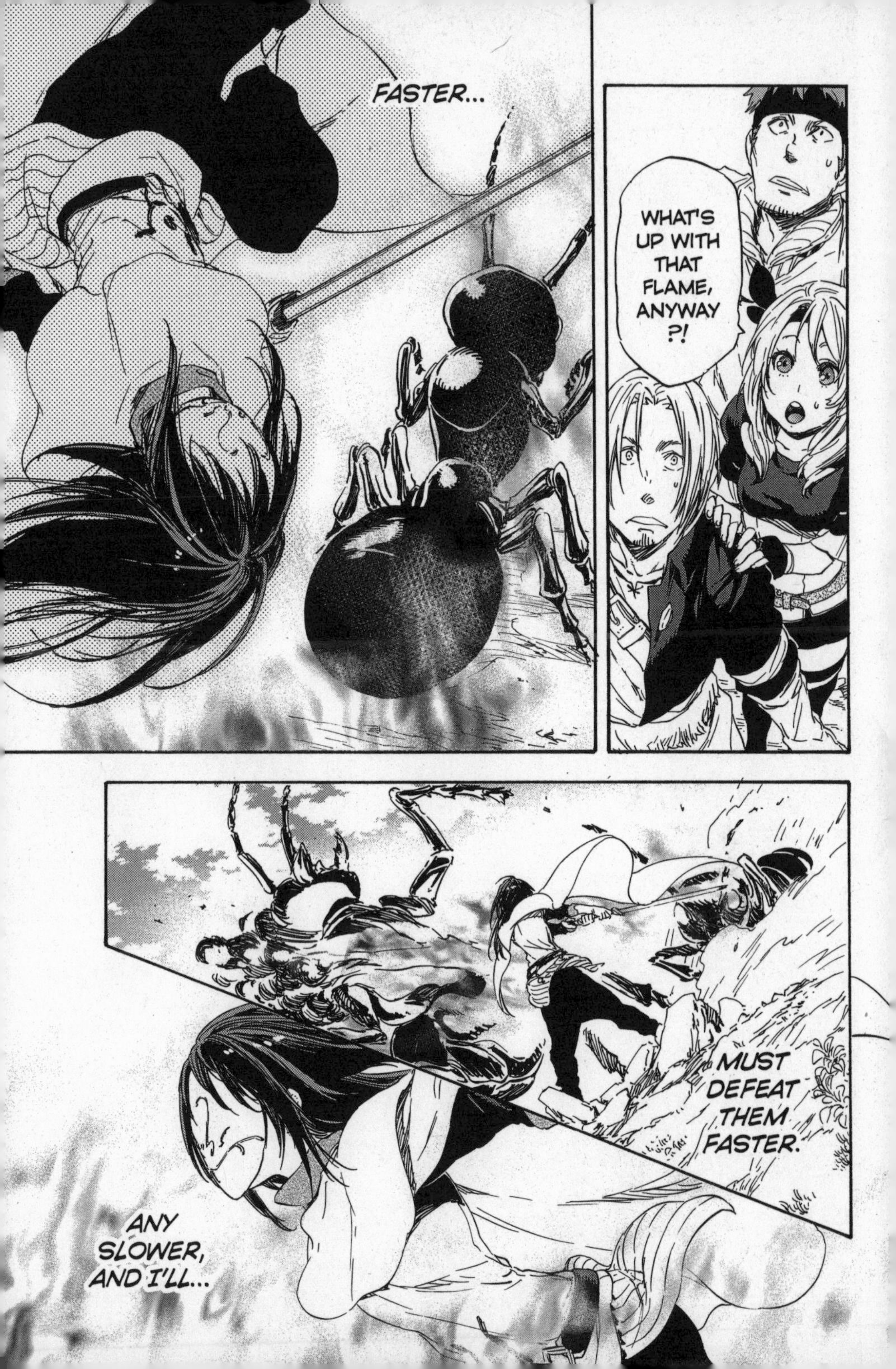
WHAT'S UP WITH THAT FLAME, ANYWAY ?!
FASTER...
MUST DEFEAT THEM FASTER.
ANY SLOWER, AND I'LL...

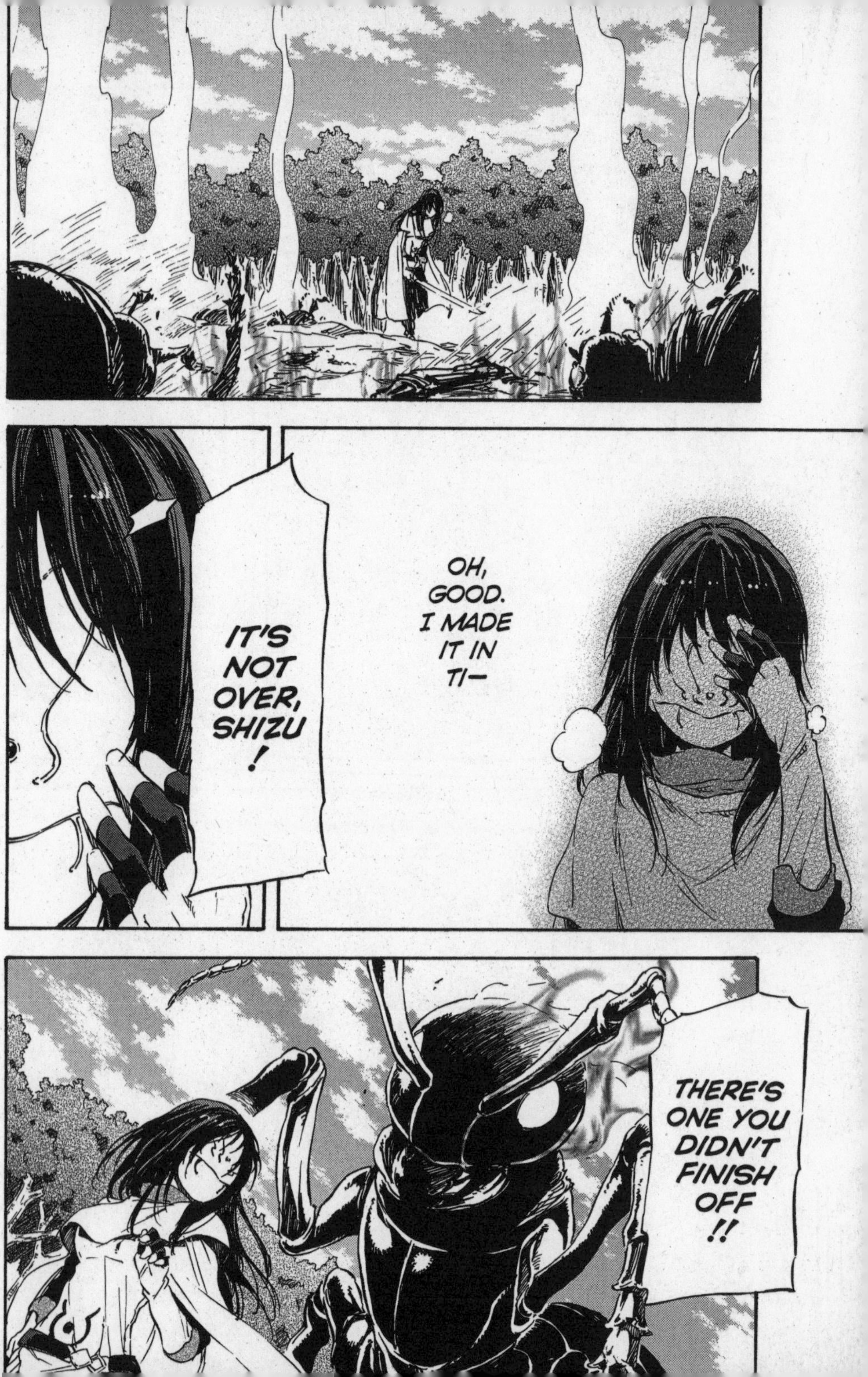
OH, GOOD. I MADE IT IN TI—
IT'S NOT OVER, SHIZU!
THERE'S ONE YOU DIDN'T FINISH OFF!!

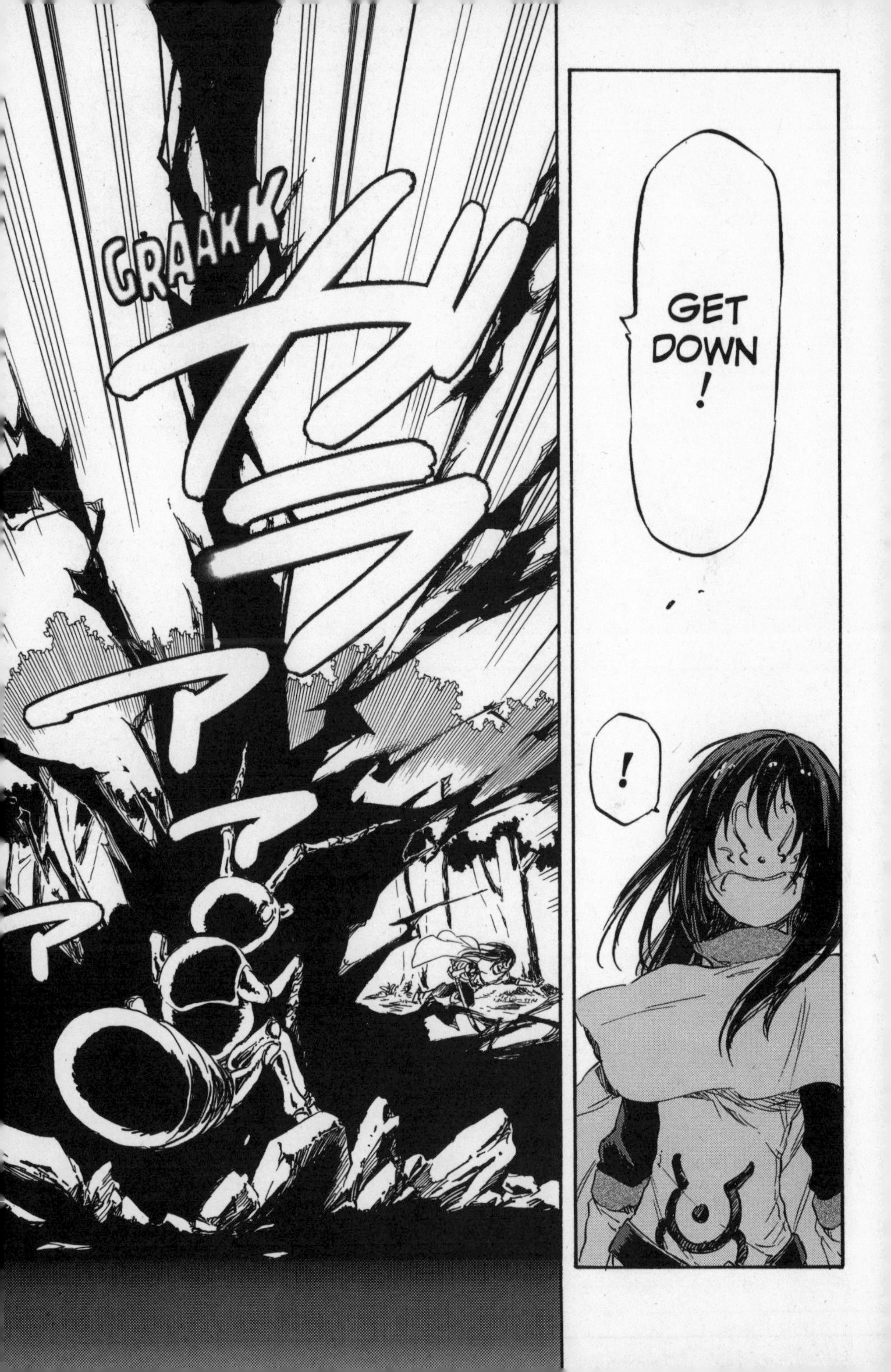
GET DOWN!
!
GRAAKK

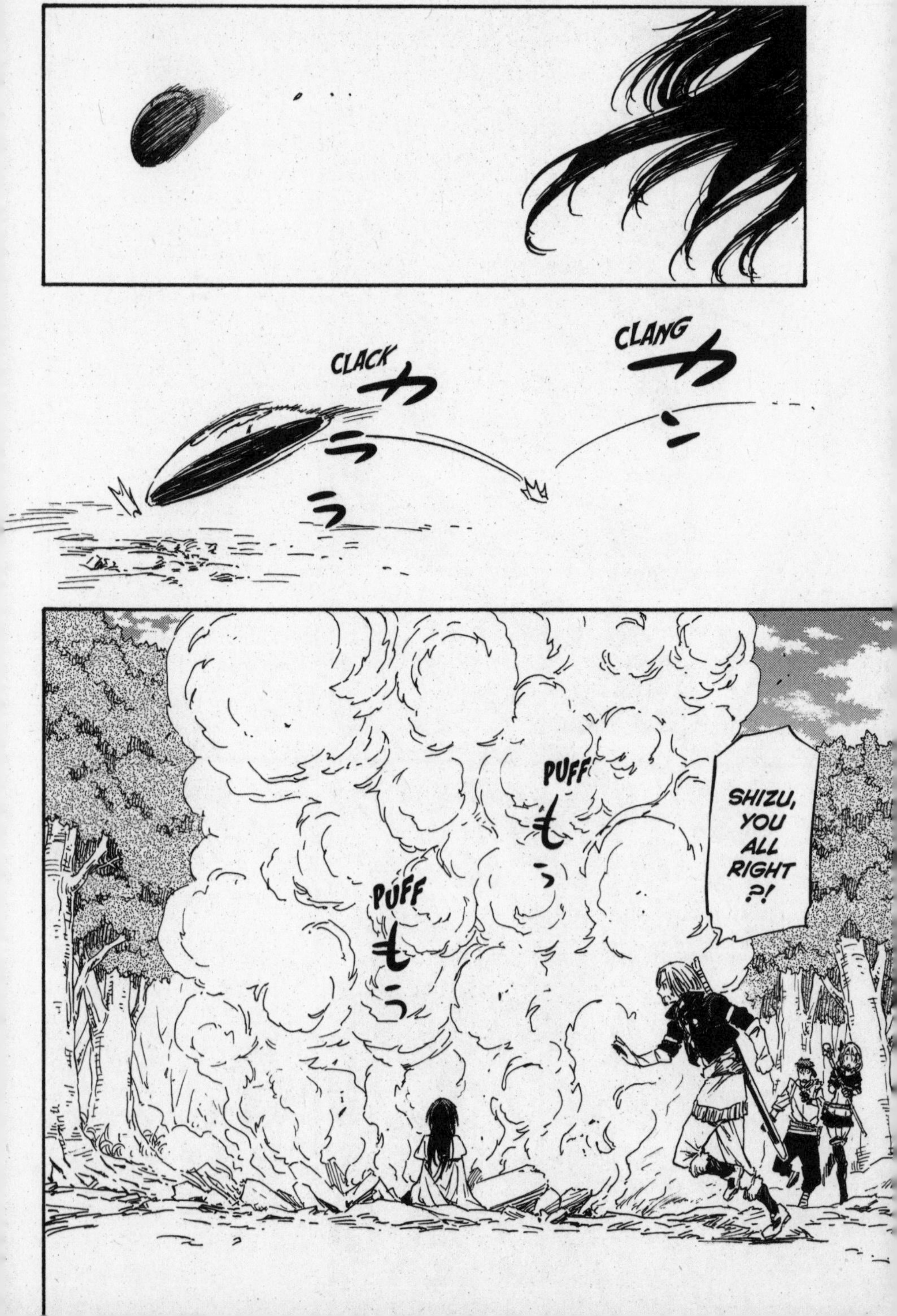
CLANG
カン
CLACK
カララ
SHIZU, YOU ALL RIGHT?!
PUFF
もう
PUFF
もう

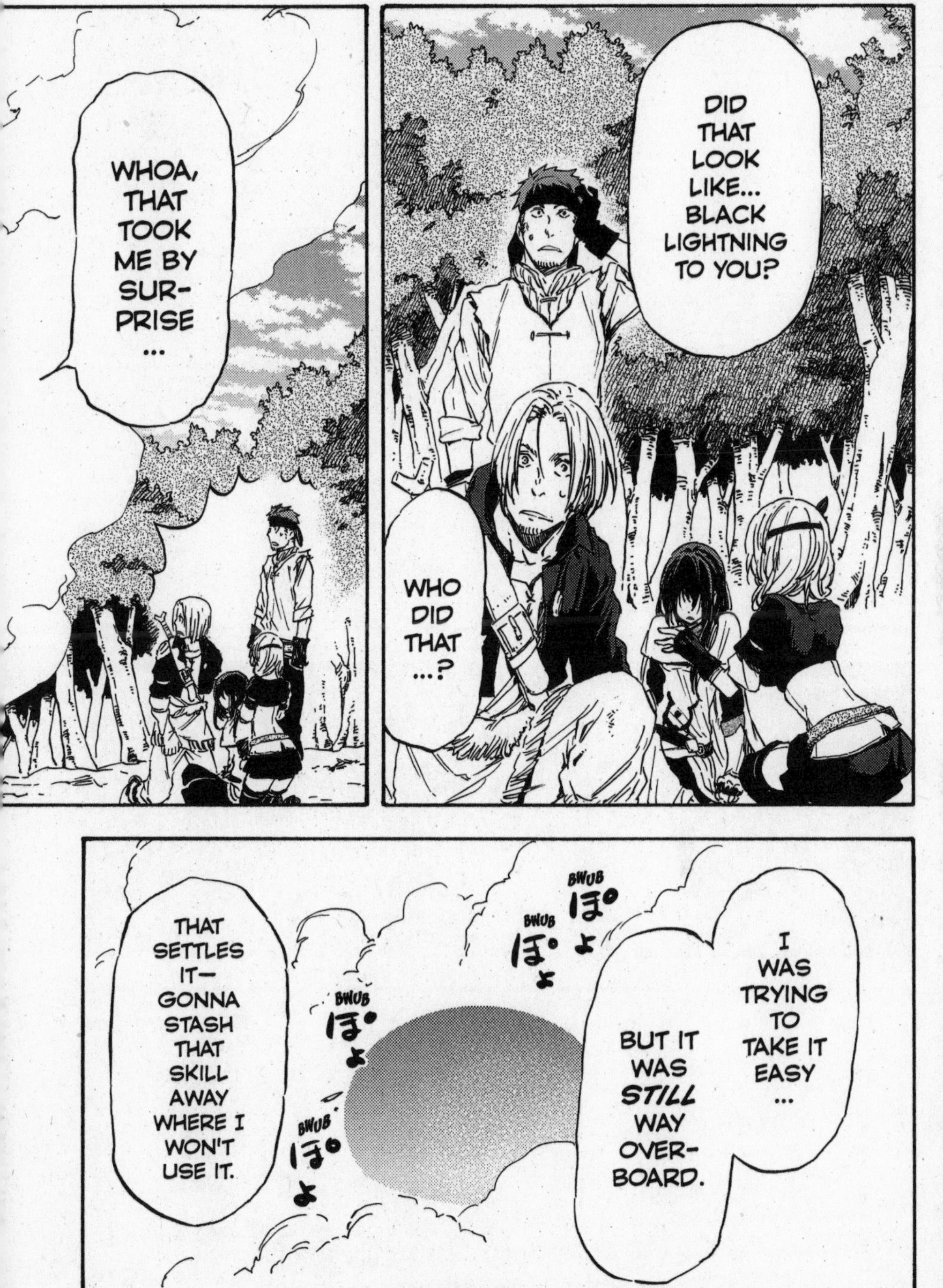
DID THAT LOOK LIKE... BLACK LIGHTNING TO YOU?
WHO DID THAT ...?
WHOA, THAT TOOK ME BY SUR-PRISE ...
I WAS TRYING TO TAKE IT EASY ...
BUT IT WAS *STILL* WAY OVER-BOARD.
BWUB ぽよ
BWUB ぽよ
BWUB ぽよ
BWUB ぽよ
THAT SETTLES IT—GONNA STASH THAT SKILL AWAY WHERE I WON'T USE IT.

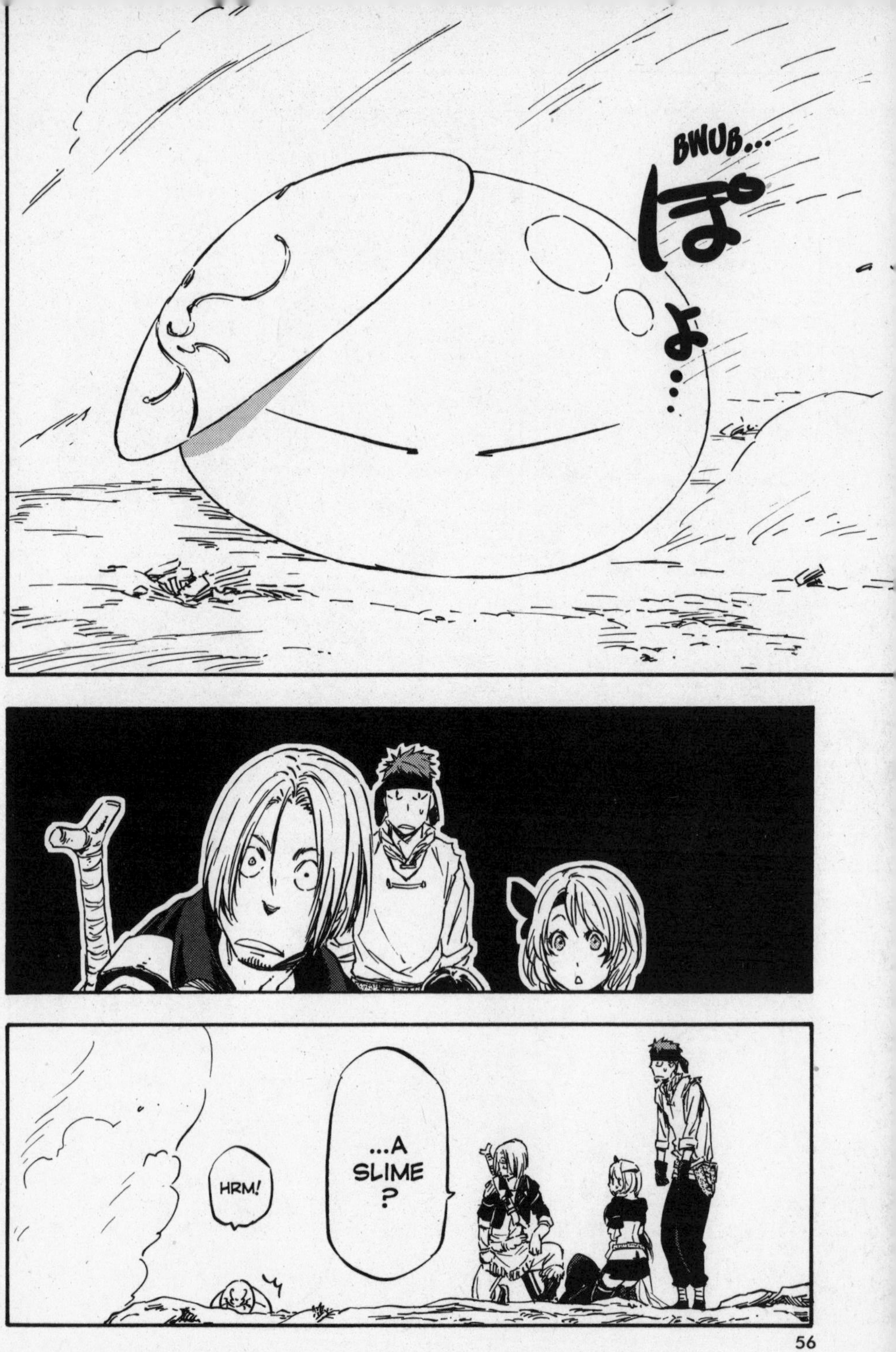
BWUB...
ぽよ...
...A SLIME?
HRM!

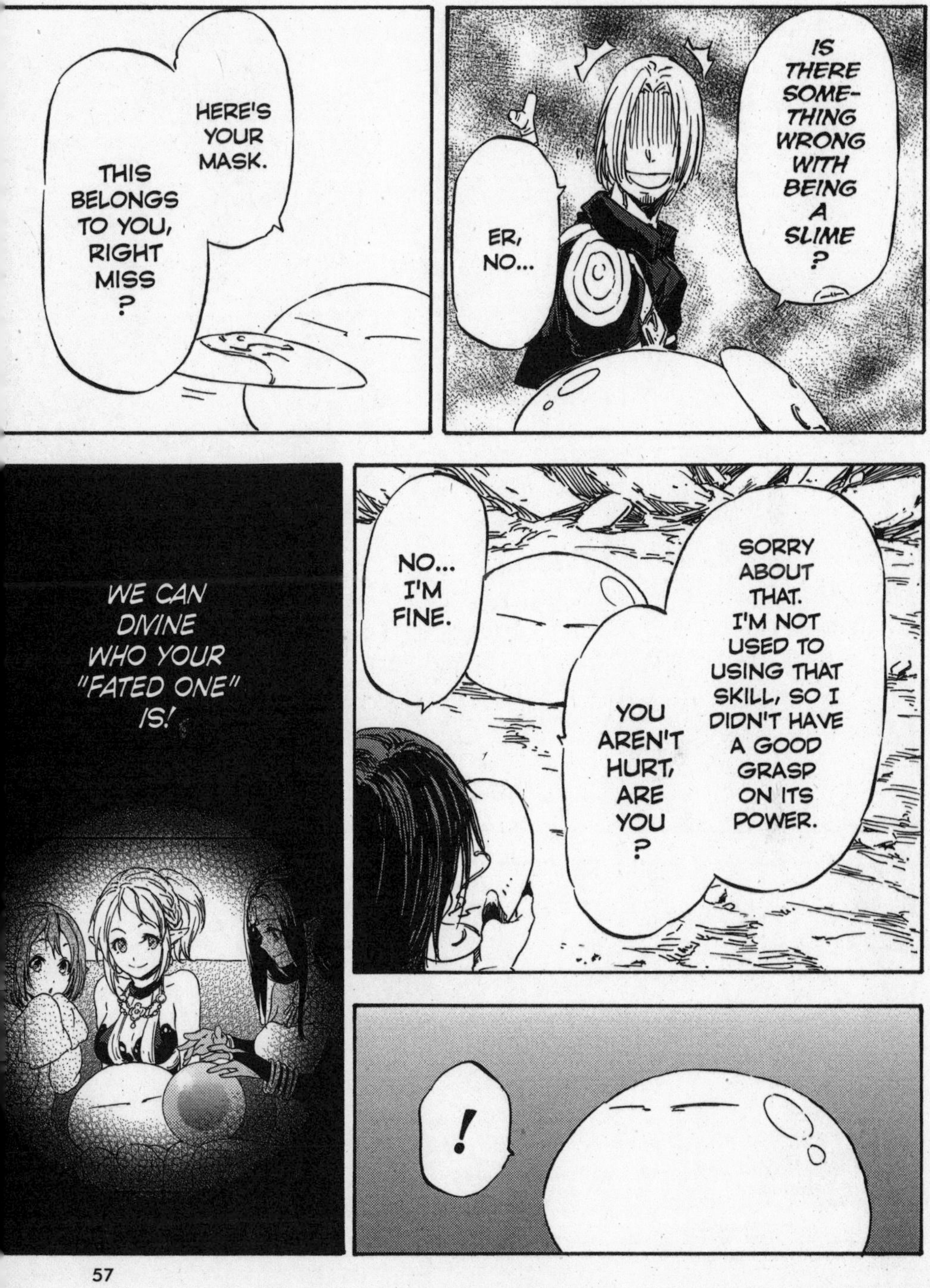
IS THERE SOME-THING WRONG WITH BEING A SLIME?
ER, NO...
HERE'S YOUR MASK.
THIS BELONGS TO YOU, RIGHT MISS?
SORRY ABOUT THAT. I'M NOT USED TO USING THAT SKILL, SO I DIDN'T HAVE A GOOD GRASP ON ITS POWER.
YOU AREN'T HURT, ARE YOU?
NO... I'M FINE.
!
WE CAN DIVINE WHO YOUR "FATED ONE" IS!

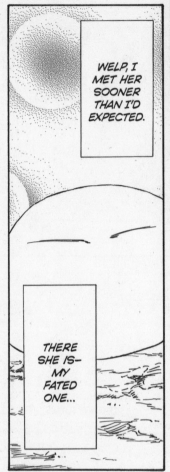

WELP, I MET HER SOONER THAN I'D EXPECTED.

THERE SHE IS— MY FATED ONE...

YOU SAVED ME.

THANK YOU.

UGHHH ...

THUMP

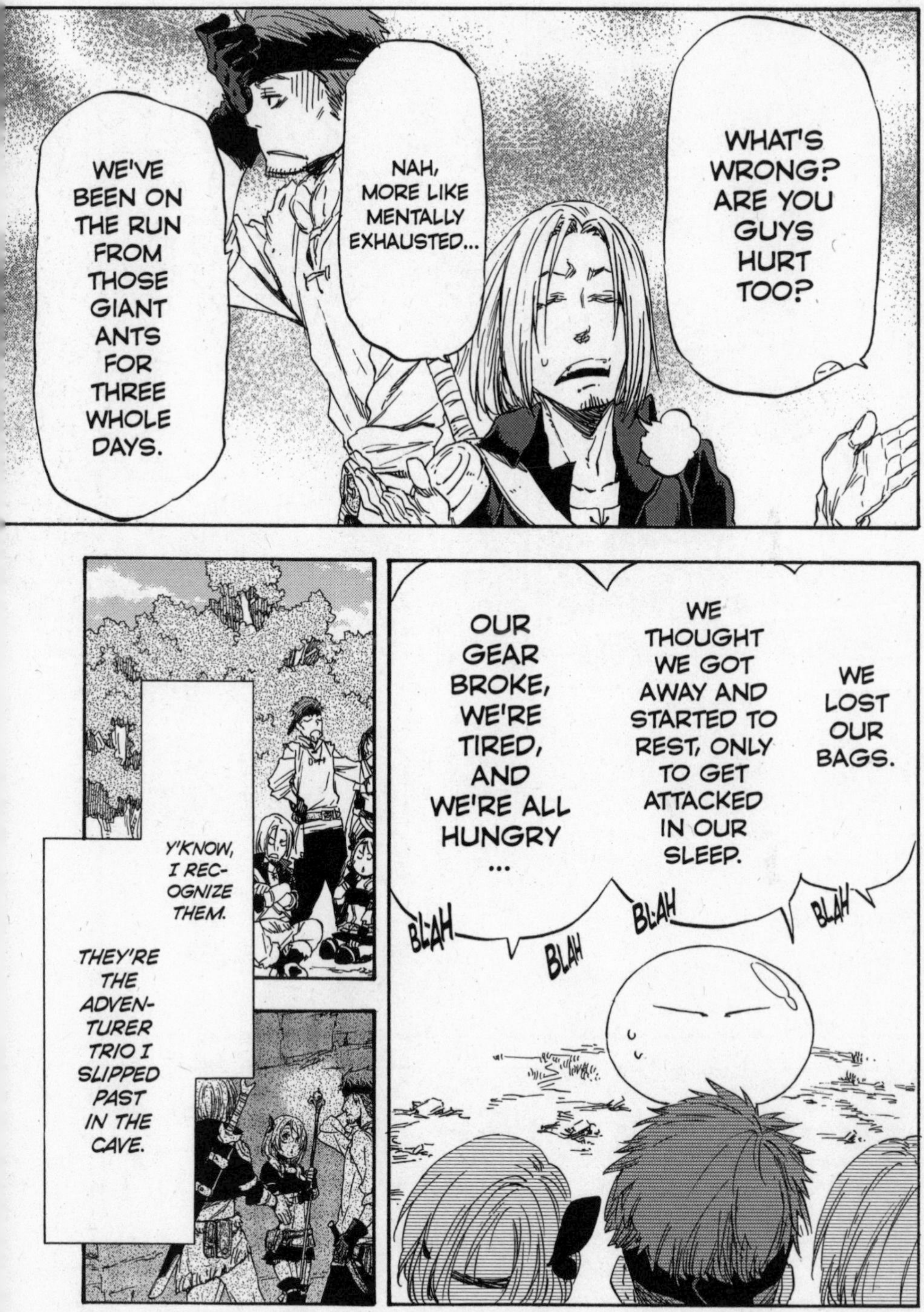
WHAT'S WRONG? ARE YOU GUYS HURT TOO?
NAH, MORE LIKE MENTALLY EXHAUSTED...
WE'VE BEEN ON THE RUN FROM THOSE GIANT ANTS FOR THREE WHOLE DAYS.
WE LOST OUR BAGS.
WE THOUGHT WE GOT AWAY AND STARTED TO REST, ONLY TO GET ATTACKED IN OUR SLEEP.
OUR GEAR BROKE, WE'RE TIRED, AND WE'RE ALL HUNGRY ...
BLAH
BLAH
BLAH
BLAH
BLAH
Y'KNOW, I RECOGNIZE THEM.
THEY'RE THE ADVENTURER TRIO I SLIPPED PAST IN THE CAVE.

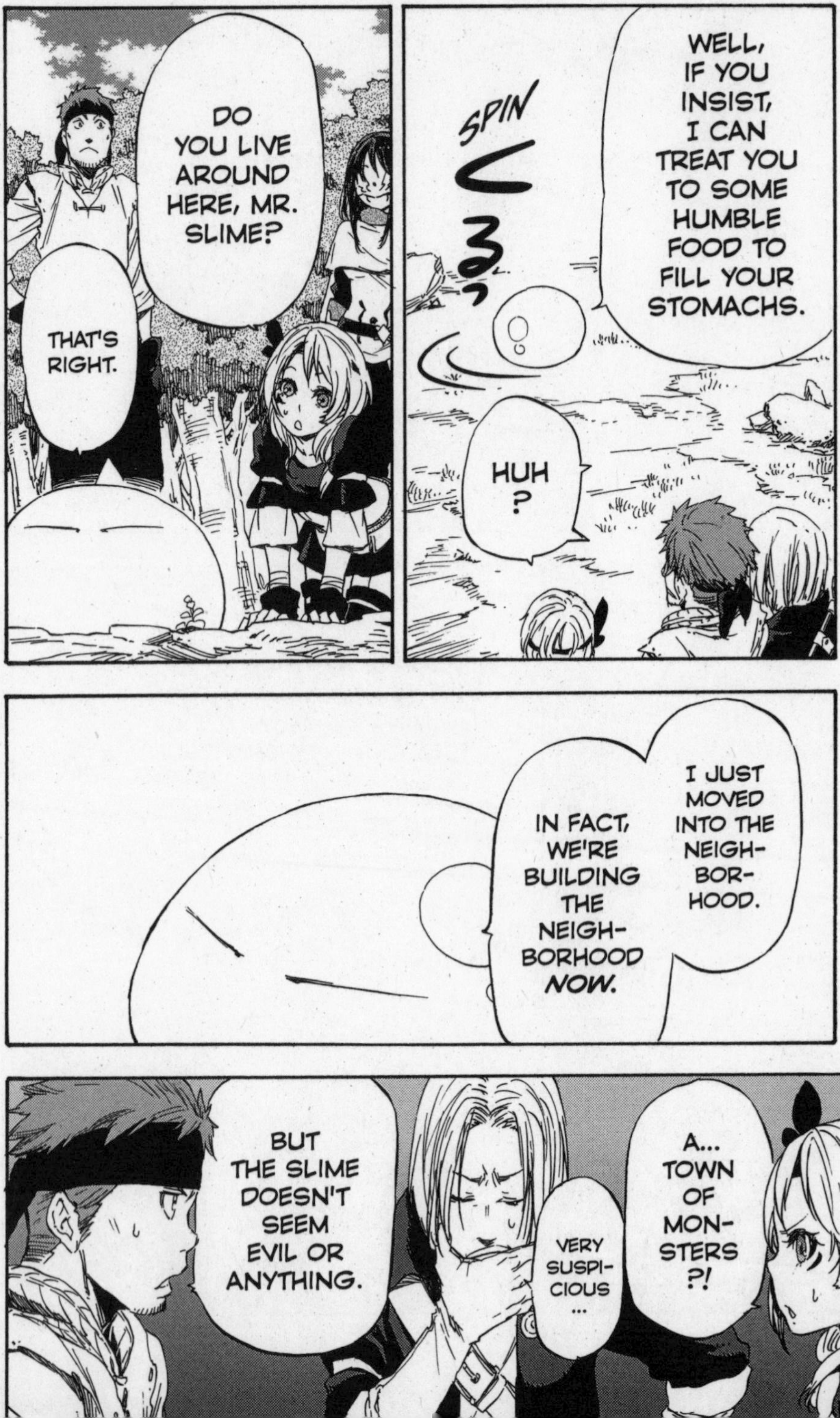
WELL, IF YOU INSIST, I CAN TREAT YOU TO SOME HUMBLE FOOD TO FILL YOUR STOMACHS.
SPIN
くる
HUH?
DO YOU LIVE AROUND HERE, MR. SLIME?
THAT'S RIGHT.
I JUST MOVED INTO THE NEIGHBORHOOD.
IN FACT, WE'RE BUILDING THE NEIGHBORHOOD *NOW*.
A... TOWN OF MONSTERS?!
VERY SUSPICIOUS...
BUT THE SLIME DOESN'T SEEM EVIL OR ANYTHING.

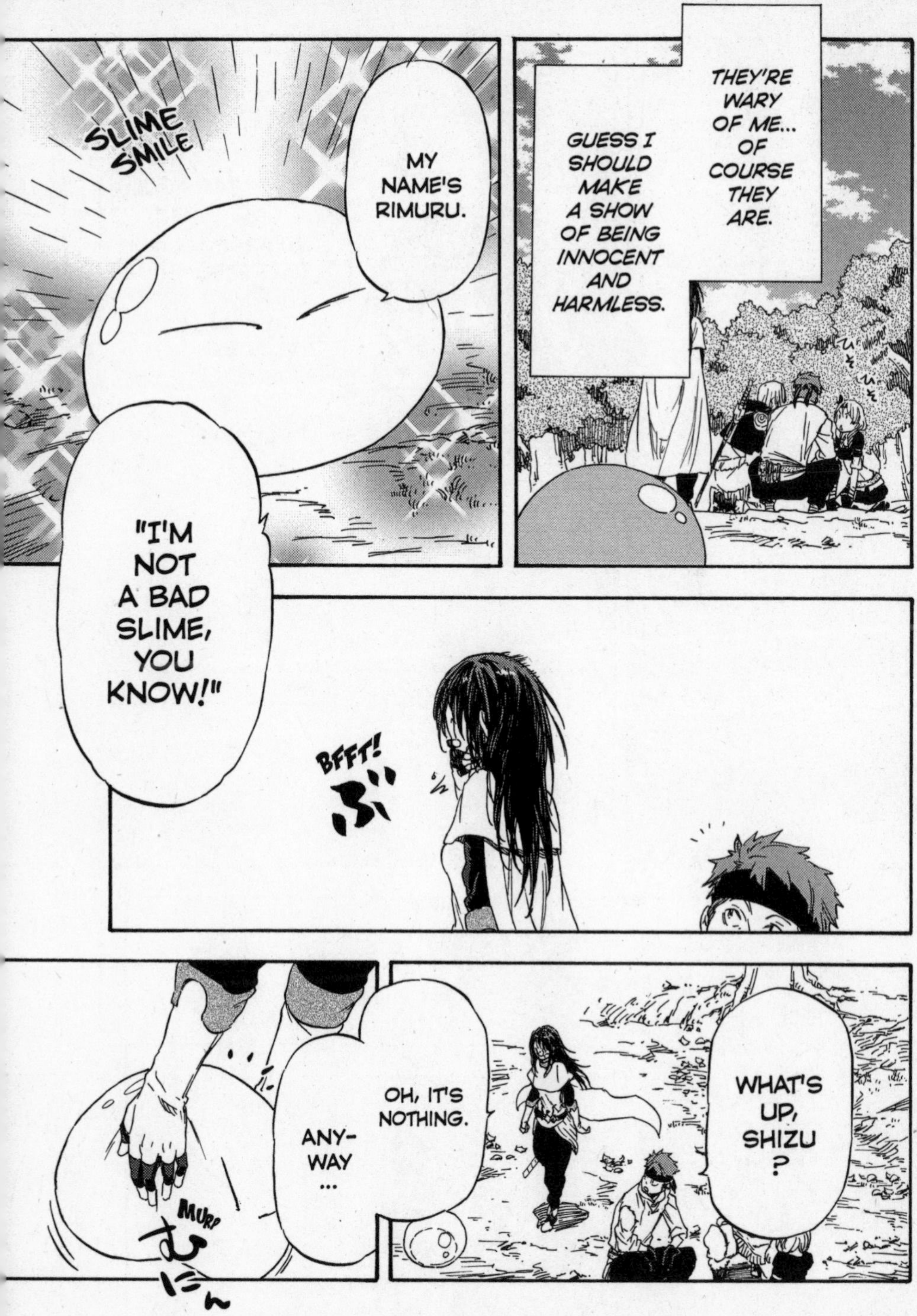
THEY'RE WARY OF ME... OF COURSE THEY ARE.
GUESS I SHOULD MAKE A SHOW OF BEING INNOCENT AND HARMLESS.
SLIME SMILE
MY NAME'S RIMURU.
"I'M NOT A BAD SLIME, YOU KNOW!"
BFFT!
ぶ
WHAT'S UP, SHIZU?
OH, IT'S NOTHING.
ANYWAY...
MURP
むにゅ

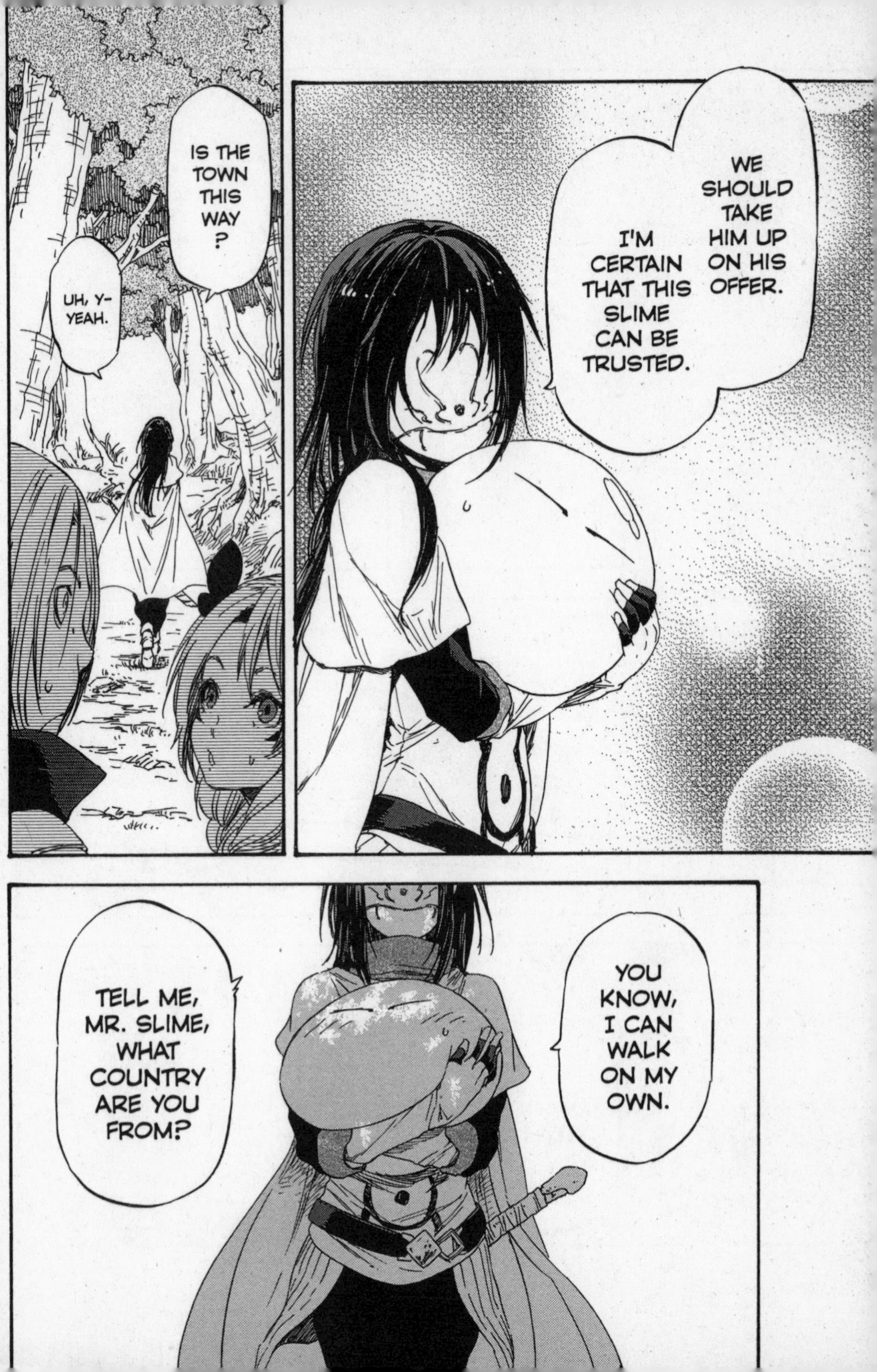
WE SHOULD TAKE HIM UP ON HIS OFFER.
I'M CERTAIN THAT THIS SLIME CAN BE TRUSTED.
IS THE TOWN THIS WAY?
UH, Y-YEAH.
YOU KNOW, I CAN WALK ON MY OWN.
TELL ME, MR. SLIME, WHAT COUNTRY ARE YOU FROM?

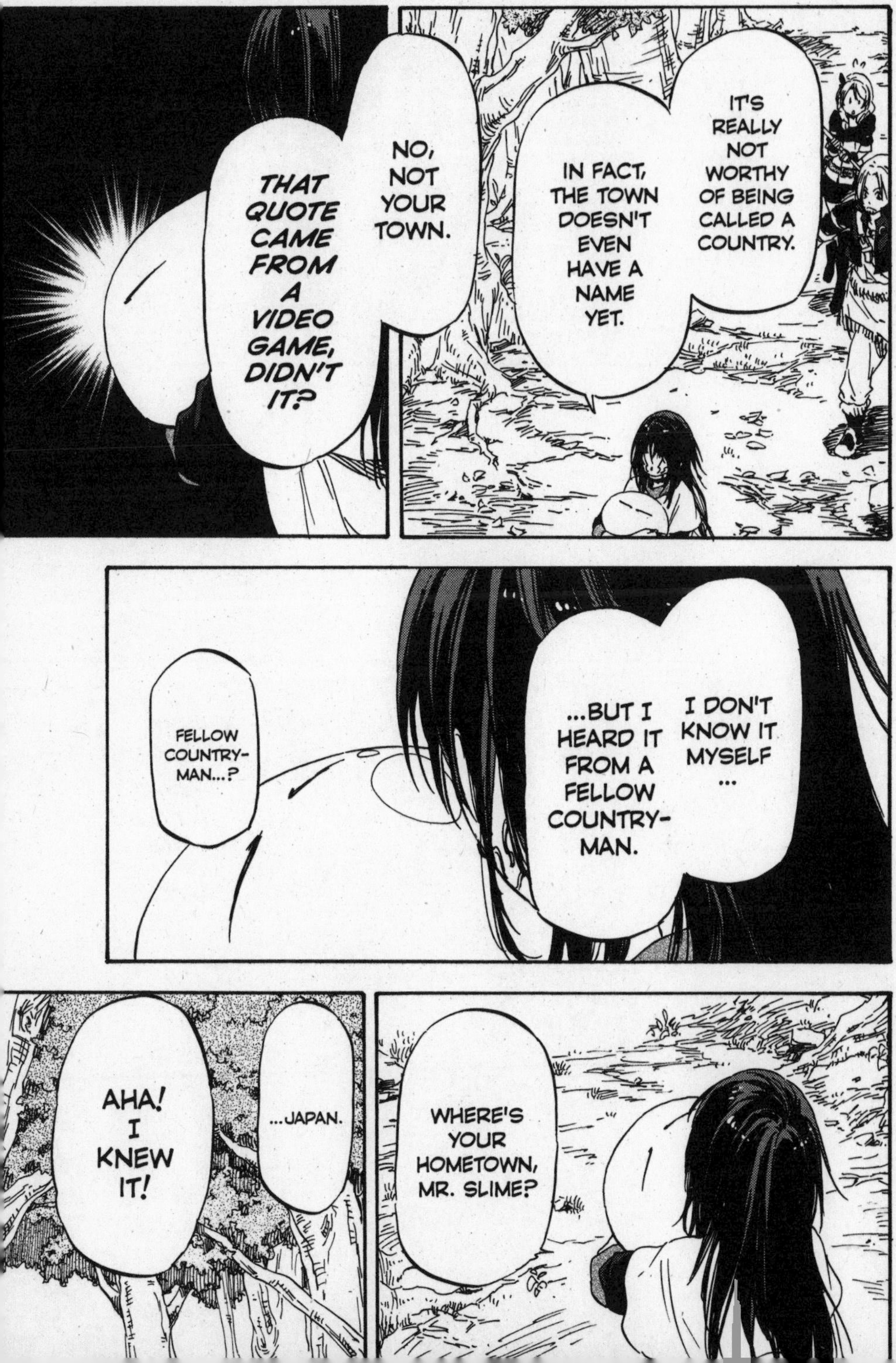
IT'S REALLY NOT WORTHY OF BEING CALLED A COUNTRY.
IN FACT, THE TOWN DOESN'T EVEN HAVE A NAME YET.
NO, NOT YOUR TOWN.
THAT QUOTE CAME FROM A VIDEO GAME, DIDN'T IT?
I DON'T KNOW IT MYSELF ...
...BUT I HEARD IT FROM A FELLOW COUNTRY-MAN.
FELLOW COUNTRY-MAN...?
WHERE'S YOUR HOMETOWN, MR. SLIME?
...JAPAN.
AHA! I KNEW IT!

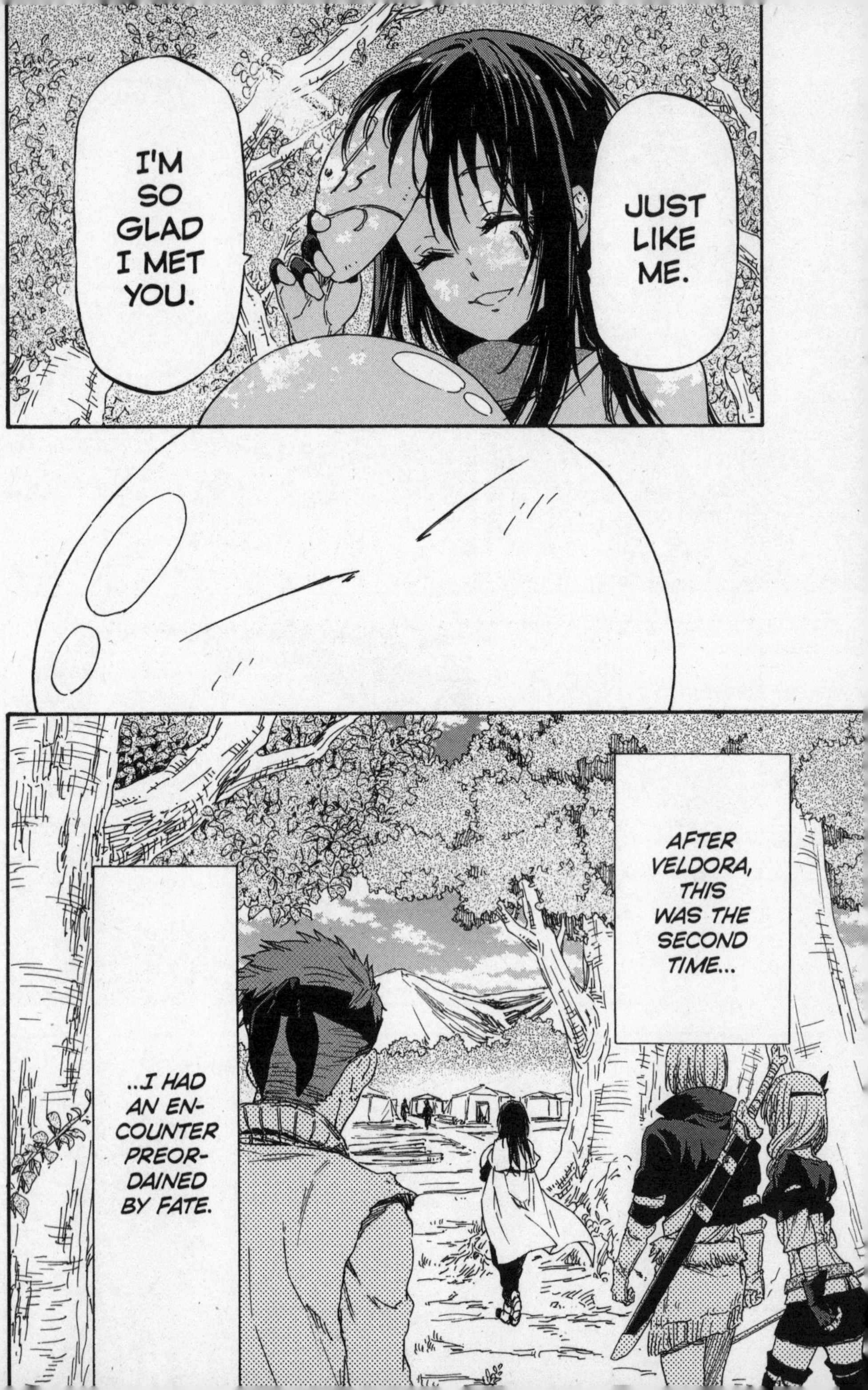
JUST LIKE ME.
I'M SO GLAD I MET YOU.
AFTER VELDORA, THIS WAS THE SECOND TIME...
...I HAD AN EN-COUNTER PREOR-DAINED BY FATE.

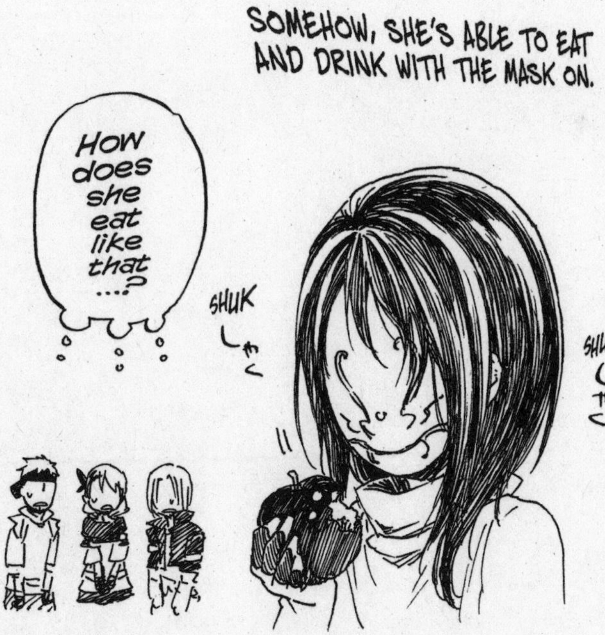
SOMEHOW, SHE'S ABLE TO EAT AND DRINK WITH THE MASK ON.
SHUK
How does she eat like that...?
SHUK

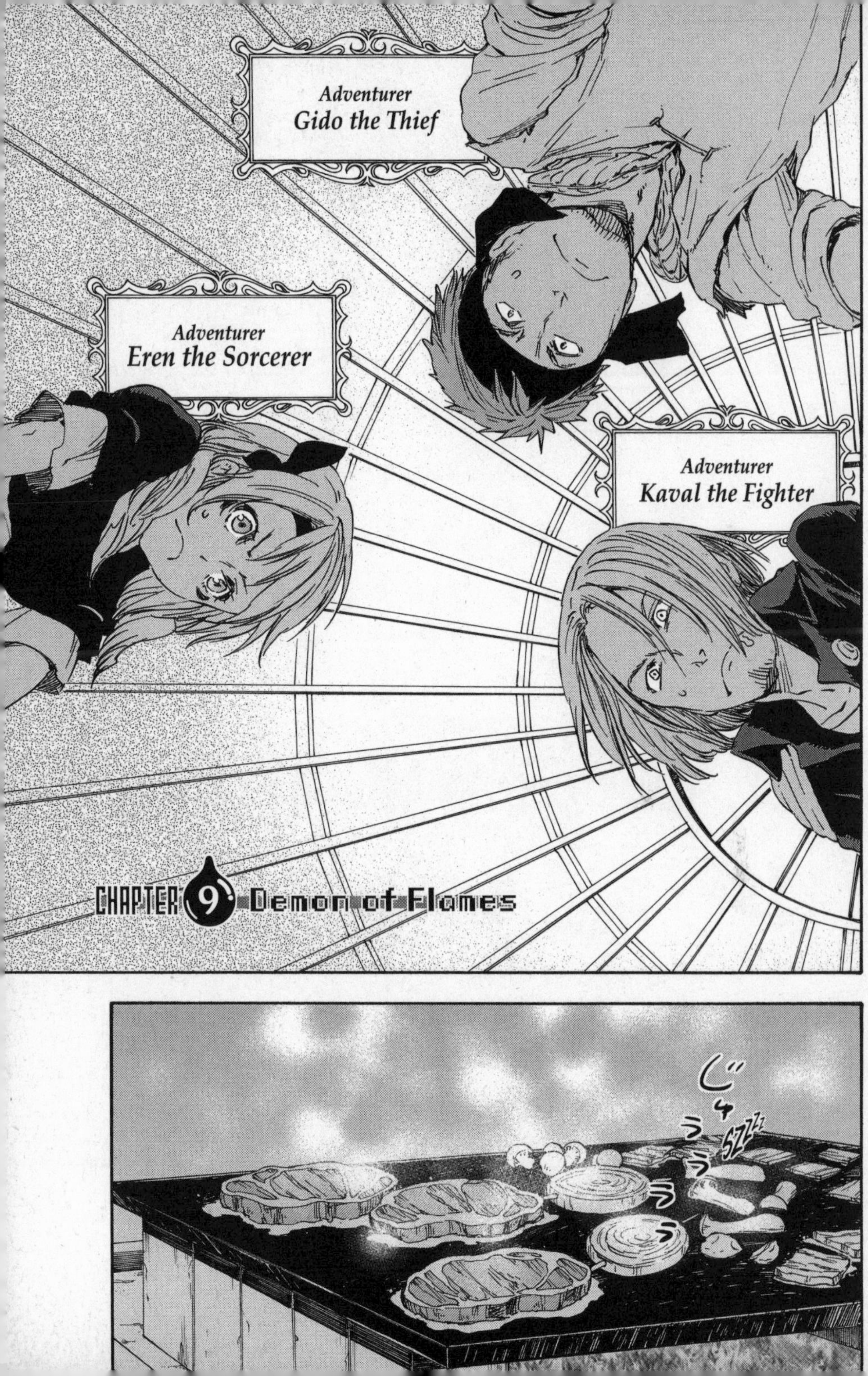
Adventurer
Gido the Thief
Adventurer
Kaval the Fighter
Adventurer
Eren the Sorcerer
CHAPTER 9 Demon of Flames
じゅうううう
SZZZZZ

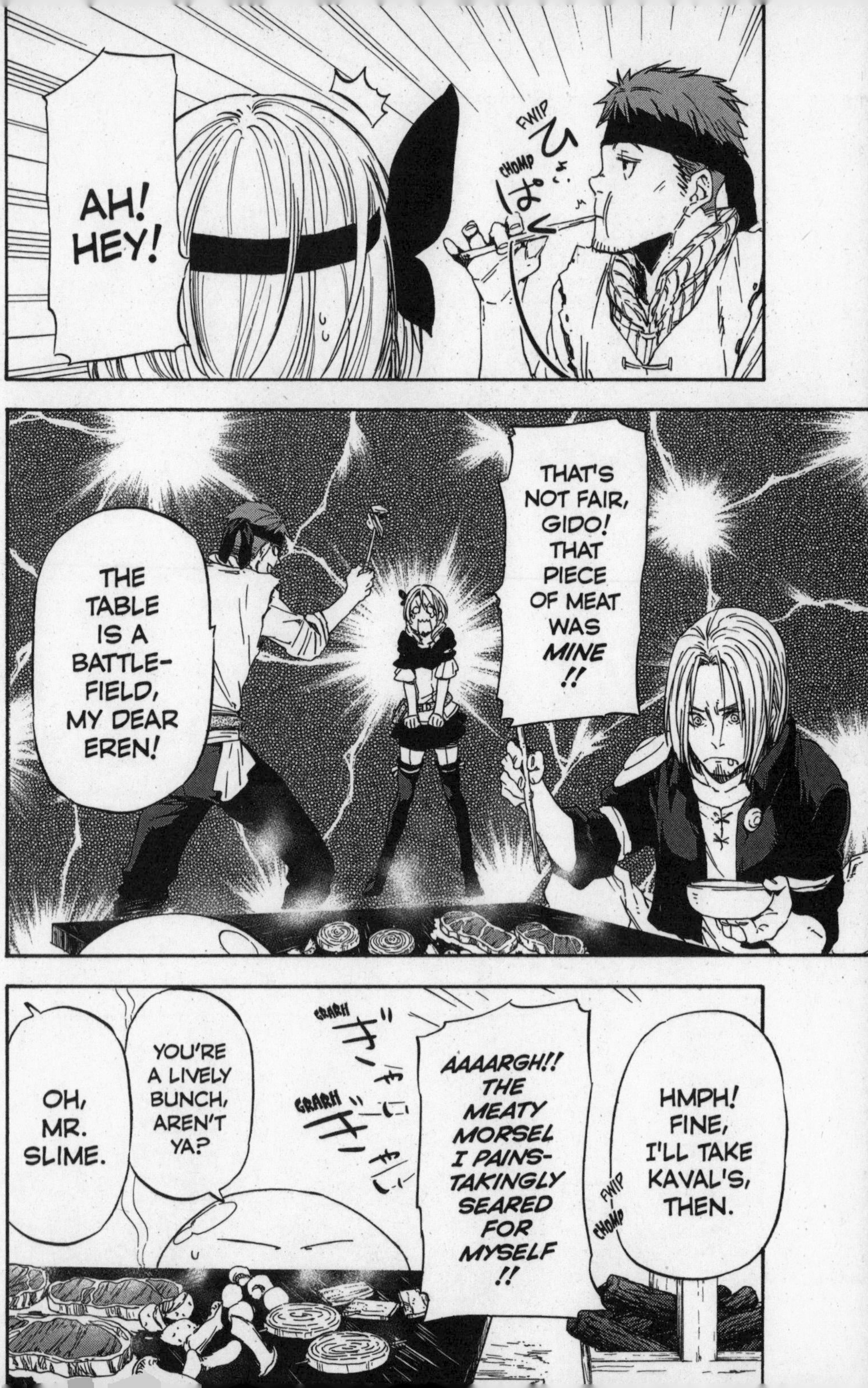

FWIP
CHOMP
AH! HEY!
THAT'S NOT FAIR, GIDO! THAT PIECE OF MEAT WAS *MINE* !!
THE TABLE IS A BATTLE-FIELD, MY DEAR EREN!
HMPH! FINE, I'LL TAKE KAVAL'S, THEN.
FWIP
CHOMP
AAAARGH!! THE MEATY MORSEL I PAINS-TAKINGLY SEARED FOR MYSELF !!
GRARH
GRARH
YOU'RE A LIVELY BUNCH, AREN'T YA?
OH, MR. SLIME.

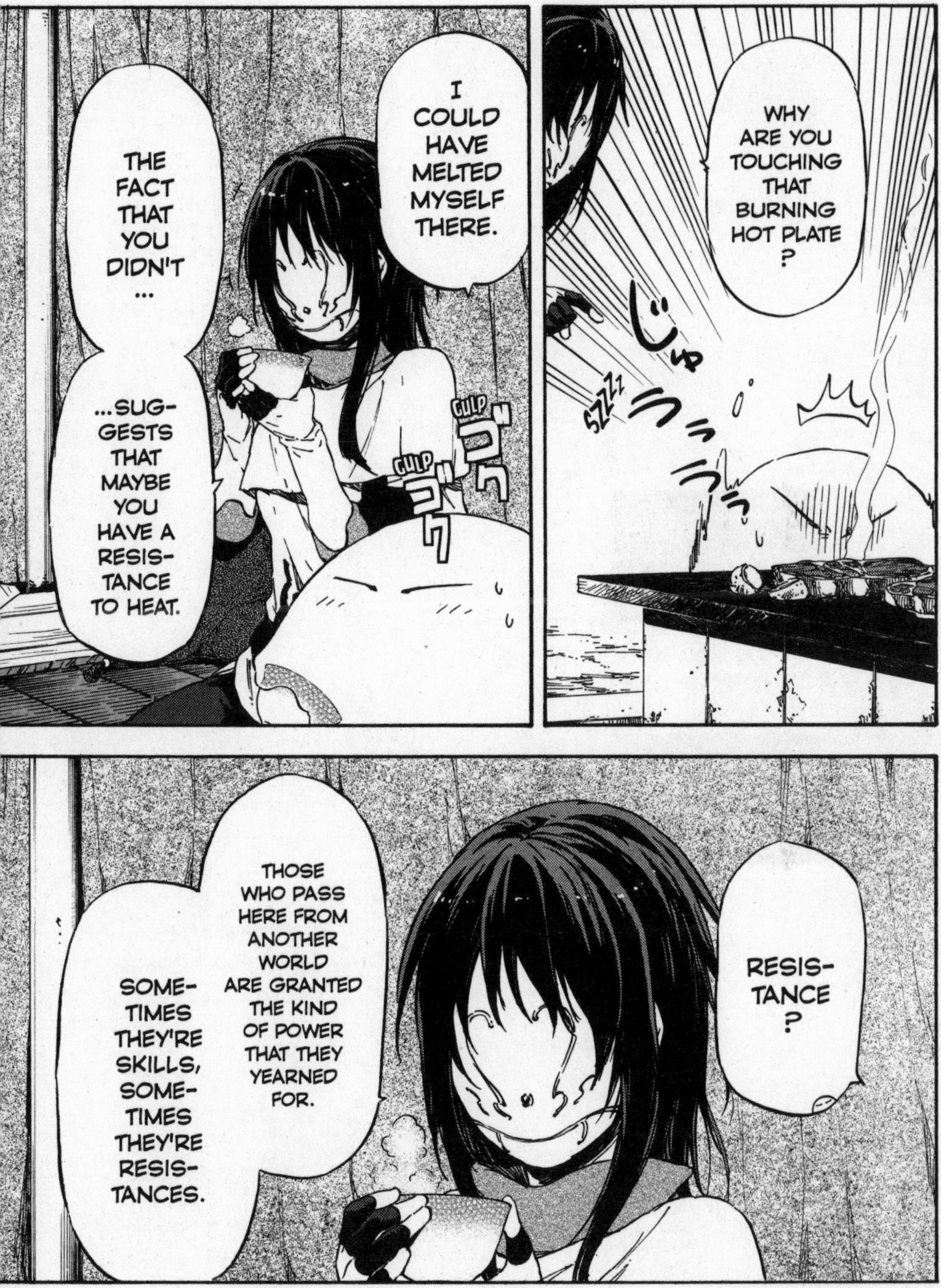
WHY ARE YOU TOUCHING THAT BURNING HOT PLATE?
じゅううう
SZZZZ
I COULD HAVE MELTED MYSELF THERE.
GULP
ゴク
GULP
ゴク
THE FACT THAT YOU DIDN'T ...
...SUGGESTS THAT MAYBE YOU HAVE A RESISTANCE TO HEAT.
RESISTANCE?
THOSE WHO PASS HERE FROM ANOTHER WORLD ARE GRANTED THE KIND OF POWER THAT THEY YEARNED FOR.
SOMETIMES THEY'RE SKILLS, SOMETIMES THEY'RE RESISTANCES.

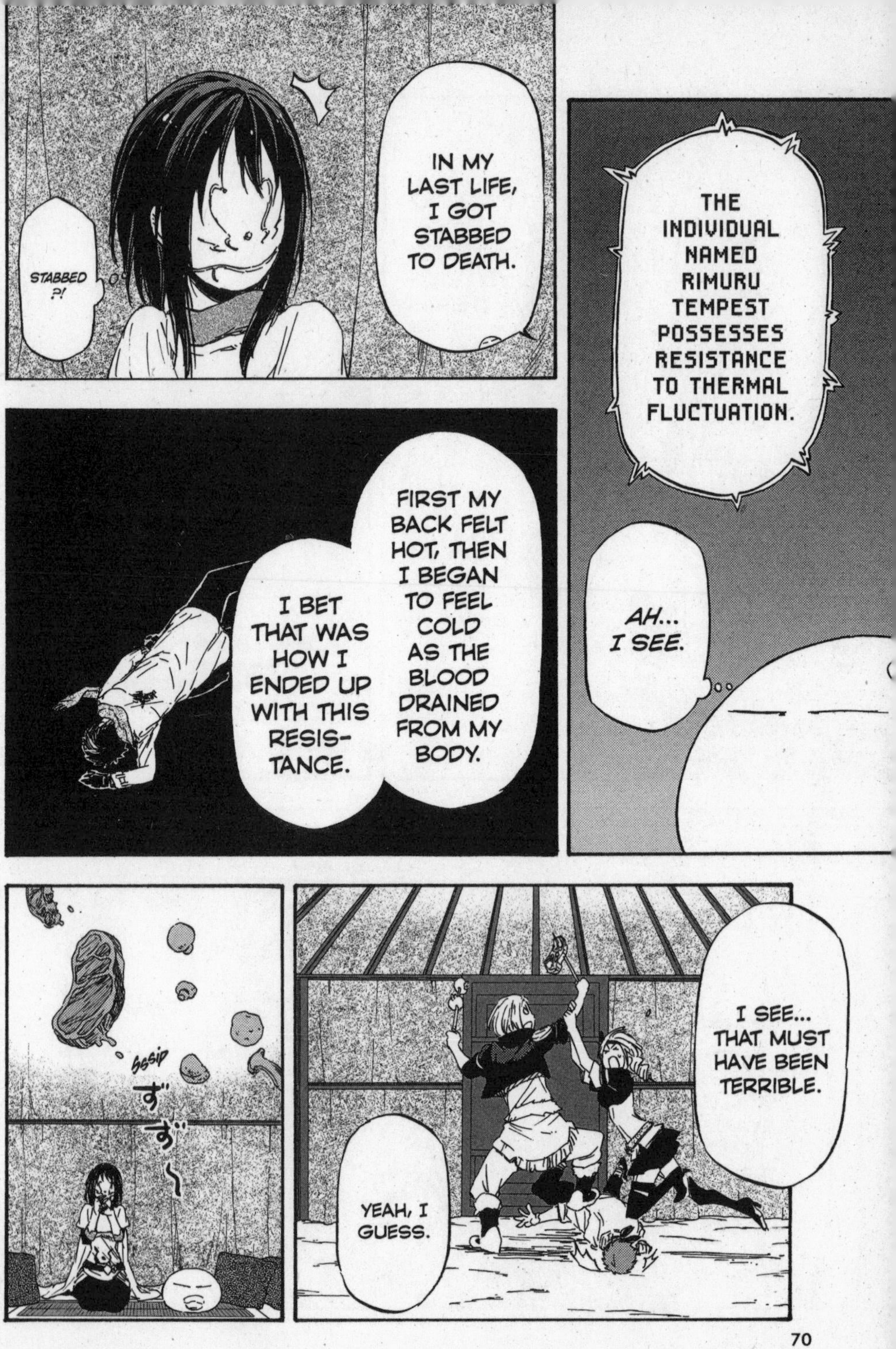
THE INDIVIDUAL NAMED RIMURU TEMPEST POSSESSES RESISTANCE TO THERMAL FLUCTUATION.
AH... I SEE.
IN MY LAST LIFE, I GOT STABBED TO DEATH.
STABBED?!
FIRST MY BACK FELT HOT, THEN I BEGAN TO FEEL COLD AS THE BLOOD DRAINED FROM MY BODY.
I BET THAT WAS HOW I ENDED UP WITH THIS RESIS-TANCE.
I SEE... THAT MUST HAVE BEEN TERRIBLE.
YEAH, I GUESS.
SSSIP
ずず~

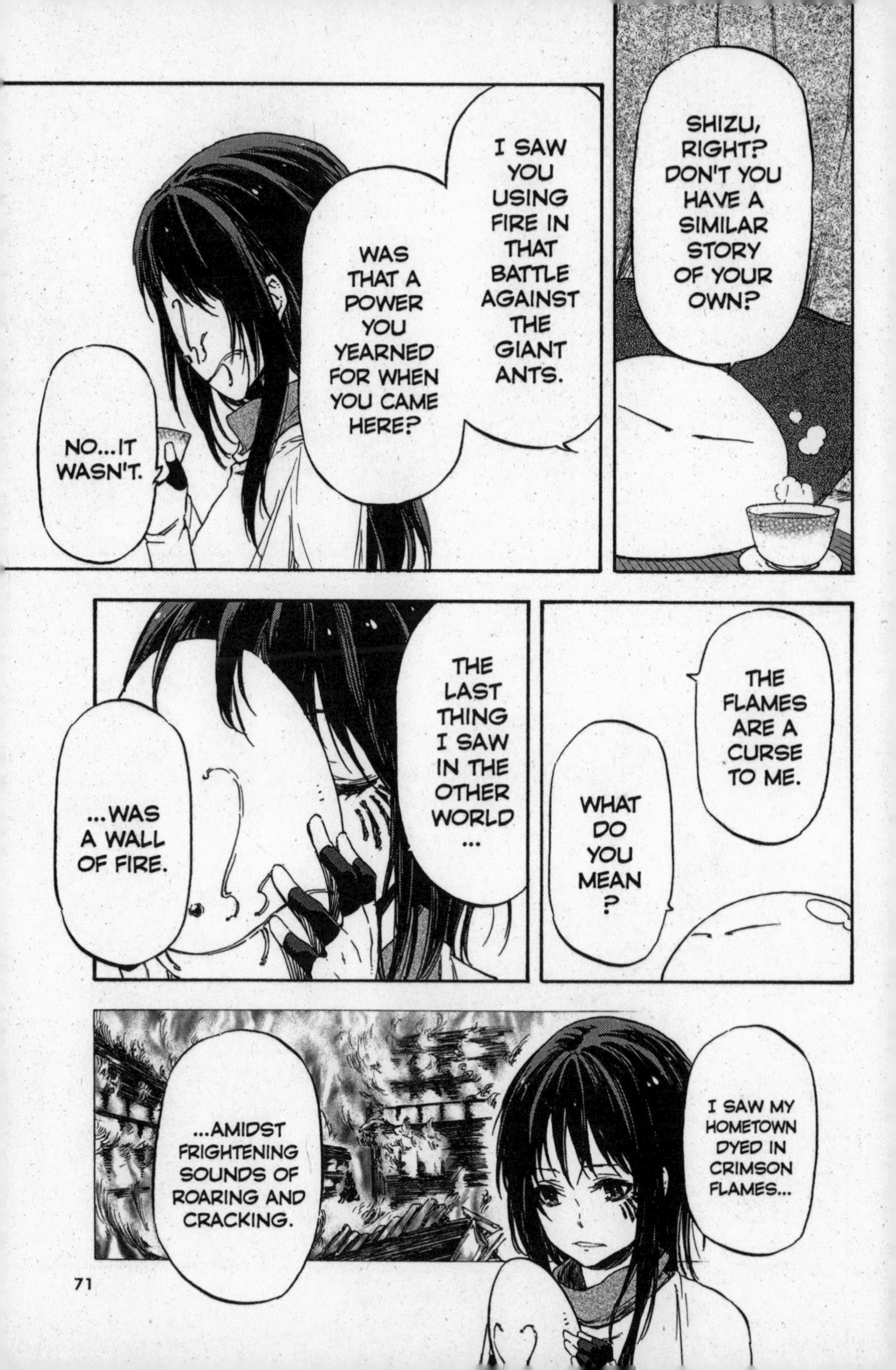
SHIZU, RIGHT? DON'T YOU HAVE A SIMILAR STORY OF YOUR OWN?
I SAW YOU USING FIRE IN THAT BATTLE AGAINST THE GIANT ANTS.
WAS THAT A POWER YOU YEARNED FOR WHEN YOU CAME HERE?
NO...IT WASN'T.
THE FLAMES ARE A CURSE TO ME.
WHAT DO YOU MEAN?
THE LAST THING I SAW IN THE OTHER WORLD...
...WAS A WALL OF FIRE.
I SAW MY HOMETOWN DYED IN CRIMSON FLAMES...
...AMIDST FRIGHTENING SOUNDS OF ROARING AND CRACKING.

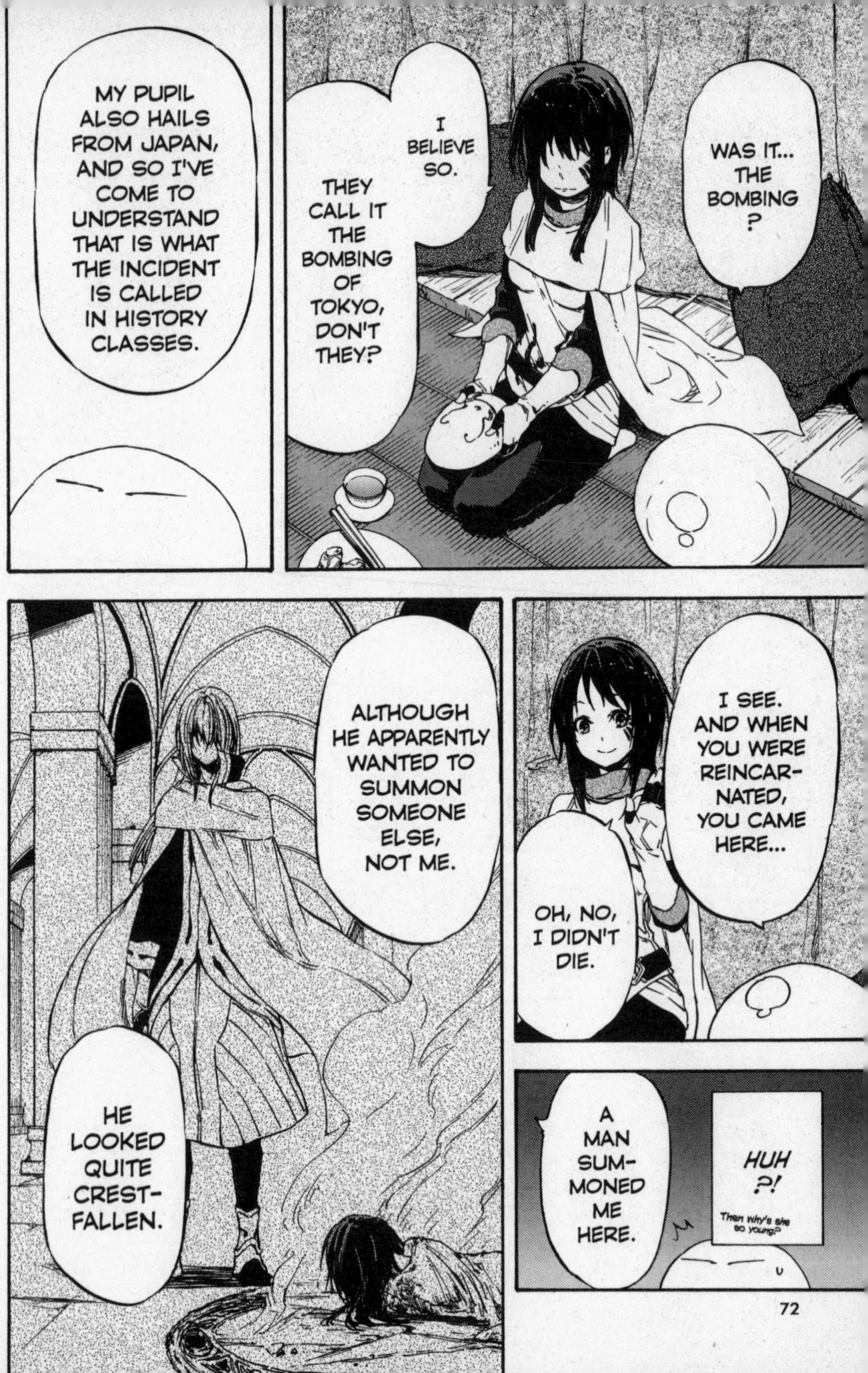
WAS IT... THE BOMBING?
I BELIEVE SO.
THEY CALL IT THE BOMBING OF TOKYO, DON'T THEY?
MY PUPIL ALSO HAILS FROM JAPAN, AND SO I'VE COME TO UNDERSTAND THAT IS WHAT THE INCIDENT IS CALLED IN HISTORY CLASSES.
I SEE. AND WHEN YOU WERE REINCAR-NATED, YOU CAME HERE...
OH, NO, I DIDN'T DIE.
HUH?!
Then why's she so young?
A MAN SUM-MONED ME HERE.
ALTHOUGH HE APPARENTLY WANTED TO SUMMON SOMEONE ELSE, NOT ME.
HE LOOKED QUITE CREST-FALLEN.

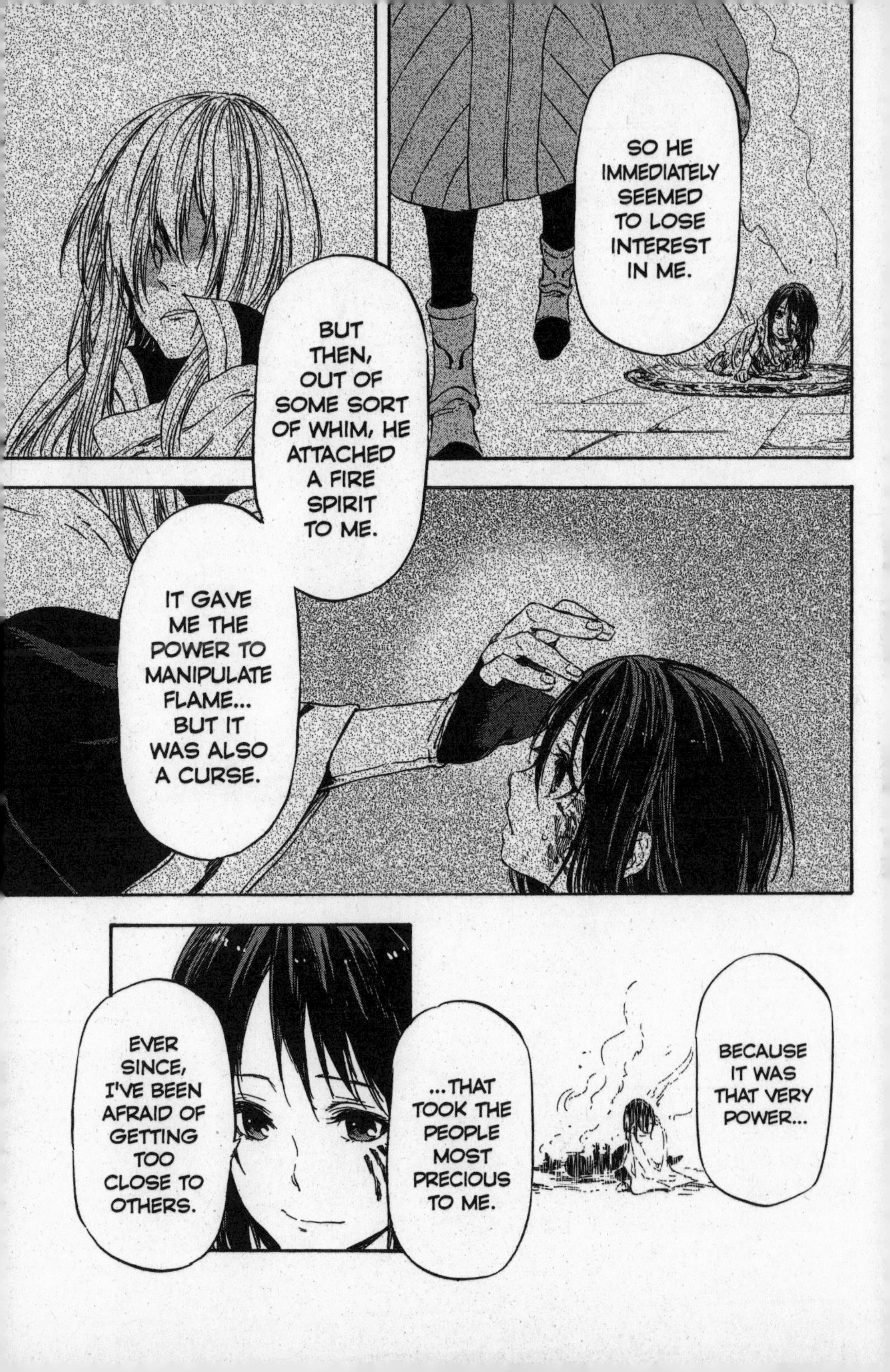
SO HE IMMEDIATELY SEEMED TO LOSE INTEREST IN ME.
BUT THEN, OUT OF SOME SORT OF WHIM, HE ATTACHED A FIRE SPIRIT TO ME.
IT GAVE ME THE POWER TO MANIPULATE FLAME... BUT IT WAS ALSO A CURSE.
BECAUSE IT WAS THAT VERY POWER...
...THAT TOOK THE PEOPLE MOST PRECIOUS TO ME.
EVER SINCE, I'VE BEEN AFRAID OF GETTING TOO CLOSE TO OTHERS.

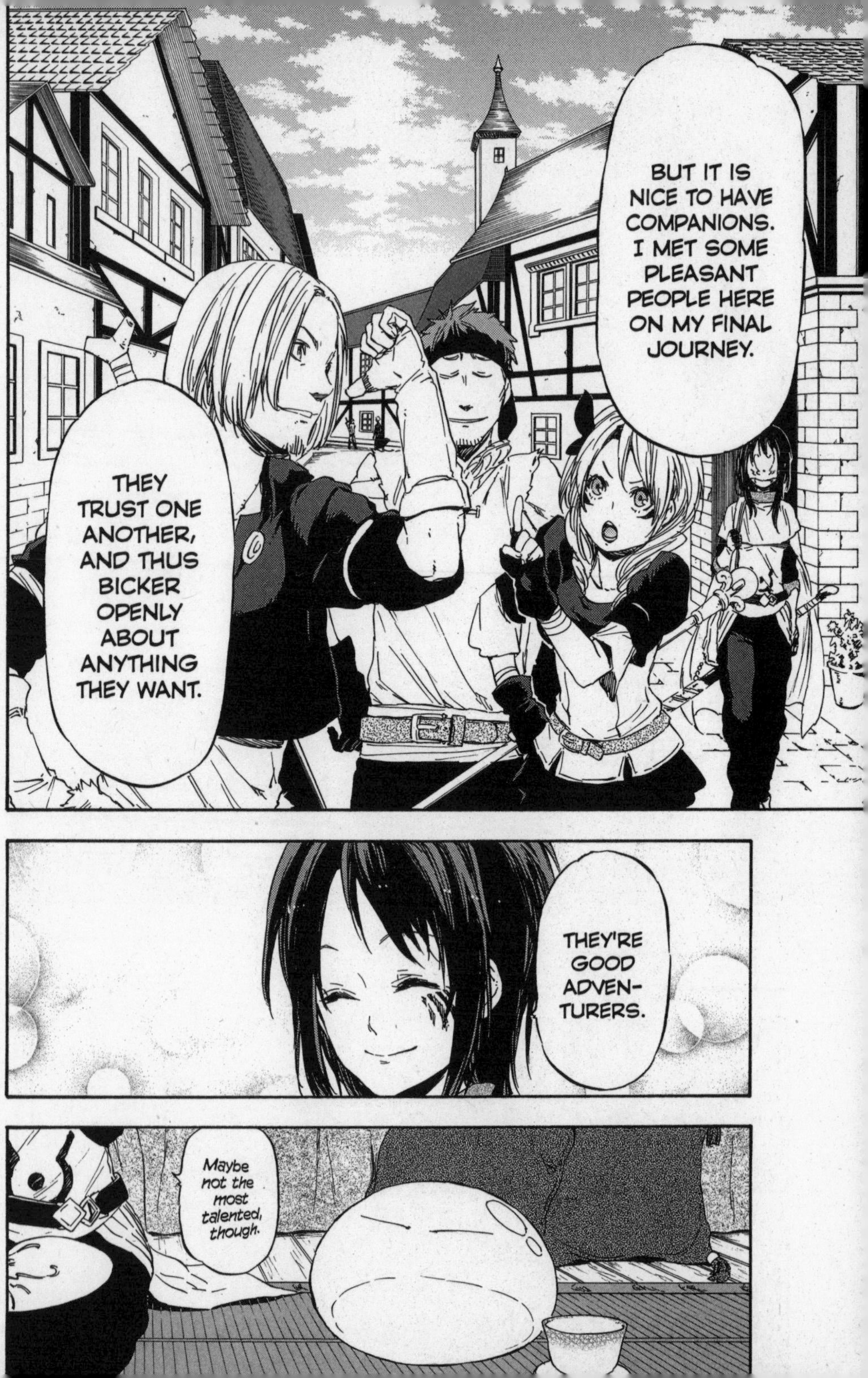
BUT IT IS NICE TO HAVE COMPANIONS. I MET SOME PLEASANT PEOPLE HERE ON MY FINAL JOURNEY.
THEY TRUST ONE ANOTHER, AND THUS BICKER OPENLY ABOUT ANYTHING THEY WANT.
THEY'RE GOOD ADVEN-TURERS.
Maybe not the most talented, though.

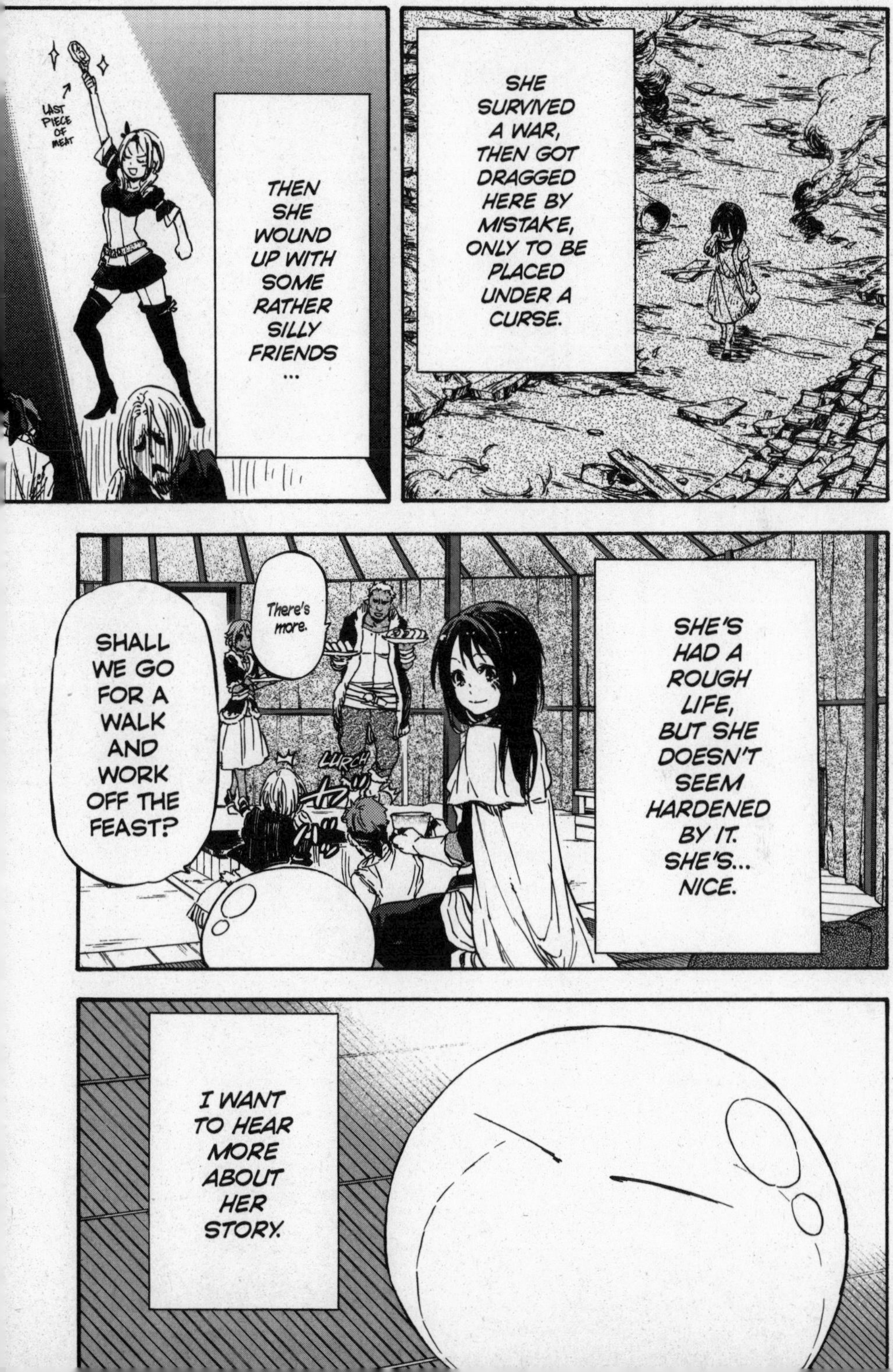
SHE SURVIVED A WAR, THEN GOT DRAGGED HERE BY MISTAKE, ONLY TO BE PLACED UNDER A CURSE.
THEN SHE WOUND UP WITH SOME RATHER SILLY FRIENDS...
LAST PIECE OF MEAT
SHE'S HAD A ROUGH LIFE, BUT SHE DOESN'T SEEM HARDENED BY IT. SHE'S... NICE.
There's more.
SHALL WE GO FOR A WALK AND WORK OFF THE FEAST?
LURCH
I WANT TO HEAR MORE ABOUT HER STORY.

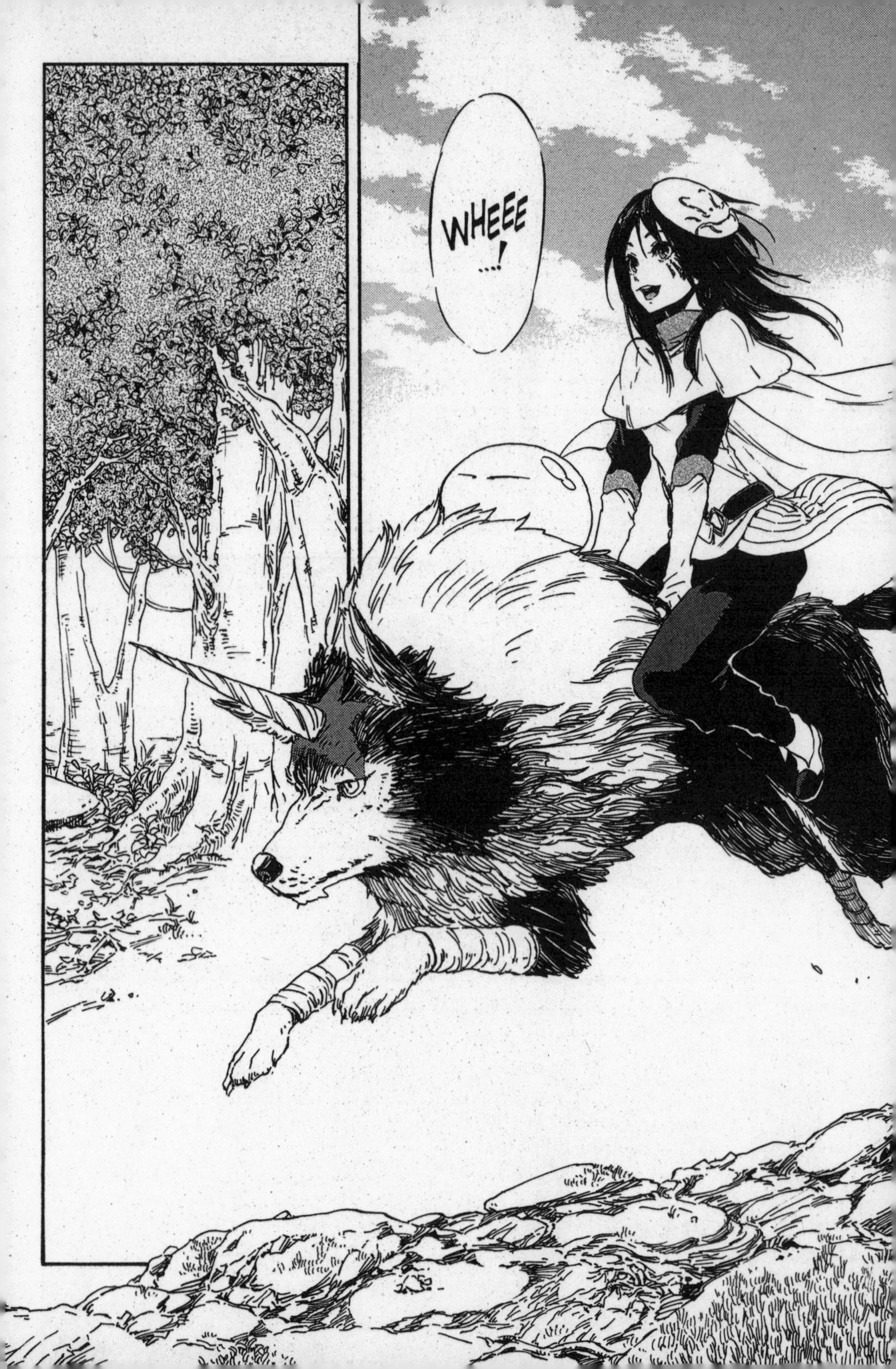
WHEEE ...!

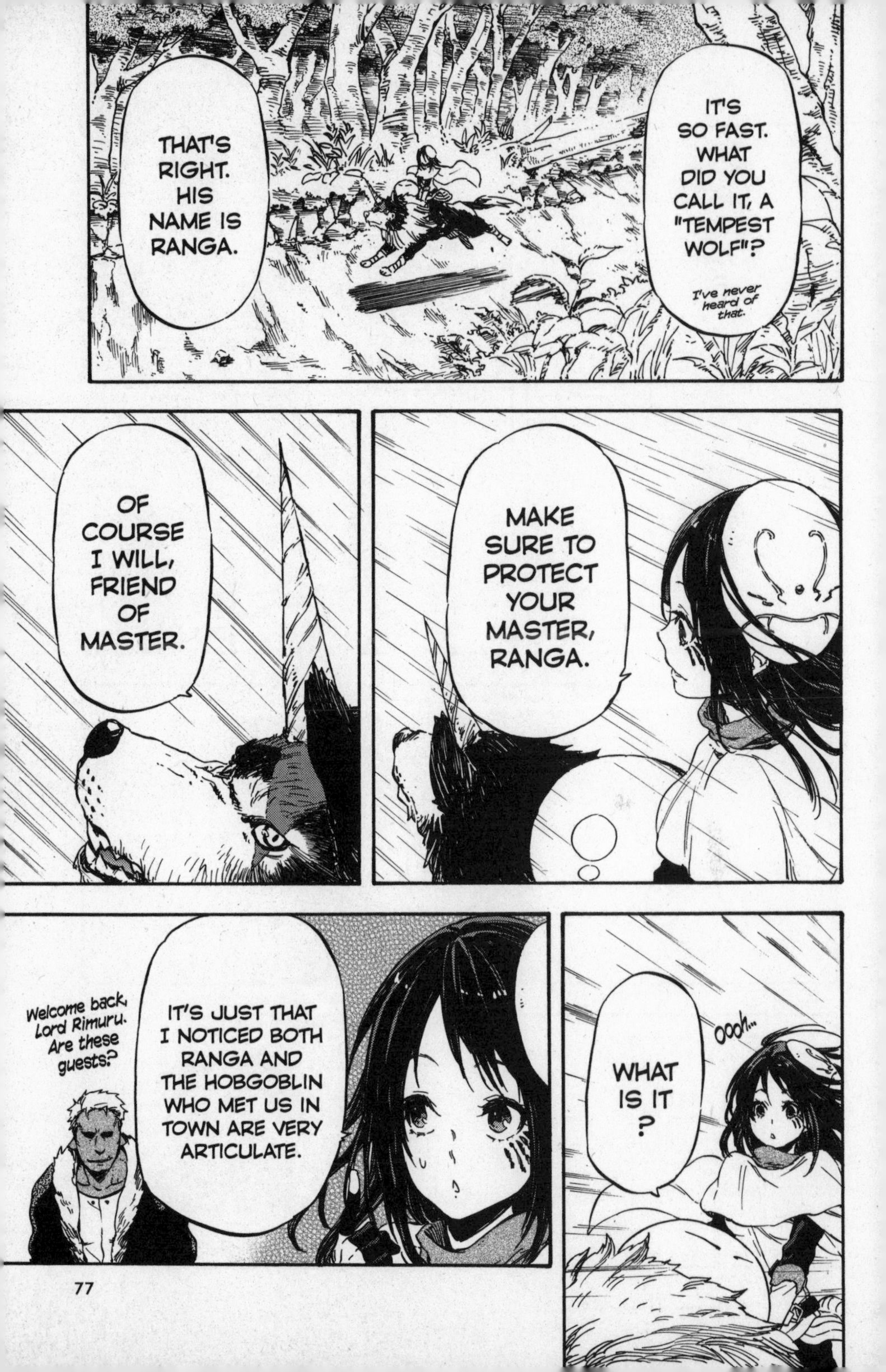
IT'S SO FAST. WHAT DID YOU CALL IT, A "TEMPEST WOLF"?
I've never heard of that.
THAT'S RIGHT. HIS NAME IS RANGA.
MAKE SURE TO PROTECT YOUR MASTER, RANGA.
OF COURSE I WILL, FRIEND OF MASTER.
Oooh...
WHAT IS IT ?
IT'S JUST THAT I NOTICED BOTH RANGA AND THE HOBGOBLIN WHO MET US IN TOWN ARE VERY ARTICULATE.
Welcome back, Lord Rimuru. Are these guests?

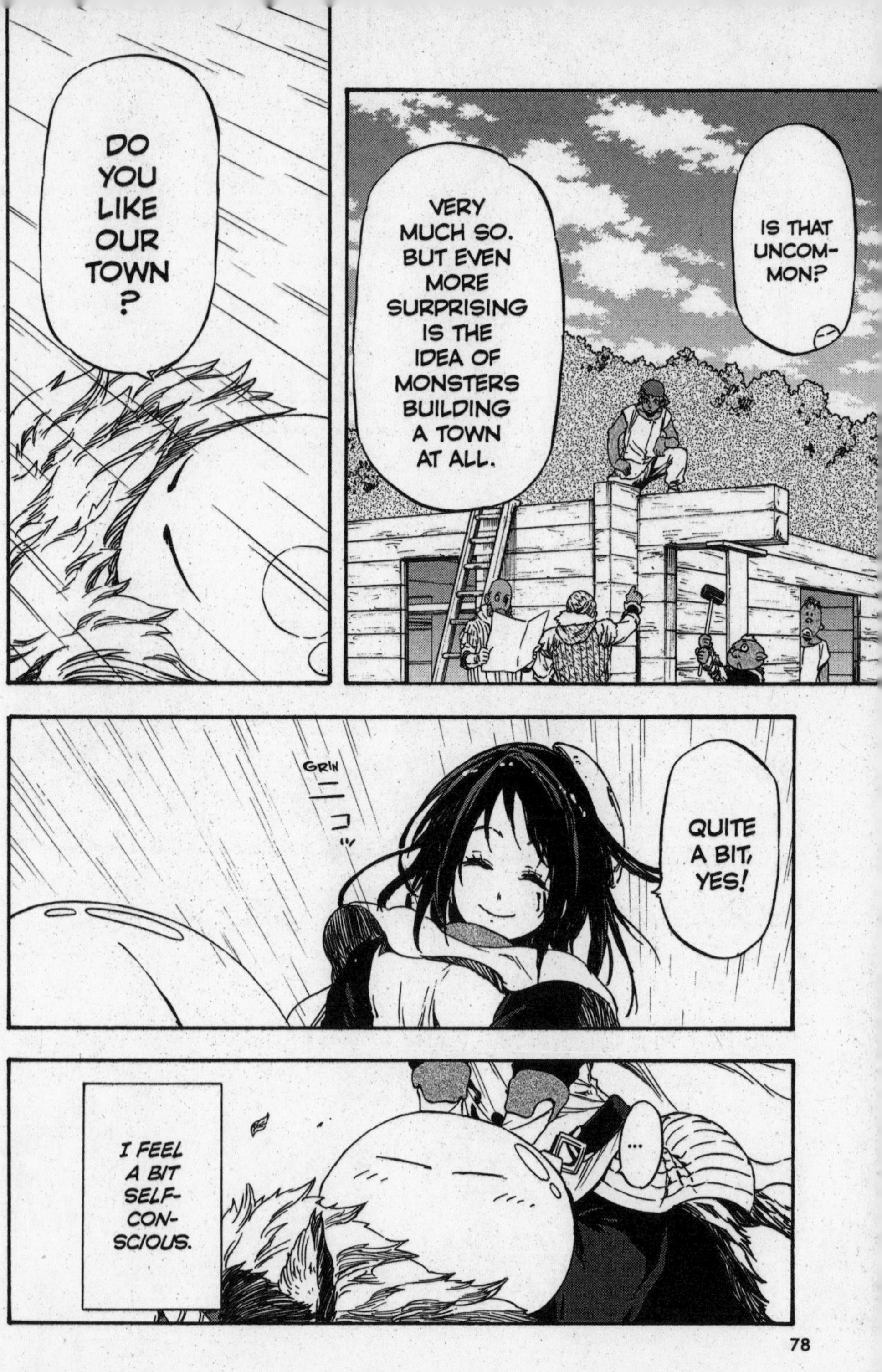
DO YOU LIKE OUR TOWN ?
VERY MUCH SO. BUT EVEN MORE SURPRISING IS THE IDEA OF MONSTERS BUILDING A TOWN AT ALL.
IS THAT UNCOM-MON?
GRIN
QUITE A BIT, YES!
I FEEL A BIT SELF-CON-SCIOUS.
...

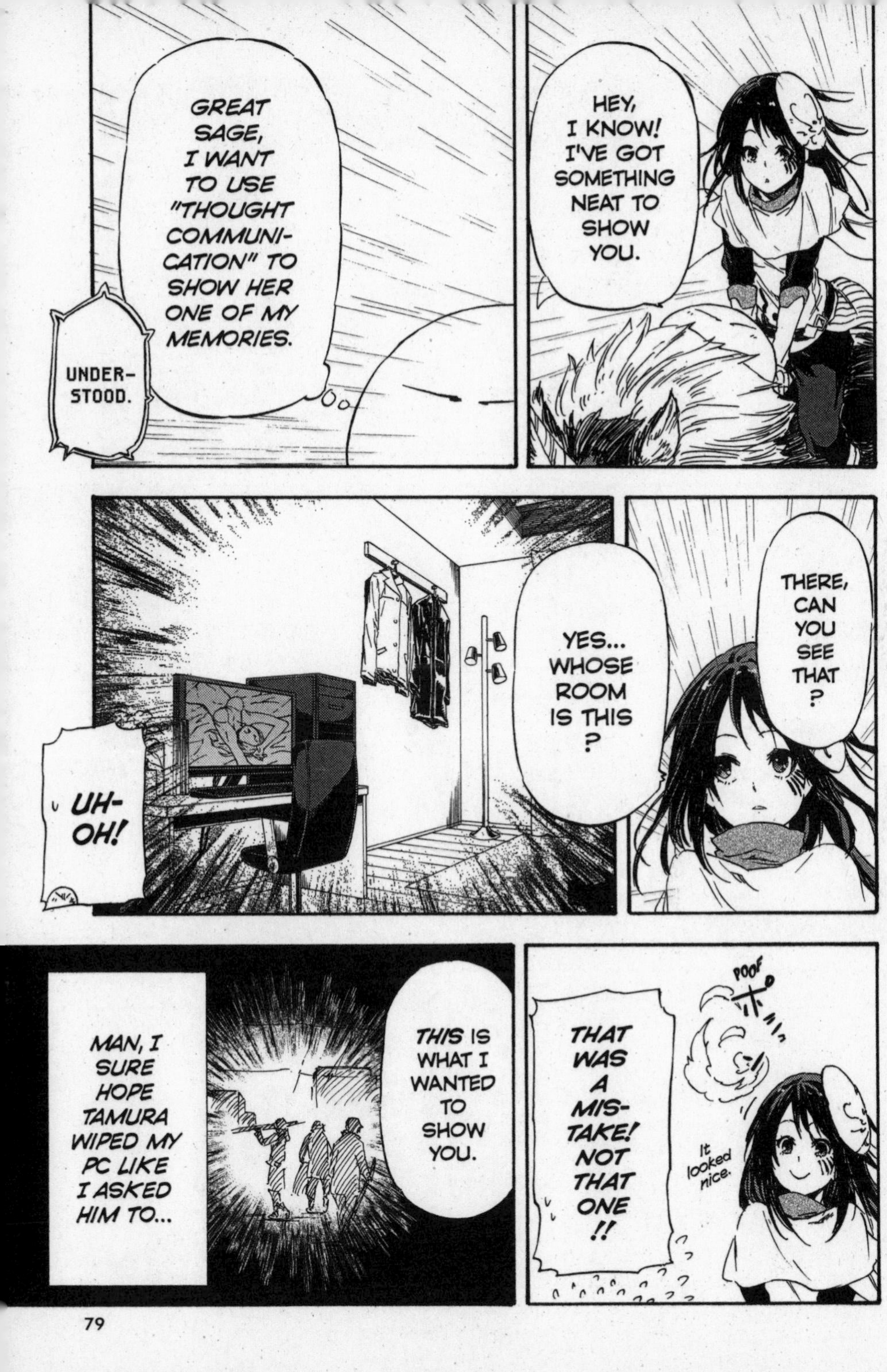
HEY, I KNOW! I'VE GOT SOMETHING NEAT TO SHOW YOU.
GREAT SAGE, I WANT TO USE "THOUGHT COMMUNICATION" TO SHOW HER ONE OF MY MEMORIES.
UNDER-STOOD.
THERE, CAN YOU SEE THAT?
YES... WHOSE ROOM IS THIS?
UH-OH!
THAT WAS A MISTAKE! NOT THAT ONE!!
It looked nice.
THIS IS WHAT I WANTED TO SHOW YOU.
MAN, I SURE HOPE TAMURA WIPED MY PC LIKE I ASKED HIM TO...

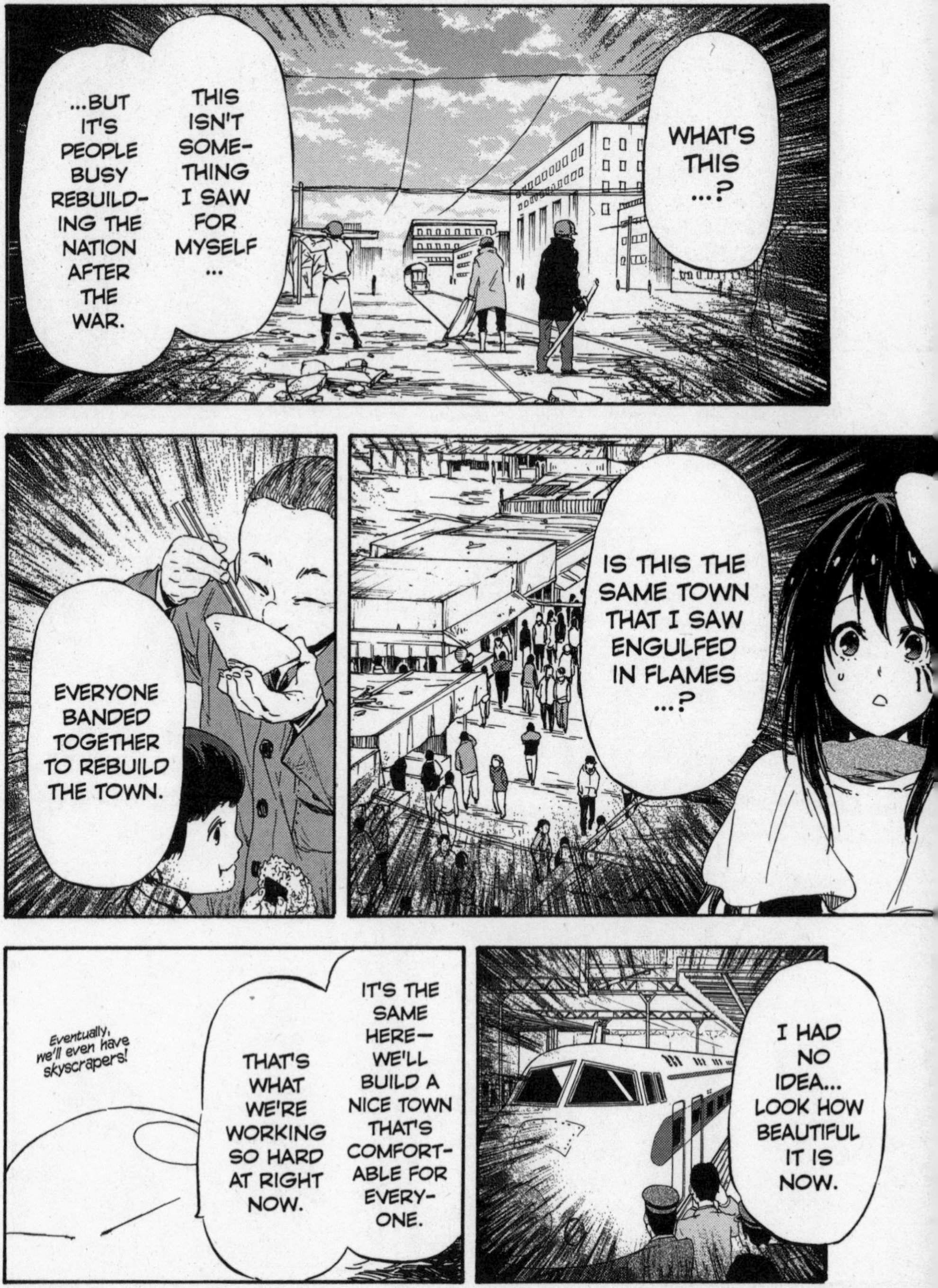
WHAT'S THIS ...?
THIS ISN'T SOMETHING I SAW FOR MYSELF ...
...BUT IT'S PEOPLE BUSY REBUILDING THE NATION AFTER THE WAR.
IS THIS THE SAME TOWN THAT I SAW ENGULFED IN FLAMES ...?
EVERYONE BANDED TOGETHER TO REBUILD THE TOWN.
I HAD NO IDEA... LOOK HOW BEAUTIFUL IT IS NOW.
IT'S THE SAME HERE—WE'LL BUILD A NICE TOWN THAT'S COMFORTABLE FOR EVERYONE.
THAT'S WHAT WE'RE WORKING SO HARD AT RIGHT NOW.
Eventually, we'll even have skyscrapers!

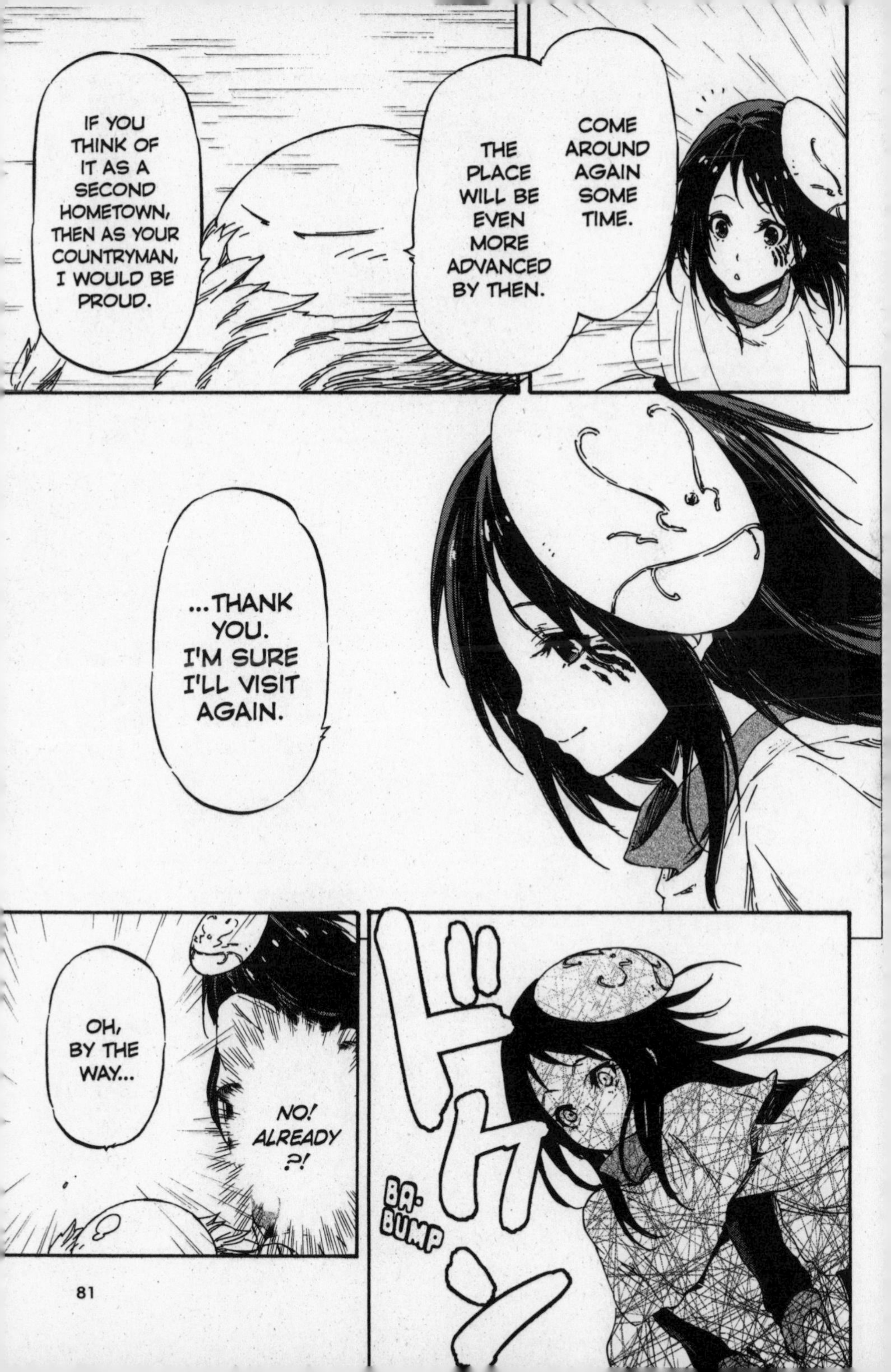
COME AROUND AGAIN SOME TIME.
THE PLACE WILL BE EVEN MORE ADVANCED BY THEN.
IF YOU THINK OF IT AS A SECOND HOMETOWN, THEN AS YOUR COUNTRYMAN, I WOULD BE PROUD.
...THANK YOU. I'M SURE I'LL VISIT AGAIN.
BA-BUMP
OH, BY THE WAY...
NO! ALREADY ?!

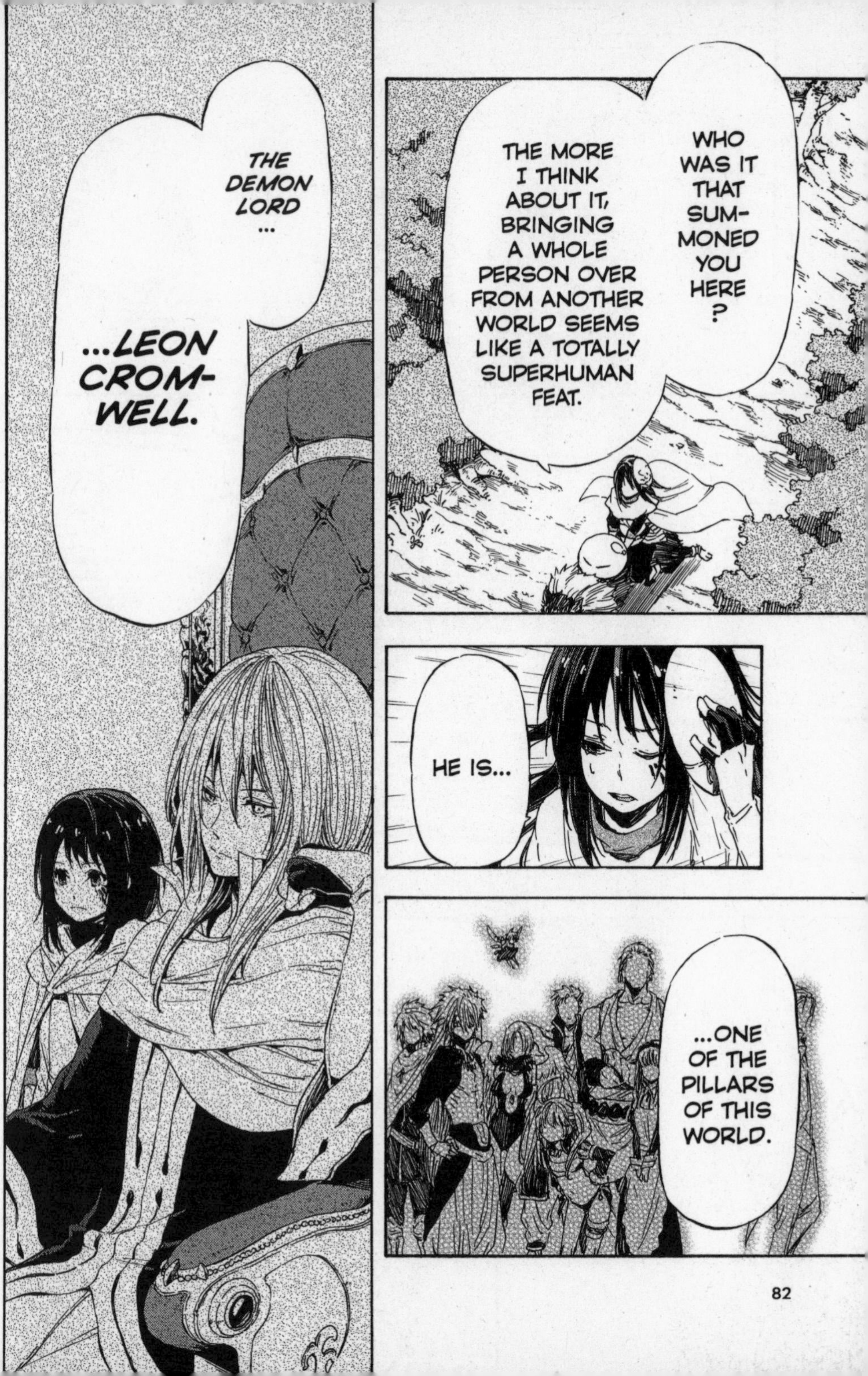
WHO WAS IT THAT SUM-MONED YOU HERE?
THE MORE I THINK ABOUT IT, BRINGING A WHOLE PERSON OVER FROM ANOTHER WORLD SEEMS LIKE A TOTALLY SUPERHUMAN FEAT.
HE IS...
...ONE OF THE PILLARS OF THIS WORLD.
THE DEMON LORD...
...LEON CROM-WELL.

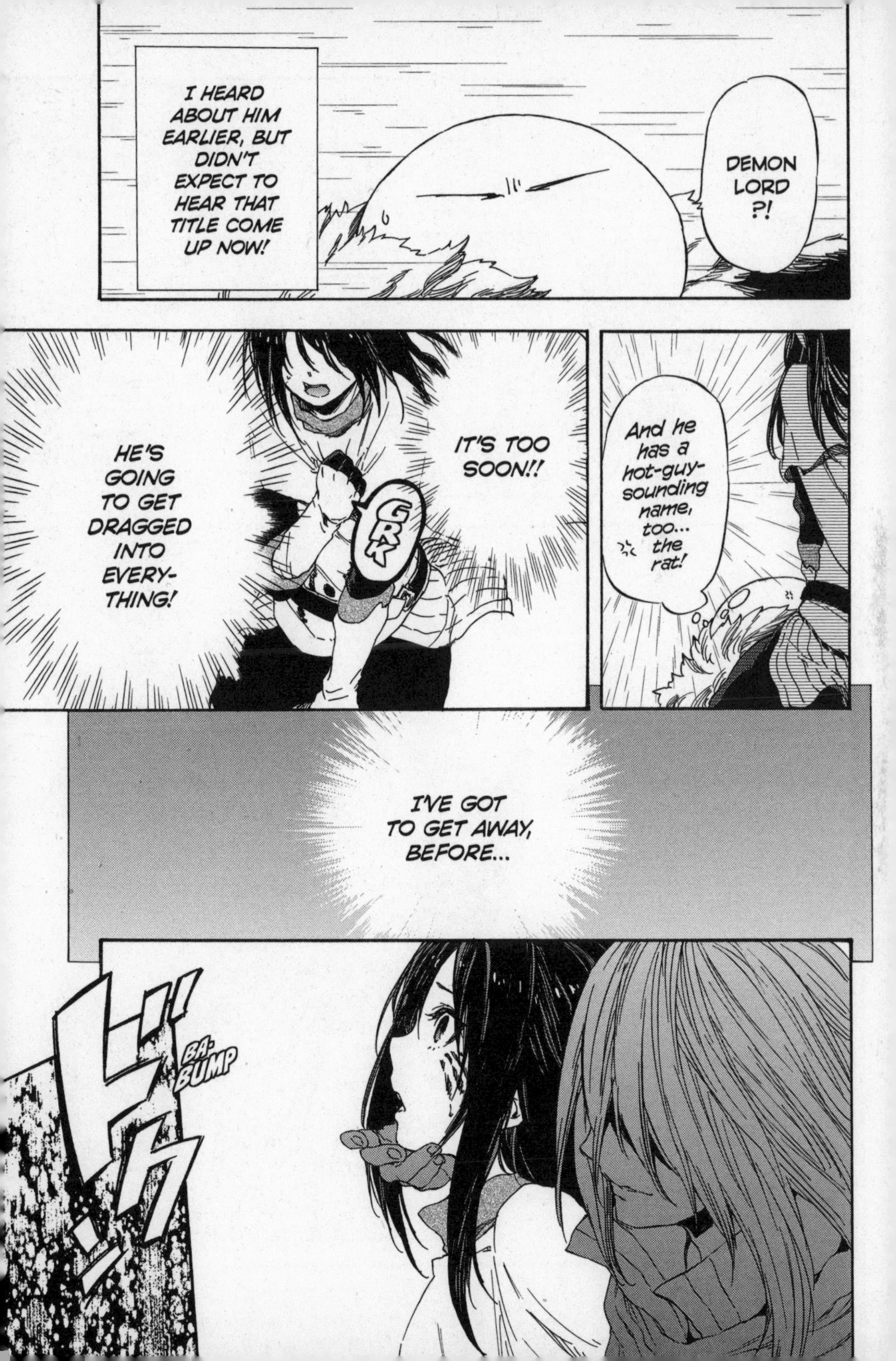
DEMON LORD?!
I HEARD ABOUT HIM EARLIER, BUT DIDN'T EXPECT TO HEAR THAT TITLE COME UP NOW!
And he has a hot-guy-sounding name, too... the rat!
IT'S TOO SOON!!
GRK
HE'S GOING TO GET DRAGGED INTO EVERYTHING!
I'VE GOT TO GET AWAY, BEFORE...
BA-BUMP

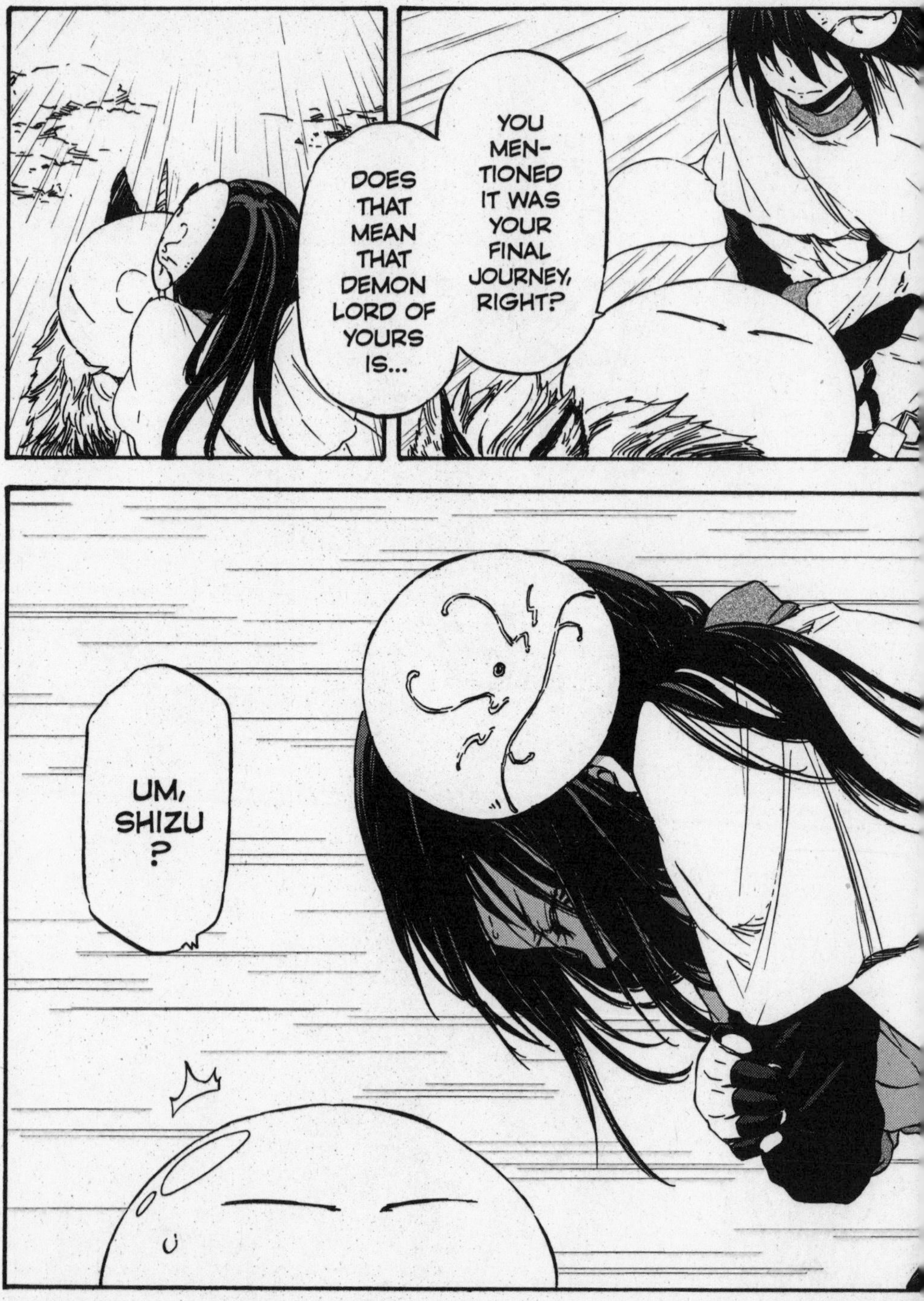
YOU MEN-TIONED IT WAS YOUR FINAL JOURNEY, RIGHT?
DOES THAT MEAN THAT DEMON LORD OF YOURS IS...
UM, SHIZU?

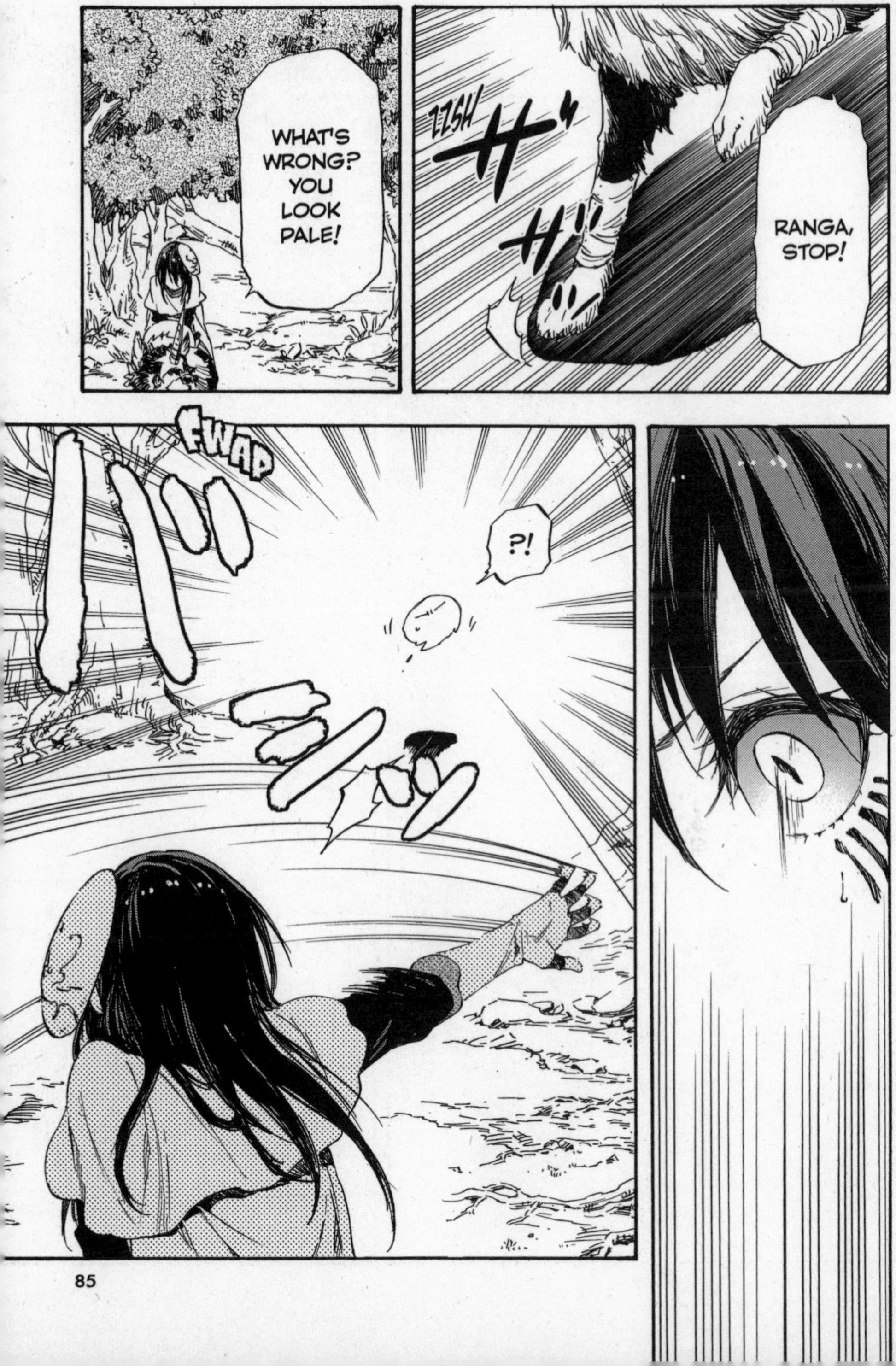
ZZSH
RANGA, STOP!
WHAT'S WRONG? YOU LOOK PALE!
FWAP
?!

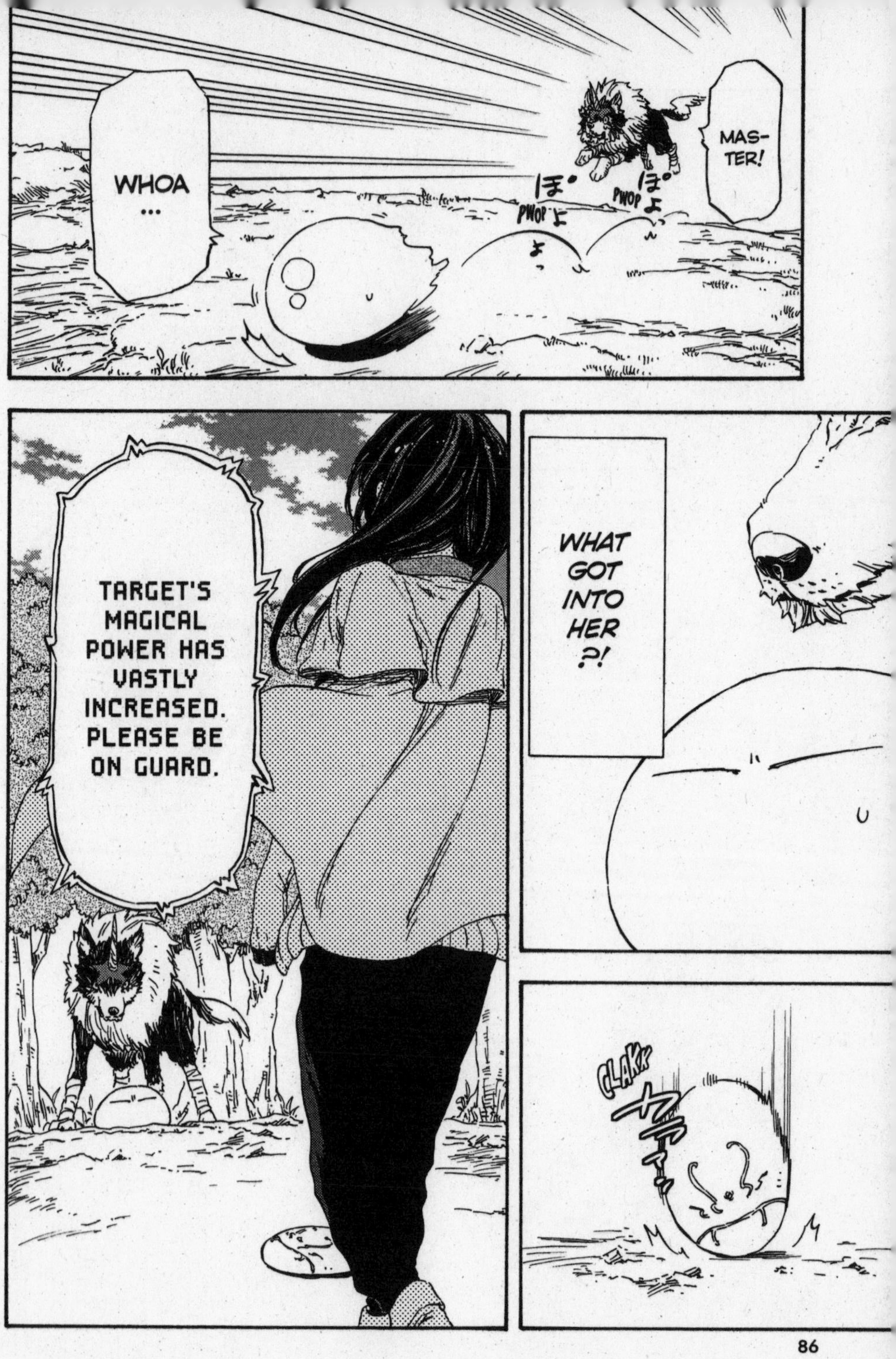
MAS-TER!
ぽよ PWOP
ぽよ PWOP
WHOA ...
WHAT GOT INTO HER ?!
CLAKK
TARGET'S MAGICAL POWER HAS VASTLY INCREASED. PLEASE BE ON GUARD.

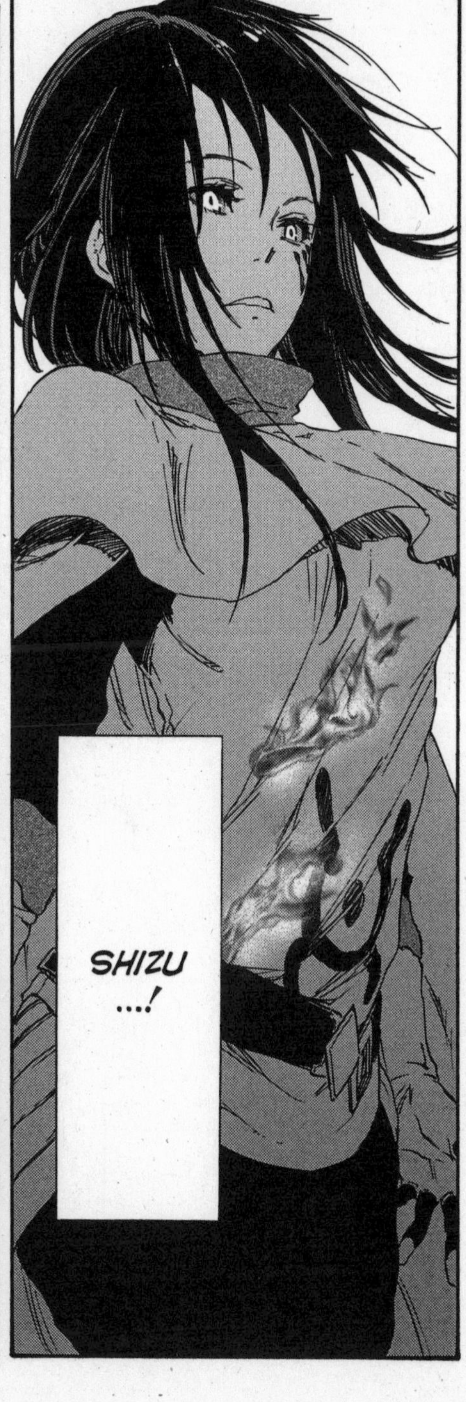
SHIZU ...!

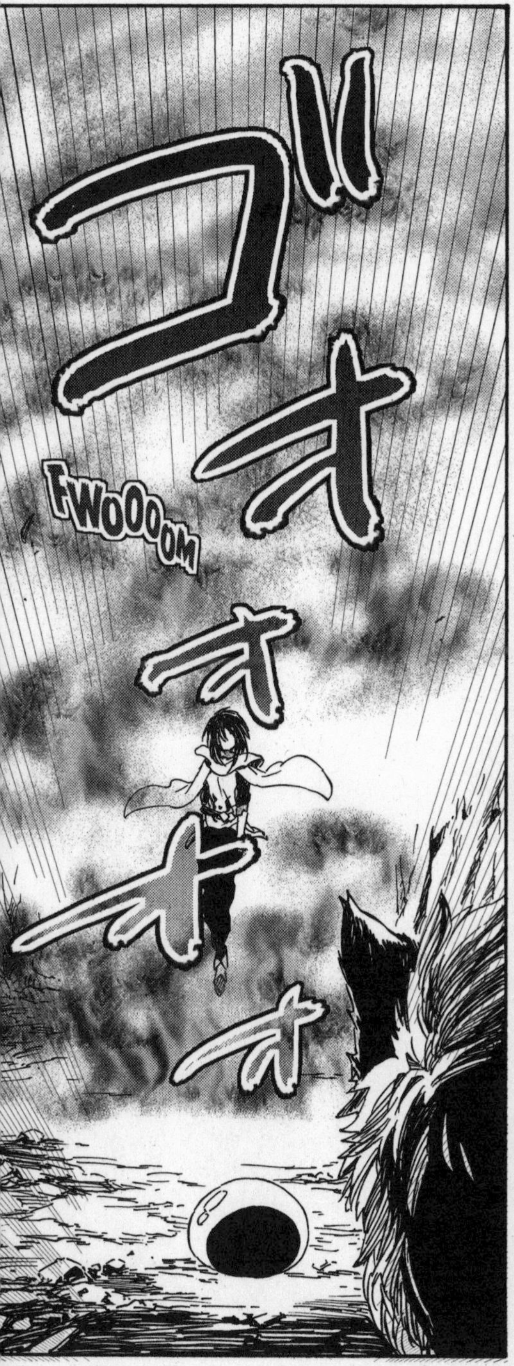
FWOOOOM

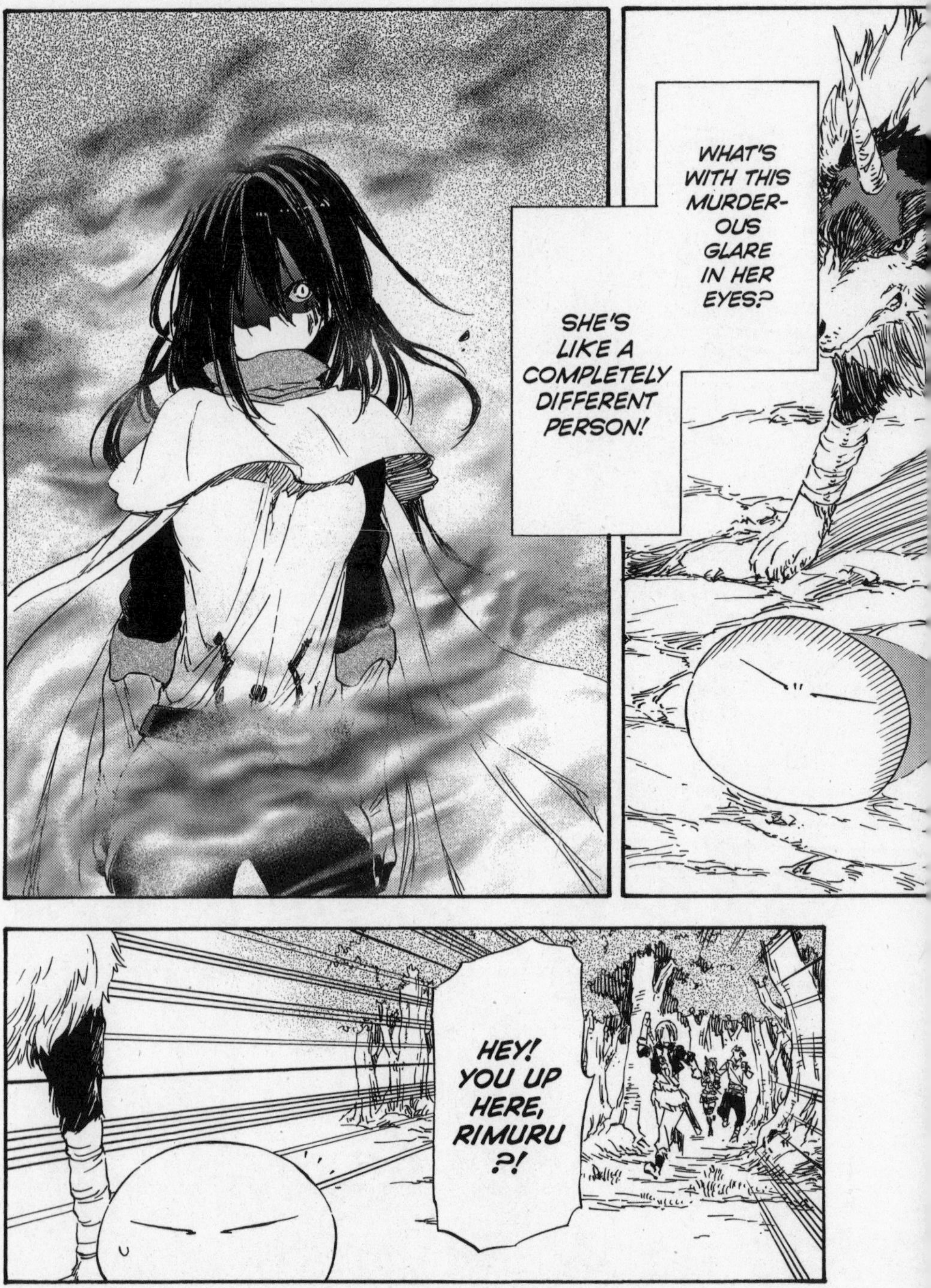
WHAT'S WITH THIS MURDER-OUS GLARE IN HER EYES?
SHE'S LIKE A COMPLETELY DIFFERENT PERSON!
HEY! YOU UP HERE, RIMURU?!

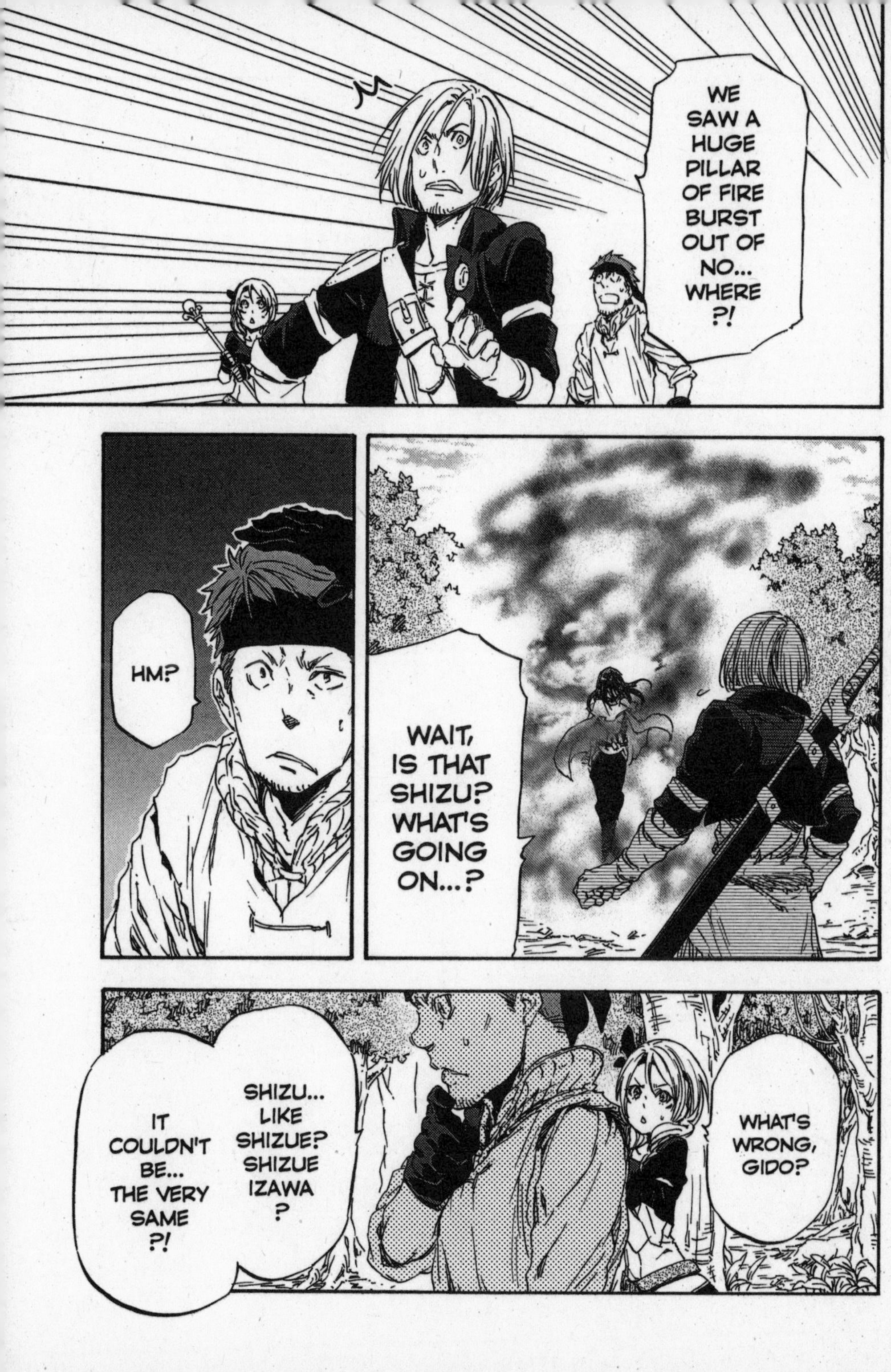
WE SAW A HUGE PILLAR OF FIRE BURST OUT OF NO... WHERE ?!
WAIT, IS THAT SHIZU? WHAT'S GOING ON...?
HM?
WHAT'S WRONG, GIDO?
SHIZU... LIKE SHIZUE? SHIZUE IZAWA ?
IT COULDN'T BE... THE VERY SAME ?!

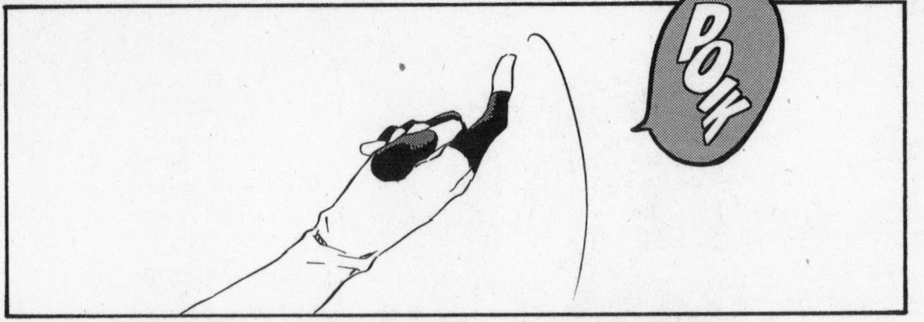
POIK

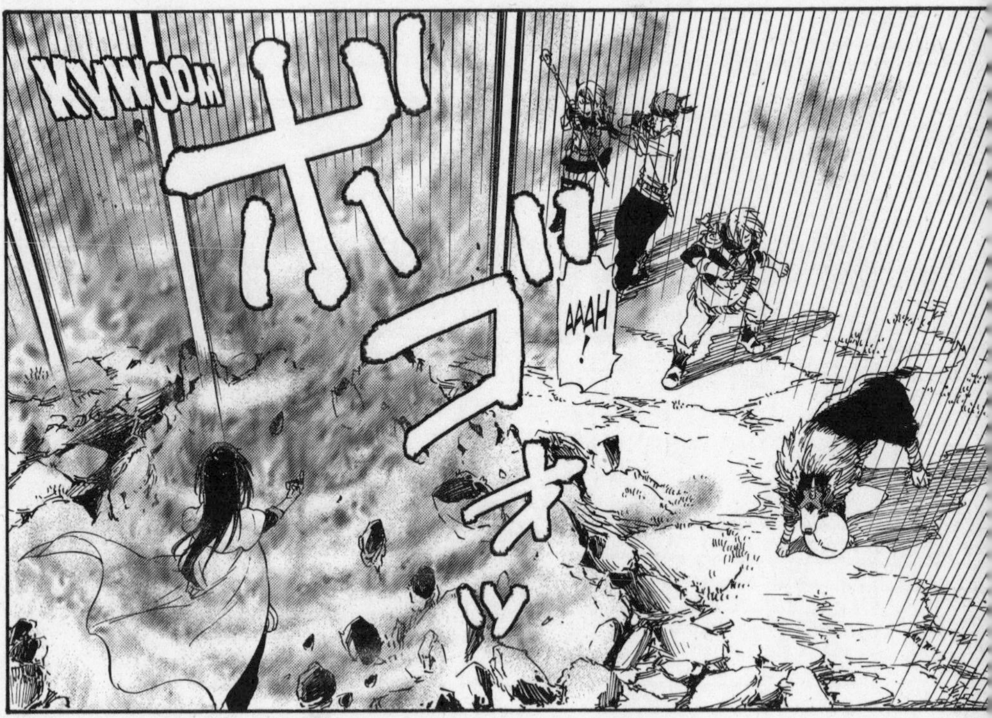
KVWOOM
AAAH!

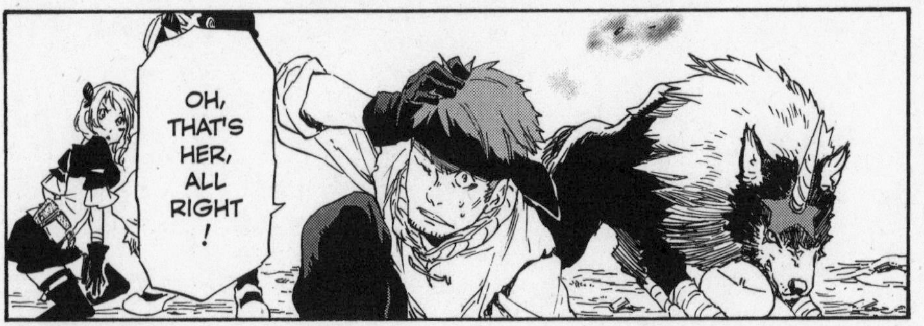
OH, THAT'S HER, ALL RIGHT!

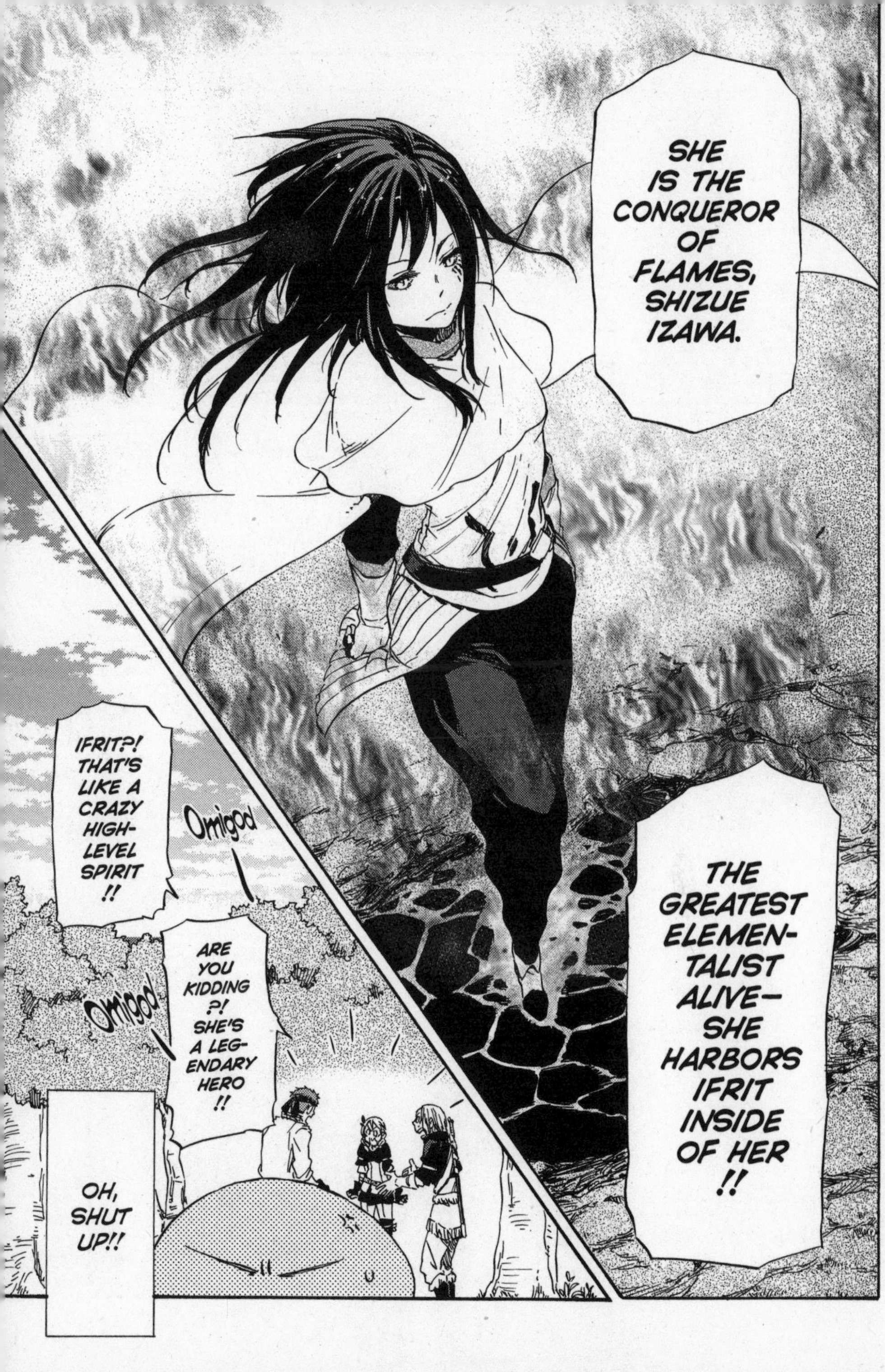
SHE IS THE CONQUEROR OF FLAMES, SHIZUE IZAWA.
THE GREATEST ELEMENTALIST ALIVE—SHE HARBORS IFRIT INSIDE OF HER!!
Omigod
IFRIT?! THAT'S LIKE A CRAZY HIGH-LEVEL SPIRIT!!
Omigod
ARE YOU KIDDING?! SHE'S A LEGENDARY HERO!!
OH, SHUT UP!!

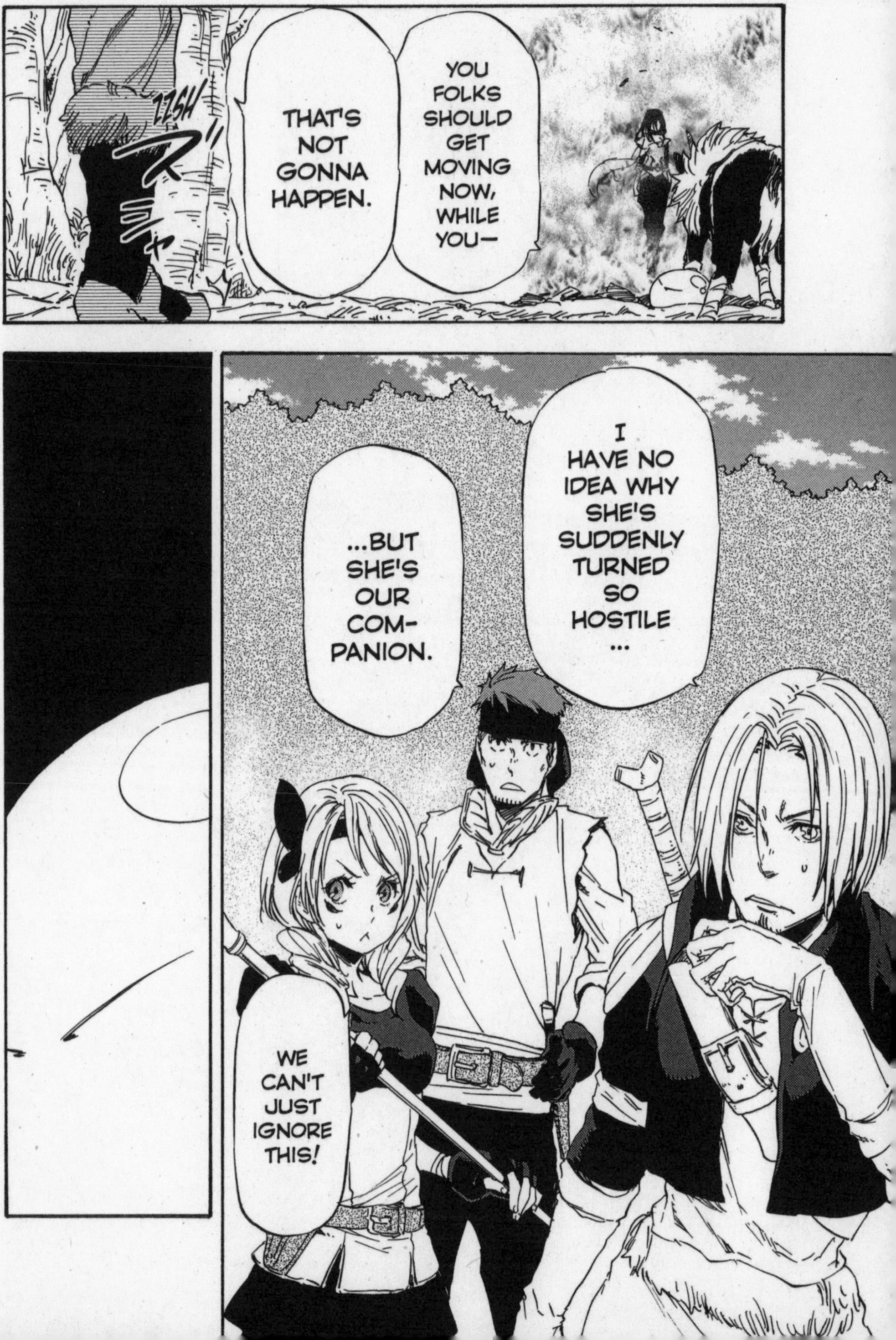
YOU FOLKS SHOULD GET MOVING NOW, WHILE YOU—
THAT'S NOT GONNA HAPPEN.
ZZSH
I HAVE NO IDEA WHY SHE'S SUDDENLY TURNED SO HOSTILE...
...BUT SHE'S OUR COMPANION.
WE CAN'T JUST IGNORE THIS!

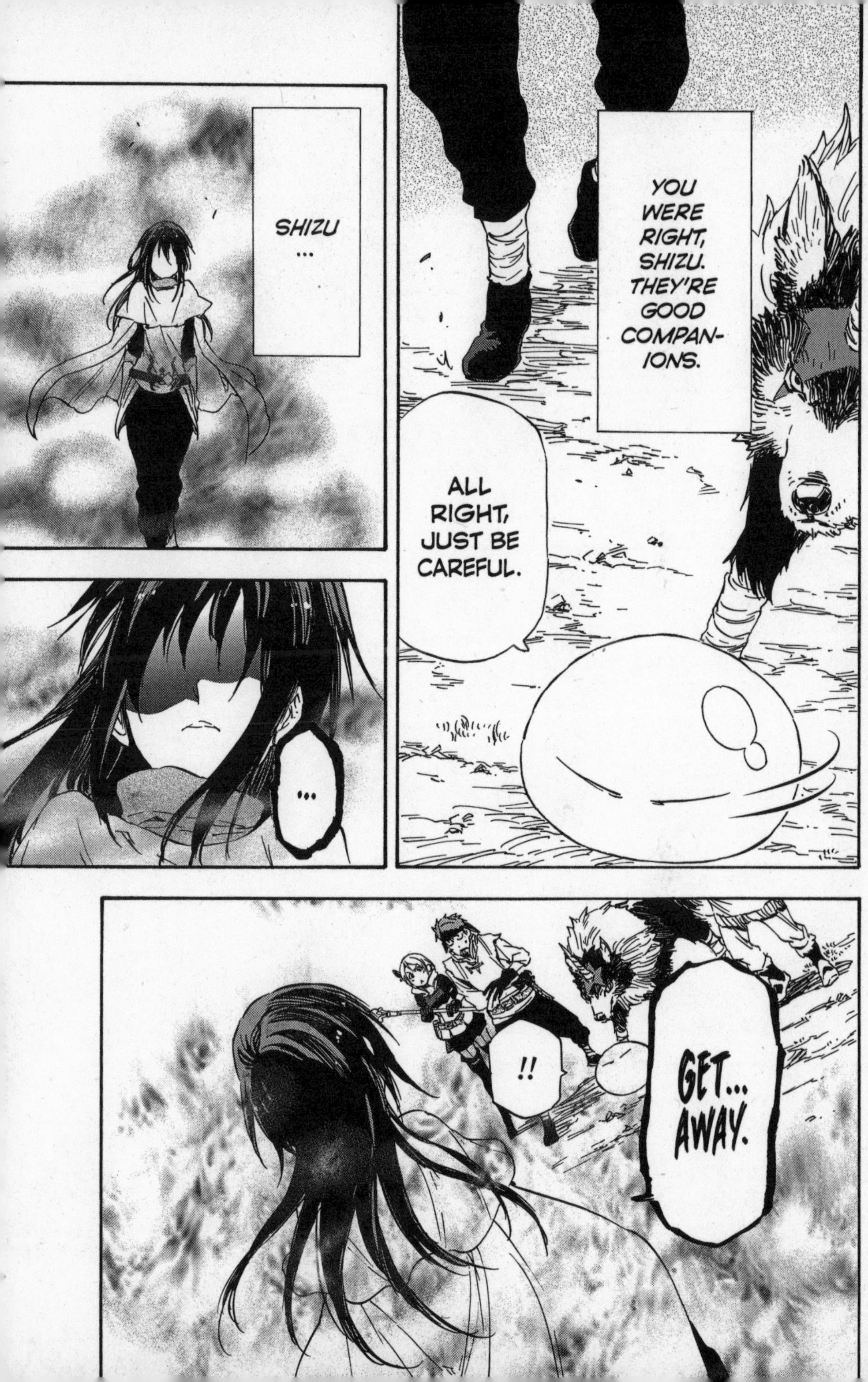
YOU WERE RIGHT, SHIZU. THEY'RE GOOD COMPAN-IONS.
ALL RIGHT, JUST BE CAREFUL.
SHIZU ...
...
GET... AWAY.
!!

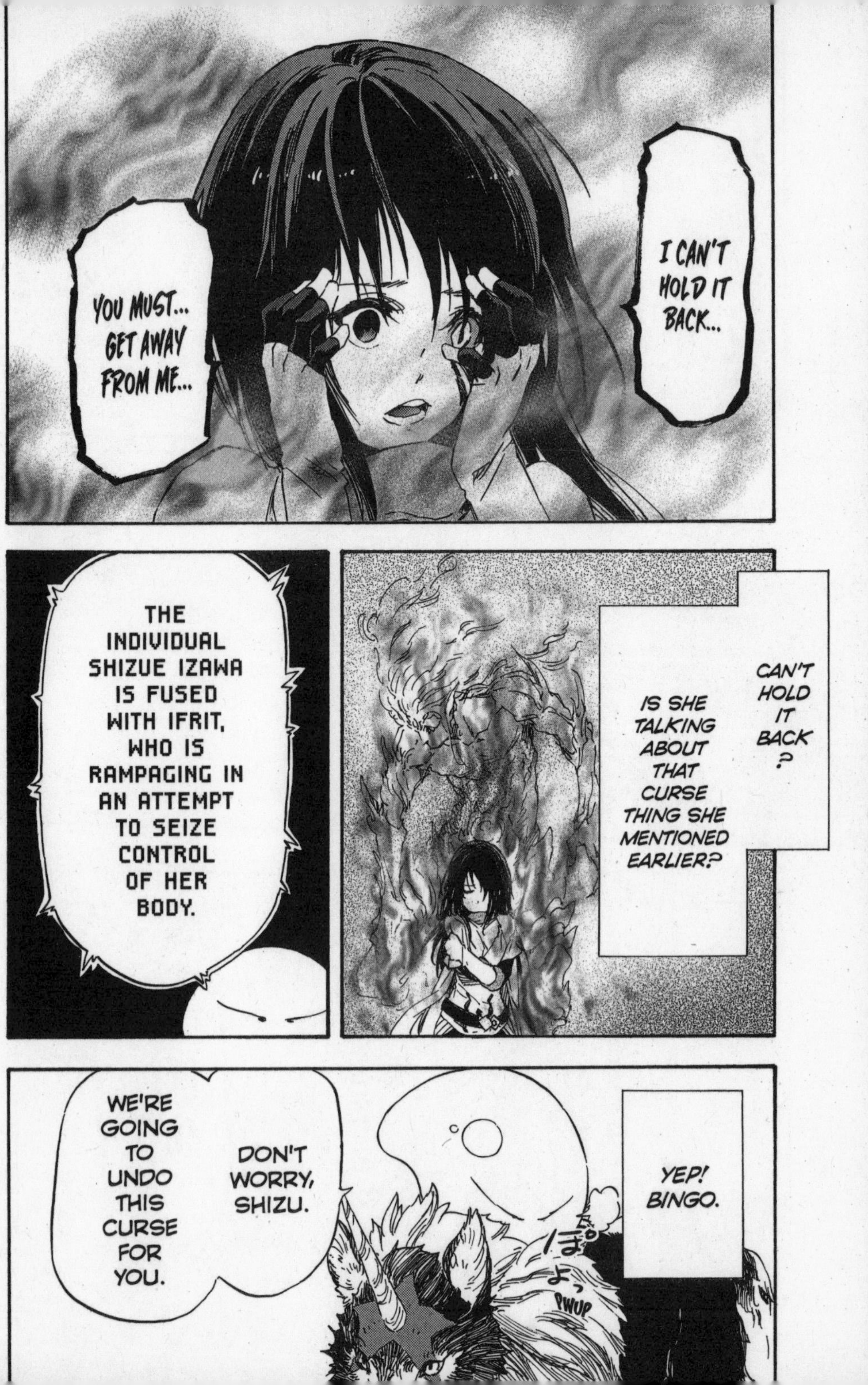
I CAN'T HOLD IT BACK...
YOU MUST... GET AWAY FROM ME...
CAN'T HOLD IT BACK?
IS SHE TALKING ABOUT THAT CURSE THING SHE MENTIONED EARLIER?
THE INDIVIDUAL SHIZUE IZAWA IS FUSED WITH IFRIT, WHO IS RAMPAGING IN AN ATTEMPT TO SEIZE CONTROL OF HER BODY.
YEP! BINGO.
ぽよっ
PWUP
DON'T WORRY, SHIZU.
WE'RE GOING TO UNDO THIS CURSE FOR YOU.

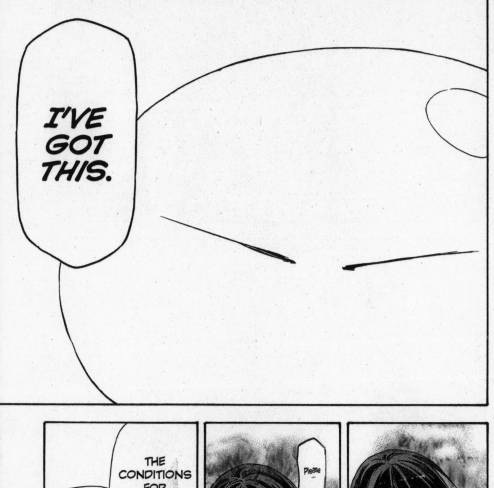

I'VE GOT THIS.

THE CONDITIONS FOR VICTORY ARE: SUBDUING IFRIT, AND RESCUING SHIZU.

Please ...

hel...

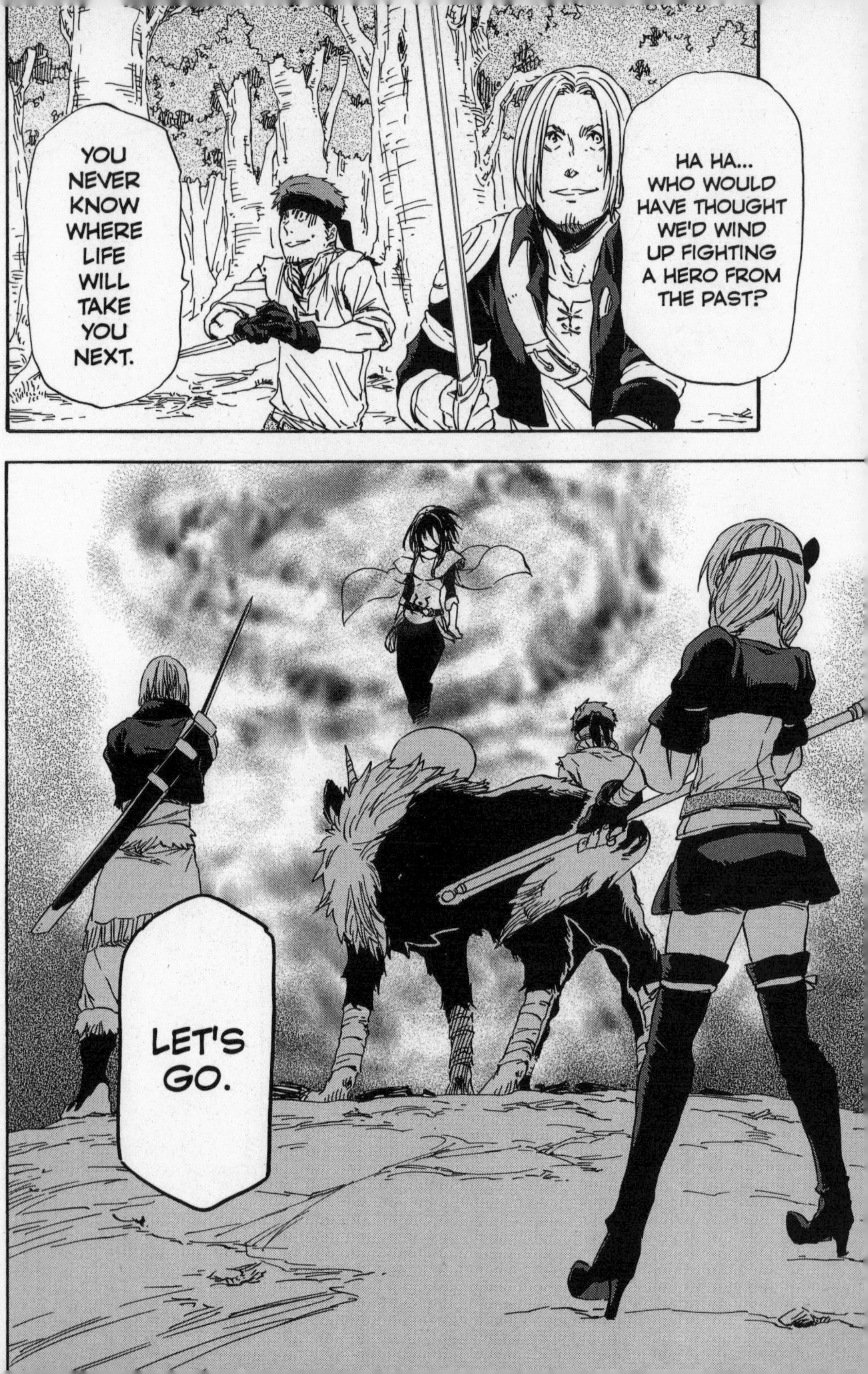
HA HA... WHO WOULD HAVE THOUGHT WE'D WIND UP FIGHTING A HERO FROM THE PAST?
YOU NEVER KNOW WHERE LIFE WILL TAKE YOU NEXT.
LET'S GO.

AFTER THE YAKINIKU PARTY

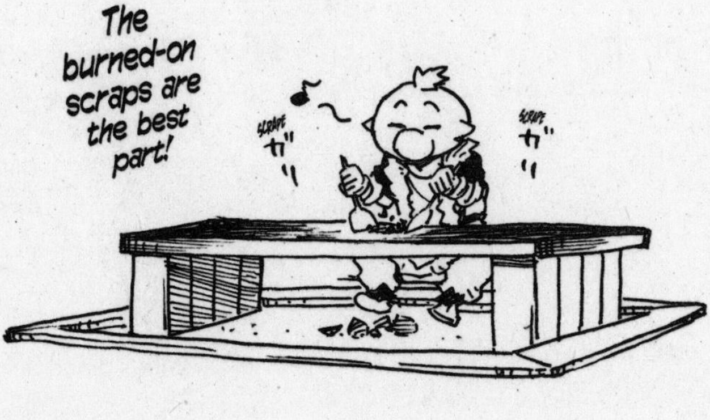
The burned-on scraps are the best part!
SCRAPE
SCRAPE

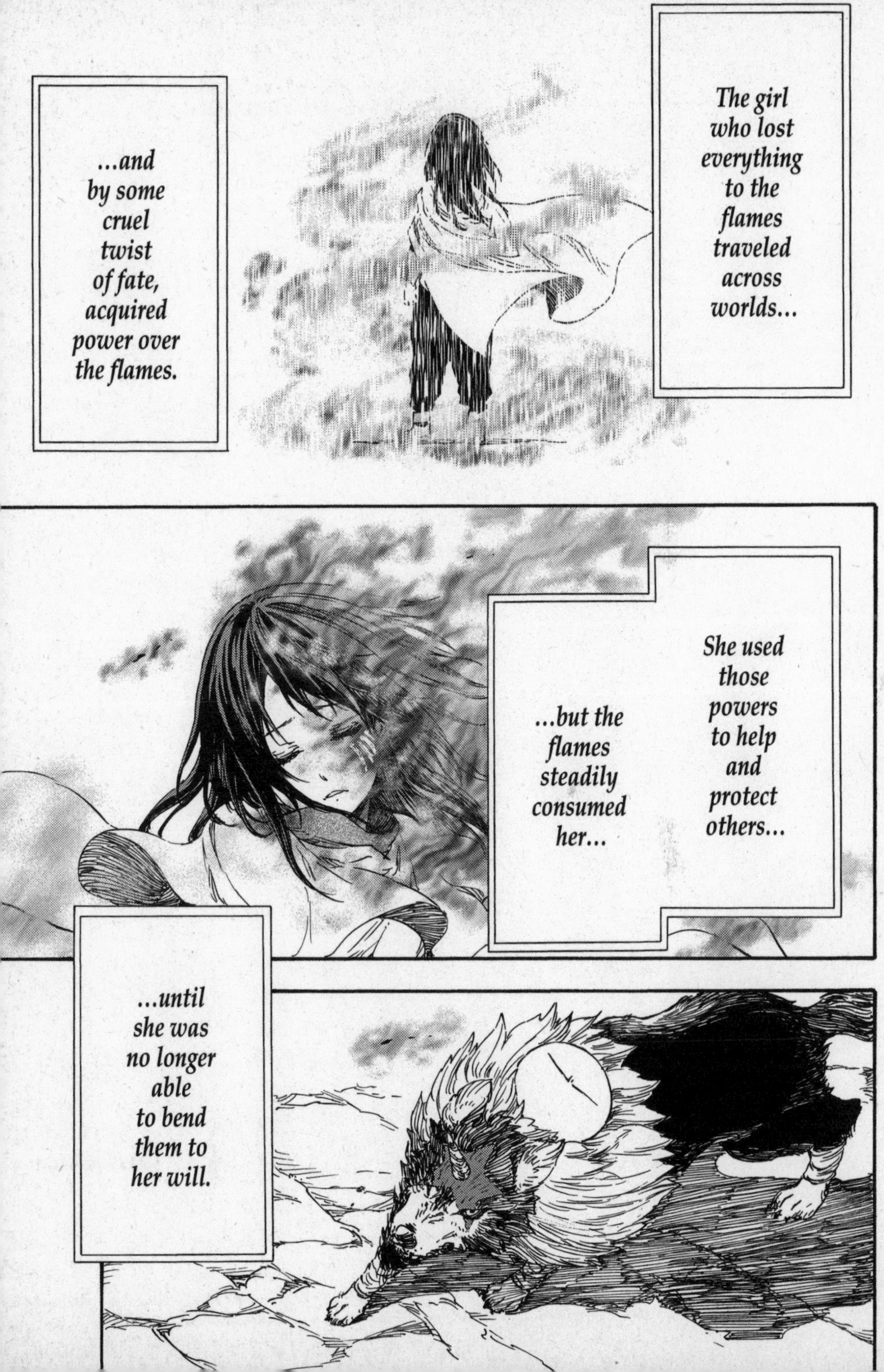
The girl who lost everything to the flames traveled across worlds...
...and by some cruel twist of fate, acquired power over the flames.
She used those powers to help and protect others...
...but the flames steadily consumed her...
...until she was no longer able to bend them to her will.

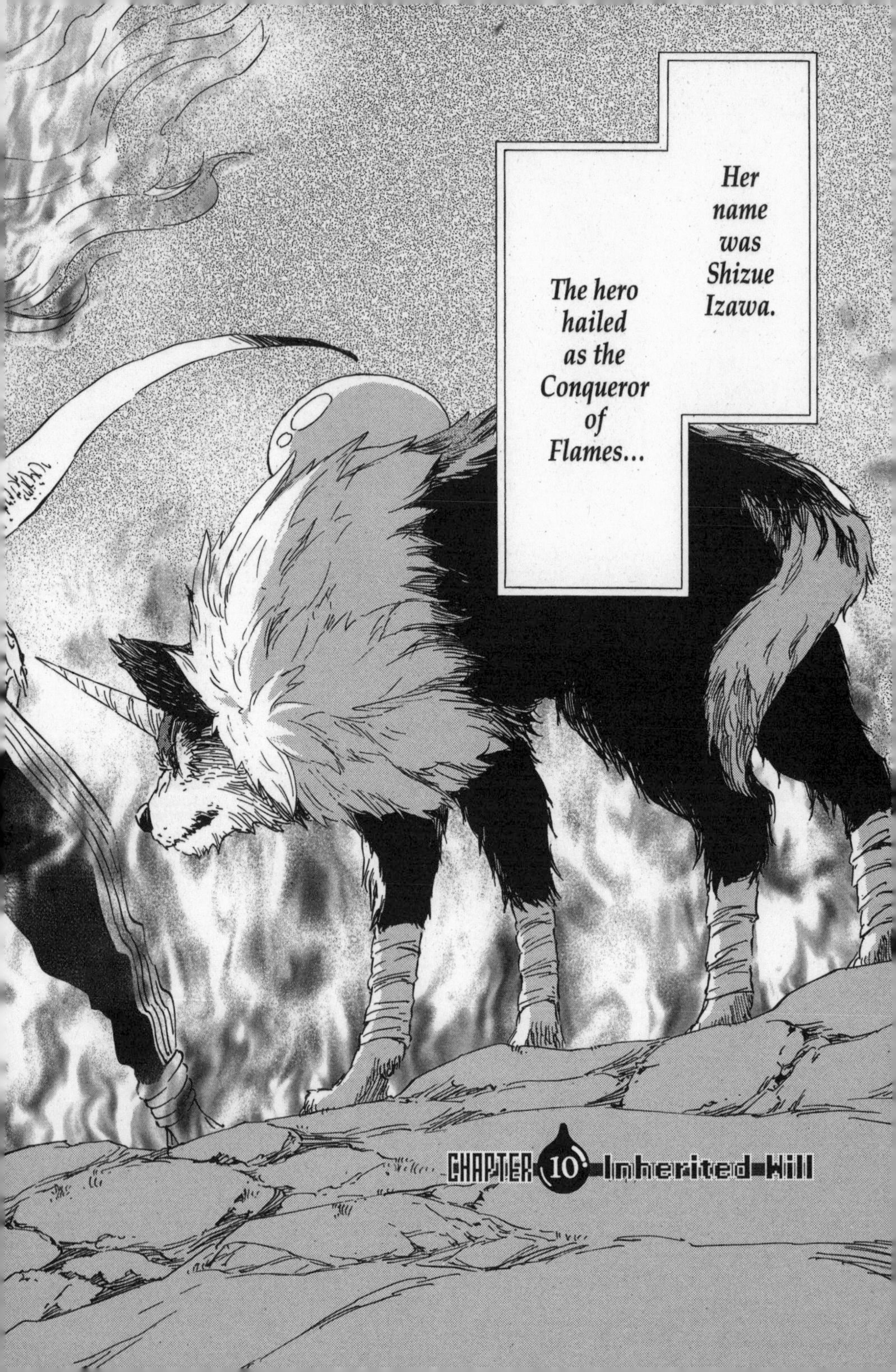
Her name was Shizue Izawa.
The hero hailed as the Conqueror of Flames...
CHAPTER 10 Inherited Will

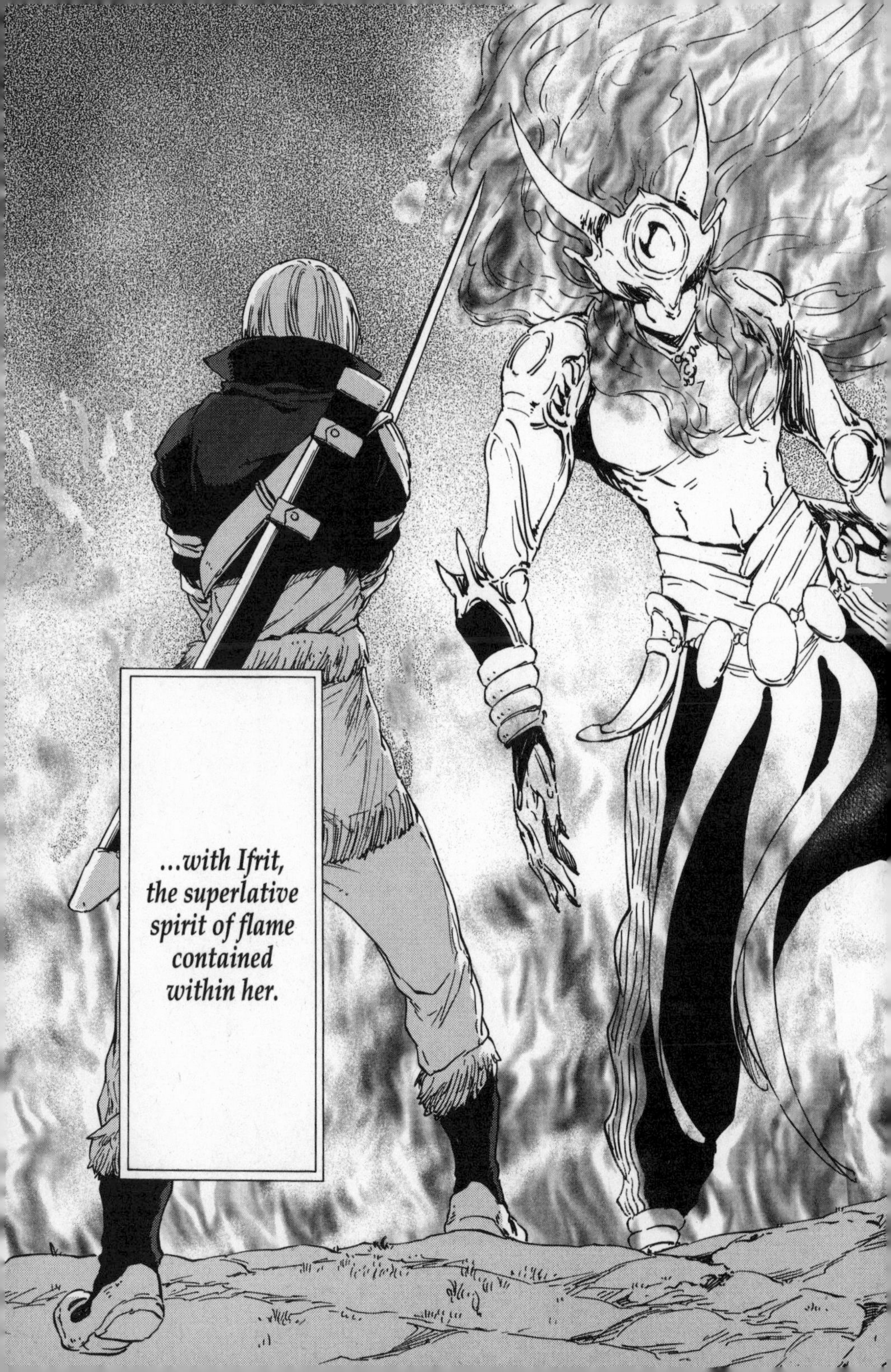
...with Ifrit, the superlative spirit of flame contained within her.

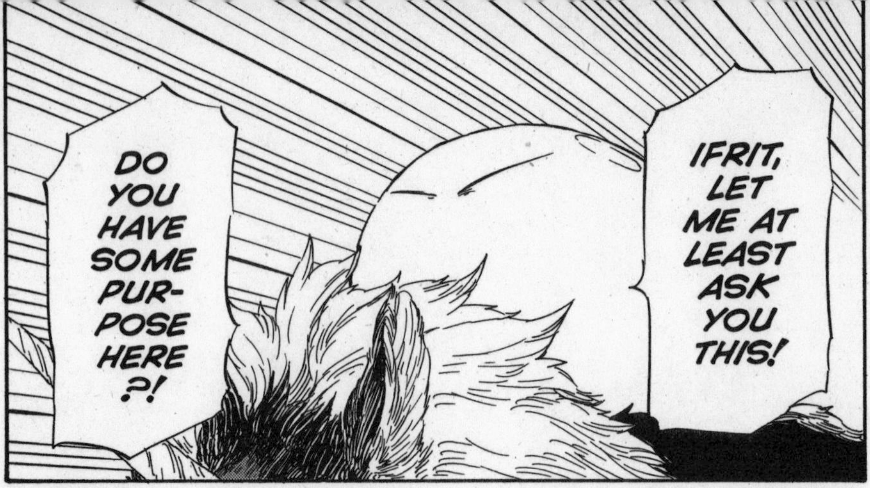
IFRIT, LET ME AT LEAST ASK YOU THIS!
DO YOU HAVE SOME PUR-POSE HERE?!

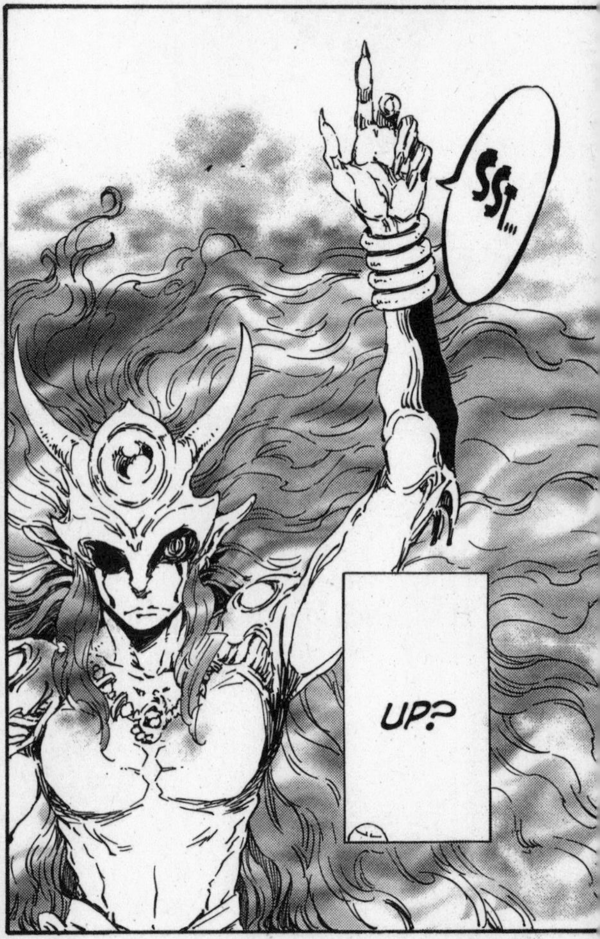
SST...
UP?

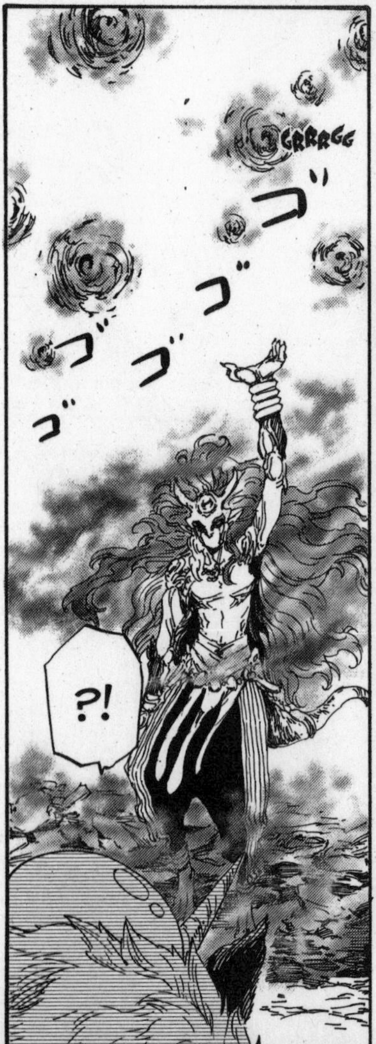
GRRRGG
ゴゴゴゴゴ
?!

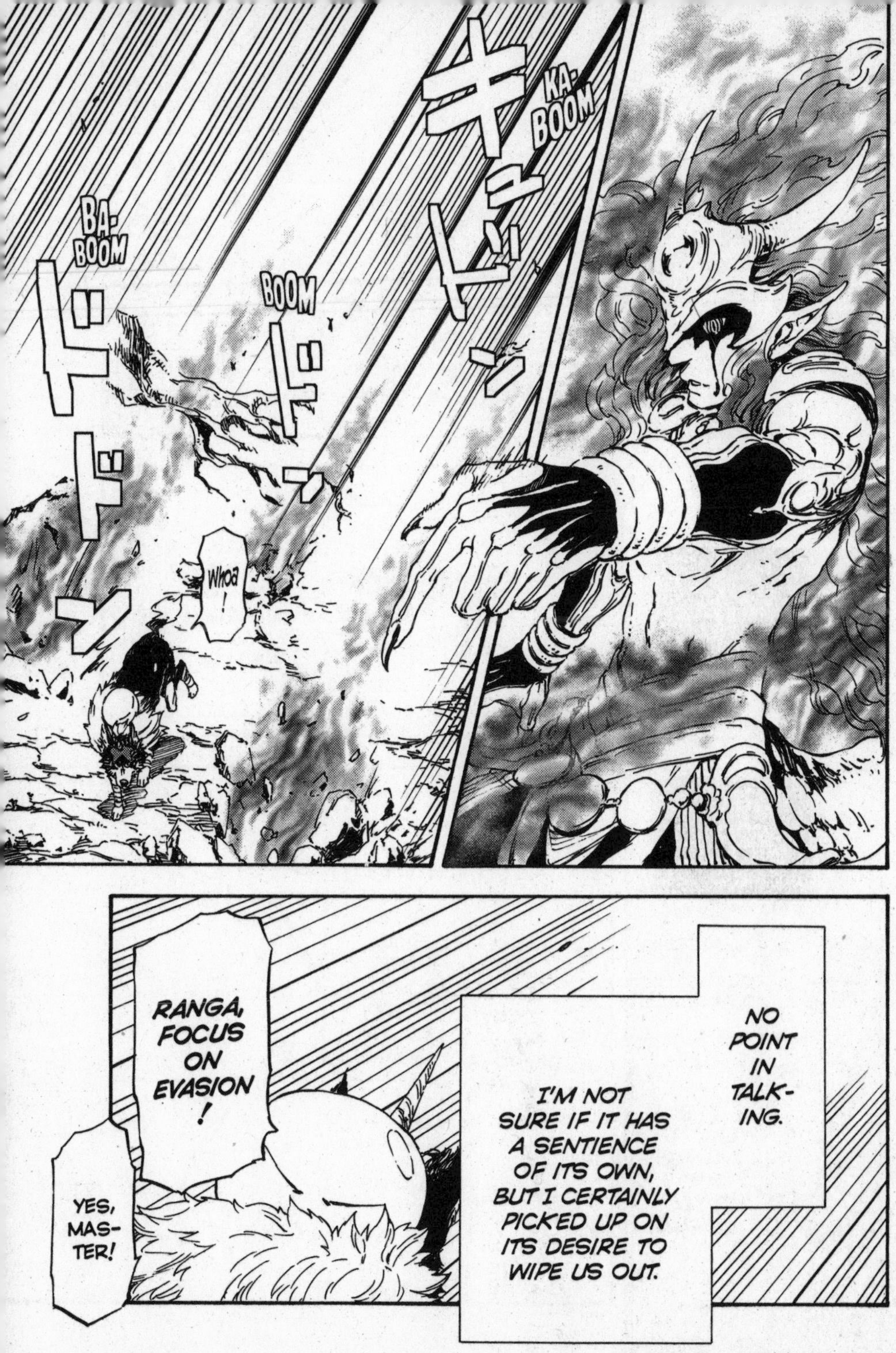
KA-BOOM
BOOM
BA-BOOM
Whoa!
NO POINT IN TALKING.
I'M NOT SURE IF IT HAS A SENTIENCE OF ITS OWN, BUT I CERTAINLY PICKED UP ON ITS DESIRE TO WIPE US OUT.
RANGA, FOCUS ON EVASION!
YES, MASTER!

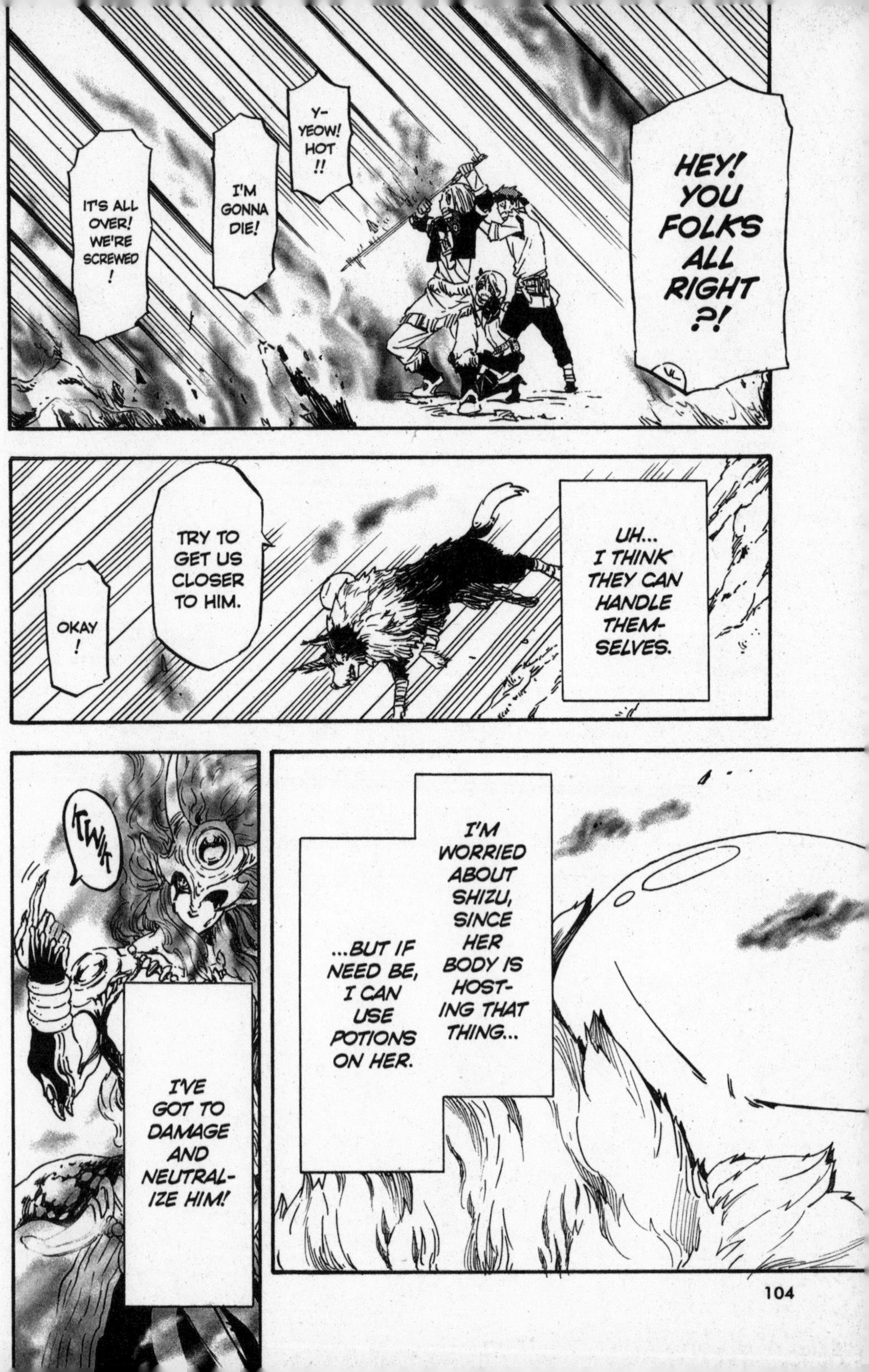
HEY! YOU FOLKS ALL RIGHT?!
Y-YEOW! HOT!!
I'M GONNA DIE!
IT'S ALL OVER! WE'RE SCREWED!
UH... I THINK THEY CAN HANDLE THEM-SELVES.
TRY TO GET US CLOSER TO HIM.
OKAY!
I'M WORRIED ABOUT SHIZU, SINCE HER BODY IS HOST-ING THAT THING...
...BUT IF NEED BE, I CAN USE POTIONS ON HER.
KWIK
I'VE GOT TO DAMAGE AND NEUTRAL-IZE HIM!

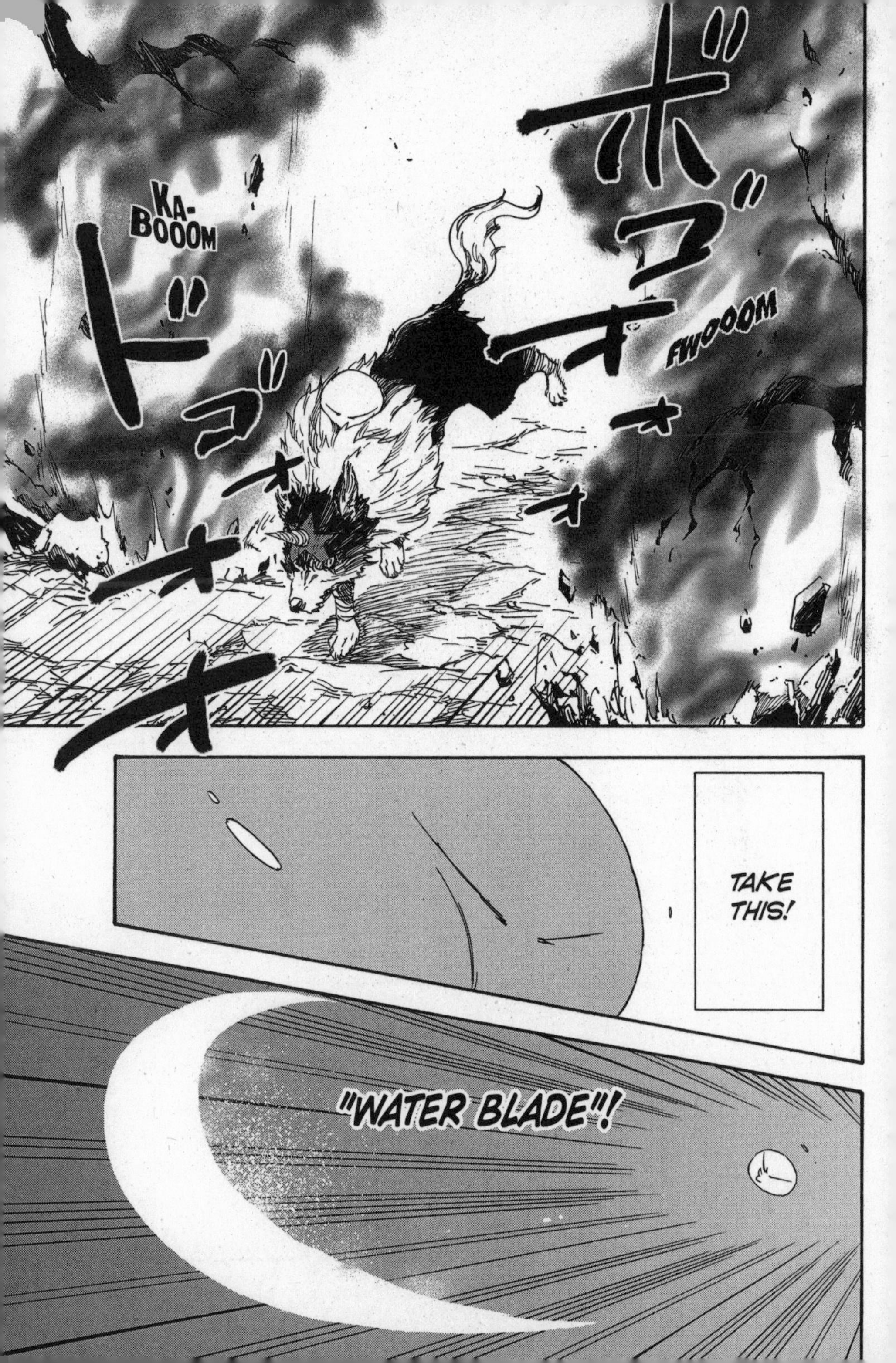

ボゴォォォ
FWOOOM
ドゴォォォ
KA-BOOOM
TAKE THIS!
"WATER BLADE"!

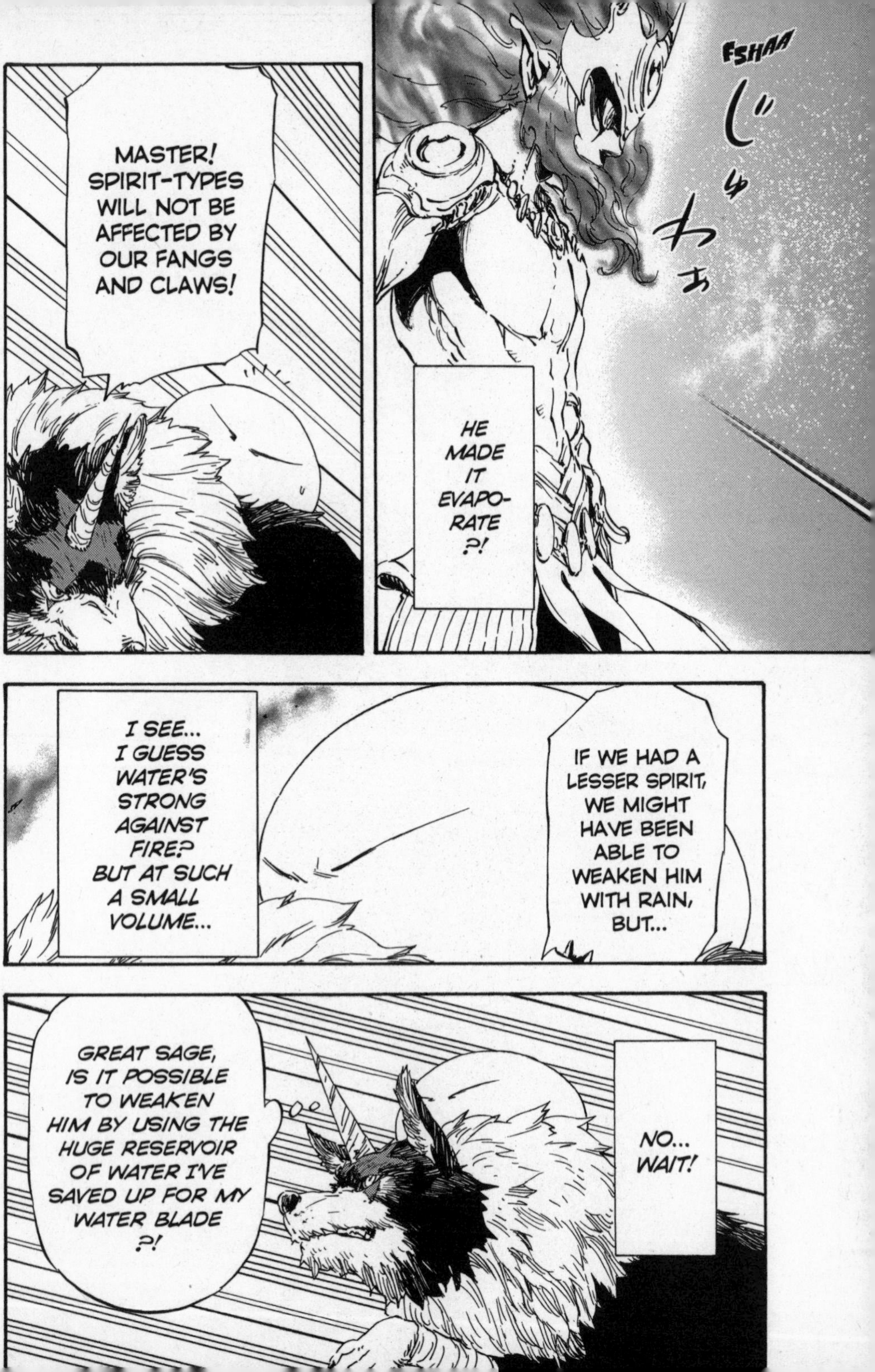
FSHAA
じゅわぁ
HE MADE IT EVAPORATE ?!
MASTER! SPIRIT-TYPES WILL NOT BE AFFECTED BY OUR FANGS AND CLAWS!
IF WE HAD A LESSER SPIRIT, WE MIGHT HAVE BEEN ABLE TO WEAKEN HIM WITH RAIN, BUT...
I SEE... I GUESS WATER'S STRONG AGAINST FIRE? BUT AT SUCH A SMALL VOLUME...
NO... WAIT!
GREAT SAGE, IS IT POSSIBLE TO WEAKEN HIM BY USING THE HUGE RESERVOIR OF WATER I'VE SAVED UP FOR MY WATER BLADE ?!

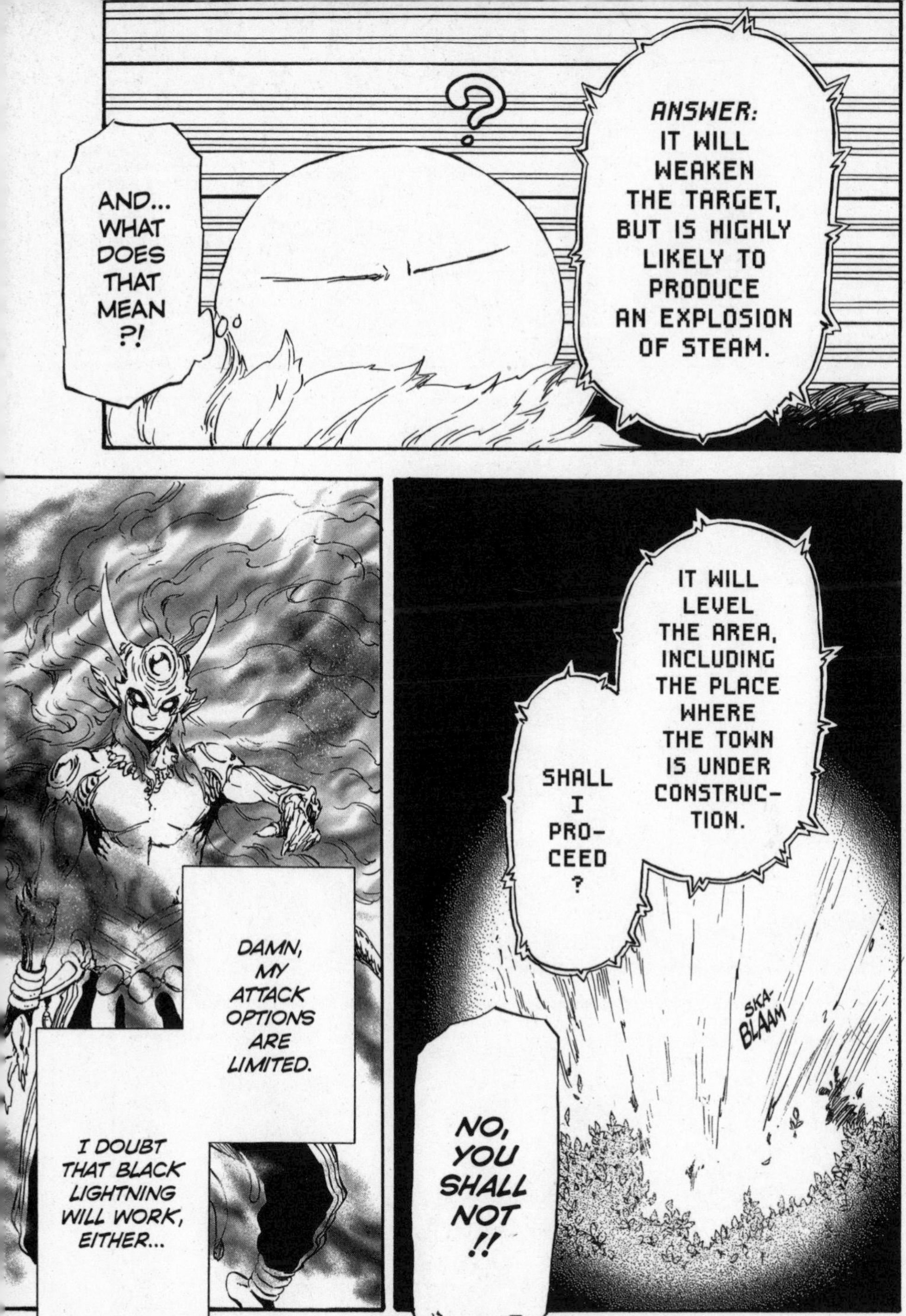
ANSWER: IT WILL WEAKEN THE TARGET, BUT IS HIGHLY LIKELY TO PRODUCE AN EXPLOSION OF STEAM.
AND... WHAT DOES THAT MEAN?!
IT WILL LEVEL THE AREA, INCLUDING THE PLACE WHERE THE TOWN IS UNDER CONSTRUC-TION.
SHALL I PRO-CEED?
SKA-BLAAM
NO, YOU SHALL NOT!!
DAMN, MY ATTACK OPTIONS ARE LIMITED.
I DOUBT THAT BLACK LIGHTNING WILL WORK, EITHER...

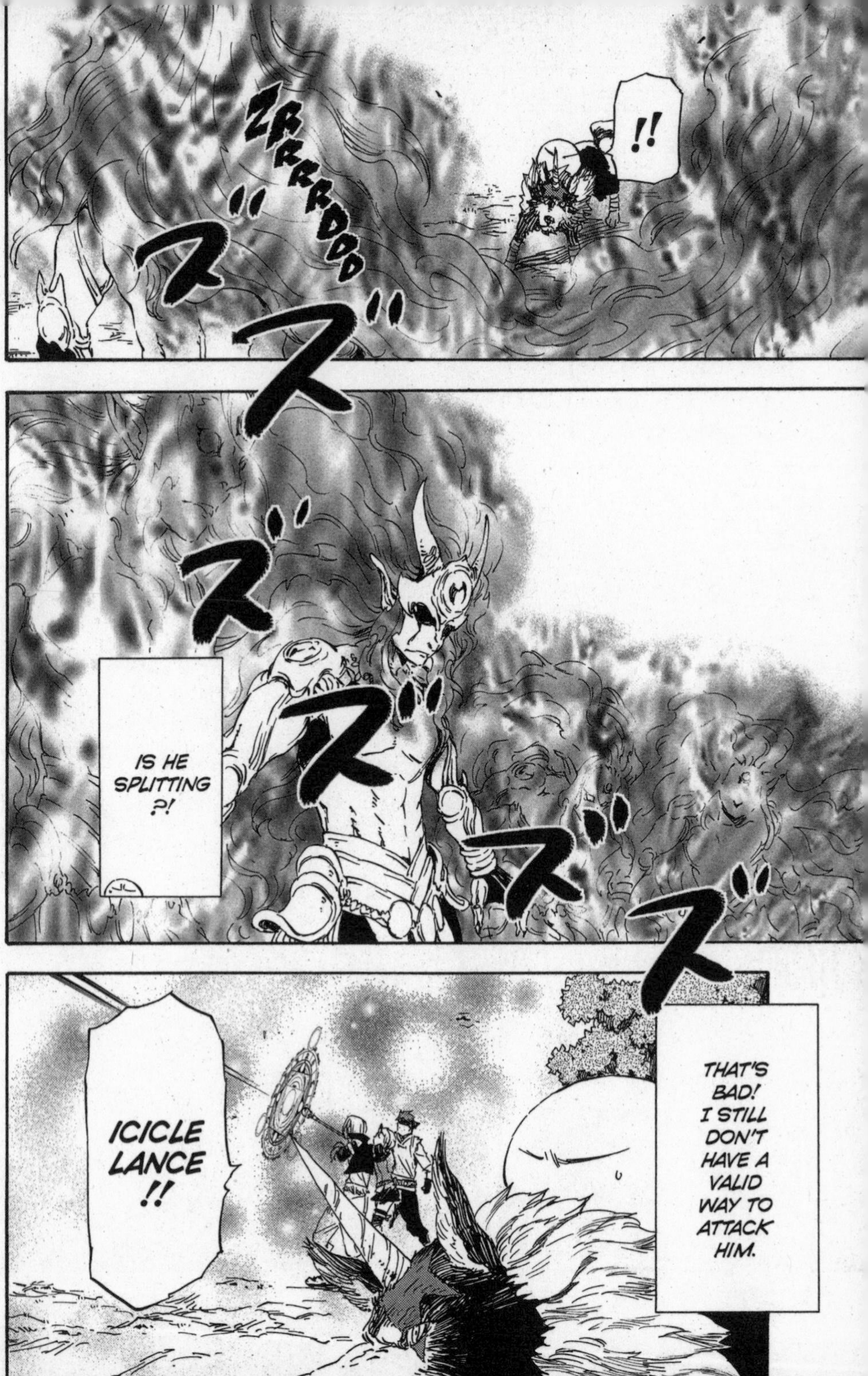
!!
ZRRRRDDDD
ズズズズズズ
IS HE SPLITTING ?!
THAT'S BAD! I STILL DON'T HAVE A VALID WAY TO ATTACK HIM.
ICICLE LANCE !!

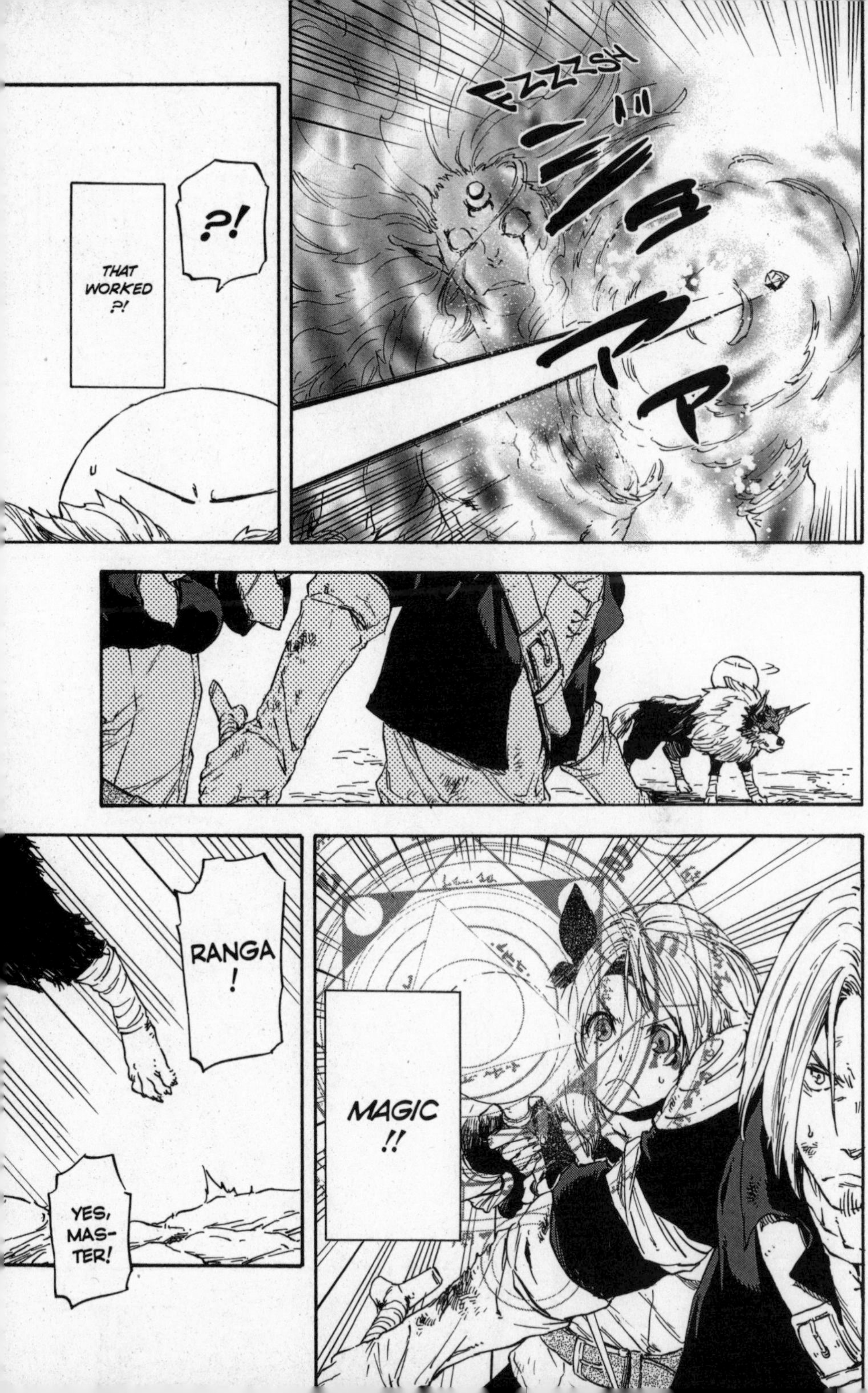

FZZZSH
?!
THAT WORKED ?!
MAGIC !!
RANGA !
YES, MASTER!

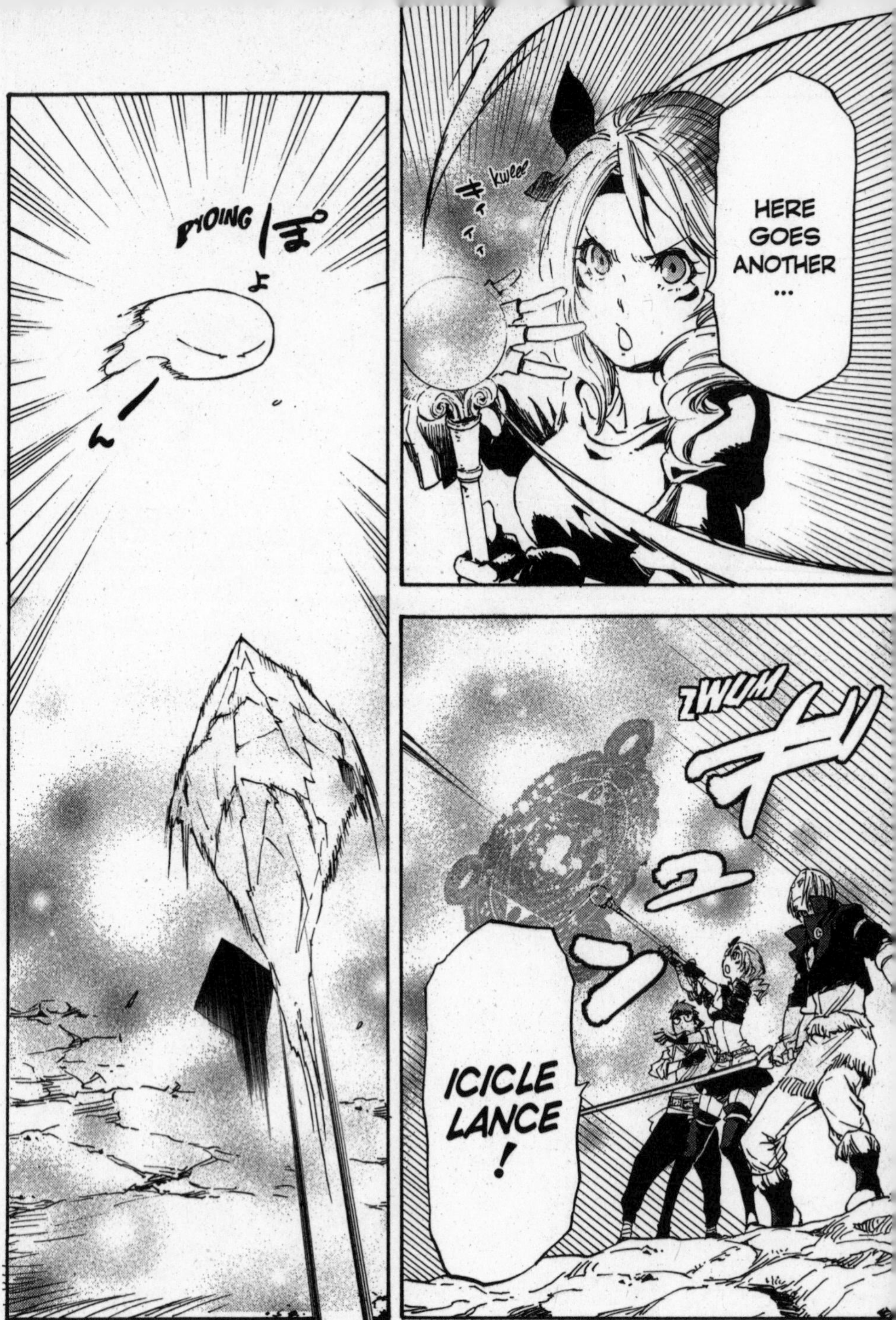
kweee
HERE GOES ANOTHER ...
ZWUM
ICICLE LANCE!
BYOING
ぽよーん

ACK!

WAIT! RIMURU, NO!

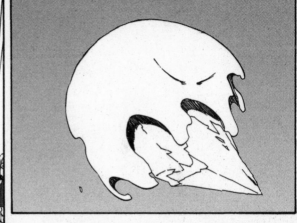

WHAAA?! WHAT HAPPENED TO MY SPELL?!

PWOOP

SORRY, I'LL EXPLAIN LATER.

SWOOP

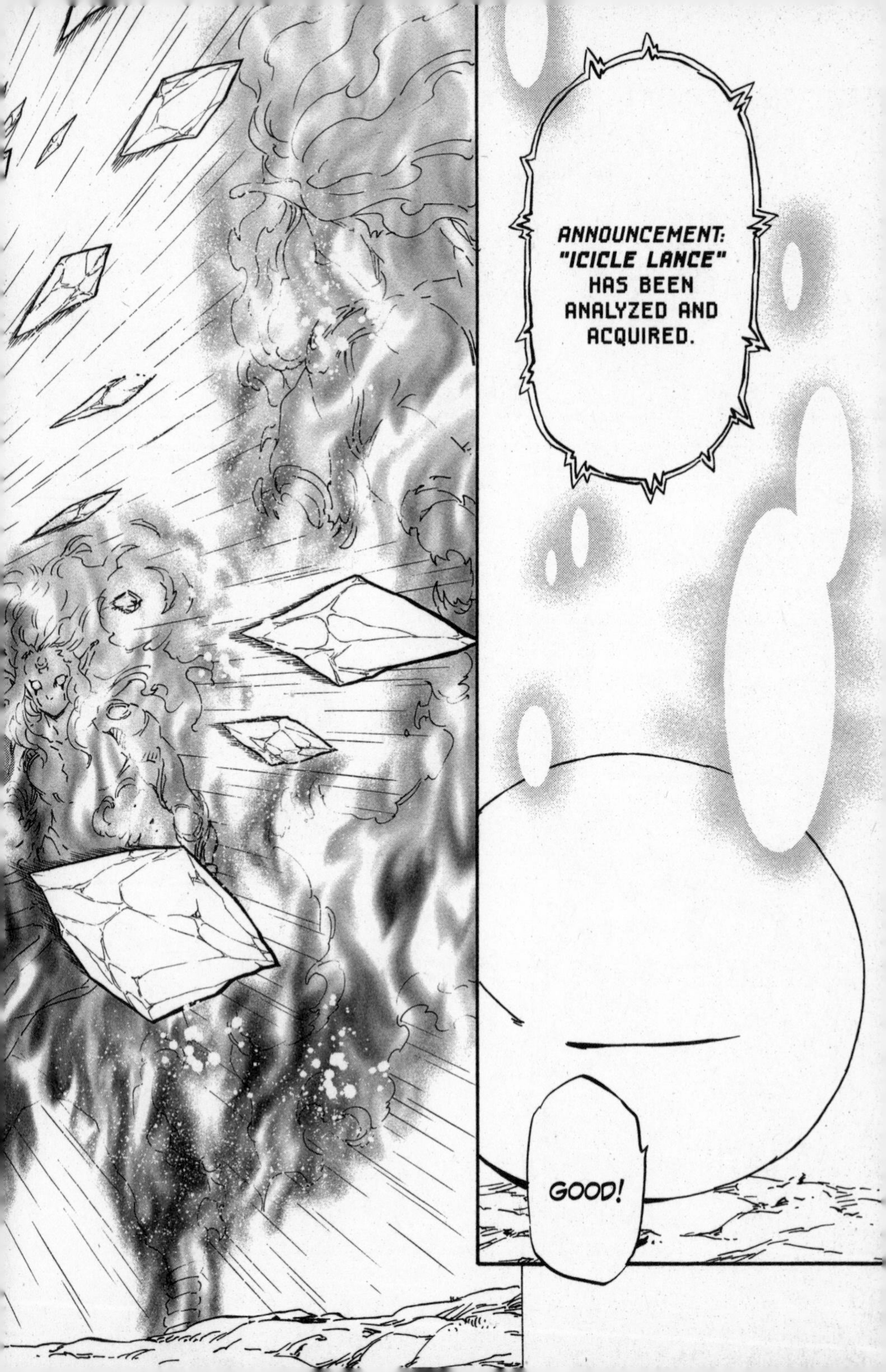
ANNOUNCEMENT: "ICICLE LANCE" HAS BEEN ANALYZED AND ACQUIRED.
GOOD!

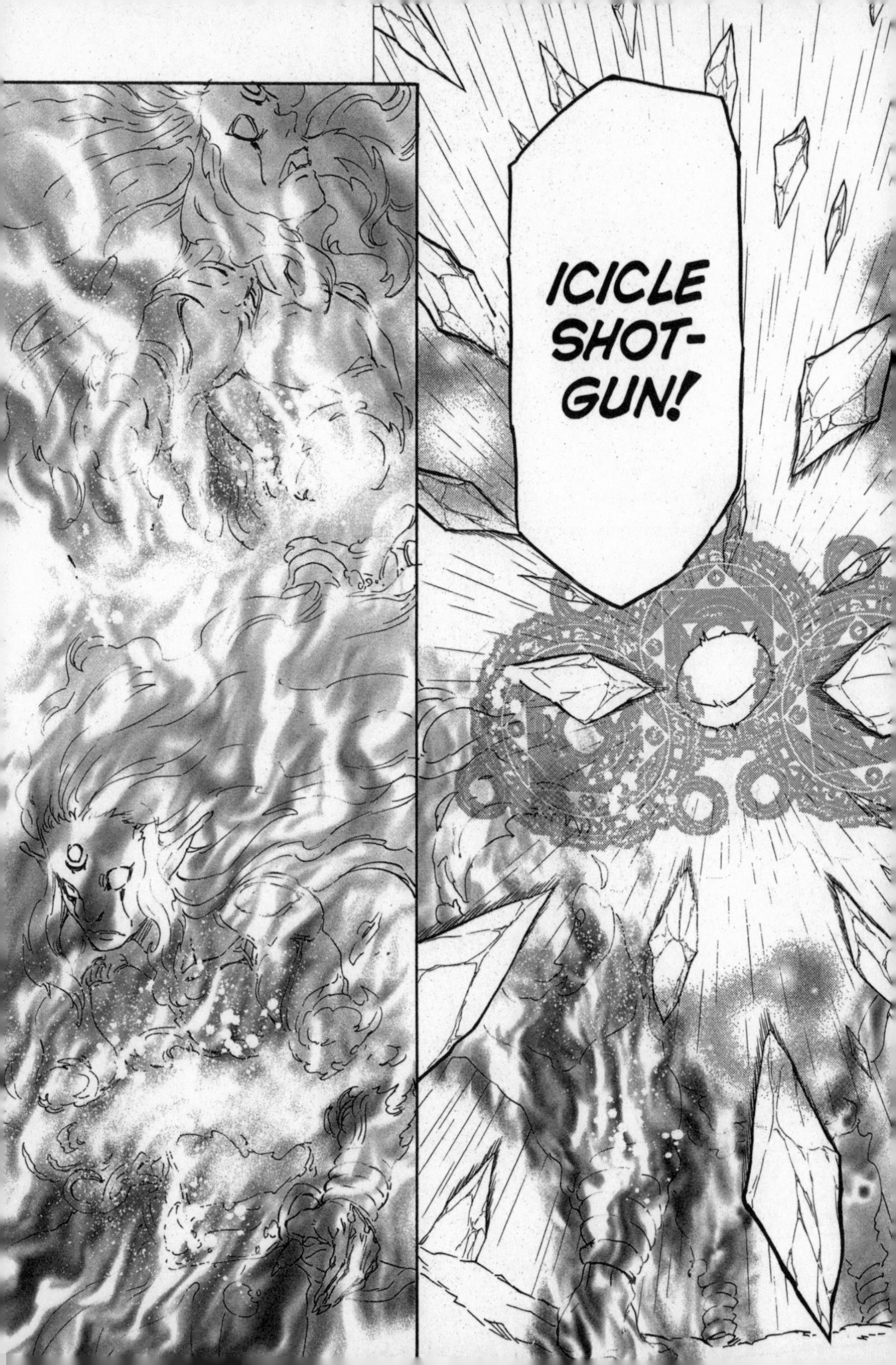
ICICLE SHOT-GUN!

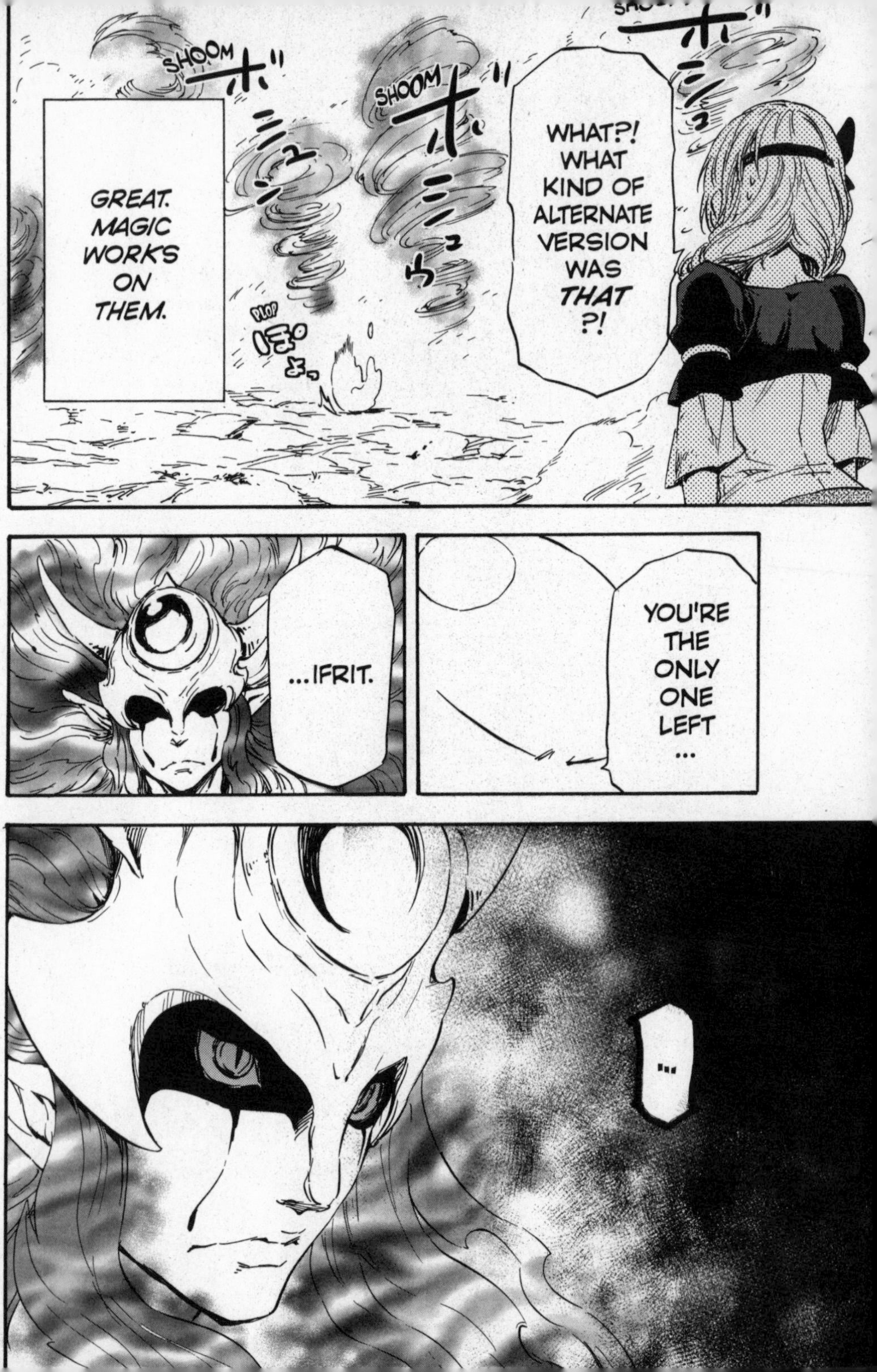
WHAT?! WHAT KIND OF ALTERNATE VERSION WAS *THAT*?!
SHOOM
SHOOM
PLOP
GREAT. MAGIC WORKS ON THEM.
YOU'RE THE ONLY ONE LEFT...
...IFRIT.
...

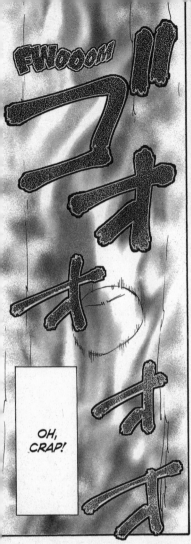

FWOOOM

OH, CRAP!

KSHAAA

FLARE CIRCLE
...

MASTER!!

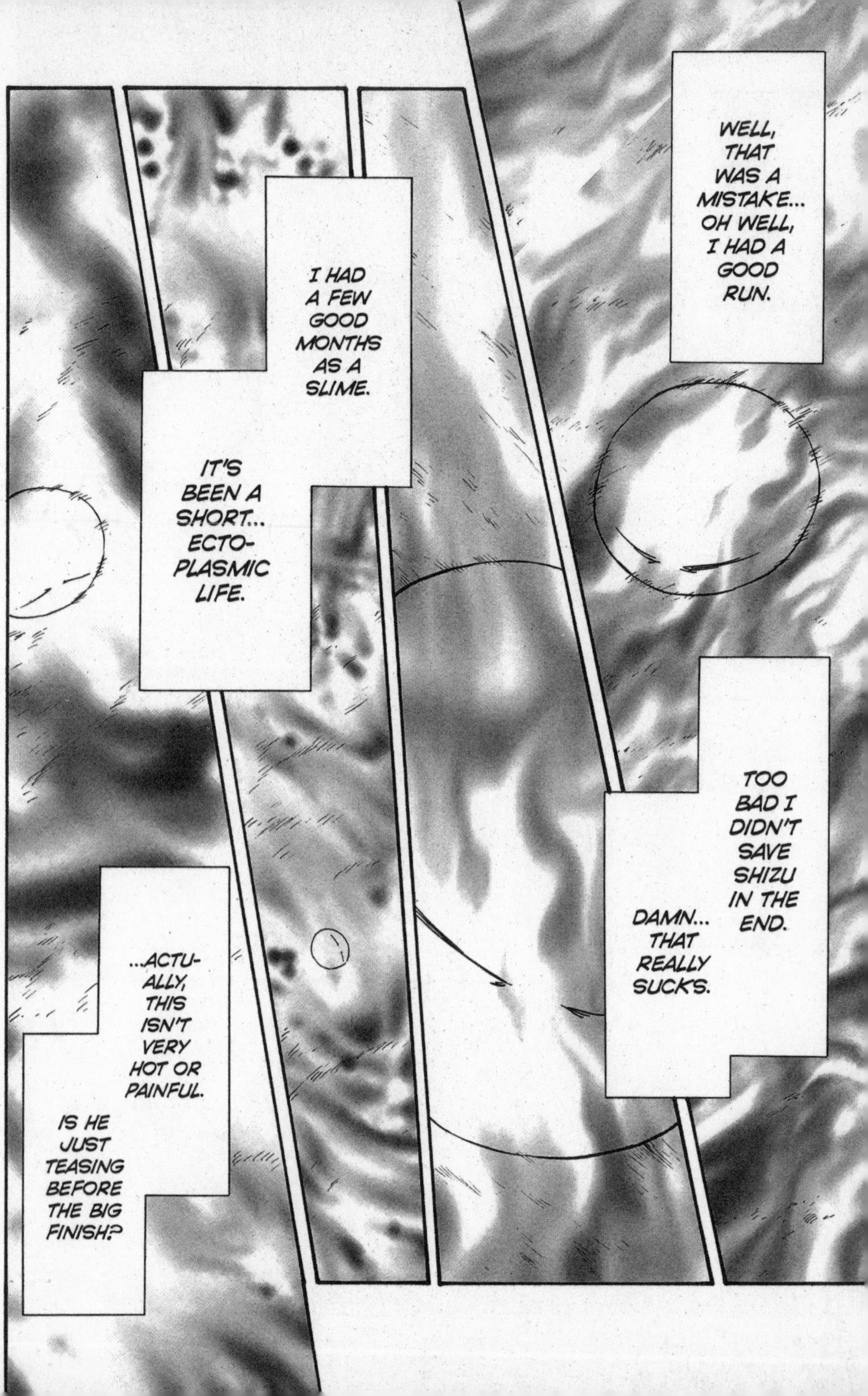
WELL, THAT WAS A MISTAKE... OH WELL, I HAD A GOOD RUN.
TOO BAD I DIDN'T SAVE SHIZU IN THE END.
DAMN... THAT REALLY SUCKS.
I HAD A FEW GOOD MONTHS AS A SLIME.
IT'S BEEN A SHORT... ECTO-PLASMIC LIFE.
...ACTU-ALLY, THIS ISN'T VERY HOT OR PAINFUL.
IS HE JUST TEASING BEFORE THE BIG FINISH?

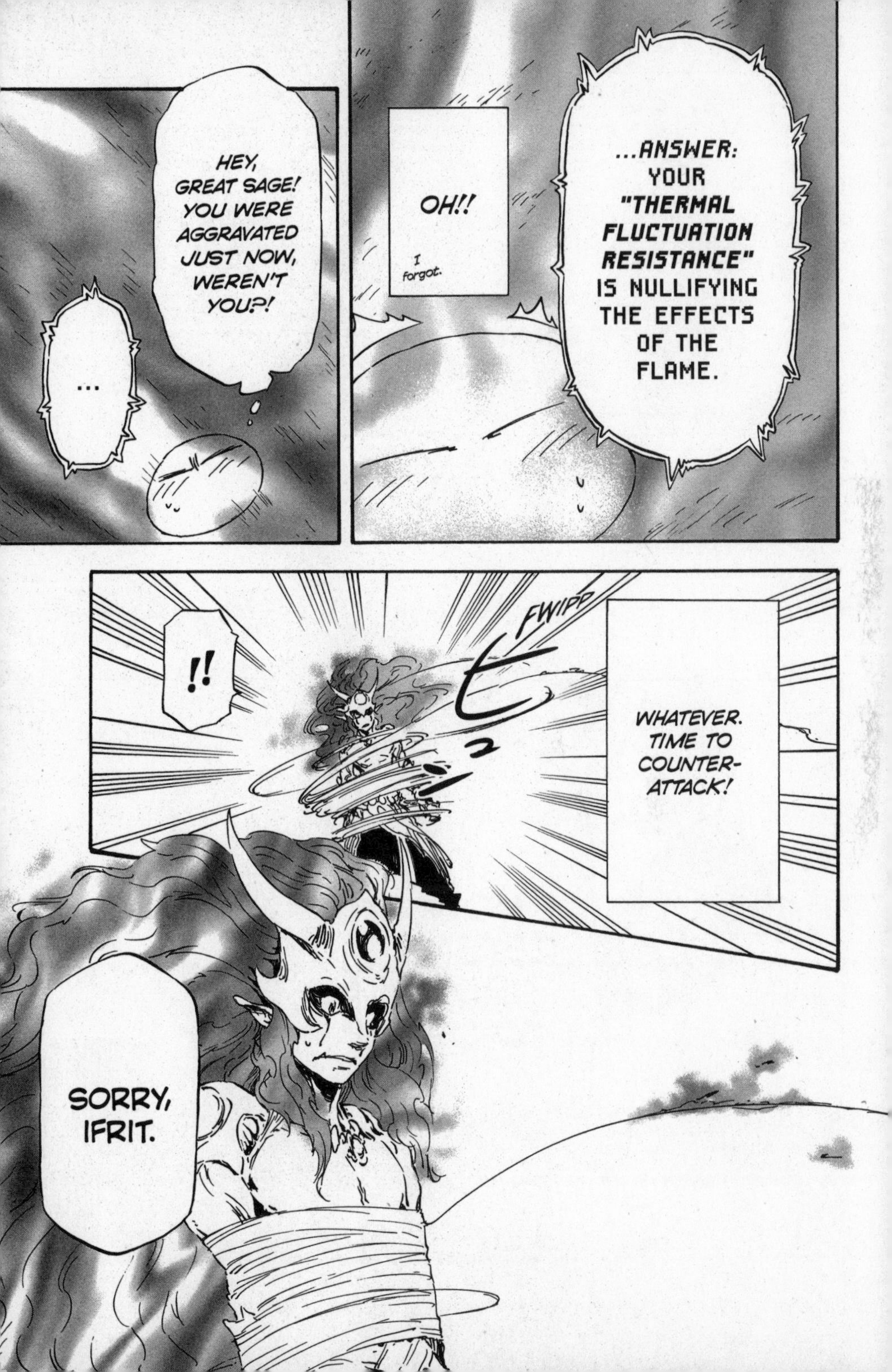

...ANSWER: YOUR "THERMAL FLUCTUATION RESISTANCE" IS NULLIFYING THE EFFECTS OF THE FLAME.
OH!!
I forgot.
HEY, GREAT SAGE! YOU WERE AGGRAVATED JUST NOW, WEREN'T YOU?!
...
WHATEVER. TIME TO COUNTER-ATTACK!
FWIPP
!!
SORRY, IFRIT.

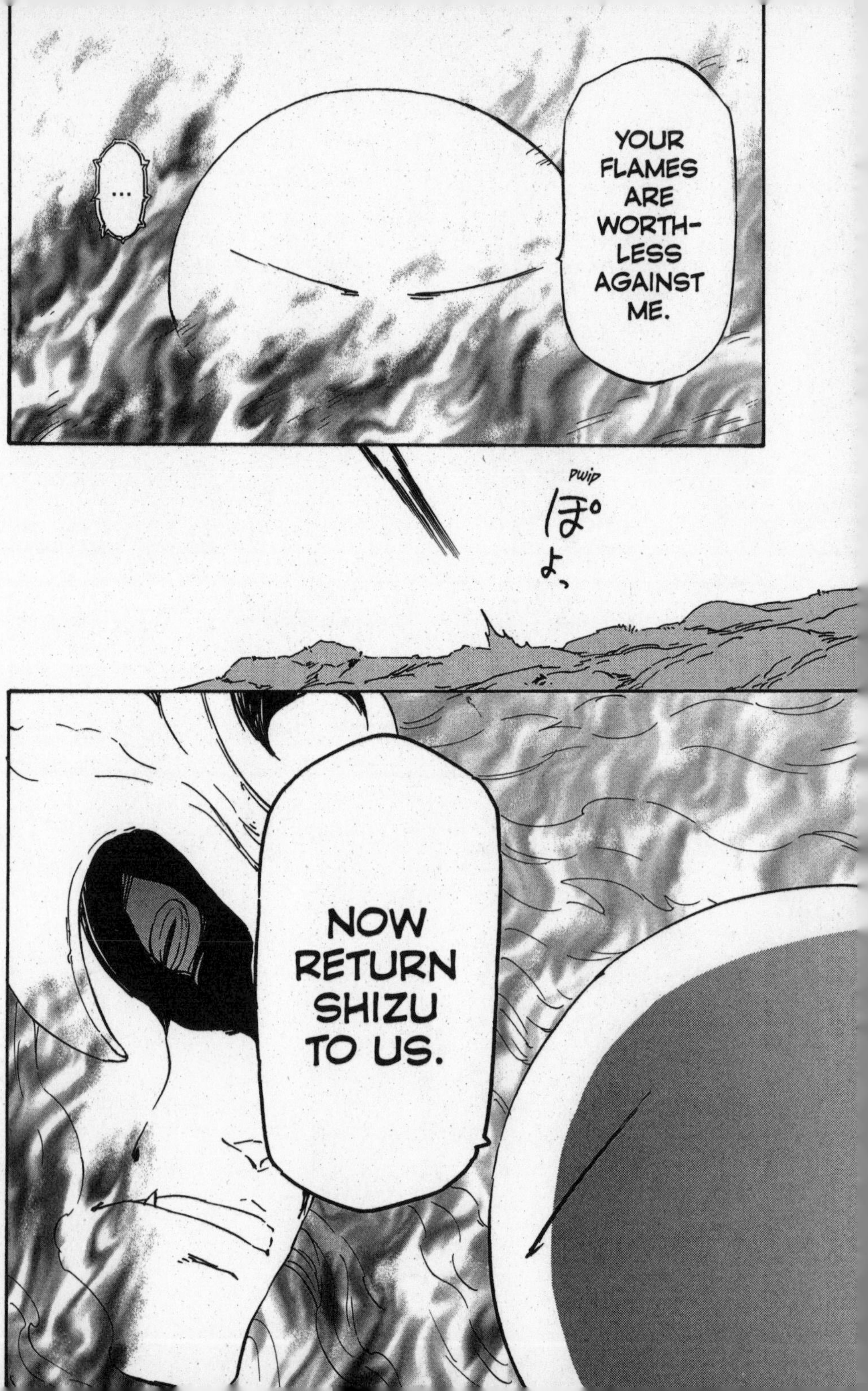
YOUR FLAMES ARE WORTHLESS AGAINST ME.
...
PWIP
ぽよ、
NOW RETURN SHIZU TO US.

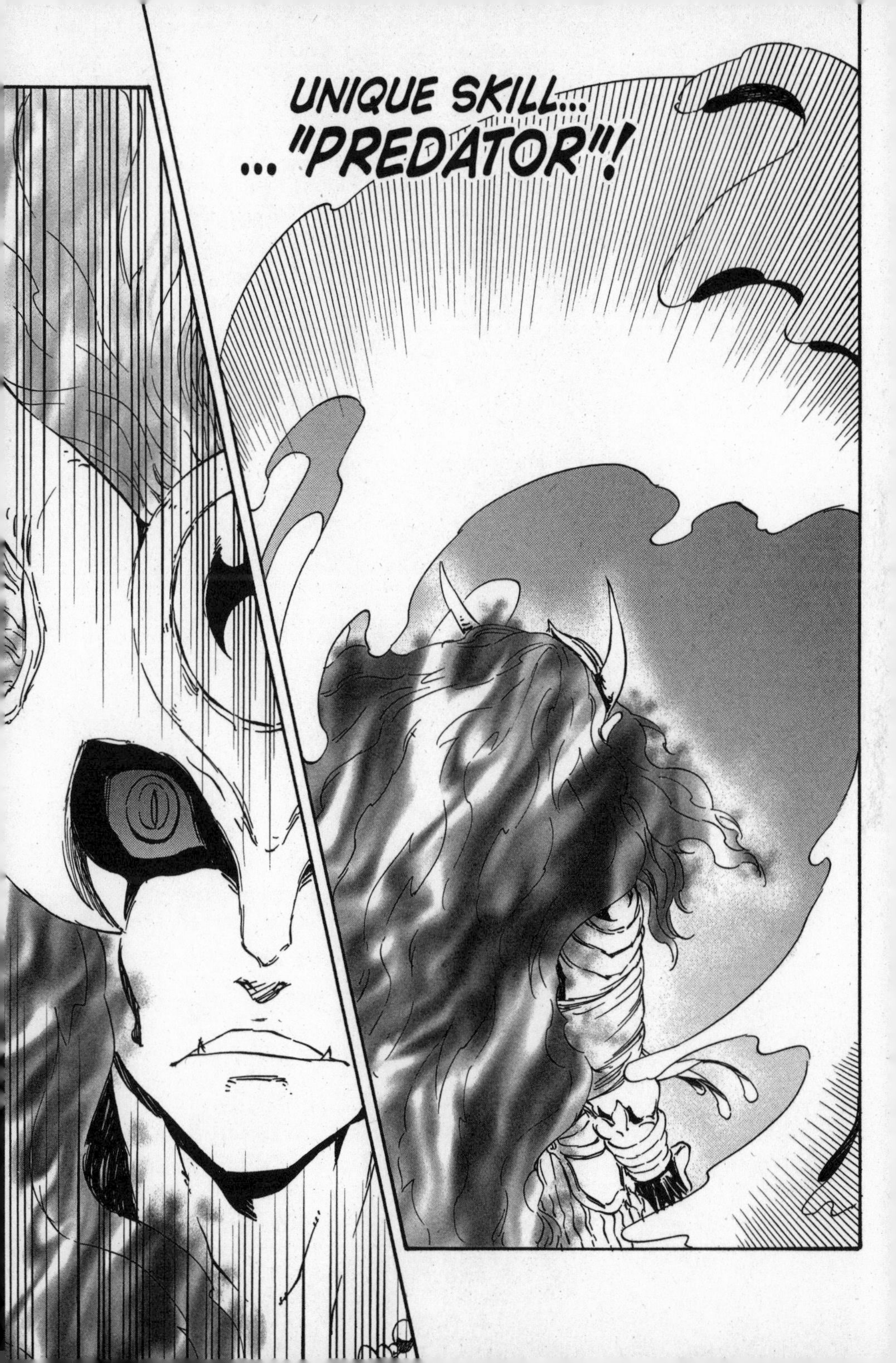
UNIQUE SKILL...
..."PREDATOR"!

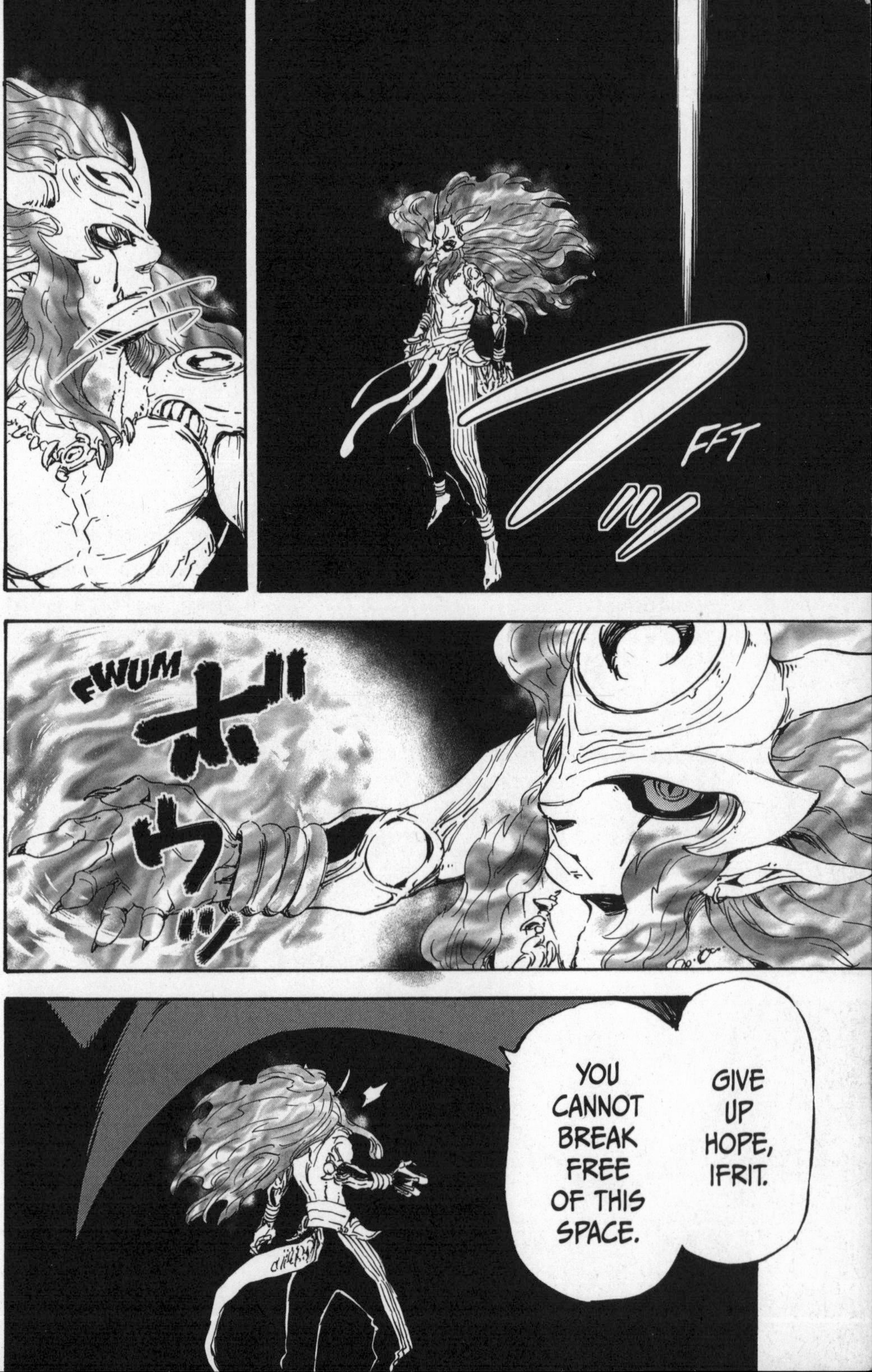
FFT
FWUM
YOU CANNOT BREAK FREE OF THIS SPACE.
GIVE UP HOPE, IFRIT.

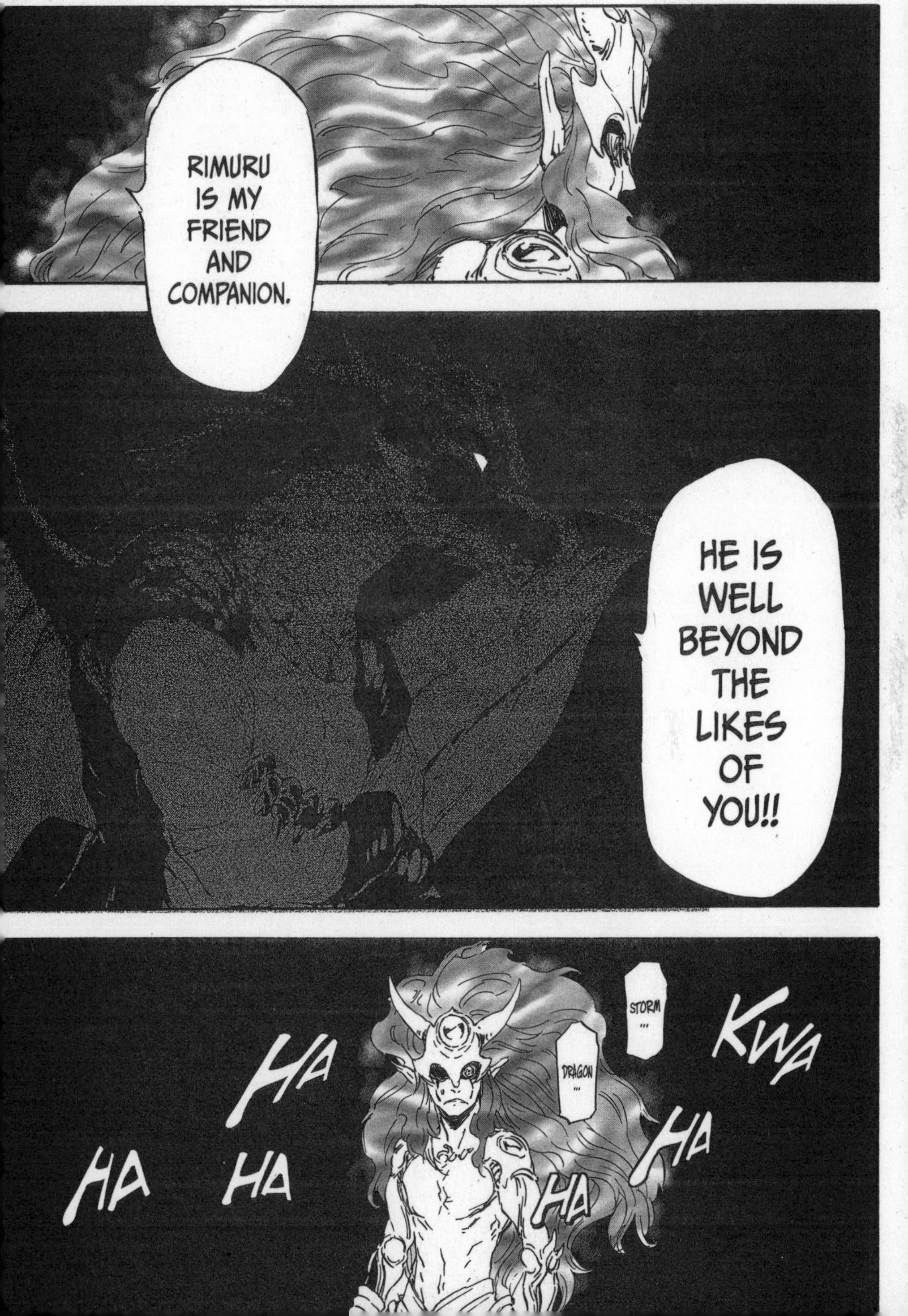
RIMURU IS MY FRIEND AND COMPANION.
HE IS WELL BEYOND THE LIKES OF YOU!!
KWA
STORM ...
DRAGON ...
HA
HA
HA
HA
HA

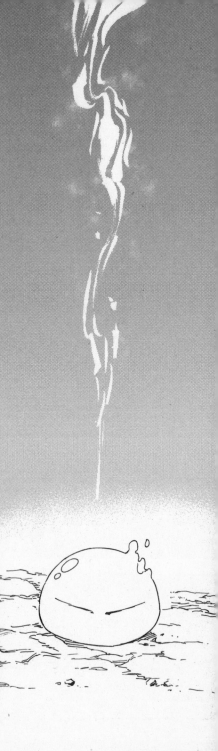

PLOP...
ぽ
よ‥

THANK YOU...

...MR. SLIME.

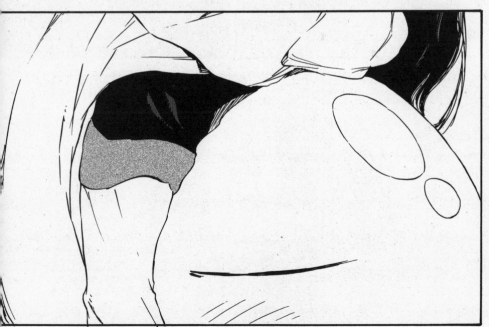

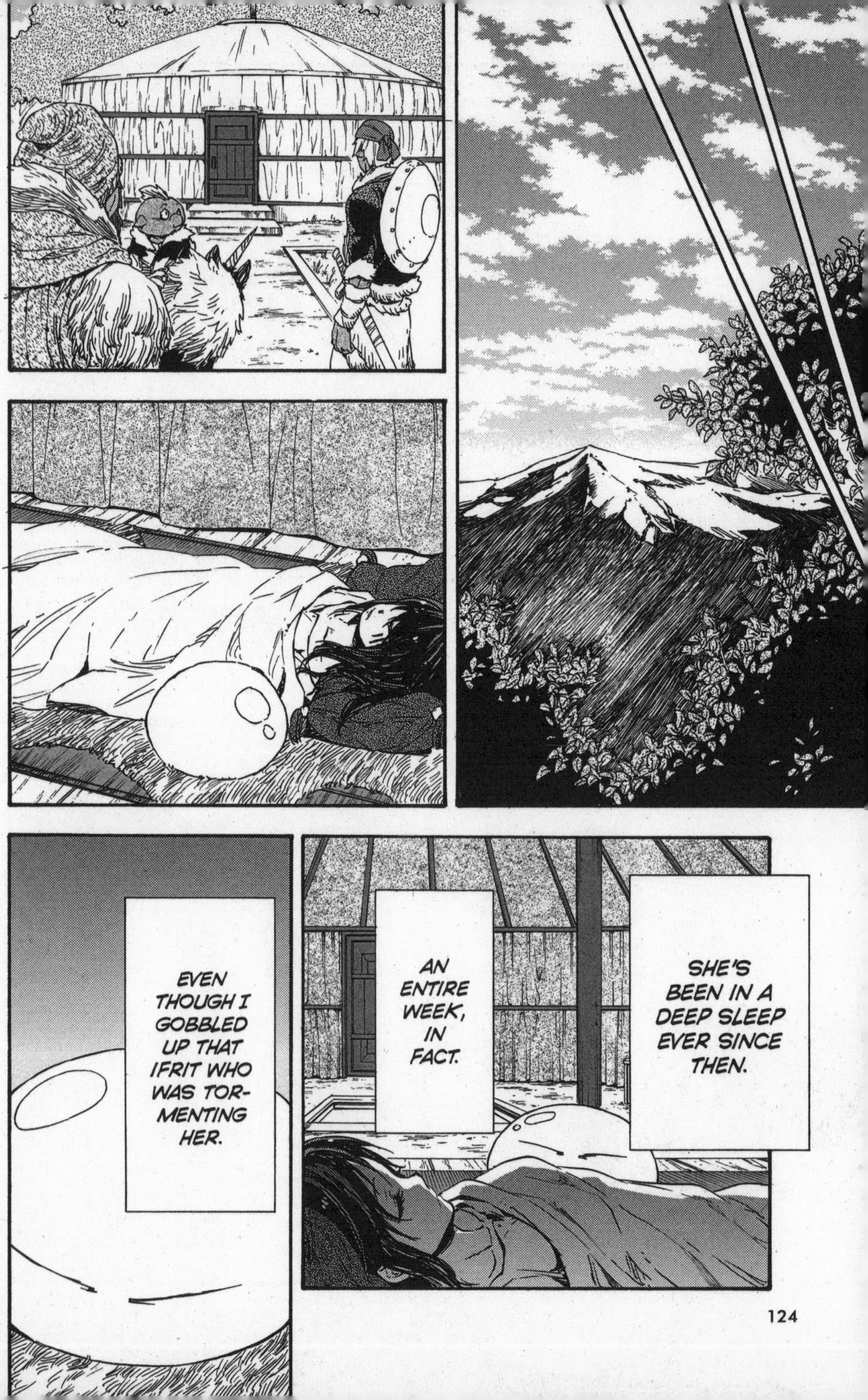
SHE'S BEEN IN A DEEP SLEEP EVER SINCE THEN.
AN ENTIRE WEEK, IN FACT.
EVEN THOUGH I GOBBLED UP THAT IFRIT WHO WAS TOR-MENTING HER.

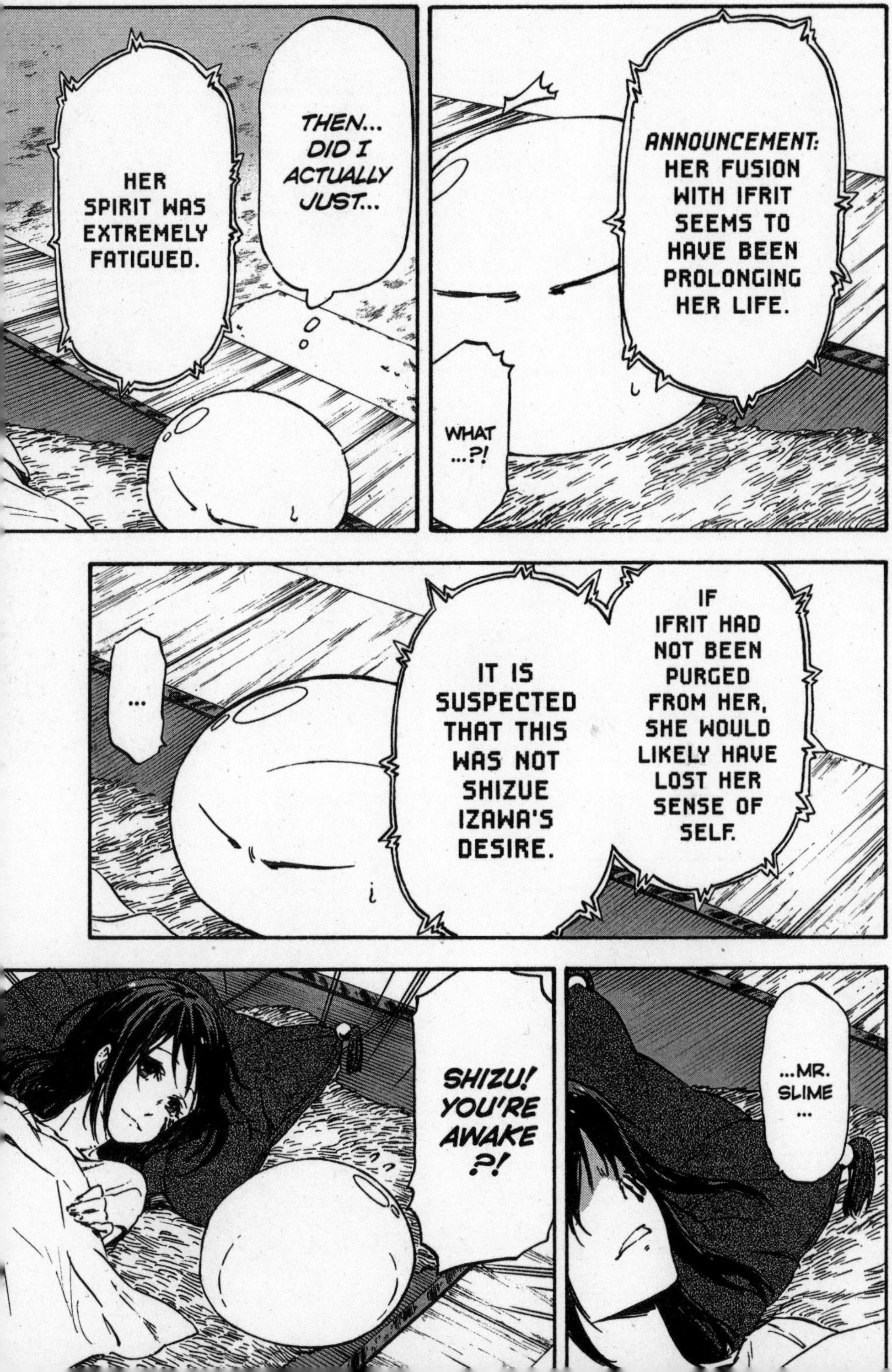
ANNOUNCEMENT: HER FUSION WITH IFRIT SEEMS TO HAVE BEEN PROLONGING HER LIFE.
WHAT ...?!
THEN... DID I ACTUALLY JUST...
HER SPIRIT WAS EXTREMELY FATIGUED.
IF IFRIT HAD NOT BEEN PURGED FROM HER, SHE WOULD LIKELY HAVE LOST HER SENSE OF SELF.
IT IS SUSPECTED THAT THIS WAS NOT SHIZUE IZAWA'S DESIRE.
...
...MR. SLIME ...
SHIZU! YOU'RE AWAKE ?!

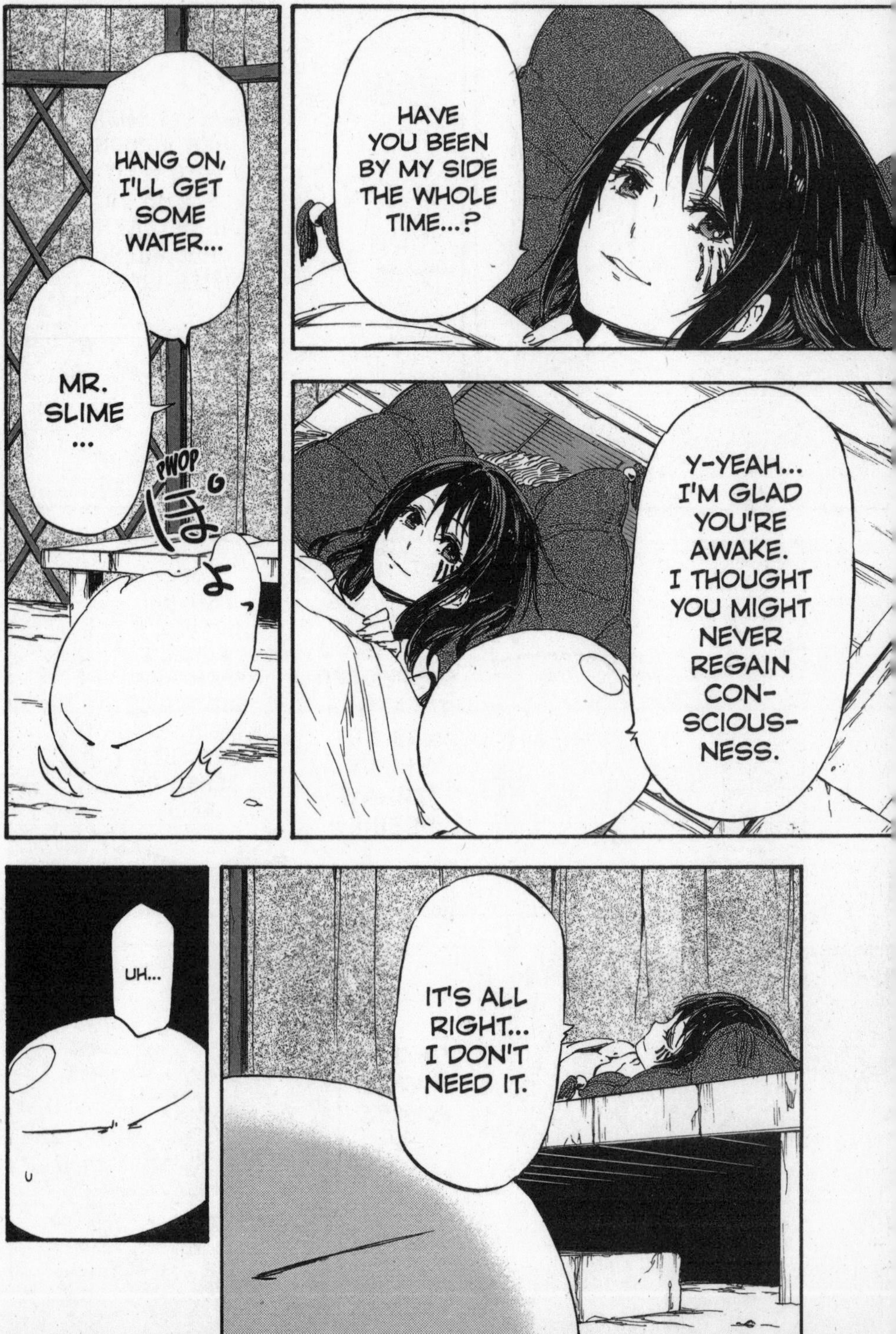
HAVE YOU BEEN BY MY SIDE THE WHOLE TIME...?
Y-YEAH... I'M GLAD YOU'RE AWAKE. I THOUGHT YOU MIGHT NEVER REGAIN CON-SCIOUS-NESS.
HANG ON, I'LL GET SOME WATER...
MR. SLIME ...
PWOP
ぽよ
IT'S ALL RIGHT... I DON'T NEED IT.
UH...

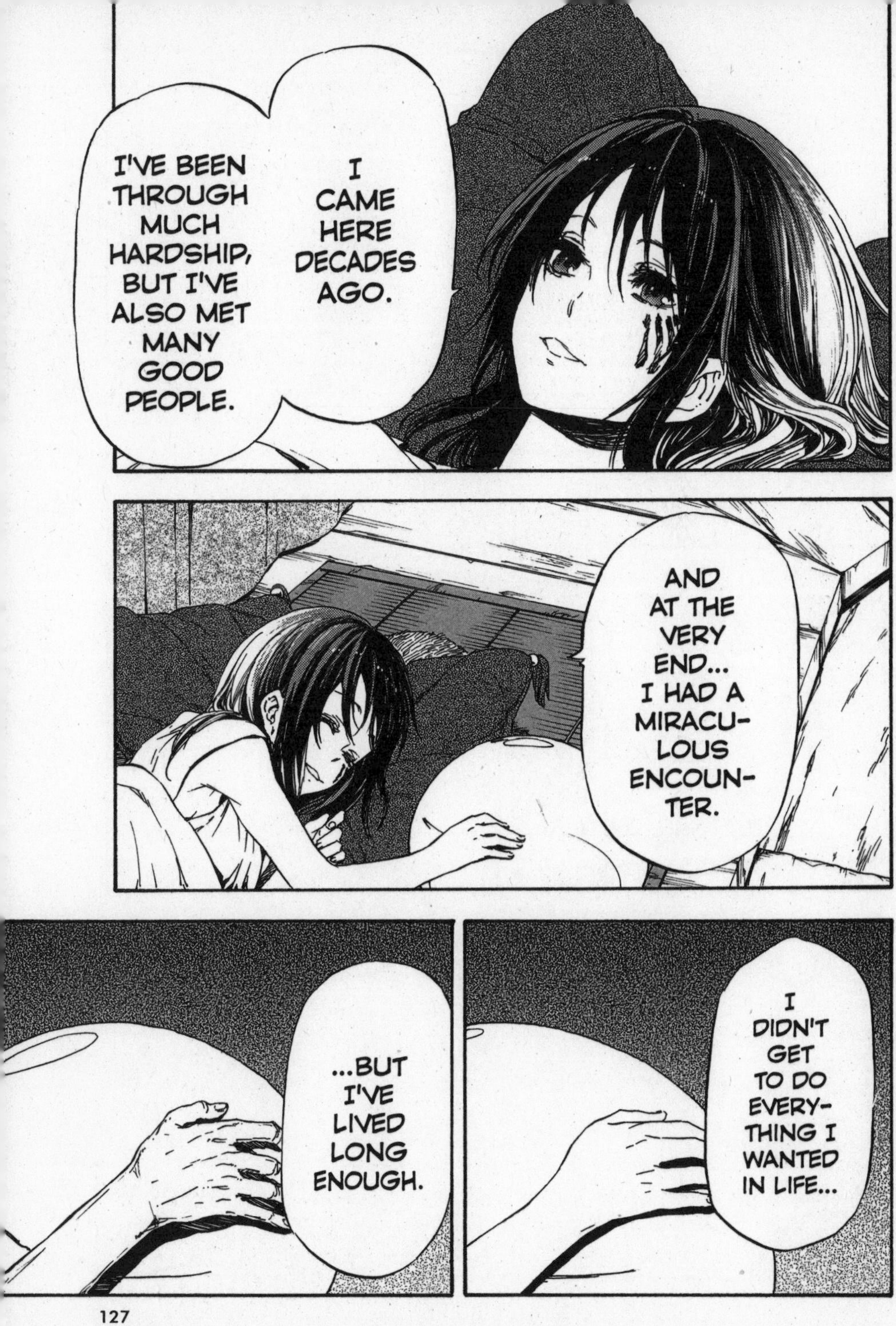
I CAME HERE DECADES AGO.
I'VE BEEN THROUGH MUCH HARDSHIP, BUT I'VE ALSO MET MANY GOOD PEOPLE.
AND AT THE VERY END... I HAD A MIRACULOUS ENCOUNTER.
I DIDN'T GET TO DO EVERYTHING I WANTED IN LIFE...
...BUT I'VE LIVED LONG ENOUGH.

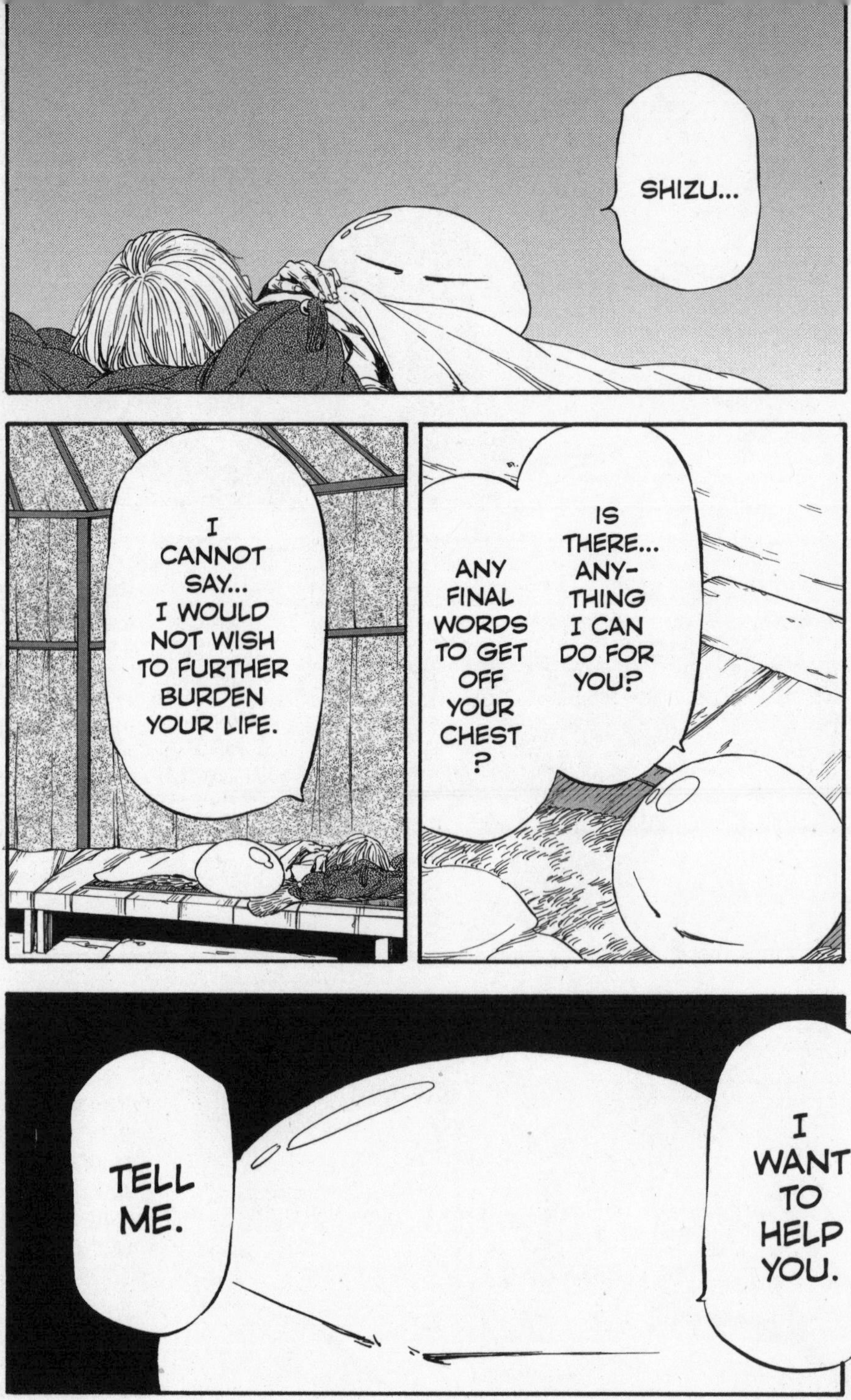
SHIZU...
IS THERE... ANYTHING I CAN DO FOR YOU?
ANY FINAL WORDS TO GET OFF YOUR CHEST?
I CANNOT SAY... I WOULD NOT WISH TO FURTHER BURDEN YOUR LIFE.
I WANT TO HELP YOU.
TELL ME.

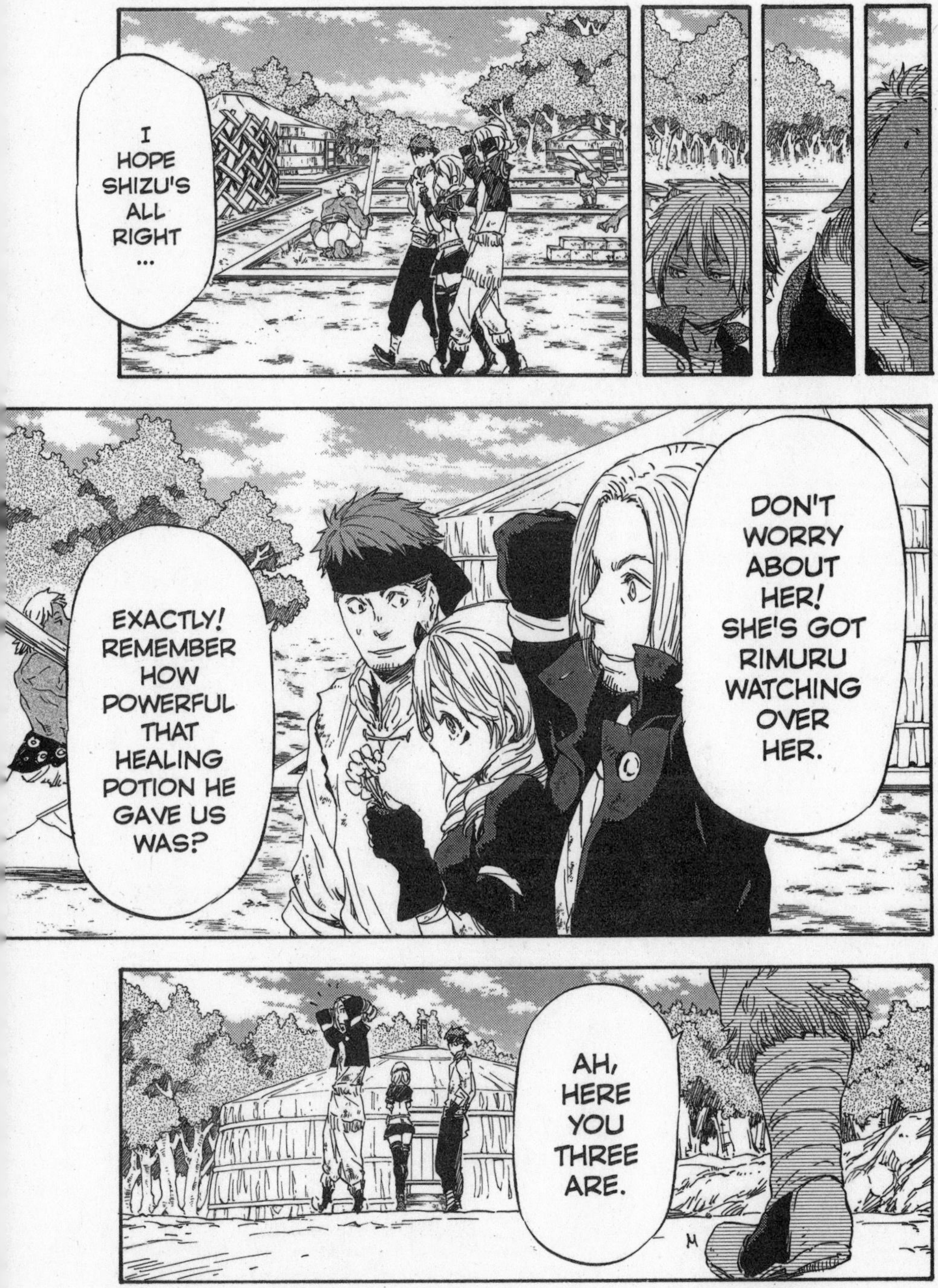
I HOPE SHIZU'S ALL RIGHT ...
DON'T WORRY ABOUT HER! SHE'S GOT RIMURU WATCHING OVER HER.
EXACTLY! REMEMBER HOW POWERFUL THAT HEALING POTION HE GAVE US WAS?
AH, HERE YOU THREE ARE.

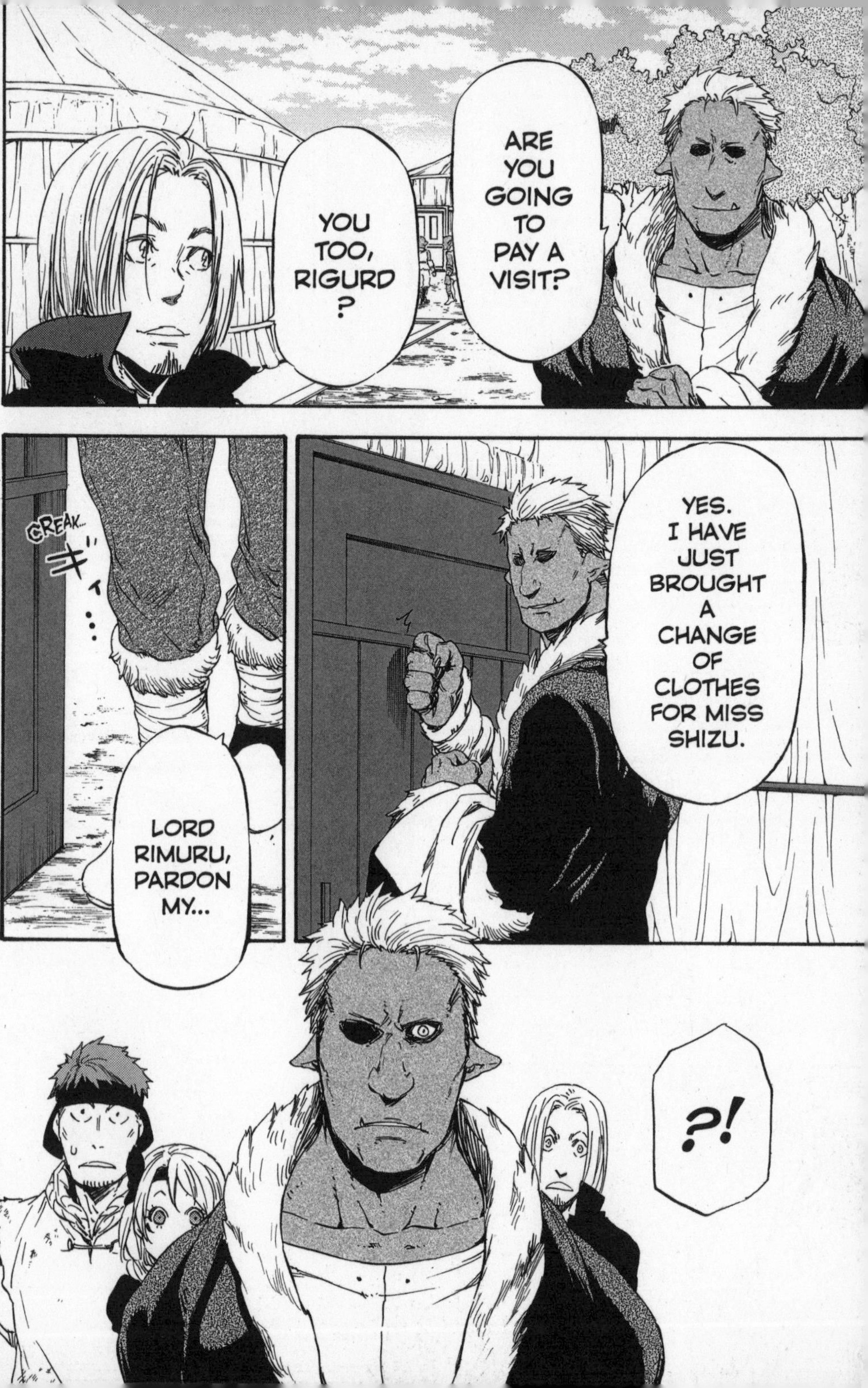
ARE YOU GOING TO PAY A VISIT?
YOU TOO, RIGURD?
YES. I HAVE JUST BROUGHT A CHANGE OF CLOTHES FOR MISS SHIZU.
CREAK...
ギィ…
LORD RIMURU, PARDON MY...
?!

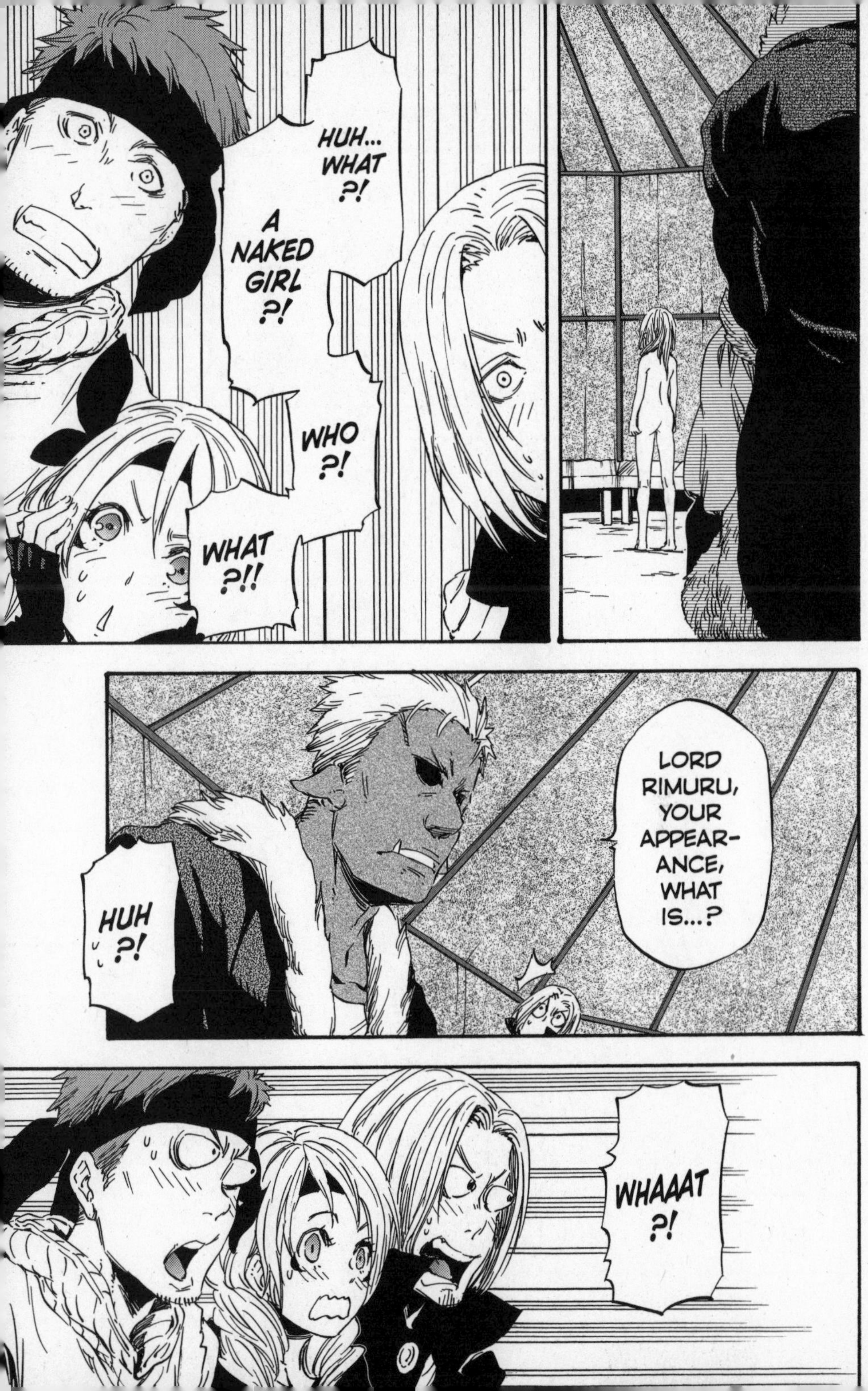
HUH... WHAT ?!
A NAKED GIRL ?!
WHO ?!
WHAT ?!!
LORD RIMURU, YOUR APPEARANCE, WHAT IS...?
HUH ?!
WHAAAT ?!

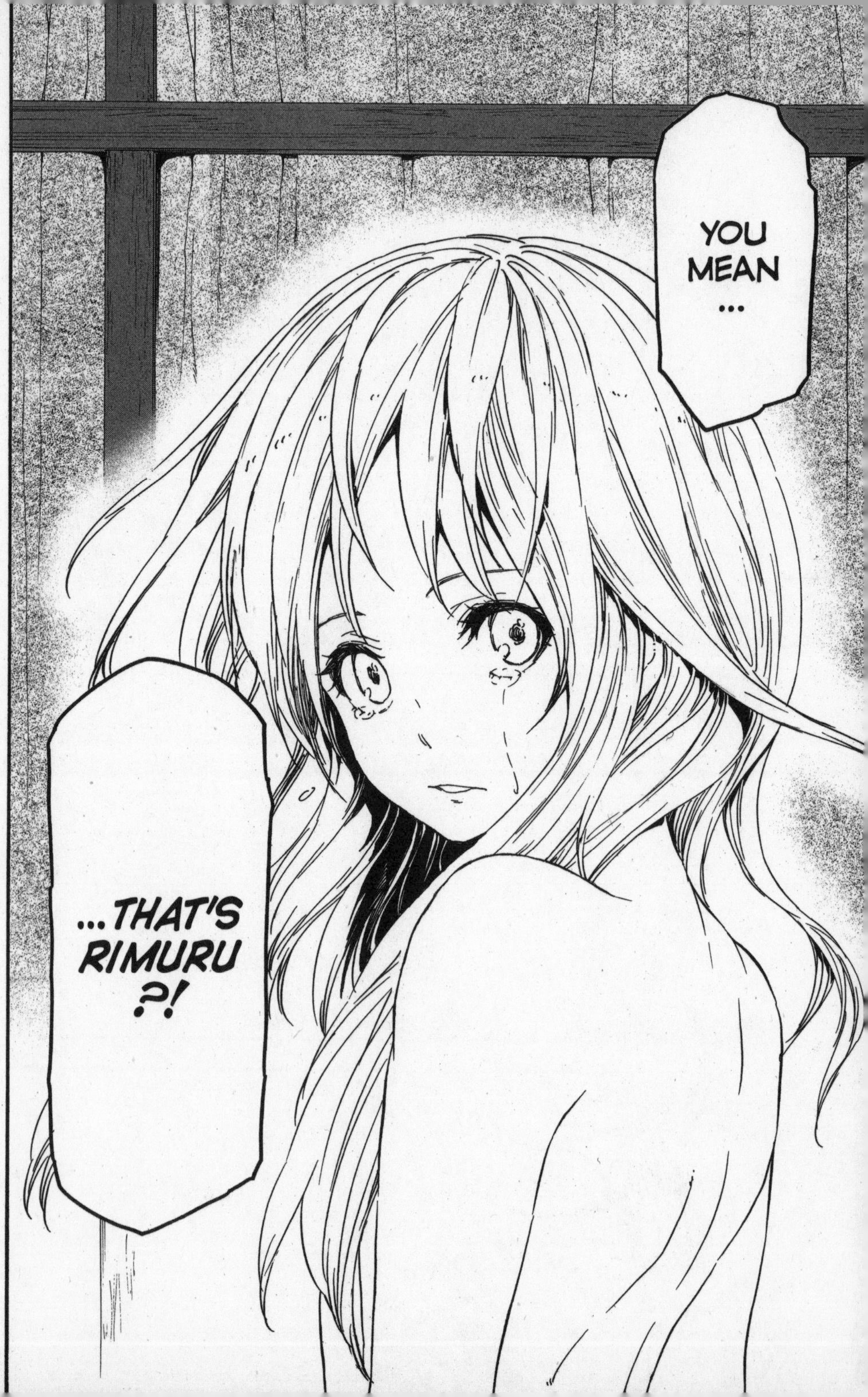
YOU MEAN ...
...THAT'S RIMURU ?!

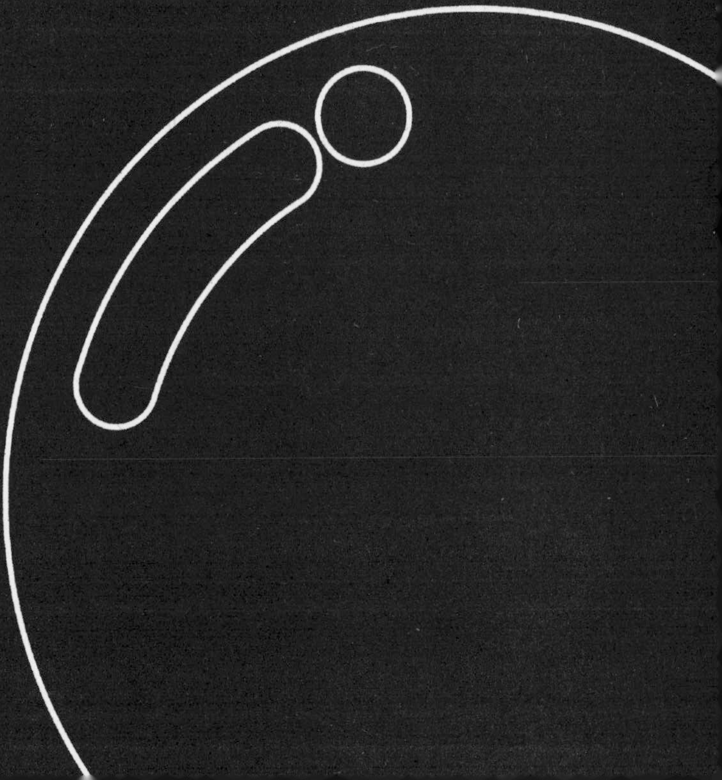

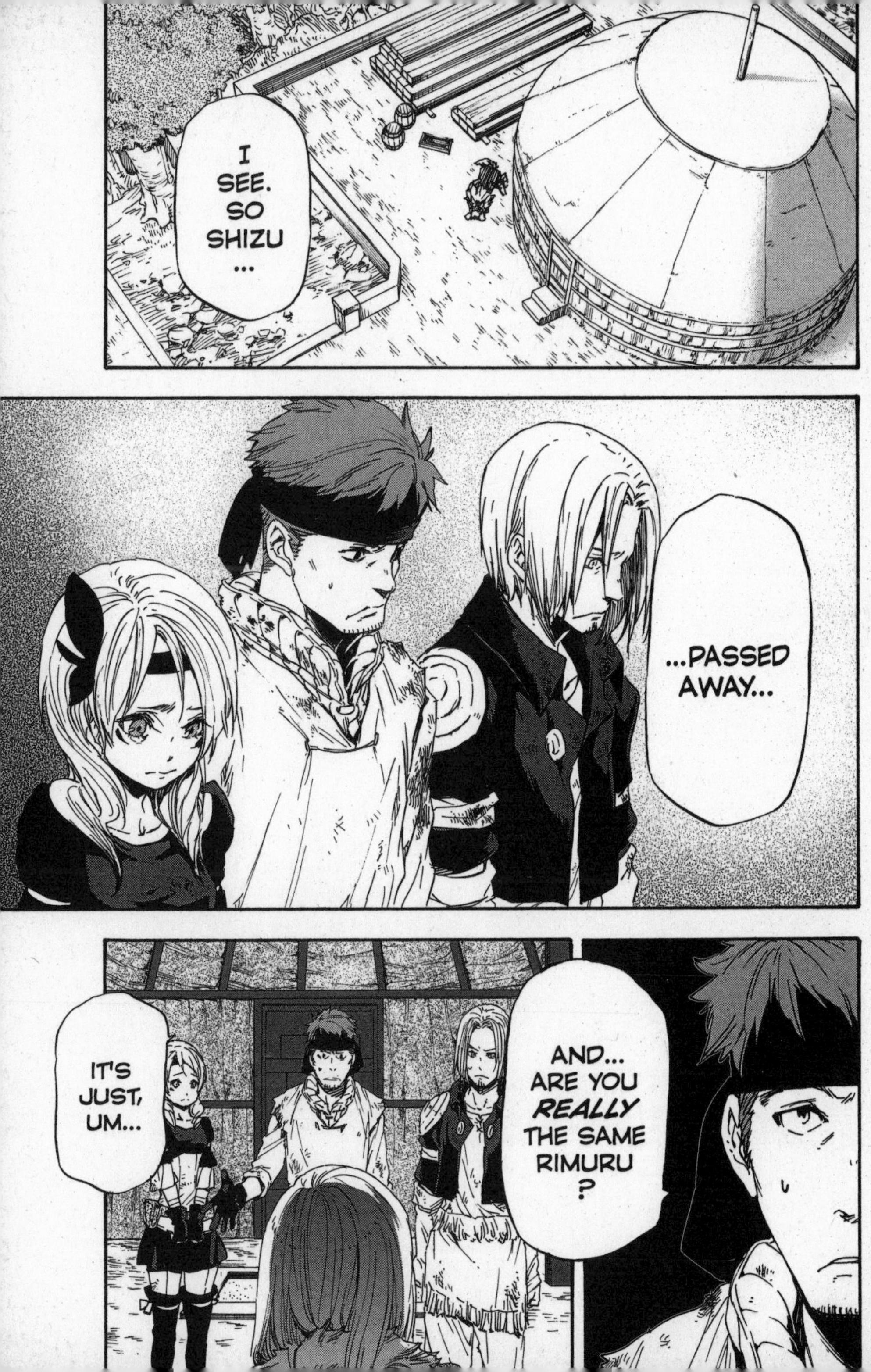
I SEE. SO SHIZU...
...PASSED AWAY...
AND... ARE YOU *REALLY* THE SAME RIMURU?
IT'S JUST, UM...

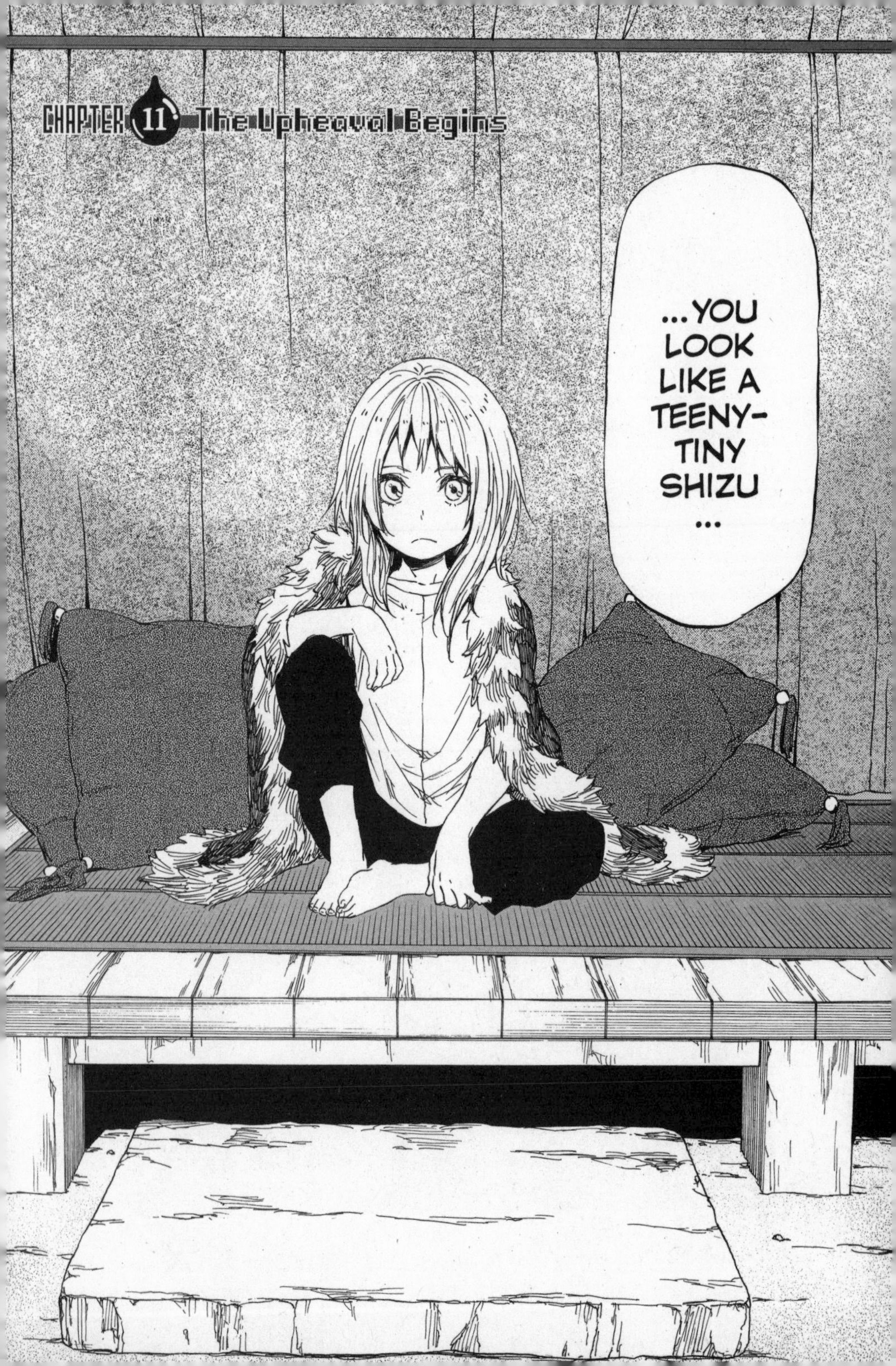
CHAPTER 11 The Upheaval Begins
...YOU LOOK LIKE A TEENY-TINY SHIZU ...

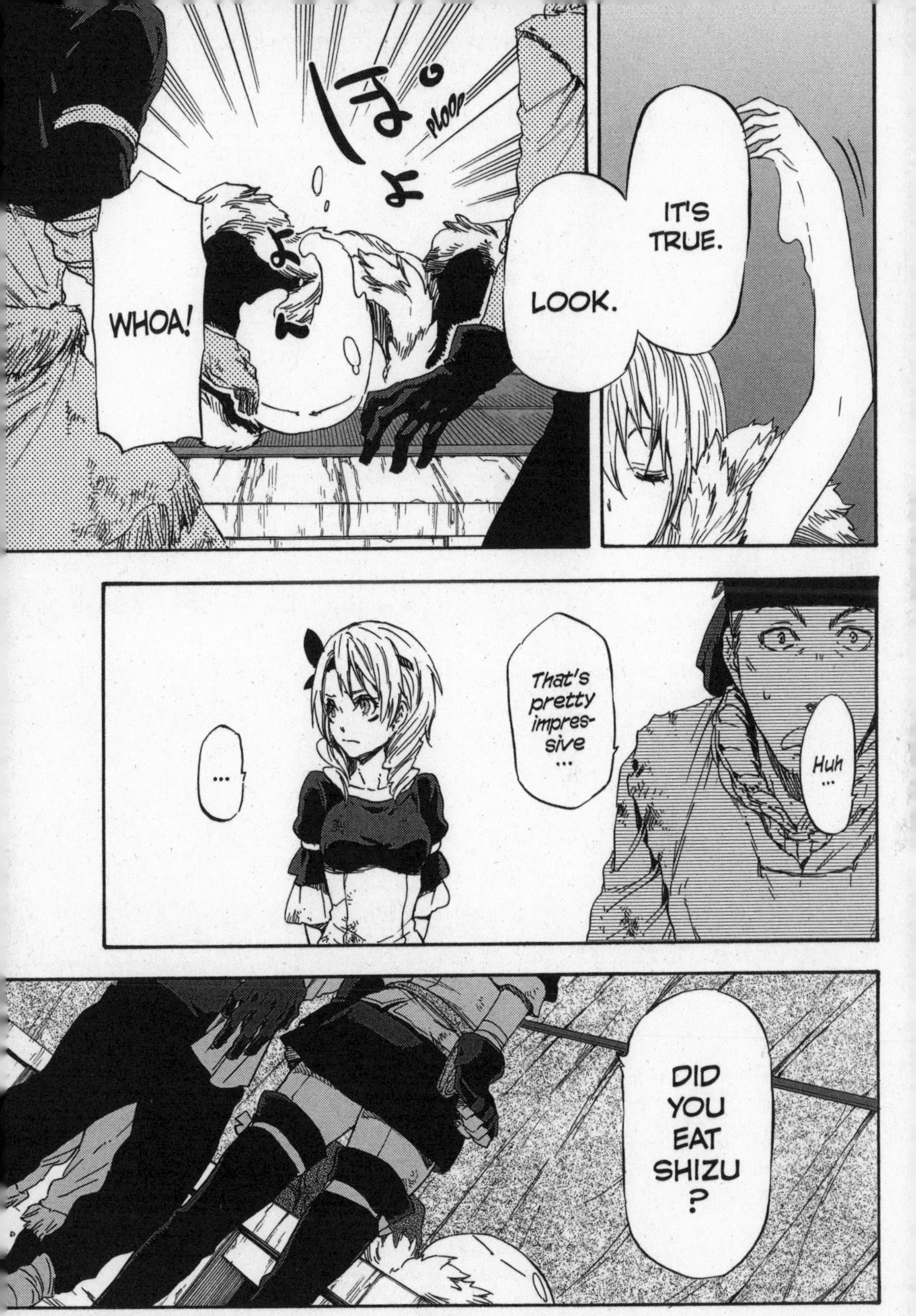
IT'S TRUE.
LOOK.
ぽよ
PLOOP
WHOA!
Huh ...
That's pretty impres- sive ...
...
DID YOU EAT SHIZU ?

THE SAME WAY YOU ATE IFRIT.

IT WAS THE ONE METHOD I HAD...

...TO SEE HER OFF.

I WANT TO GO TO MY ETERNAL SLEEP...

...AMID THE FAMILIAR SIGHT OF MY OLD HOME, LIKE YOU SHOWED ME...

NO... IF THAT WAS HER WISH, THEN WE COULDN'T ARGUE AGAINST IT.

I'M SORRY TO HAVE DONE THAT WITHOUT CONSULTING YOU, HER COMPAN-IONS.

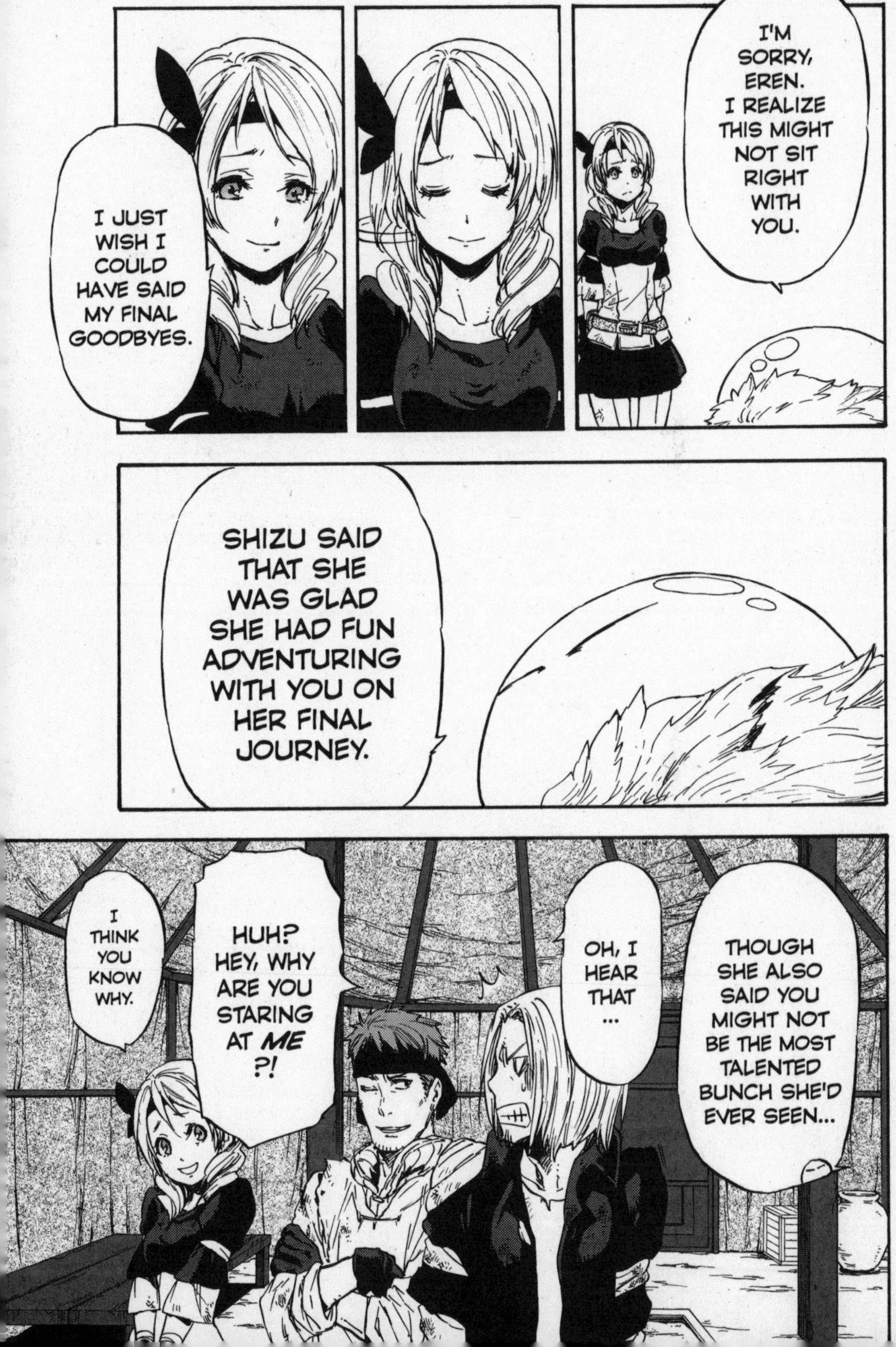
I'M SORRY, EREN. I REALIZE THIS MIGHT NOT SIT RIGHT WITH YOU.
I JUST WISH I COULD HAVE SAID MY FINAL GOODBYES.
SHIZU SAID THAT SHE WAS GLAD SHE HAD FUN ADVENTURING WITH YOU ON HER FINAL JOURNEY.
THOUGH SHE ALSO SAID YOU MIGHT NOT BE THE MOST TALENTED BUNCH SHE'D EVER SEEN...
OH, I HEAR THAT ...
HUH? HEY, WHY ARE YOU STARING AT *ME* ?!
I THINK YOU KNOW WHY.

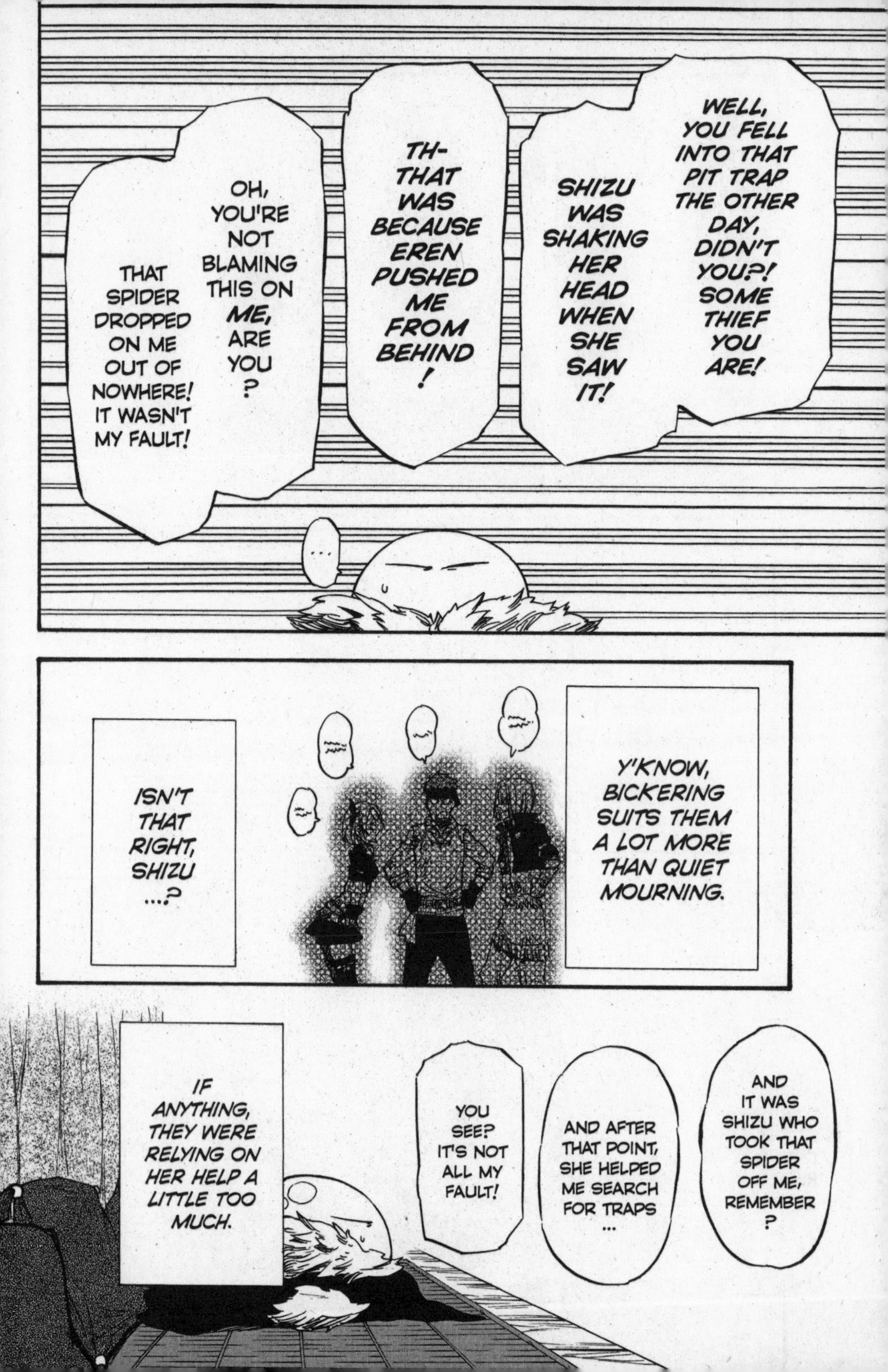
WELL, YOU FELL INTO THAT PIT TRAP THE OTHER DAY, DIDN'T YOU?! SOME THIEF YOU ARE!
SHIZU WAS SHAKING HER HEAD WHEN SHE SAW IT!
TH-THAT WAS BECAUSE EREN PUSHED ME FROM BEHIND!
OH, YOU'RE NOT BLAMING THIS ON ME, ARE YOU?
THAT SPIDER DROPPED ON ME OUT OF NOWHERE! IT WASN'T MY FAULT!
...
Y'KNOW, BICKERING SUITS THEM A LOT MORE THAN QUIET MOURNING.
ISN'T THAT RIGHT, SHIZU...?
AND IT WAS SHIZU WHO TOOK THAT SPIDER OFF ME, REMEMBER?
AND AFTER THAT POINT, SHE HELPED ME SEARCH FOR TRAPS...
YOU SEE? IT'S NOT ALL MY FAULT!
IF ANYTHING, THEY WERE RELYING ON HER HELP A LITTLE TOO MUCH.

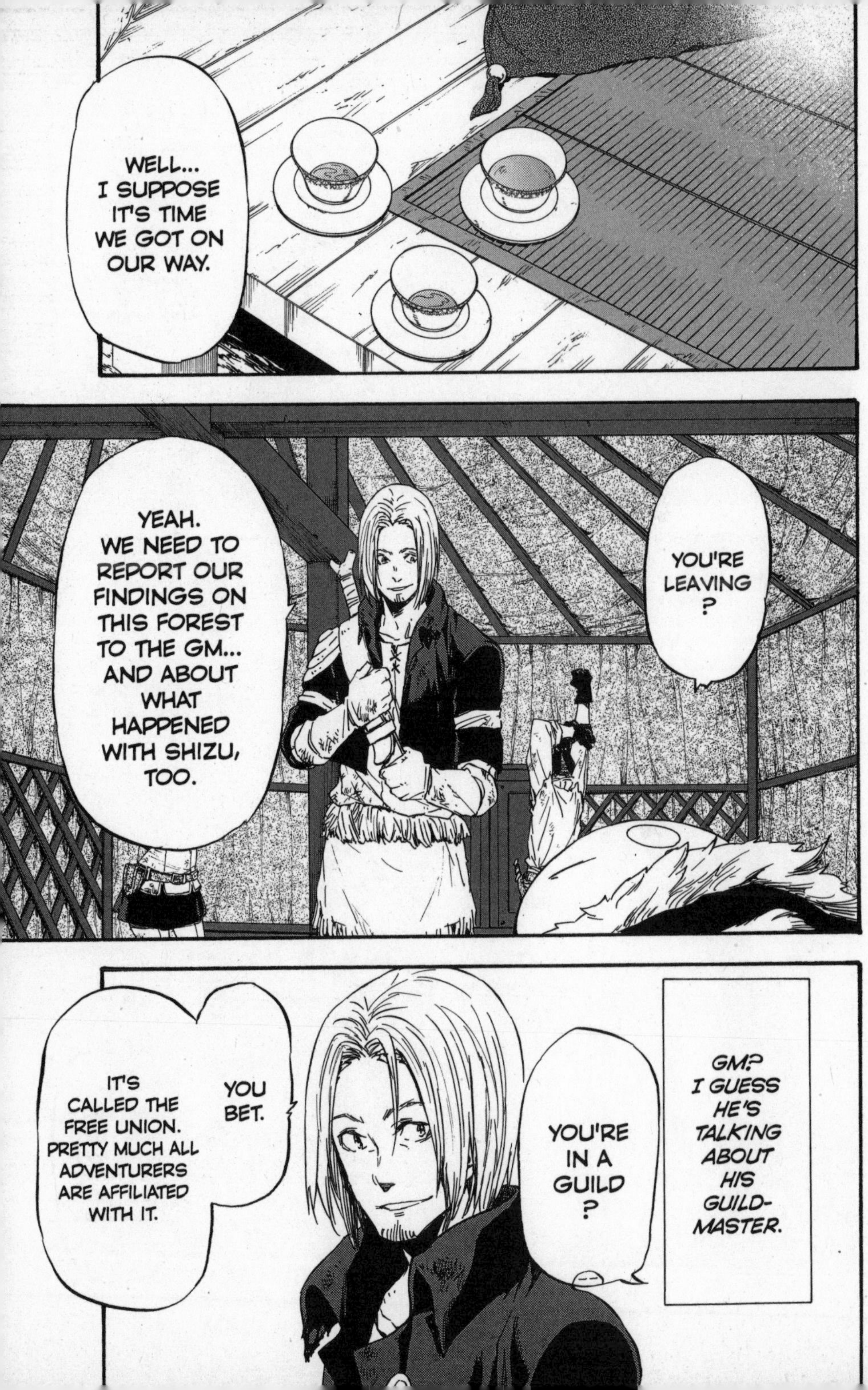
WELL... I SUPPOSE IT'S TIME WE GOT ON OUR WAY.
YOU'RE LEAVING?
YEAH. WE NEED TO REPORT OUR FINDINGS ON THIS FOREST TO THE GM... AND ABOUT WHAT HAPPENED WITH SHIZU, TOO.
GM? I GUESS HE'S TALKING ABOUT HIS GUILD-MASTER.
YOU'RE IN A GUILD?
YOU BET.
IT'S CALLED THE FREE UNION. PRETTY MUCH ALL ADVENTURERS ARE AFFILIATED WITH IT.

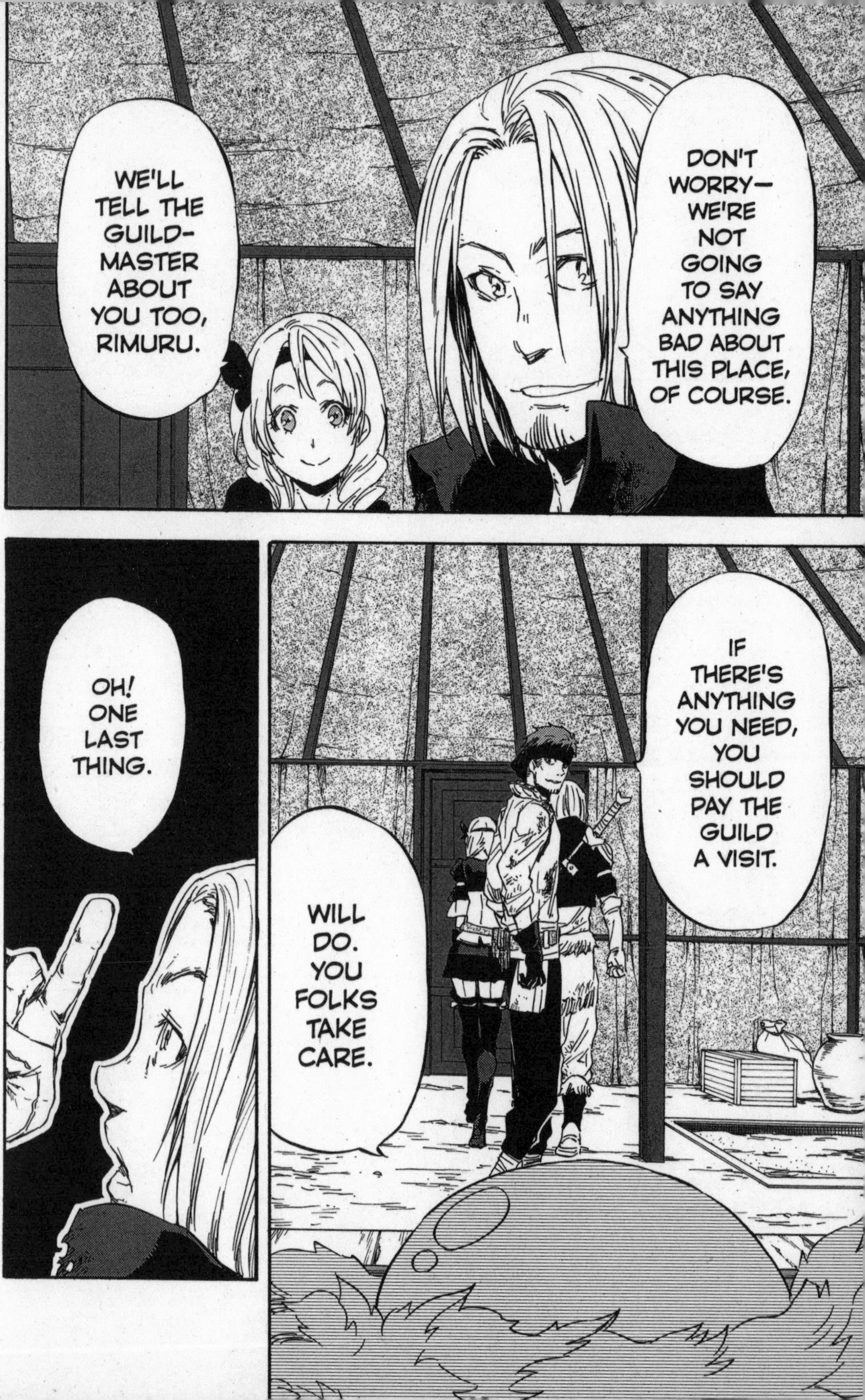
DON'T WORRY—WE'RE NOT GOING TO SAY ANYTHING BAD ABOUT THIS PLACE, OF COURSE.
WE'LL TELL THE GUILD-MASTER ABOUT YOU TOO, RIMURU.
IF THERE'S ANYTHING YOU NEED, YOU SHOULD PAY THE GUILD A VISIT.
WILL DO. YOU FOLKS TAKE CARE.
OH! ONE LAST THING.

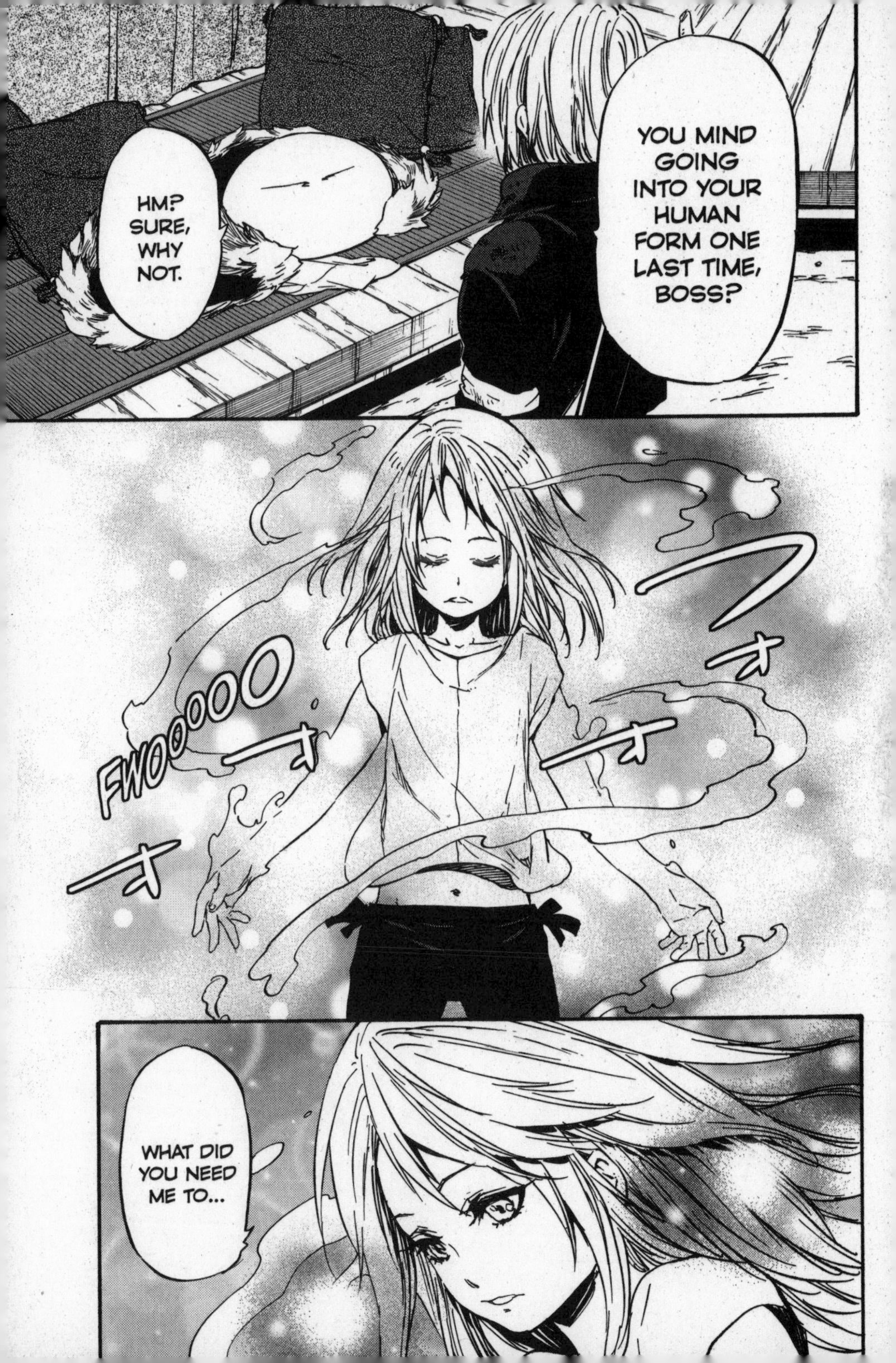
YOU MIND GOING INTO YOUR HUMAN FORM ONE LAST TIME, BOSS?
HM? SURE, WHY NOT.
FWOOOOO
WHAT DID YOU NEED ME TO...

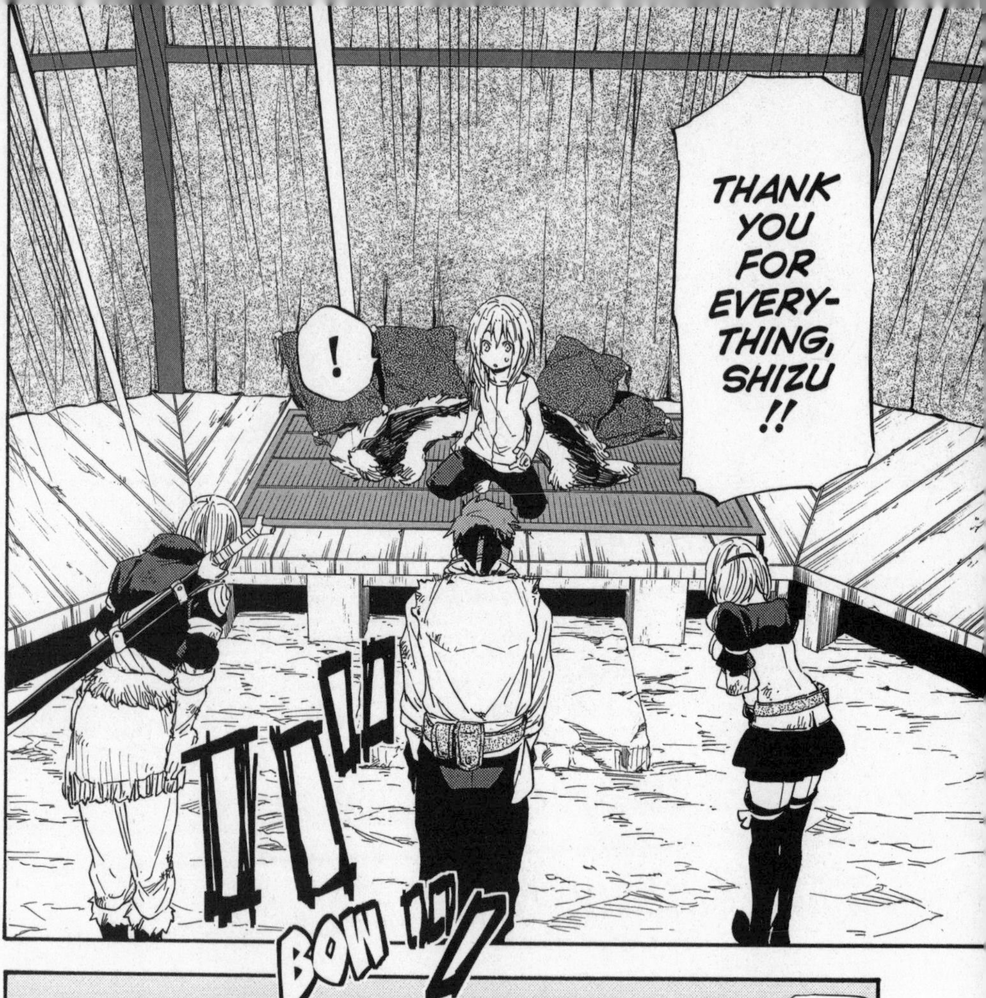
THANK YOU FOR EVERY-THING, SHIZU!!
!
BOW

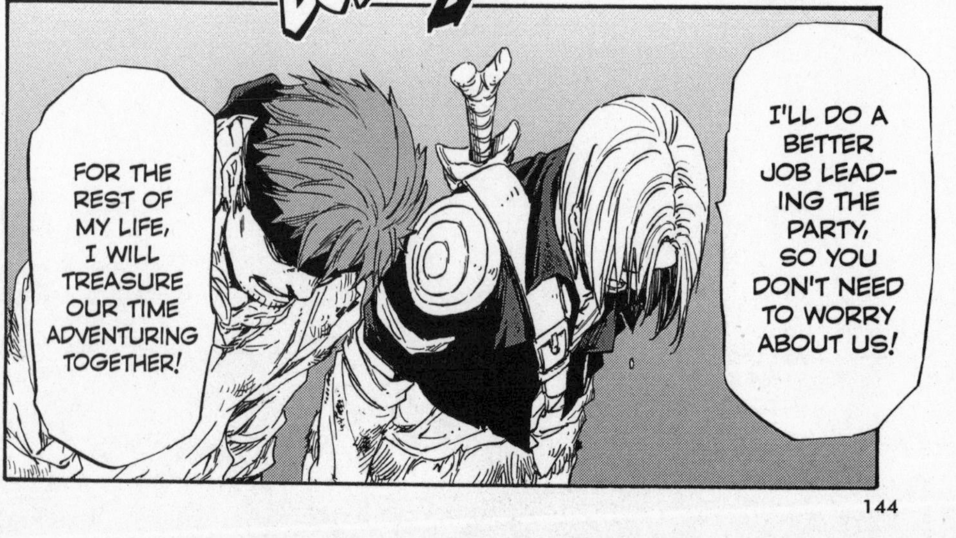
I'LL DO A BETTER JOB LEAD-ING THE PARTY, SO YOU DON'T NEED TO WORRY ABOUT US!
FOR THE REST OF MY LIFE, I WILL TREASURE OUR TIME ADVENTURING TOGETHER!

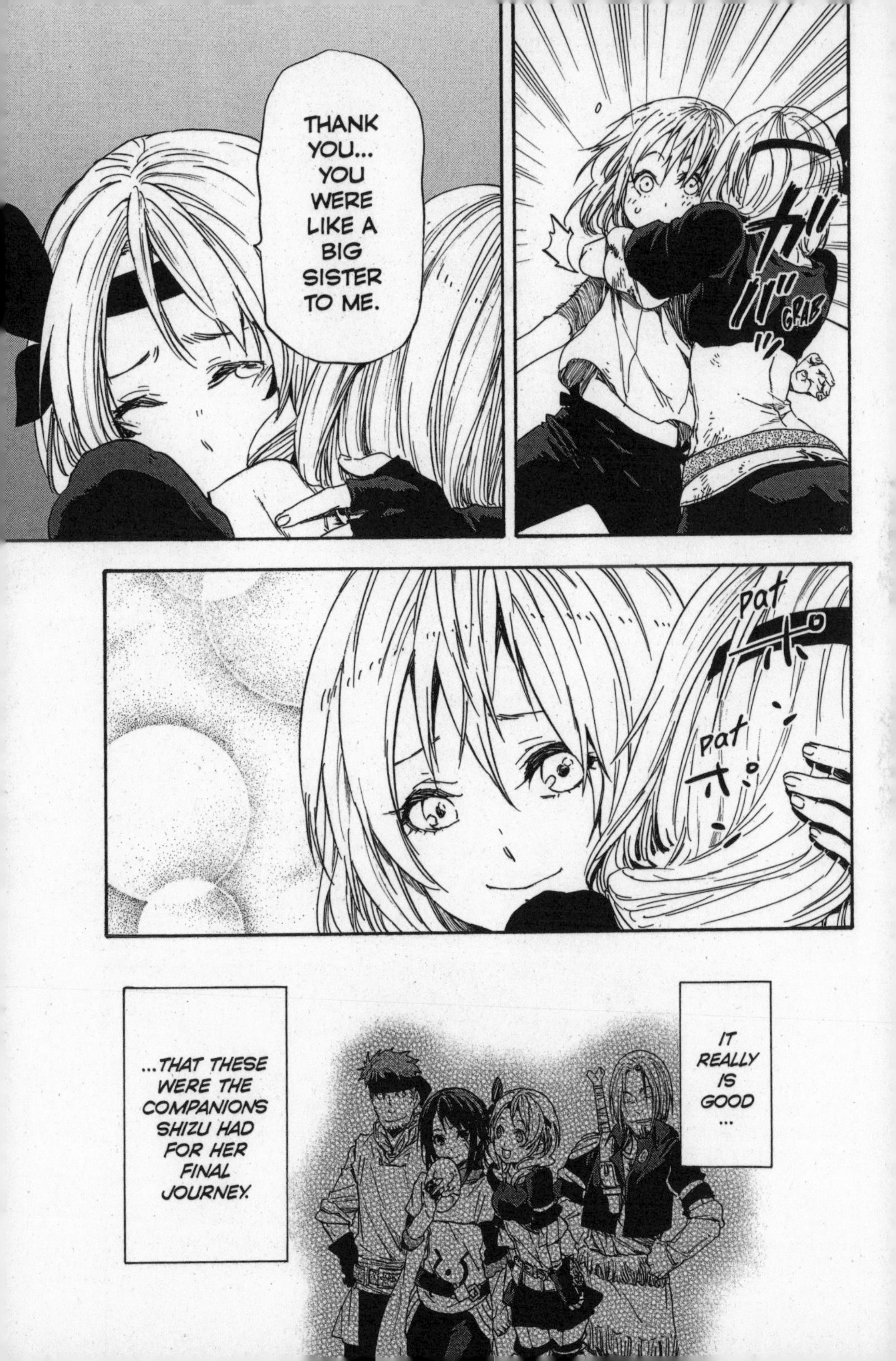
GRAB
THANK YOU... YOU WERE LIKE A BIG SISTER TO ME.
pat
pat
IT REALLY IS GOOD ...
...THAT THESE WERE THE COMPANIONS SHIZU HAD FOR HER FINAL JOURNEY.

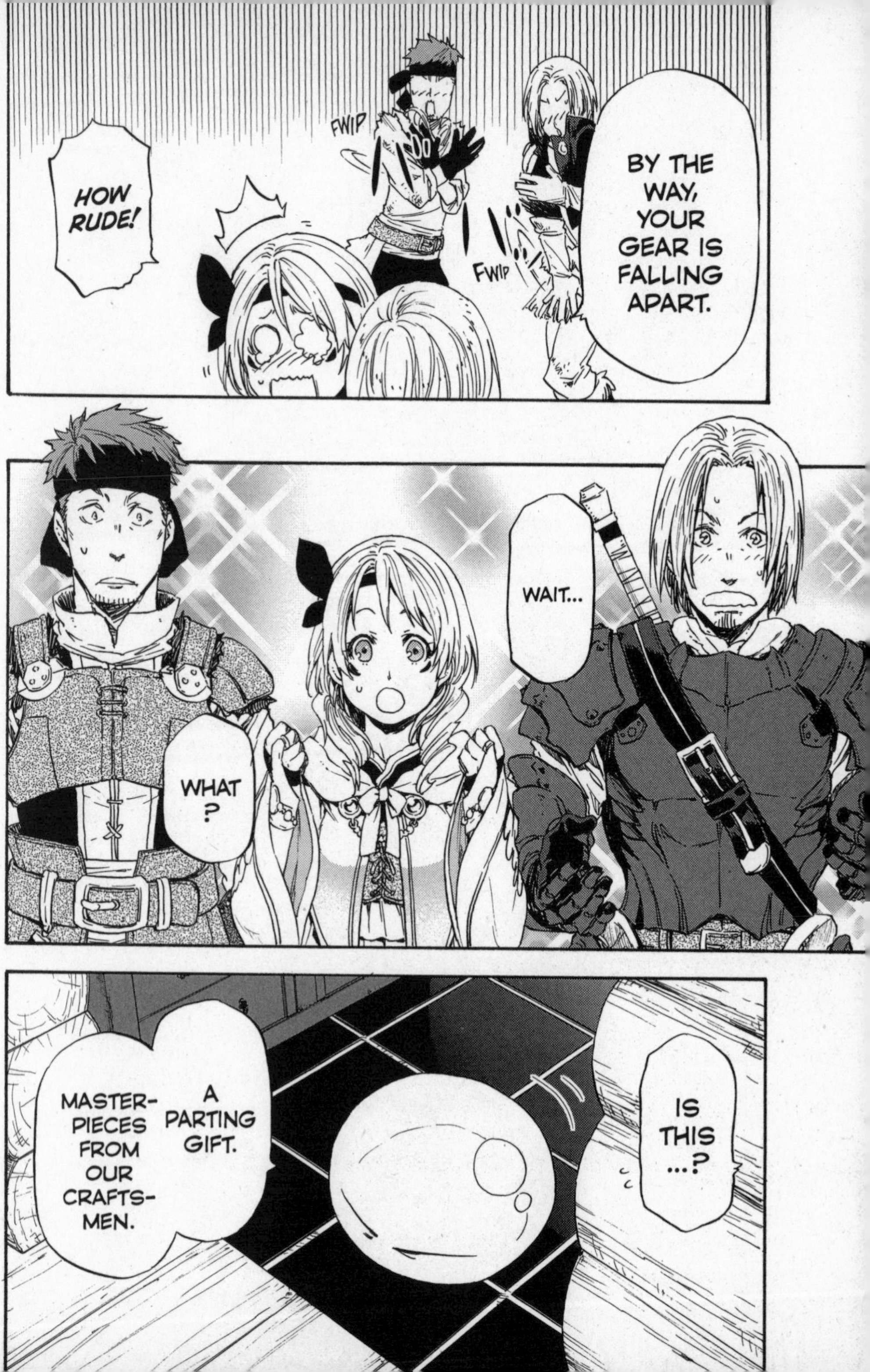
BY THE WAY, YOUR GEAR IS FALLING APART.
FWIP
FWIP
HOW RUDE!
WAIT...
WHAT?
IS THIS ...?
A PARTING GIFT.
MASTER-PIECES FROM OUR CRAFTSMEN.

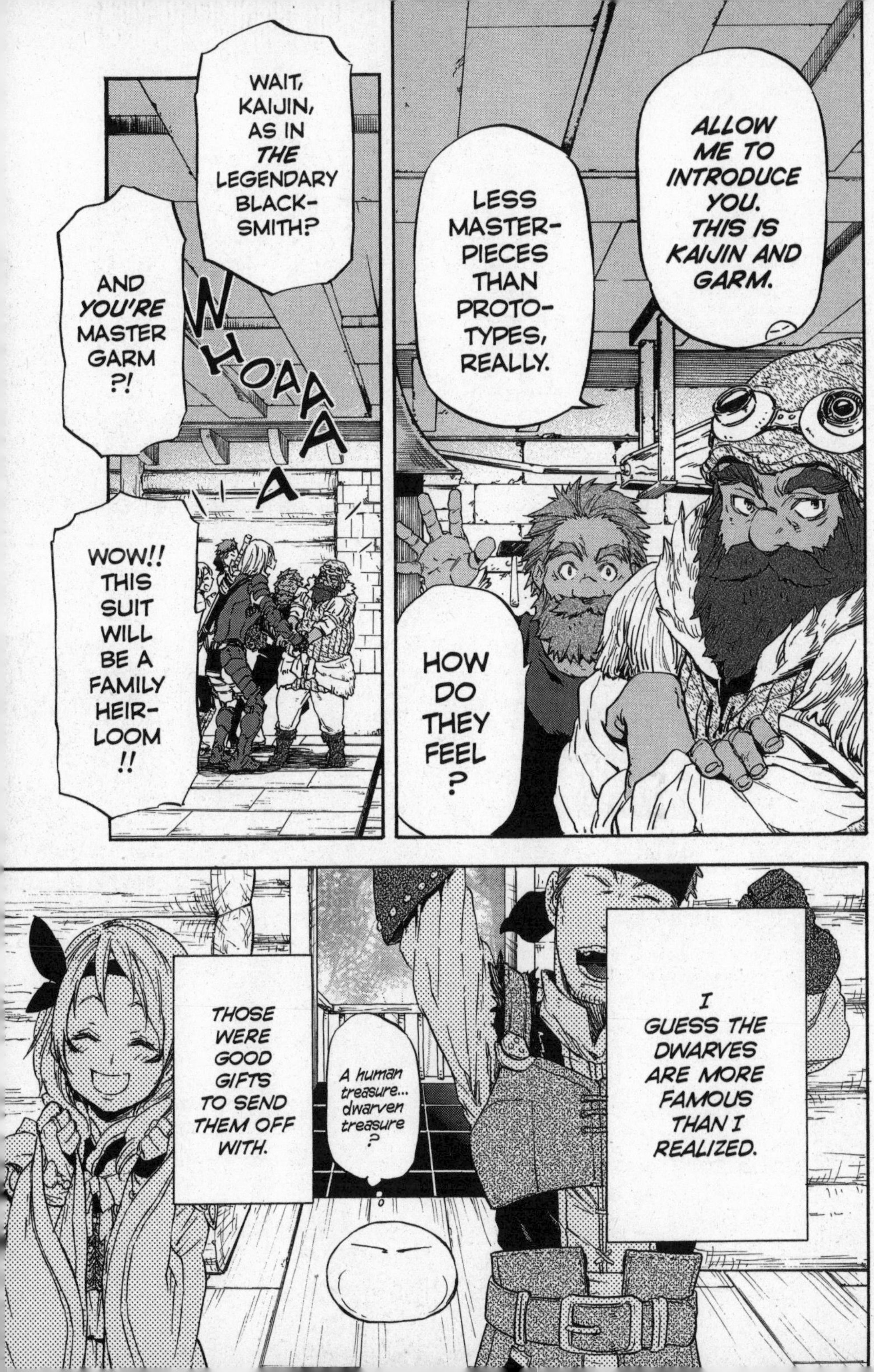
ALLOW ME TO INTRODUCE YOU. THIS IS KAIJIN AND GARM.
LESS MASTER-PIECES THAN PROTO-TYPES, REALLY.
HOW DO THEY FEEL?
WAIT, KAIJIN, AS IN THE LEGENDARY BLACK-SMITH?
AND YOU'RE MASTER GARM?!
WHOAAAA
WOW!! THIS SUIT WILL BE A FAMILY HEIR-LOOM!!
I GUESS THE DWARVES ARE MORE FAMOUS THAN I REALIZED.
A human treasure... dwarven treasure?
THOSE WERE GOOD GIFTS TO SEND THEM OFF WITH.

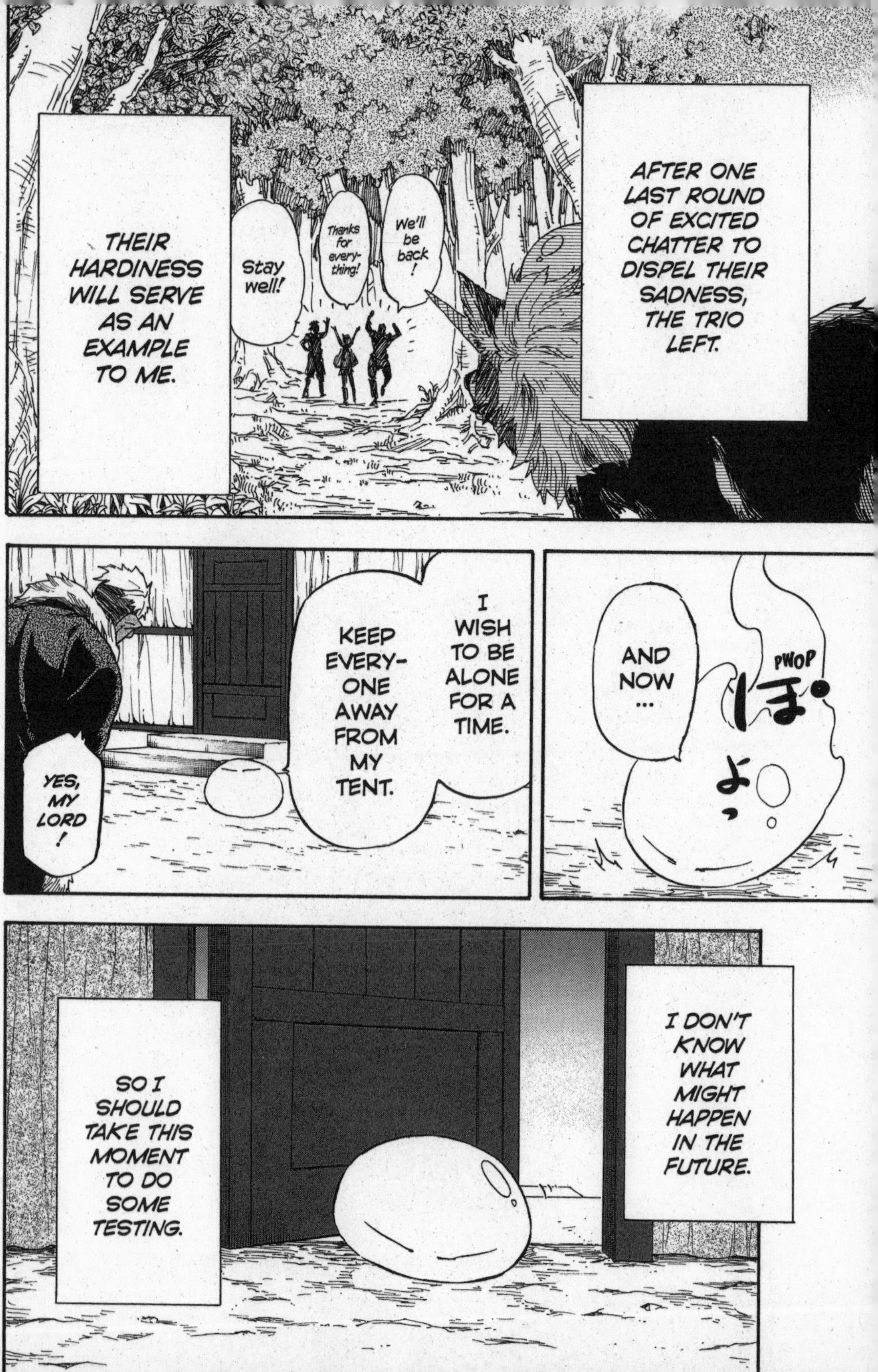
AFTER ONE LAST ROUND OF EXCITED CHATTER TO DISPEL THEIR SADNESS, THE TRIO LEFT.
We'll be back!
Thanks for every-thing!
Stay well!
THEIR HARDINESS WILL SERVE AS AN EXAMPLE TO ME.
AND NOW ...
PWOP
ぽよっ
I WISH TO BE ALONE FOR A TIME.
KEEP EVERY-ONE AWAY FROM MY TENT.
YES, MY LORD!
I DON'T KNOW WHAT MIGHT HAPPEN IN THE FUTURE.
SO I SHOULD TAKE THIS MOMENT TO DO SOME TESTING.

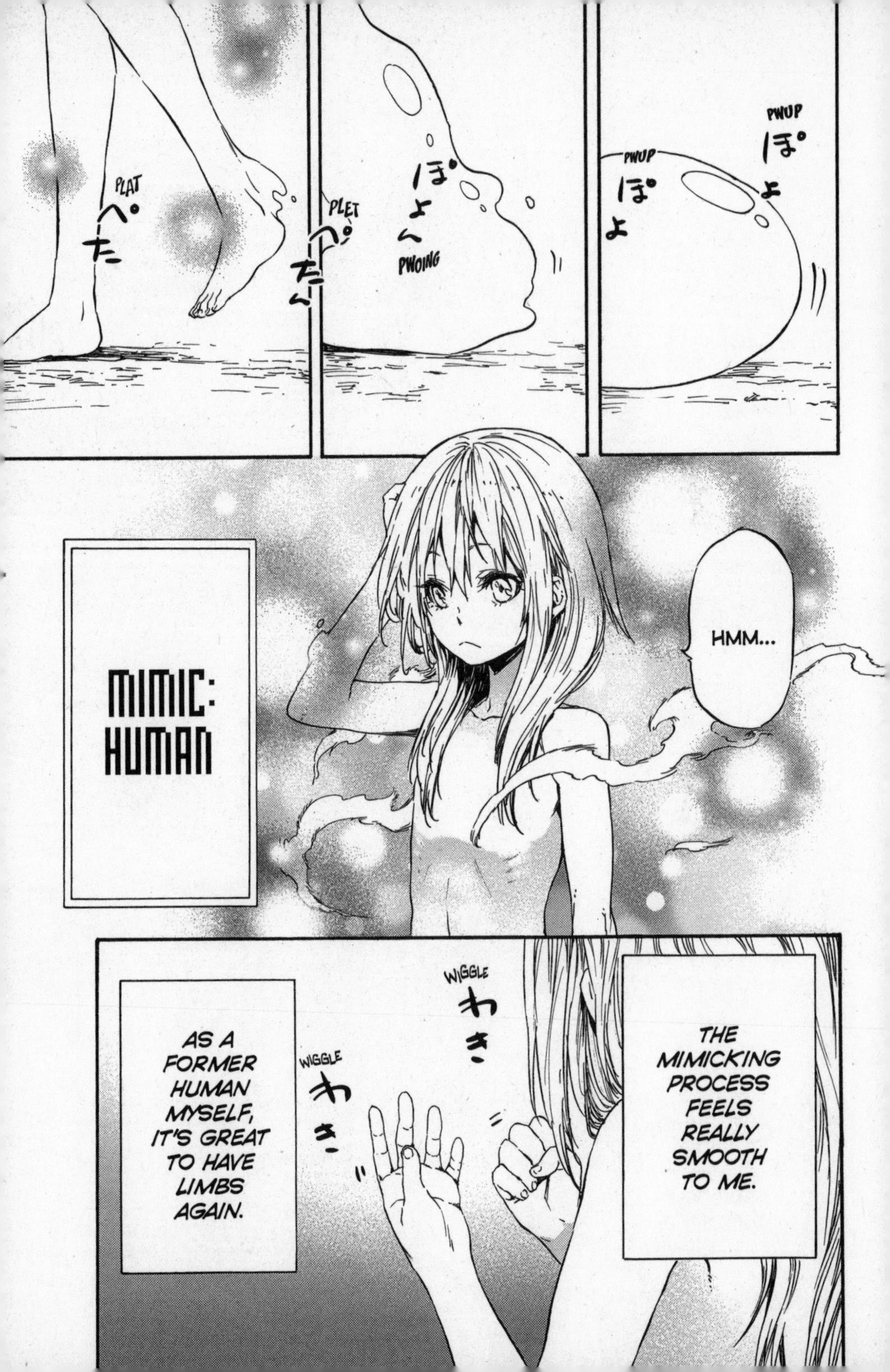
PWUP
ぽよ
PWUP
ぽよ
ぽよん
PWOING
PLET
ぺたん
PLAT
ぺた
HMM...
MIMIC: HUMAN
THE MIMICKING PROCESS FEELS REALLY SMOOTH TO ME.
WIGGLE
わき
WIGGLE
わき
AS A FORMER HUMAN MYSELF, IT'S GREAT TO HAVE LIMBS AGAIN.

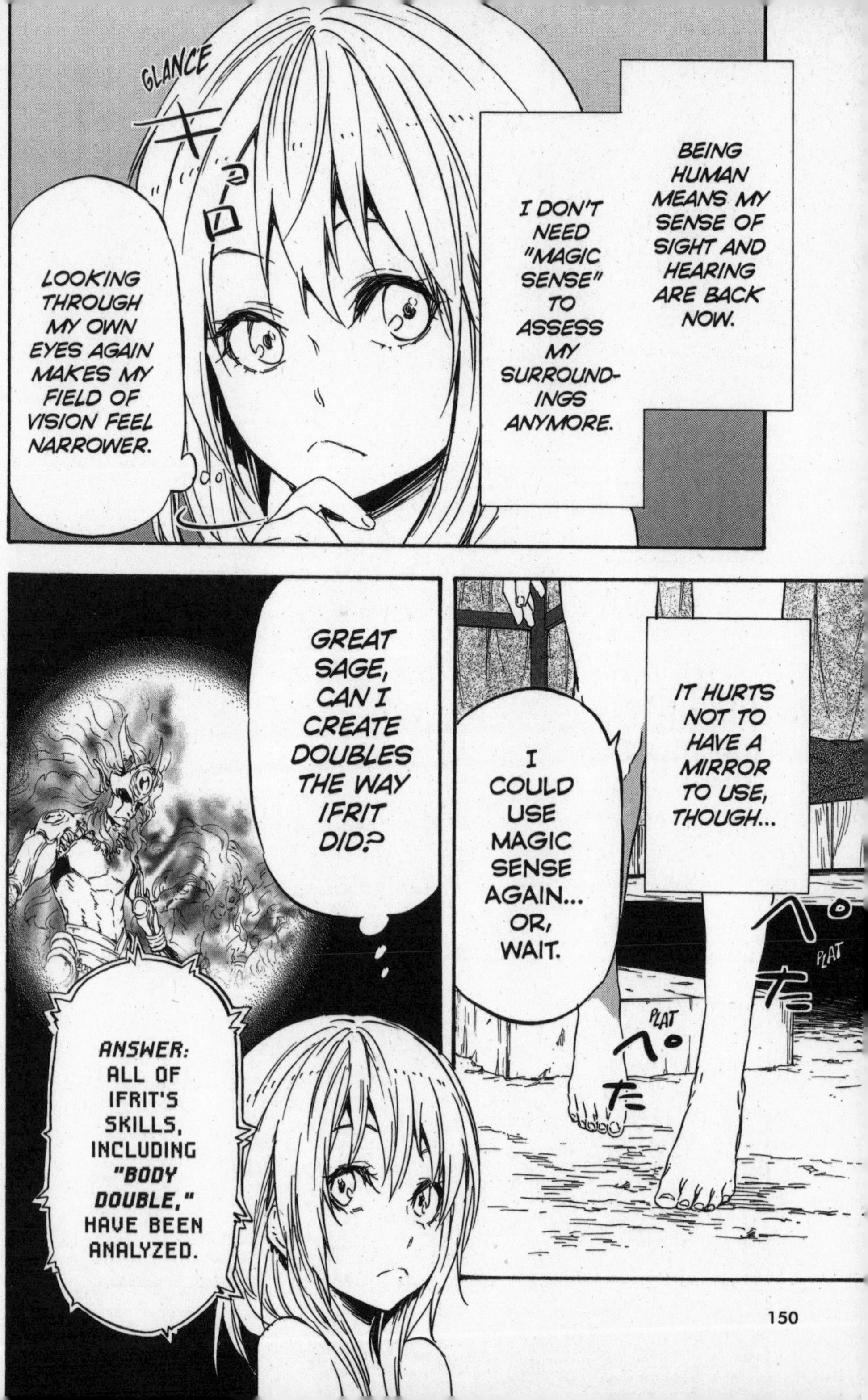
BEING HUMAN MEANS MY SENSE OF SIGHT AND HEARING ARE BACK NOW.
I DON'T NEED "MAGIC SENSE" TO ASSESS MY SURROUNDINGS ANYMORE.
GLANCE
LOOKING THROUGH MY OWN EYES AGAIN MAKES MY FIELD OF VISION FEEL NARROWER.
IT HURTS NOT TO HAVE A MIRROR TO USE, THOUGH...
I COULD USE MAGIC SENSE AGAIN... OR, WAIT.
PLAT
PLAT
GREAT SAGE, CAN I CREATE DOUBLES THE WAY IFRIT DID?
ANSWER: ALL OF IFRIT'S SKILLS, INCLUDING "BODY DOUBLE," HAVE BEEN ANALYZED.

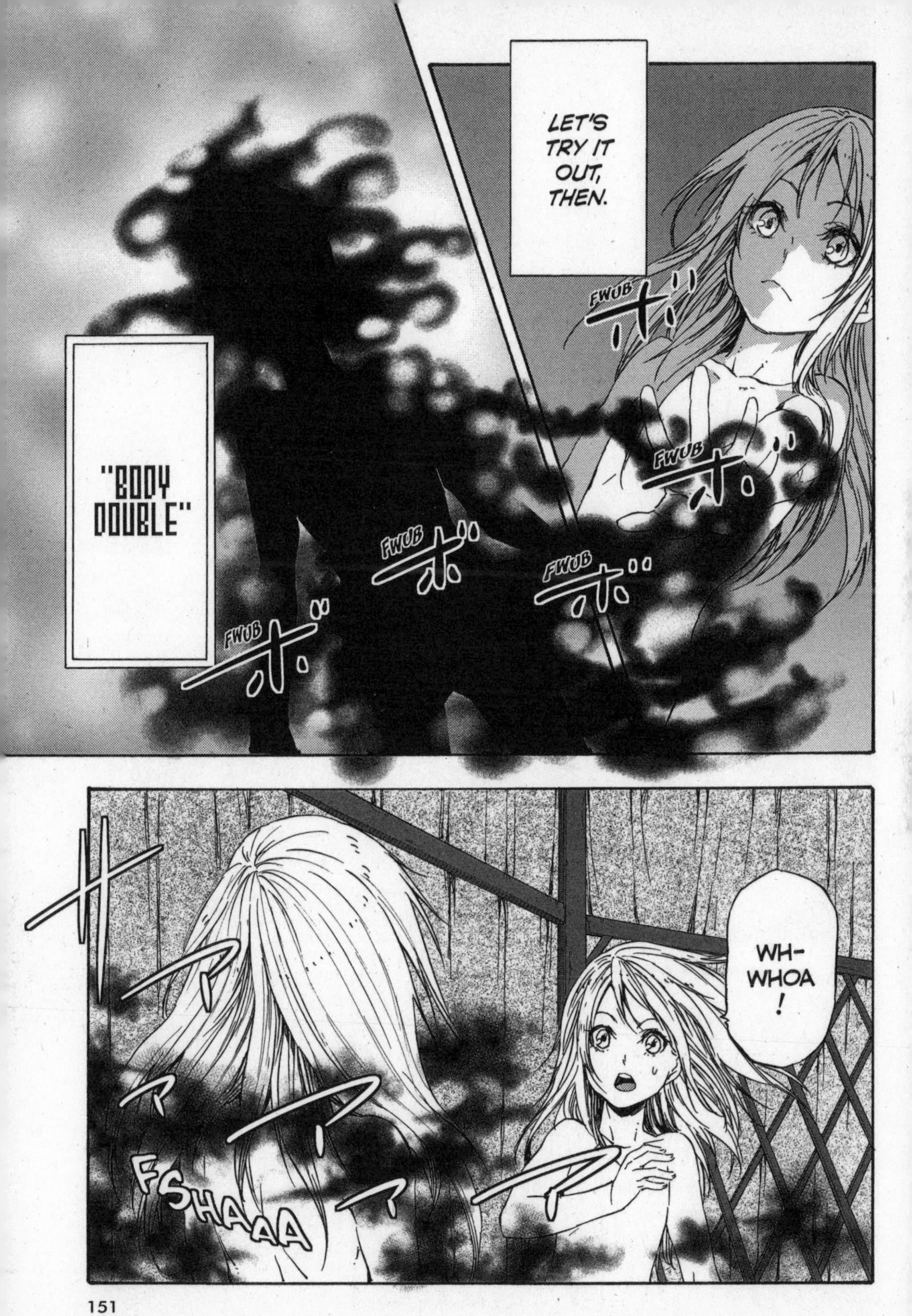
LET'S TRY IT OUT, THEN.
FWUB
FWUB
FWUB
FWUB
FWUB
"BODY DOUBLE"
WH-WHOA!
FSHAAA

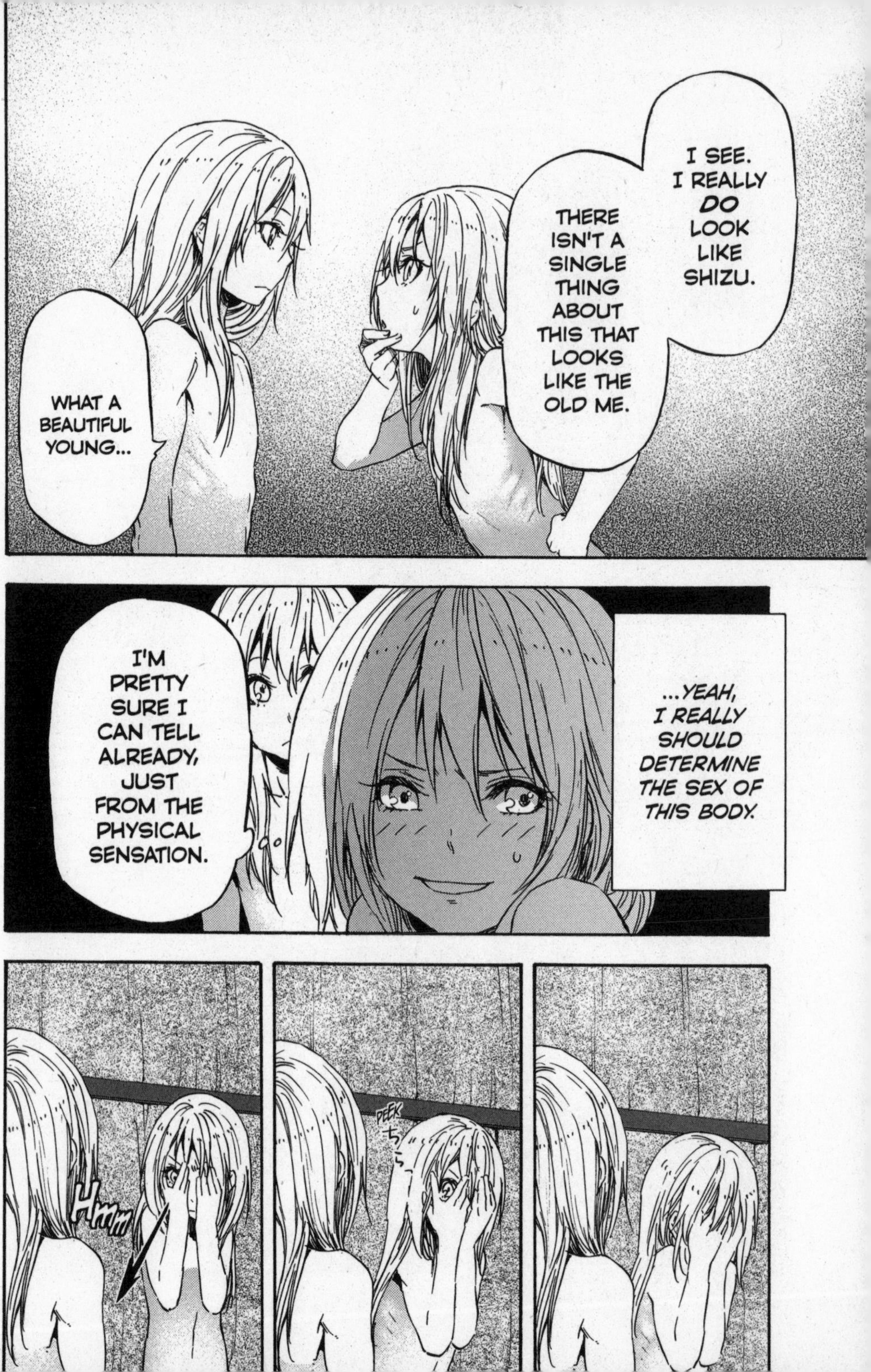
I SEE. I REALLY *DO* LOOK LIKE SHIZU.
THERE ISN'T A SINGLE THING ABOUT THIS THAT LOOKS LIKE THE OLD ME.
WHAT A BEAUTIFUL YOUNG...
...YEAH, I REALLY SHOULD DETERMINE THE SEX OF THIS BODY.
I'M PRETTY SURE I CAN TELL ALREADY, JUST FROM THE PHYSICAL SENSATION.
PEEK
Hmm

IN FACT...

NOPE. NO LITTLE GUY DOWN THERE.

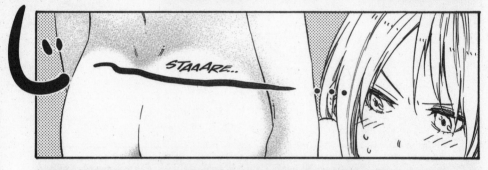

STAAARE...

IT'S INTERSEX... NO, SEXLESS.

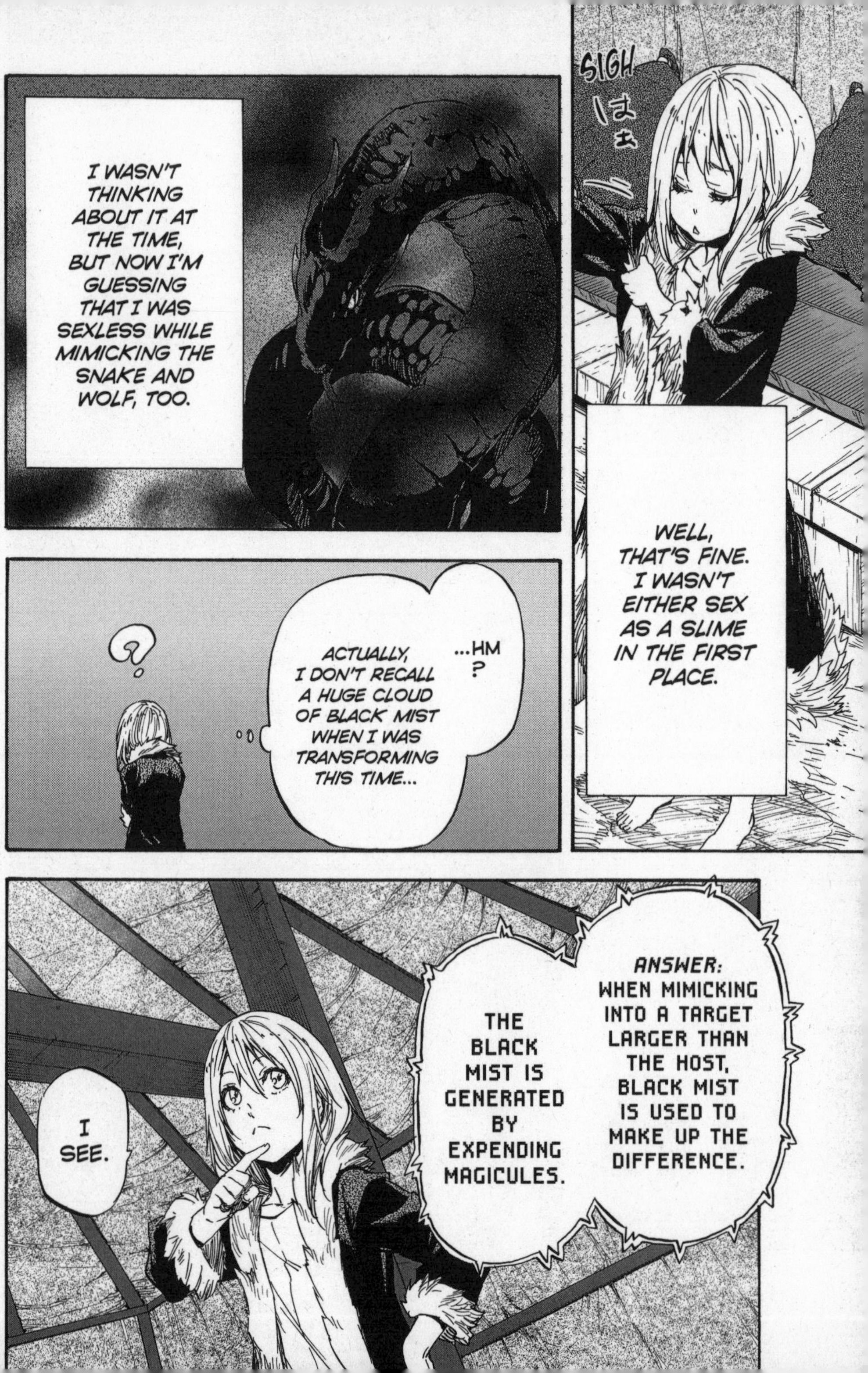
SIGH
はぁ
WELL, THAT'S FINE. I WASN'T EITHER SEX AS A SLIME IN THE FIRST PLACE.
I WASN'T THINKING ABOUT IT AT THE TIME, BUT NOW I'M GUESSING THAT I WAS SEXLESS WHILE MIMICKING THE SNAKE AND WOLF, TOO.
...HM ?
ACTUALLY, I DON'T RECALL A HUGE CLOUD OF BLACK MIST WHEN I WAS TRANSFORMING THIS TIME...
?
ANSWER: WHEN MIMICKING INTO A TARGET LARGER THAN THE HOST, BLACK MIST IS USED TO MAKE UP THE DIFFERENCE.
THE BLACK MIST IS GENERATED BY EXPENDING MAGICULES.
I SEE.

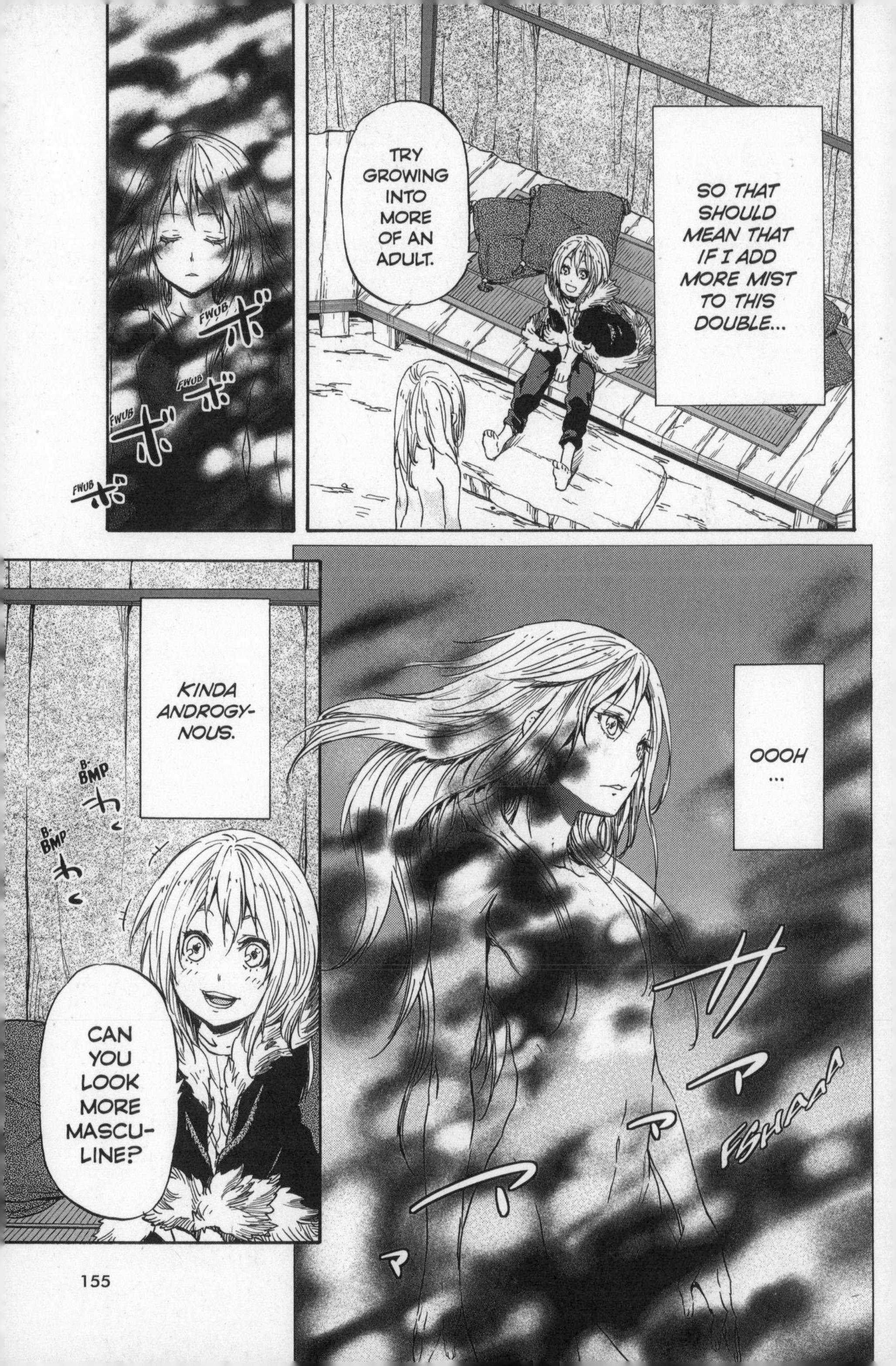
SO THAT SHOULD MEAN THAT IF I ADD MORE MIST TO THIS DOUBLE...
TRY GROWING INTO MORE OF AN ADULT.
FWUB
FWUB
FWUB
FWUB
OOOH ...
FSHAAA
KINDA ANDROGYNOUS.
B-BMP
B-BMP
CAN YOU LOOK MORE MASCULINE?

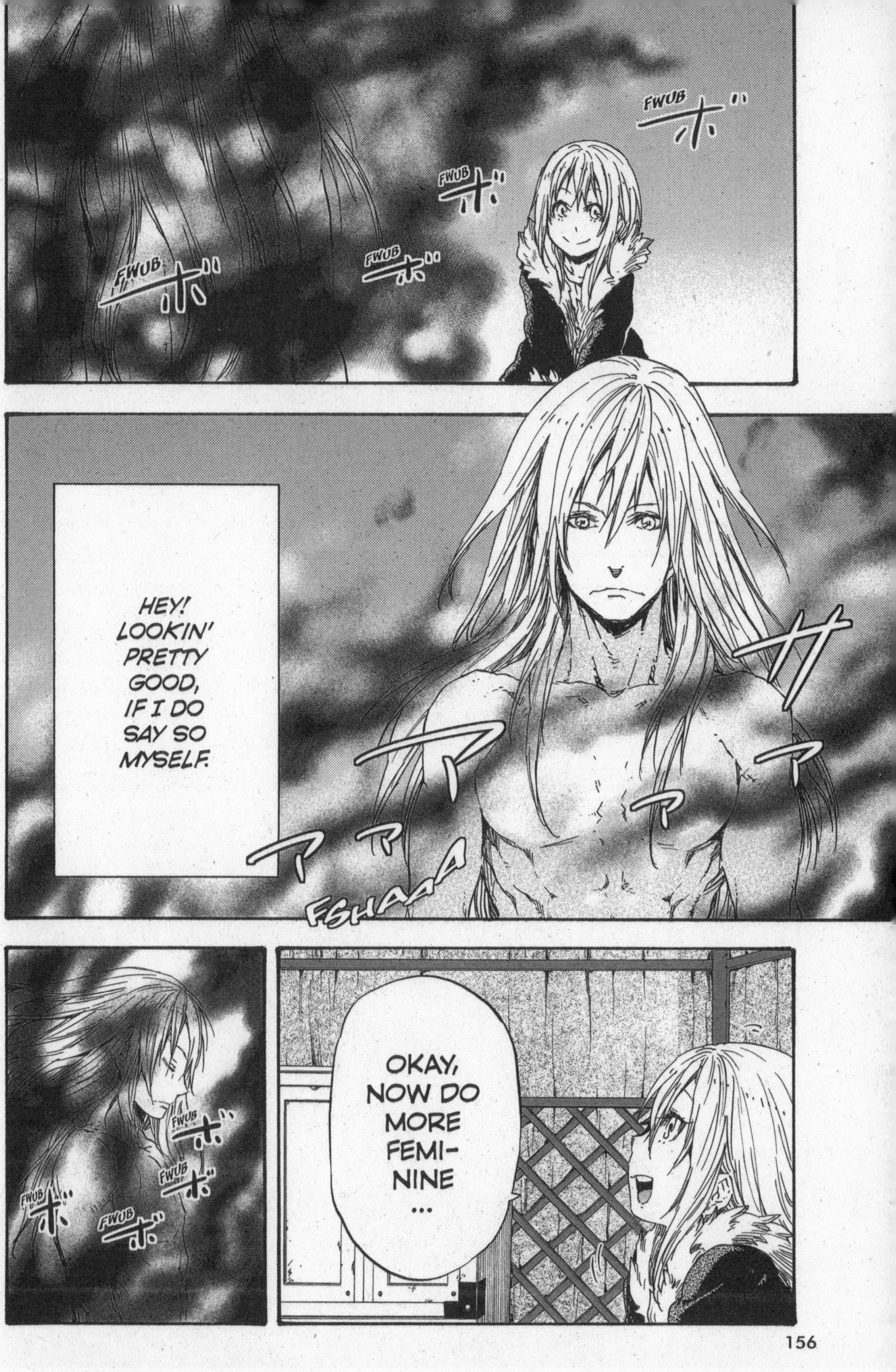
FWUB
FWUB
FWUB
FWUB
HEY! LOOKIN' PRETTY GOOD, IF I DO SAY SO MYSELF.
FSHAAA
OKAY, NOW DO MORE FEMI-NINE ...
FWUB
FWUB
FWUB
FWUB

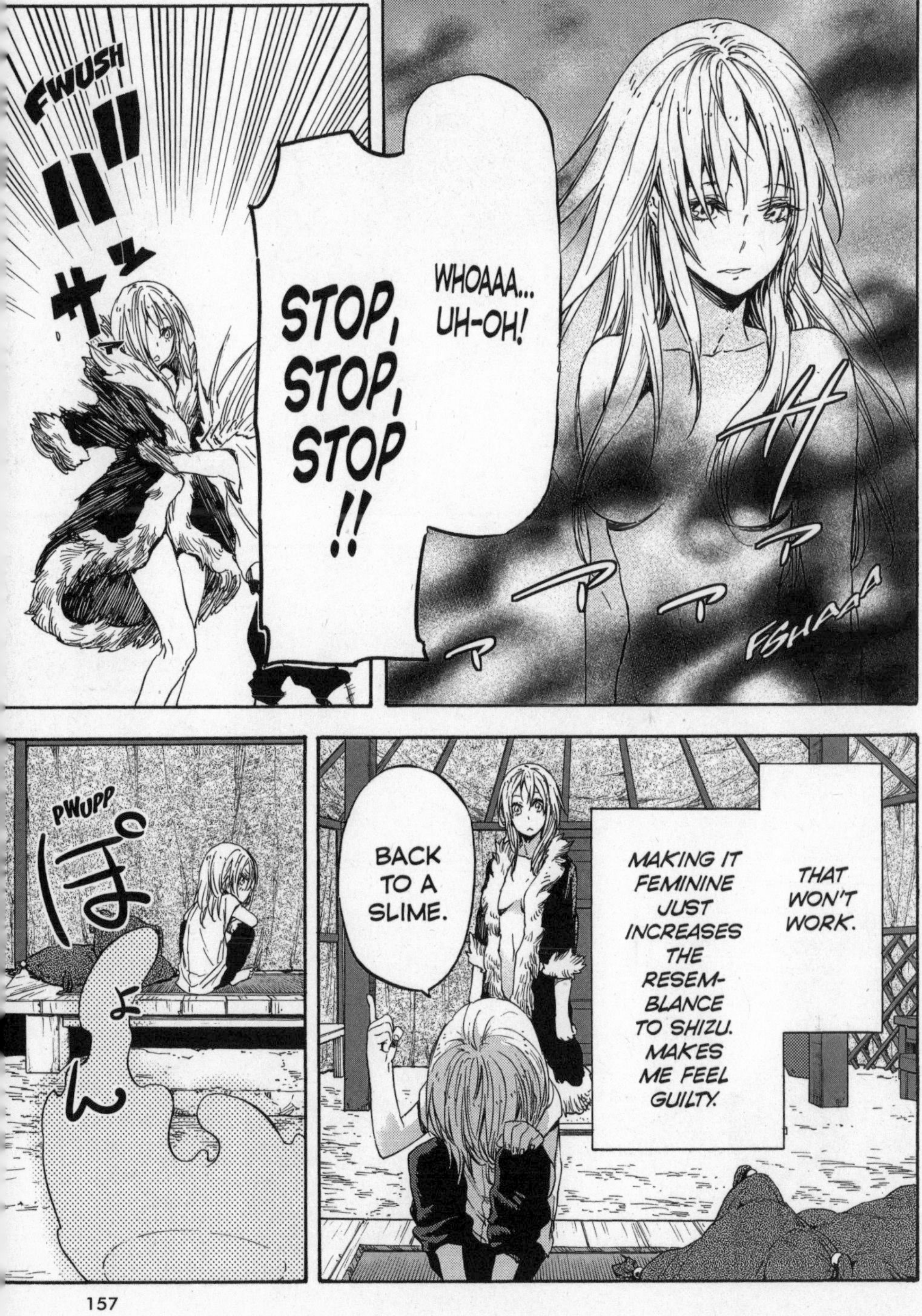
WHOAAA... UH-OH!
STOP, STOP, STOP!!
FSHAAA
FWUSH
バッ
サッ
THAT WON'T WORK.
MAKING IT FEMININE JUST INCREASES THE RESEM-BLANCE TO SHIZU. MAKES ME FEEL GUILTY.
BACK TO A SLIME.
PWUPP
ぽよん

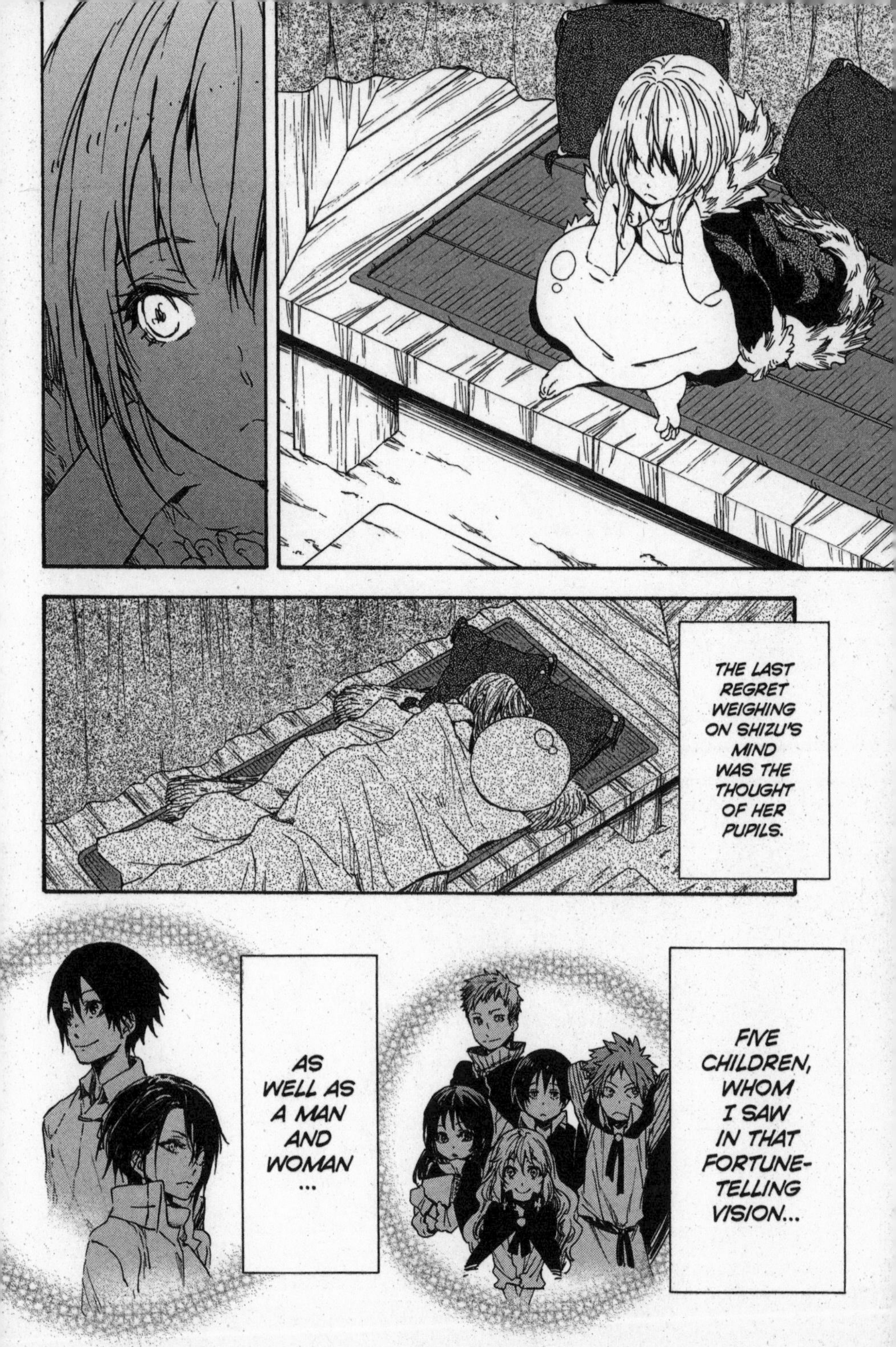
THE LAST REGRET WEIGHING ON SHIZU'S MIND WAS THE THOUGHT OF HER PUPILS.
FIVE CHILDREN, WHOM I SAW IN THAT FORTUNE-TELLING VISION...
AS WELL AS A MAN AND WOMAN ...

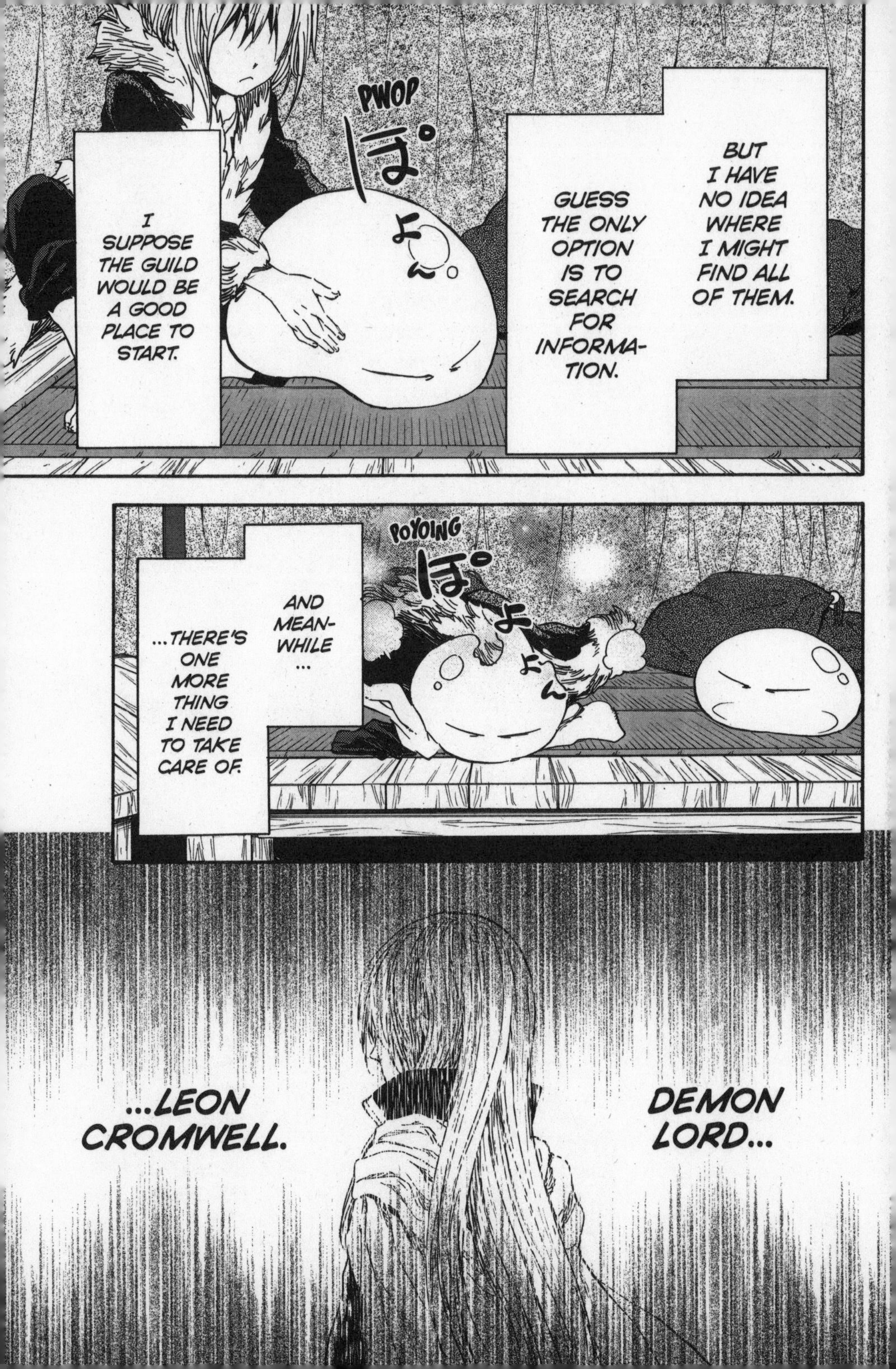
BUT I HAVE NO IDEA WHERE I MIGHT FIND ALL OF THEM.
GUESS THE ONLY OPTION IS TO SEARCH FOR INFORMATION.
PWOP
ぽよん
I SUPPOSE THE GUILD WOULD BE A GOOD PLACE TO START.
POYOING
ぽよん
AND MEANWHILE...
...THERE'S ONE MORE THING I NEED TO TAKE CARE OF.
DEMON LORD...
...LEON CROMWELL.

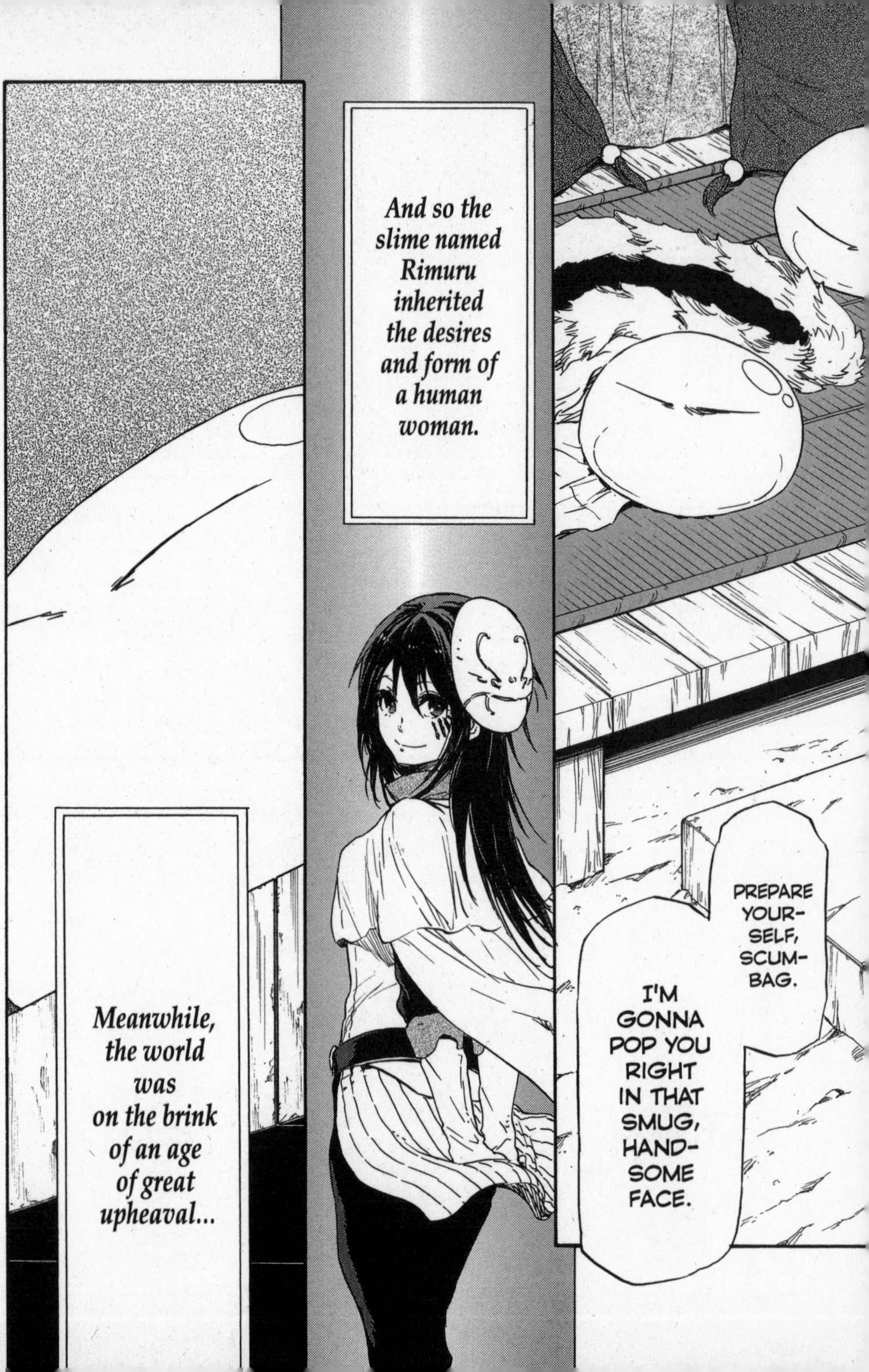
PREPARE YOUR-SELF, SCUM-BAG.
I'M GONNA POP YOU RIGHT IN THAT SMUG, HAND-SOME FACE.
And so the slime named Rimuru inherited the desires and form of a human woman.
Meanwhile, the world was on the brink of an age of great upheaval...

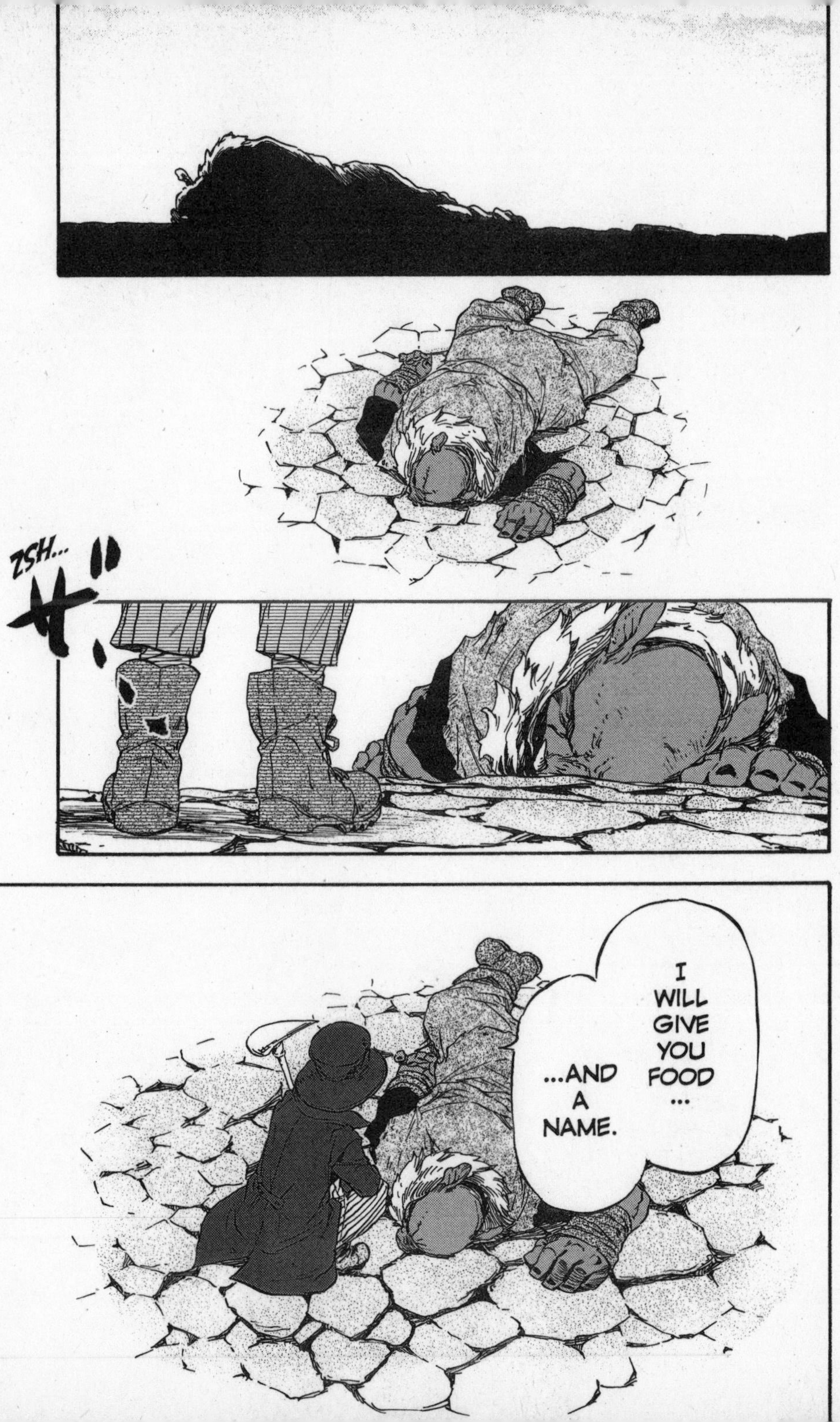
ZSH...
ザッ
I WILL GIVE YOU FOOD...
...AND A NAME.

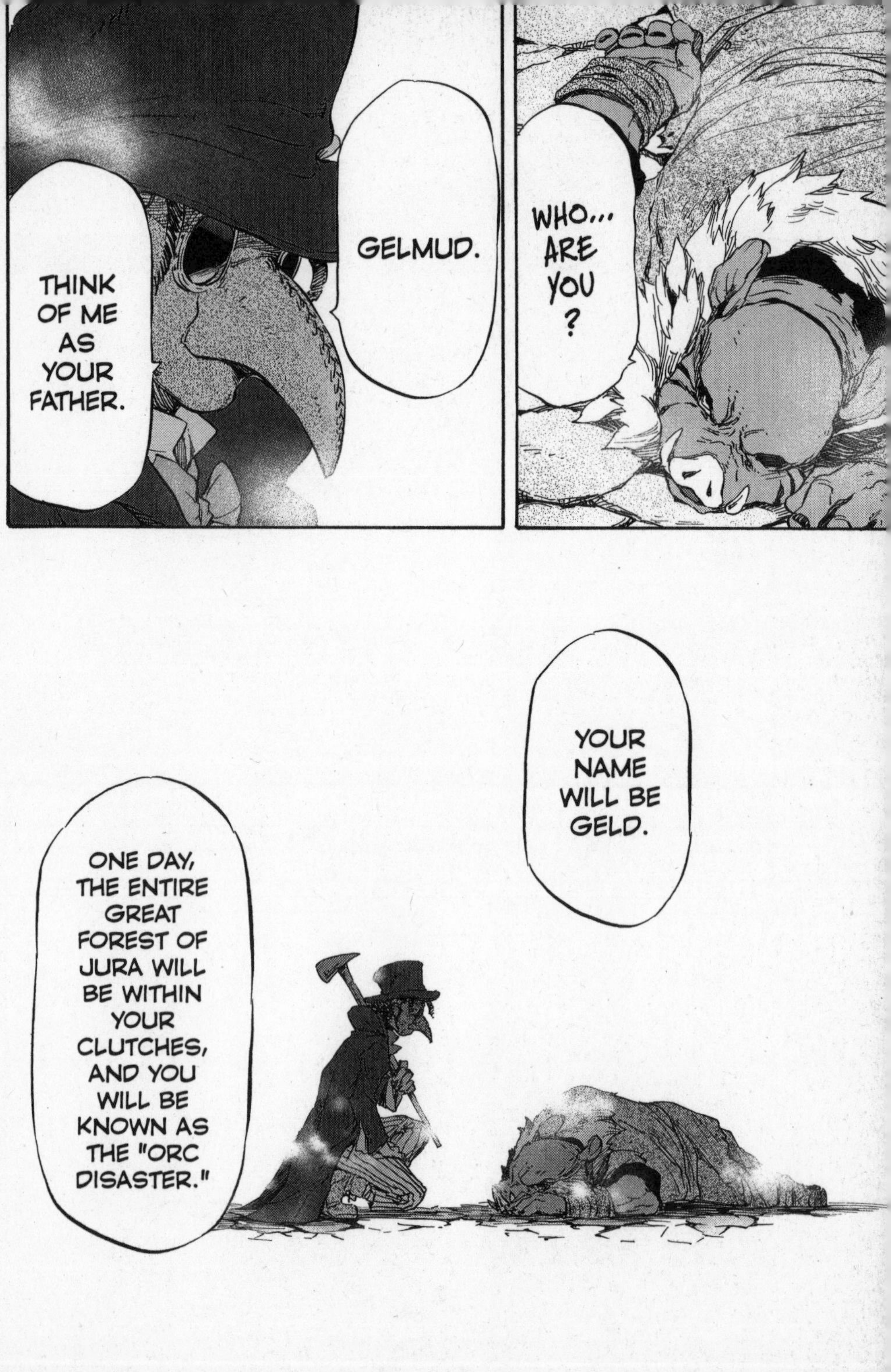
WHO... ARE YOU?
GELMUD.
THINK OF ME AS YOUR FATHER.
YOUR NAME WILL BE GELD.
ONE DAY, THE ENTIRE GREAT FOREST OF JURA WILL BE WITHIN YOUR CLUTCHES, AND YOU WILL BE KNOWN AS THE "ORC DISASTER."

Reincarnate
in Volume 3?

→YES

NO

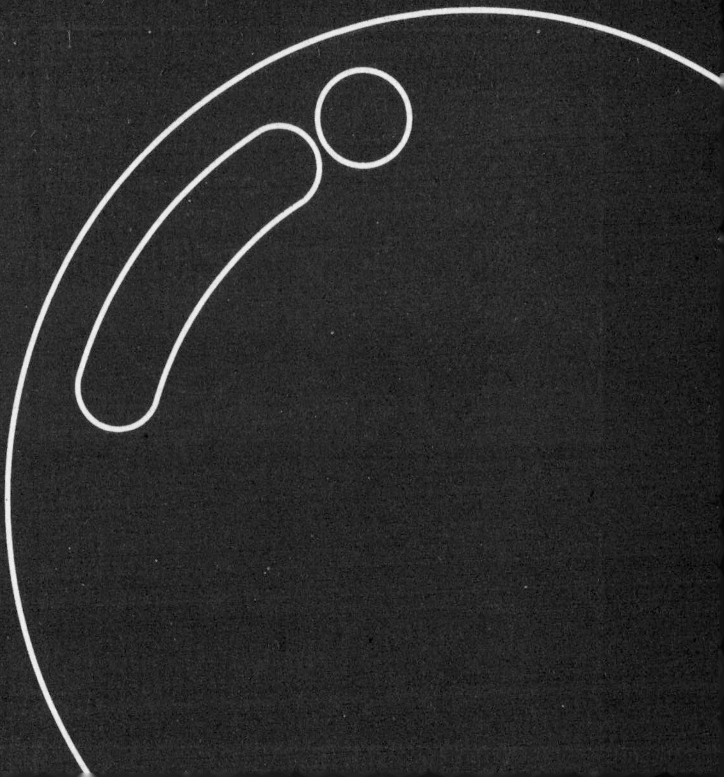

Bonus
Short Story

Veldora's Slime Observation Journal
~STUNNING DEVELOPMENTS~

Veldora's Slime Observation Journal
~STUNNING DEVELOPMENTS~

◆THE HERO-KING'S JUDGMENT◆

The trial began.

Excitement coursed through me as I waited and watched. A suspect-looking man begins to explain things on his own. Rimuru is content to remain calm and quiet for now, so I realize that perhaps my expectations were off-base.

The entire group is groveling before the mighty dwarf king. However, as all those before the king bow their heads in fealty, Rimiru alone has been standing proud and upright. It seems that they do not realize from his appearance that he is not bowing in the least. While his words are polite, he maintains his same proud, challenging attitude. Given that he is the equal to one such as me, that is only natural.

I will need him to continue to maintain our proud status, but it seems that might prove difficult. A curious facet of human society is that strength alone is not enough to solve all matters. This instance is a good example of that.

I would have assumed that those involved would have beaten one another in an effort to establish dominance. But for some reason, they intend to determine the winner and loser through words alone.

But what if one of the parties is lying?

As if in answer, the man appointed to argue Rimuru's case acts to betray them. They must have known from the very start that he was a tricky and untrustworthy fellow... And yet they allowed him to bring them to ruin. I would have engaged in some minor rampaging to silence his lying tongue.

Human society is such a vexing thing. I had thought that my recent studies would have granted me some understanding of its ways. However, this incident proves that I have still more to learn. I must search out a more detailed text on the matter.

And yet it seems that Rimuru's choice was correct this time. If he had started a fight, he would not stand a chance against that man—that...Gazel Dwargo fellow. He is apparently the sovereign of this dwarven kingdom, but his power seems to transcend that of the humanoid peoples.

Of course, he is no match for the hero who sealed me away in my prison, but I might admit that is he is at least worthy of standing in my presence. In fact, the way he looked at us, it appeared that he could see right through Rimuru.

"Interference with deep psyche detected. Attempt rebuffed."

There, you see? Even such a natural action from Gazel was capable of penetrating to Rimuru's deep psyche. Rimuru didn't seem to realize it, but I could tell that this Gazel fellow was capable of reading minds.

Regardless of the kind of skill he used, it is clear enough that this bodes ill. This is the very reason that Rimuru cannot best the man.

But perhaps it is not Gazel's capabilities that I should be worried about but Rimuru's. At first, I thought it a trick of my own imagination, but it seems that Rimuru's skill had activated on its own, without his input. This skill did not activate when Gazel read Rimuru's surface thoughts, but it did prevent him from interacting with his deep psyche.

I found my own attempts to connect to his deep memories blocked in the past—could it have been the same process?

Is it autonomous?!

No, that would be silly. My mind is getting carried away, I imagine. I have never heard of such a skill, nor do I believe it exists. No powers can take effect without the intentional bidding of the user.

Then how to explain this? Unless—but, wait...

Rimuru is too cautious for any other explanation. He must have anticipated such an outcome and ordered this skill of his to autonomously guard against any contact. Doubtless he sensed Gazel probing his surface thoughts, and ordered for his subliminal defense systems to act autonomously.

Kwaaaa ha ha ha! I very nearly fell victim to Rimuru's deceptions, myself. But it is his fault for seeming so thoughtless. Actually, upon closer examination, he does appear rather thoughtful. It is strange that the more one comes to know Rimuru, the more capable he seems.

And just as he expected, Gazel is taken aback. He is confused that he could easily read the surface thoughts, but not peer into the depths. Moreover, the surface of Rimuru's mind shows no signs of awareness that Gazel is reading his thoughts. No wonder the man was confused.

But this was Rimuru's trap. He knew that he could not win through prowess alone, and thus lured the other into a battle of wits. Now Gazel is totally unaware that he has been taken in by Rimuru's scheme.

A manga text contained this piece of wisdom: "To fool your enemies, first fool your friends." I was not fooled, of course, but Gazel is now beset by paranoia. Gazel must have recognized Rimuru as a slime who, though he appears easy to defeat, hides a great and powerful mind, and so released him and his companions. Thus, Rimuru passed safely through the dangers of the trial.

I am quite impressed by his skill.

Rimuru left the dwarven kingdom and rejoined his fellows at the entrance to the forest. Then he explained the series of events to them and concluded that, "It ended up pretty much as expected."

I knew it. He holds everything in the palm of his hand. What a formidable slime.

Strength cannot be measured solely by might, it seems. It is clear to me now that being able to manipulate others to join your side is another form of strength. Those he has bent to his will understand it as well. They all accept and agree with Rimuru's words. And now we have four dwarves among our group.

Just as Rimuru began to journey back to his forest dwelling, a young whelp charged from behind, lamenting, "How could you do this to me?!" I recognized him as the one Rimuru named Gobta.

Rimuru appeared to have forgotten him, but he hid this fact well, promising to take the lad to a business full of beautiful women in the future—yet I found this strange. The group had just been banished from the dwarven kingdom—could it be that Rimuru was simply lying? After all, I had wished to see such a place for myself, so we must address this situation. I suppose I shall have to trust Rimuru to come up with a plan to meet these beautiful women again by the time I have recovered my powers. The thought of this brings me excitement and joy.

◆ A FAMILIAR SCENT ◆

With the addition of the dwarves, Rimuru's village quickly became a bustling town. Garments of wild animal pelts are being assembled and distributed to all. And the dwarves taught their techniques to the hobgoblins. This is, I have no doubt, on Rimuru's orders.

Plans are also underway to cut down trees for the wood to construct new dwellings. How I lament that I am unable to take part in the excitement of progress, imprisoned as I am. Watching Gobta show off his pitiful skills made me itch to unleash my truly impressive tricks for all to admire.

Perhaps I should start thinking of a fantastic new finishing move to demonstrate when I am freed. With that in mind, I tore through more and more holy manga texts for inspiration.

Gwuaaaah?!

Suddenly, I felt a terrible loss of strength. To my dismay, I found that Rimuru hadn't learned his lesson from the last round of naming monsters, and was doing it again. I figuratively cradled my head in my hands at his seeming folly.

He already failed at this once. Why would he attempt it again...? And there is a truly daunting number of subjects awaiting him— five hundred in all. Again, I was forced to desperately brace myself against the outward flow of energy, when...

"Announcement. Total level of magical energy required to complete task has been successfully calculated. Your assistance is requested to ensure safety until the calculated value is reached."

What's this?!

Despite being locked inside the "Unlimited Imprisonment," the voice spoke directly to me! How is such a thing possible...?

"Answer: By using 'Words of the World,' successful communication of will is possible."

What nonsense is this?! I am sealed from the world, in an "alternate space," and yet this message can reach me from the outside...?

No, wait. Now I recall that in order to decipher Rimuru's knowledge, I made the process of sharing information smoother. I suppose that would make it possible to communicate in a way through information alone.

Because Rimuru has not learned how to read my knowledge, it is difficult to make my will known to him. On the other hand, it is possible for me to understand his desires. In other words, Rimuru is aware that I am reading his thoughts, and utilizing that to his ends— the devious runt.

I suppose I must offer some begrudging respect to the fact that he thought to make use of "Words of the World" as a means to express his will to me. That idea never occurred to me, and I had not thought it possible. Regardless of the means by which it came about, the fact remains that it happened.

Come to think of it, I glossed over something that I should be grappling with. What is this "safety until the calculated value is reached" nonsense? Surely it can't mean...

"Answer: The data collected during the previous experience has helped to improve the safety factor. The amount of magical energy available to use without risking the loss of maximum energy value is estimated to be..."

So that skill was collecting data during the last naming round? I don't know whether to call it overly cautious or just plain shrewd...

But enough of this! I believe you. I believe you already! My friend Rimuru has placed his trust in me. I must meet that level of trust. And so I steeled myself for the consequences and allowed him to borrow my energy.

As part of my promise to help, I expected to suffer some loss of power. Naming is a dangerous act, and there is no guarantee that the energy expended in the process will ever fully return. In fact, I have never heard of such an outcome... But my concerns turned out to be unnecessary. As Rimuru said, my magical energy stores returned to their full value.

As a consequence, however, he was once more forced into a three-day hibernation. Perhaps he should realize that his helpful personality ought to have limits. Common sense would tell him that naming five hundred individuals is simply madness. Strange as it is for me to lecture about common sense, Rimuru's recklessness makes even one such as me seem almost rational.

In fact, perhaps I was the rational type all along. Perhaps it is the views of the rest of the world that are excessively dramatized. I let these thoughts entertain me as I settled back to recover my energy.

With the naming finished and a large addition to the village population, Rimuru and his brain trust are considering moving the settlement. They are surveying the lands near the cave in which I was sealed. They've cut down a number of trees and opened up a sizable plot of land to use.

With Rimuru's new servants, and the evolution from goblins to hobgoblins, the group's physical abilities are much higher than before. The work proceeds quicker than I thought possible. As for Rimuru himself...he appears absorbed in developing various new techniques.

I am itching to test out some new spectacular moves of my own—how does he have all the luck?! Alas, all I can do is grumble and complain to myself.

Oh, it seems that he has discovered something. Are those...humans?

Four adventurers, under attack by a nest of giant ants. Rimuru being Rimuru, he has of course decided to help them.

No, wait! That's "Black Lightning"...

But my warning did not reach Rimuru. Despite his attempt to limit the power as much as possible, the Black Lightning spell possesses devastating force. The bolt lashed out faster than sound and obliterated its target. His skill exhibited a power and effectiveness many times that of ordinary magic; it had heavy shades of the dark lightning that is a feature of my Tempest Magic.

Lightning is powerful on its own—with my influence, it was bound to be a deadly assault—certainly not suited for such puny threats. That adventurer woman was sure to die, which seemed a pity. However, to my surprise, she was not caught in the blast; she had evaded one of the most powerful spells in existence.

Kwaaa ha ha ha! This is why I find humans so entertaining.

The woman could very well be the equal of Gazel the Dwarf King.

On short notice yet again, Rimuru has somehow managed to unexpectedly acquaint himself with an extraordinary figure. I continued my observation from within Rimuru, more convinced than ever that his exploits must be seen to be believed.

◆DEMON OF FLAMES◆

Meat sizzles as it cooks atop a rectangular sheet of metal.

I'd wondered what this sheet would be used for when Rimuru ordered it fashioned. Lacking any handles, it seemed rather too awkward to be a shield. And yet, to use such a thing for this! A most satisfying resolution to my curiosity.

This was my first encounter with the concept of "teppanyaki."

The adventurers Rimuru saved are now cooking strips of meat on the hot plate. I've never eaten it—in fact, I have no need to eat at all—but it does look quite delicious. Even Rimuru is looking at the humans with envy.

He doesn't seem to realize that his body is touching the burning plate, because it isn't hurting him. Apparently the slime has a resistance to heat.

"The individual named Rimuru Tempest possesses resistance to thermal fluctuation."

So my suspicions were correct. But how did he acquire "Thermal Fluctuation Resistance" from being stabbed in the back? I do not understand. It makes no sense.

I would understand "Piercing Resistance", but one does not gain resistance to thermal fluctuation from being stabbed. The woman with him hears his explanation and accepts it at face value, showing her own keen mind. Even I, sagacious as I am, cannot follow the thread of logic.

Apparently, the woman hails from the same world from which Rimuru came. But unlike Rimuru, she is a complete "otherworlder" who made the transition in her own flesh. She was summoned here, in fact. And yet, summoning requires a grand ritual with many arcane requirements, and from the way she describes it, she was summoned by a lone individual.

Whoever it is, that summoner must be mighty, indeed.

I had a hunch about this woman; the stench of trouble seemed to hang thick and heavy around her. And my hunch was soon proven correct. The summoner who brought her here is one of the very pillars of the world: the Demon Lord, Leon Cromwell. However, I do not know this Lord Leon.

Some neophyte who appeared during the time that I was sealed in that cave, perhaps? One as powerful as I am can maintain knowledge of the world's power balance, even from behind a magical seal. With my Unique Skill "Inquirer," I can collect information even while confined by the hero's "Unlimited Imprisonment" curse. But sadly, its powers are not infinite.

The best I could manage was an infrequent influx of limited amounts of information. Ultimately, there was little I could do about this. Even a top-level being such as a demon lord could not be monitored on an individual basis.

However, if he is a recent arrival to the world, then he surely cannot be that great of a threat. Compared to those frequent foes of mine, such as the giants and that lady vampire, a newborn demon lord is but a trifle.

That reminds me of the time I destroyed the city built by the vampiress. She was absolutely livid about it, and I think I might understand a sliver of that emotion now. The sight of Rimuru happily creating a town with his hobgoblin and dwarf companions made me realize that I, too, would be furious if it were all torn down. Perhaps my past actions were unkind. I might even consider an apology, if I should run into her again.

But back to the topic of the Demon Lord, Leon. The part that concerns me is his summoning of this woman. Gathering hardy warriors and expanding territory has been a common strategy of all demon lords throughout time. Like Rimuru, some of them named their subjects, though never with such abandon, considering the risk of permanent power loss.

Instead, the most common tactic is to conscript powerful demons to do their bidding. I dare say none of them ever thought of summoning otherworlders before. From what I recall, the crossing over infuses the body with a great rush of magicules. Most die in the process, but those who survive receive a great influx of power to their souls, which is then shaped according to their desires. Just as the woman named Shizu explained.

There is no difference between one who crosses out of coincidence, and one who crosses in a summons. The problem is that when one is summoned by means of a ritual, absolute obedience can be etched into the target's soul.

Naturally, that depends on the intention of the summoner. Assuming it is a success, the ritual is typically undertaken in the hopes of gaining a faithful and powerful servant. This is common to demon lords in particular, and yet I do not sense such compulsion from Shizu's soul.

If only I weren't behind this seal, I could analyze the situation in more detail... But if my suspicion is correct, then why would Demon Lord Leon have summoned her? If he was not seeking a follower, then what...

Hrm?!

I was shaken from my thoughts as I felt a tremendous aura bloom. It was coming from right next to Rimuru—from that Shizu woman. And this presence is burning with fierce flames—the presence of a higher-order flame spirit!

As I recognized this, Shizu tossed Rimuru aside.

No, she did not do so of her own volition. The spirit within her is controlling her.

What a surprising level of synchronization! And even in the face of such power, Shizu has the strength of will to defy the spirit's command. I suspect that she was able to hold back the inferno raging within her to allow Rimuru to escape.

The barbecue-eating adventurers have noticed something is wrong and come to investigate. They're all staring at Shizu in shock. One of them even says, "She is the Conqueror of Flames, Shizue Izawa. The greatest elementalist alive—she harbors Ifrit inside of her!!"

Ifrit is considered a threat to humanity, I believe. His menace has been categorized as a "calamity," or a "special A-Rank threat," or some such. In his current state, Rimuru will likely not fare well against a being whose power transcends that of even a greater demon.

What? Me?

Do not associate me with such puny beings. I am known as a "catastrophe": the greatest of all menaces. I am of the most powerful rank of all beings; Special S-Rank.

Kwaaaa ha ha ha! But despite my bold and haughty laughter, I am currently helpless. So I have no choice but to stay put and observe the battle for now.

◆INHERITED WILL◆

The battle has commenced.

I can see that Ifrit's status as a superior flame spirit is well earned. He wields fire with such skill that he might as well be made from fire himself. But the biggest shock was the trio of adventurers. Ifrit's each and every attack is on the level of a Fireball spell, yet they persist in the fight. It seems there is more to them than meets the eye. Rimuru must have determined the same, because he is leaving them to their own devices and focusing directly on Ifrit.

Rimuru's first attempt was a Water Blade—a poor choice. He wants to damage and neutralize Ifrit, which is wise, but Water Blade will do nothing. It merely fizzled and dissipated in an instant. It is a high-velocity spray of magicule-infused water, and thus possesses a severing effect. It is, therefore, a physical attack power.

But an elemental is a spiritual being, and is essentially immune to physical attacks. Adding spin might increase its power, but none of that will have any effect. Even if Ifrit hadn't evaporated the Water Blade with his heat, the attack itself would have done nothing.

Rimuru seems to have learned his lesson. I can feel him running through a rapid sequence of questions and answers inside his mind in search of a new plan. Conferring with one's own skill is a fascinating fighting style.

"Icicle Lance!" shouts the woman adventurer, while Rimuru considers his next move. Ahh, most impressive. That seems to have done the trick against Ifrit's body doubles. Sadly, even hundreds of such attacks would not finish the fight if they do not hit the main body…

"Here goes another…" That's Eren, I believe her name was? She should have known it was pointless, but she prepared another attack on Ifrit. Her companions are backing her up, placing all their hopes on this meager chance. Their boldness is admirable. Weak though they may be, I enjoy the attitude of these humans.

Suddenly, Rimuru launches into an unthinkable action. He actually rushes forward to protect Ifrit, taking the full brunt of Eren's Icicle Lance.

What is he thinking…?

But in the next moment, Rimuru shouts, "Icicle Shotgun!" and sprays out the Icicle Lance as countless blades. Even I was stunned at this development. Rimuru didn't know magic, as far as I was aware, so he must have acquired the skill in that moment.

The spray of ice wiped out all of the Ifrit copies. This is utter madness.

Ever since the beginning, when my efforts to interface had first been blocked, I knew that Rimuru's skills were highly suited to strategy and analysis. But after this, I must admit that his ability to analyze is at least the equal of my "Inquirer" skill, if not greater.

Simply stunning. He instantly analyzed the Icicle Lance and made it his own, even though his resources have been divided for the purposes of unlocking my prison. It is impossible not to be amazed.

He owns "Predator," which can devour anything, and some other, mystery skill that can analyze and reuse anything he absorbs…

Wait. Is it just me…or is this an extraordinarily convenient pairing of Unique Skills to have?! The synergistic capabilities of such a pair are unfathomable. I cannot imagine its limits.

Ifrit seems to have realized this as well. His expression has changed, and now he brings out his best attack to force a conclusion.

"Flare Circle…" The widest-area flame attack, perhaps to prevent his prey from escaping. But this was a poor choice. It won't work on Rimu—

"Oh, well…I had a good run."

What?! For whatever reason, Rimuru seems to believe that he's lost. *What nonsense!* I wish I could lecture him directly and remind him that he has Thermal Fluctuation Resistance.

If it were a concentrated, individual heat attack on Rimuru, he might have suffered damage. With enough accumulated damage, he might even be defeated. But Ifrit's choice of attack was dispersed over a wide range. An attack that an ordinary being might not survive, but which is meaningless with Rimuru's resistance.

This was the reason for your failure, Ifrit. And Rimuru eventually realized it.

"Sorry, Ifrit. Your flames are worthless against me," he said cockily.

A bold statement from one who was panicked just moments ago. That was when Ifrit made his fatal mistake. He let Rimuru's words rattle him, and paused. Rimuru seized on the opportunity, sealing the spirit's fate.

His Unique Skill, "Predator," ushered Ifrit into my little domain. I believe he was meant to be isolated in his own space, but I was able to probe outward with my thoughts and draw him closer. A forceful method, perhaps, but there is no other way that I can have this conversation partner.

"Storm...Dragon..."

Ifrit was shocked to see me. And now, I have gained a new playmate in my stomach prison.

◆THE UPHEAVAL BEGINS◆

While I played with Ifrit, Rimuru finished his farewells with the woman named Shizu. And in the time that I was looking away, he learned how to take human form.

How regrettable! Why must I divert my attention at such a pivotal moment? Perhaps my failing lies in my obsession with the game "shogi" that I found in Rimuru's memory and challenged Ifrit to...

"Please don't blame me for that, Storm Dragon..."
"I told you to call me Veldora."

Ifrit is a most stubborn fool. Apparently he was ill-suited to his bodily host, the woman named Shizue.

Not in terms of synchronization, but in terms of their nature, you might say. Ifrit worshipped the Demon Lord Leon. Shizue, meanwhile, held a deep-seated grudge against him.

Of course these two would not find common purpose. It was Shizue's skill that kept Ifrit's power bottled up. That speaks to the source of her weakness. She was unable to take full advantage of Ifrit's mighty powers. If she had been able to share her mind with the spirit's, her abilities would have far surpassed such limitations. And I doubt she would have reached the end of her life at this moment...

But because she was not more adept, Rimuru has now inherited Shizue's will and gained her appearance for his own. I suppose it was simply a matter of fate.

The three adventurers happily receive new test equipment from the dwarven smiths as they take their leave. It may seem heartless of them to rush off so promptly, but that is the way of things.

The world is a cruel place, and those with the strength to survive must set their sights on the future, not the past. One must have the strength to accept the life and death of others in order to survive. That applies to Rimuru as well.

He might seem to have gifted them the equipment out of generosity, but there is keen calculation behind it. It seems he has chosen this course of action out of a desire to build a friendly relationship with the humans.

I agree with his plan. Now that I have gained an interest in the ways of the human world, I do not oppose Rimuru in this. And now, his new, human form has endowed him with an array of new abilities. In all honesty, I am jealous. I wish to take human form and frolic amongst them, too.

I am a spiritual being, so I can take any form I wish...but I have never tested it until now. There's no telling if it will go well or not. I am unsure.

I suppose I can just leave the human transforming to Rimuru. That unfathomable slime is a creature of endless delights. No doubt he has some idea in mind.

I then sat back and waited, allowing my mind to run wild with possibilities.

To be reincarnated in Volume 3!

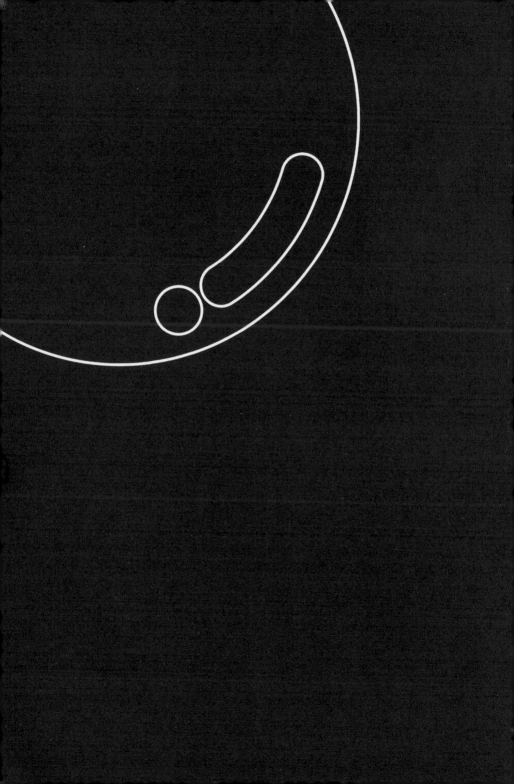

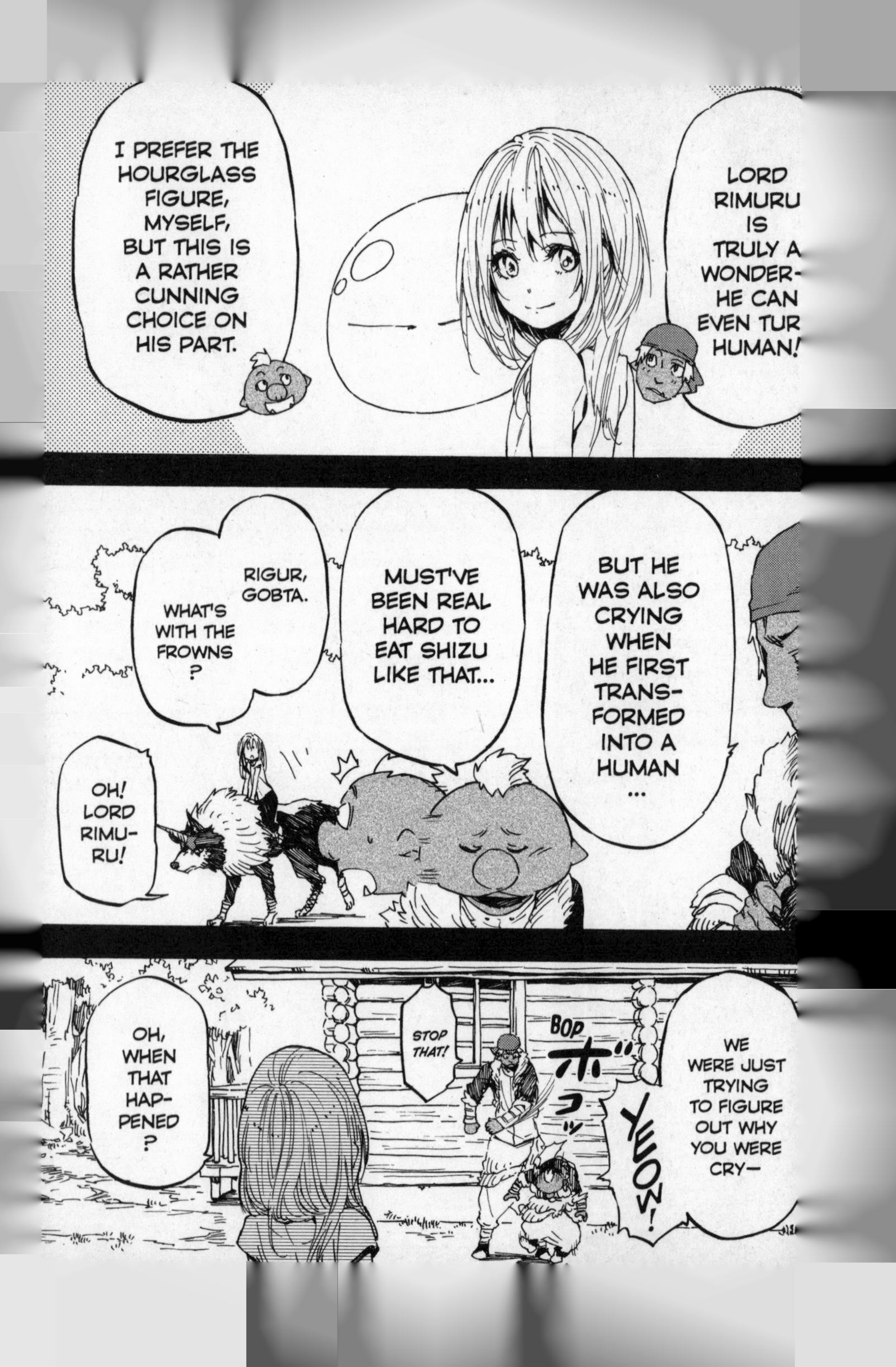
LORD RIMURU IS TRULY A WONDER- HE CAN EVEN TUR HUMAN!
I PREFER THE HOURGLASS FIGURE, MYSELF, BUT THIS IS A RATHER CUNNING CHOICE ON HIS PART.
BUT HE WAS ALSO CRYING WHEN HE FIRST TRANS-FORMED INTO A HUMAN...
MUST'VE BEEN REAL HARD TO EAT SHIZU LIKE THAT...
RIGUR, GOBTA.
WHAT'S WITH THE FROWNS?
OH! LORD RIMU-RU!
WE WERE JUST TRYING TO FIGURE OUT WHY YOU WERE CRY—
YEOW!
BOP
ボゴッ
STOP THAT!
OH, WHEN THAT HAP-PENED?

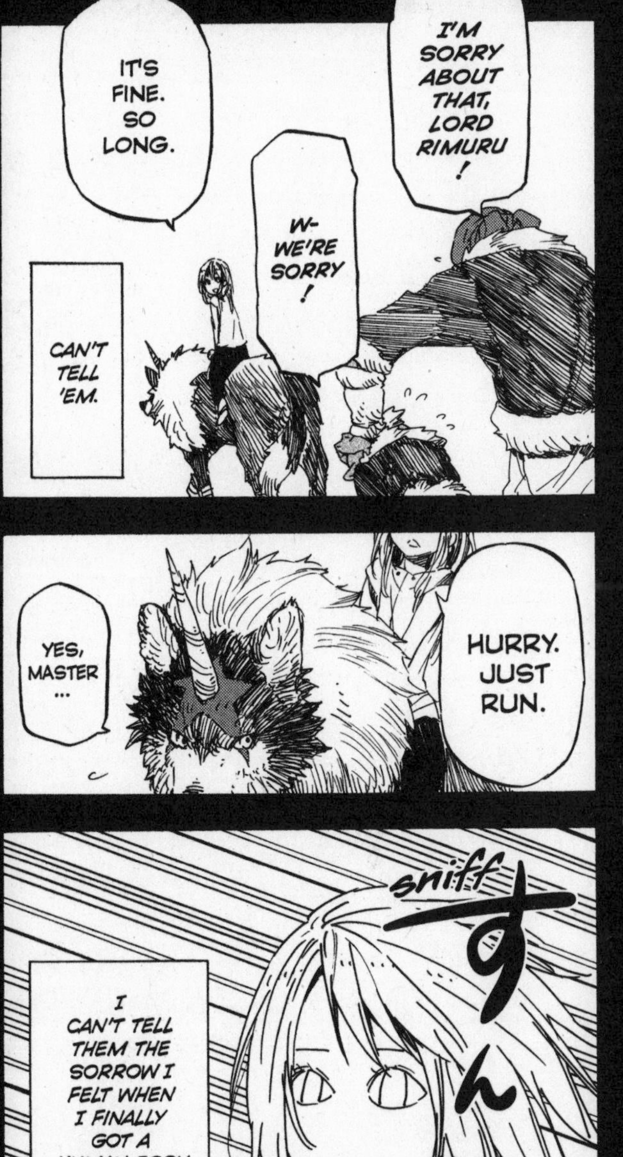
I'M SORRY ABOUT THAT, LORD RIMURU!
W-WE'RE SORRY!
IT'S FINE. SO LONG.
CAN'T TELL 'EM.
HURRY. JUST RUN.
YES, MASTER...
sniff
I CAN'T TELL THEM THE SORROW I FELT WHEN I FINALLY GOT A HUMAN BODY AGAIN, AND LEARNED MY LITTLE GUY DIDN'T COME WITH IT...

*Please take this as an "extra" little story.

LIST OF ACKNOWLEDGMENTS

AUTHOR:
Fuse-sensei

ASSISTANTS:
Taku Arao-san
Takuya Nishida-san
Muraichi-san
Hino-san
Daiki Haraguchi-san
Kiritani-sensei

Congrats on your series!!

Everyone at the editorial department

And You!!

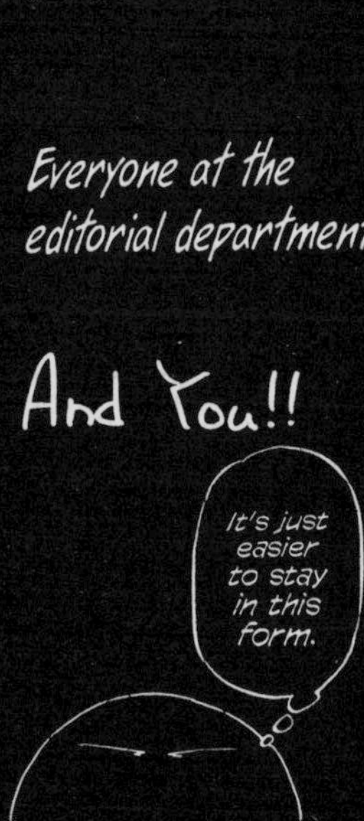
It's just easier to stay in this form.

AFTERWORD from the author, Fuse

Well, well, we've made it to the second volume of the manga adaptation of *That Time I Got Reincarnated as a Slime!* I was afraid of the reaction for Volume 1, given that it had no heroine, but I'm glad to see that most people accepted it. It seems like some folks read the manga, then were interested enough to check out the online and print versions of my original novels, which is just wonderful! As those who have read both can tell you, there are actually significant differences between the online and print editions. If those can be different despite being written by the same person (that would be me), then naturally the manga will also be different. There are alterations here and there to the sequence of events and other fine details. Don't think of them as a major issue, though. Just laugh off anything that seems odd.

"The online version is just a rough plot!!"

That's the excuse I often tell myself. Sure, the major movements should be the same, but it's fine for the little details to change! At our very first planning meeting, I told Kawakami-sensei that it's perfectly fine to draw things as you see fit, up to a point. We do have significant meetings before every chapter, however! The print version is the fundamental base we start with, but my hope as the creator is for the manga and novel to be distinctly different things. My role in the manga adaptation, as the story creator, is simply to ensure that there aren't jarring discrepancies. Not so that the stories are exactly the same, but perhaps to preserve the feel of the novel in a different medium. As long as you readers don't react like, "This is all wrong!" then I consider it a success. There will be enjoyable features of the manga version that aren't in the novels, so I just hope that I don't get in the way of that.

So that's my afterword for this volume. I really had a lot of fun rereading this book and spotting all of Kawakami-sensei's little original touches. It's too bad that I can't go overboard in gushing about the end result, or else it'll sound like I'm singing my own praises! Now that Rimuru has a human form at last, the story's about to get into the real meat of things. Please do check out the next volume of *That Time I Got Reincarnated as a Slime!!*

From character designer Mitz Vah-sensei

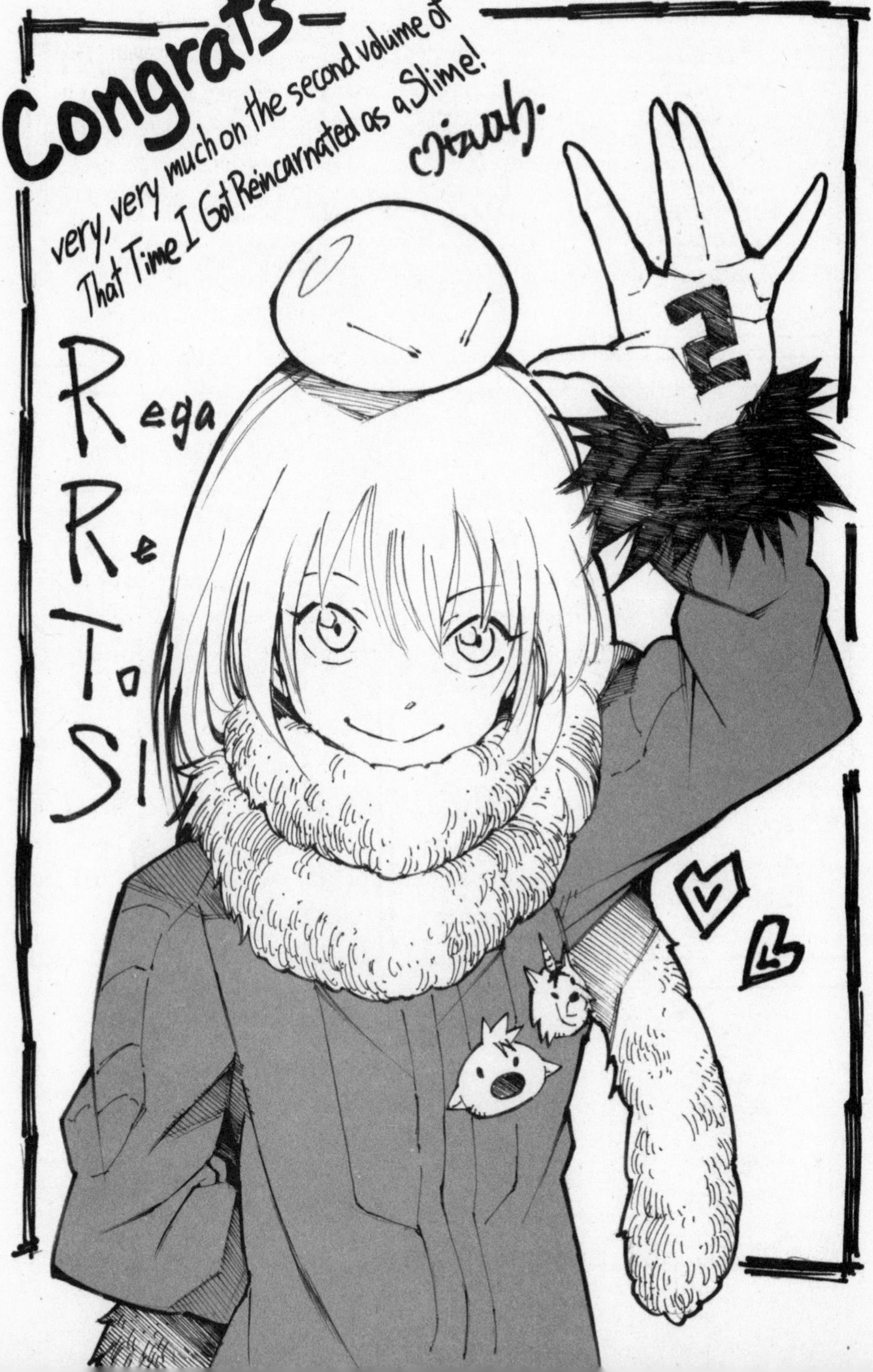
Congrats—
very, very much on the second volume of
That Time I Got Reincarnated as a Slime!
Mitz Vah.
Rega
Re
To
Sl
2

MEAL REPORT

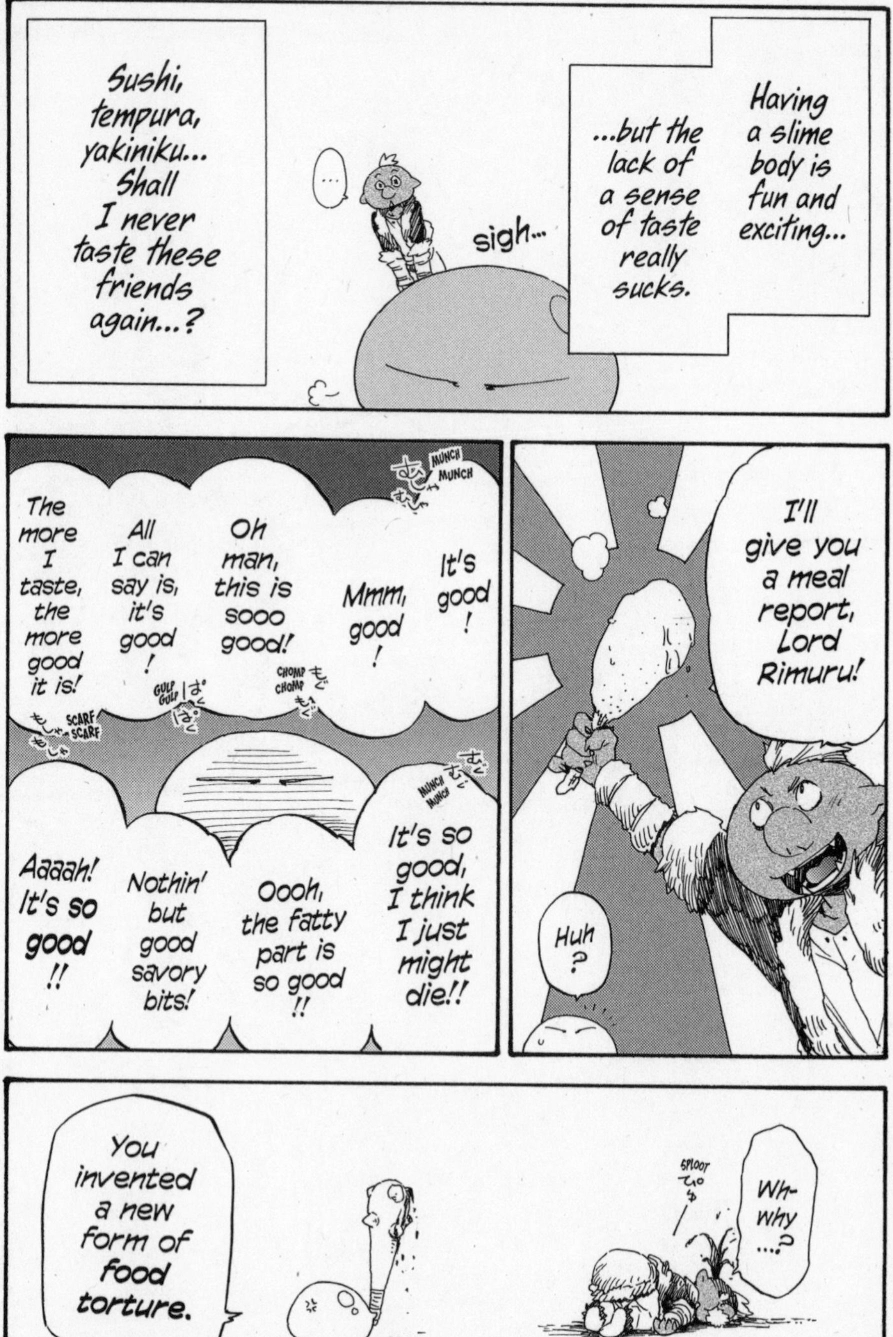

Having a slime body is fun and exciting...
...but the lack of a sense of taste really sucks.
sigh...
...
Sushi, tempura, yakiniku... Shall I never taste these friends again...?
I'll give you a meal report, Lord Rimuru!
Huh?
MUNCH MUNCH
It's good!
Mmm, good!
CHOMP CHOMP
Oh man, this is sooo good!
GULP GULP
All I can say is, it's good!
The more I taste, the more good it is!
SCARF SCARF
MUNCH MUNCH
It's so good, I think I just might die!!
Oooh, the fatty part is so good!!
Nothin' but good savory bits!
Aaaah! It's so good!!
Wh-why...?
SPLOOT
You invented a new form of food torture.

The "Three Brothers" theory.

TRANSLATION NOTES

"I'M NOT A BAD SLIME, YOU KNOW!"

page 61

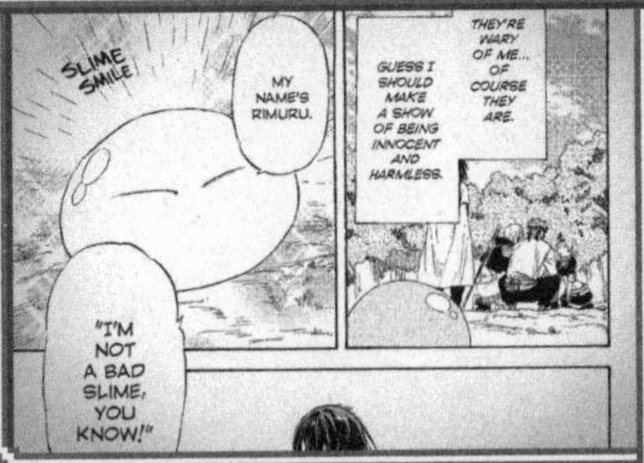
THEY'RE WARY OF ME... OF COURSE THEY ARE.
GUESS I SHOULD MAKE A SHOW OF BEING INNOCENT AND HARMLESS.
MY NAME'S RIMURU.
SLIME SMILE
"I'M NOT A BAD SLIME, YOU KNOW!"

Though it may not be obvious at first, the quotation marks in Rimuru's speech are a sign that he's quoting a line from something else—in this case, it's a well-known bit of dialogue from the *Dragon Quest* RPG series, in which the cute and largely harmless blue slimes are an iconic foe, the easiest in the game. Over time, it's become a bit of a staple for the games in the series to feature an NPC (non-player character, as opposed to a generic enemy) slime who can be conversed with, rather than fought. The first line of dialogue the slime says will always be something along the lines of, "Don't be mean to me. I'm not a bad slime, you know!"

YAKINIKU

page 97

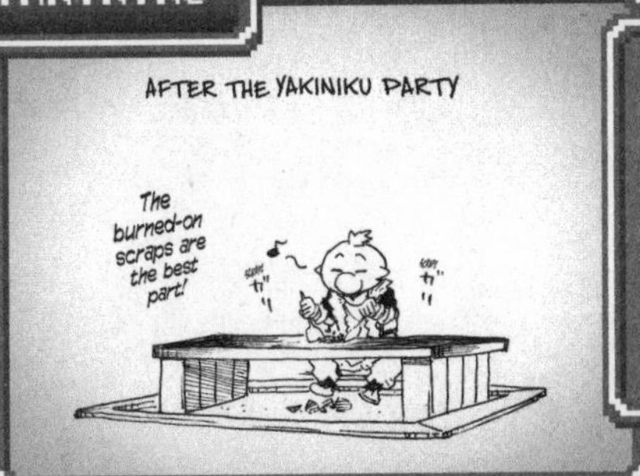
AFTER THE YAKINIKU PARTY
The burned-on scraps are the best part!

The Japanese name for grilled meat, which is often styled "Korean BBQ" in English. While yakiniku is usually done over a grilled surface, the *teppanyaki* style is also popular, as seen here: a flat metal surface like a griddle that cooks more evenly. Many Western *teppanyaki* restaurants feature cooks who put on flashy presentations, but the key to any good *yakiniku* party is placing the pieces of meat yourself and watching them cook until they're just right.

Three Brothers

page 18

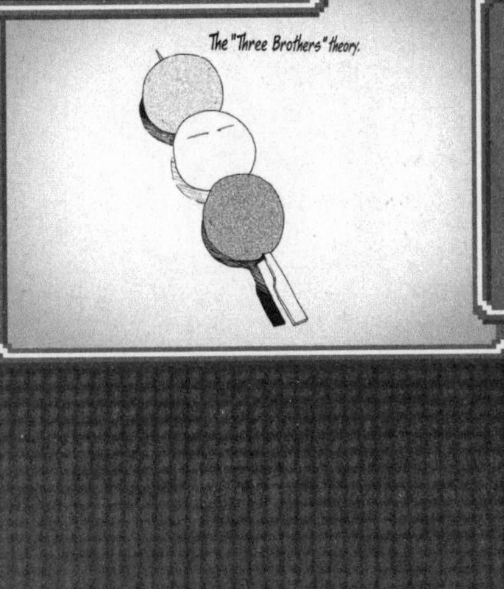
The "Three Brothers" theory.

A reference to the ultra-popular "Dango San-Kyôdai" song, meaning "Three Dango Brothers." Dango are little cakes made with rice flour, similar to mochi, and typically served on skewers. The Dango song originated on an NHK children's program and exploded in popularity around the turn of the millennium. The song's lyrics imagine that the three dango on the skewer are brothers with their own personalities. Appropriately, the song itself was a tango.

The Black Museum: The Ghost and the Lady

By Kazuhiro Fujita

Deep in Scotland Yard in London sits an evidence room dedicated to the greatest mysteries of British history. In this "Black Museum" sits a misshapen hunk of lead—two bullets fused together—the key to a wartime encounter between Florence Nightingale, the mother of modern nursing, and a supernatural Man in Grey. This story is unknown to most scholars of history, but a special guest of the museum will tell the tale of The Ghost and the Lady...

Praise for Kazuhiro Fujita's *Ushio and Tora*

"A charming revival that combines a classic look with modern depth and pacing... **Essential viewing both for curmudgeons and new fans alike.**" — Anime News Network

"**GREAT!** The first episode of Ushio and Tora captures the essence of '90s anime." — IGN

A new
series
from the
creator
of *Soul
Eater*, the
megahit
manga and
anime seen
on Toonami!

"Fun and lively...
a great start!"
-Adventures in
Poor Taste

FIRE FORCE

By Atsushi Ohkubo

The city of Tokyo is plagued by a deadly phenomenon: spontaneous human combustion! Luckily, a special team is there to quench the inferno: The Fire Force! The fire soldiers at Special Fire Cathedral 8 are about to get a unique addition. Enter Shinra, a boy who possesses the power to run at the speed of a rocket, leaving behind the famous "devil's footprints" (and destroying his shoes in the process). Can Shinra and his colleagues discover the source of this strange epidemic before the city burns to ashes?

KC KODANSHA COMICS

The award-winning manga about what happens inside you!

"Far more entertaining than it ought to be... what kid doesn't want to think that every time they sneeze a torpedo shoots out their nose?"
–Anime News Network

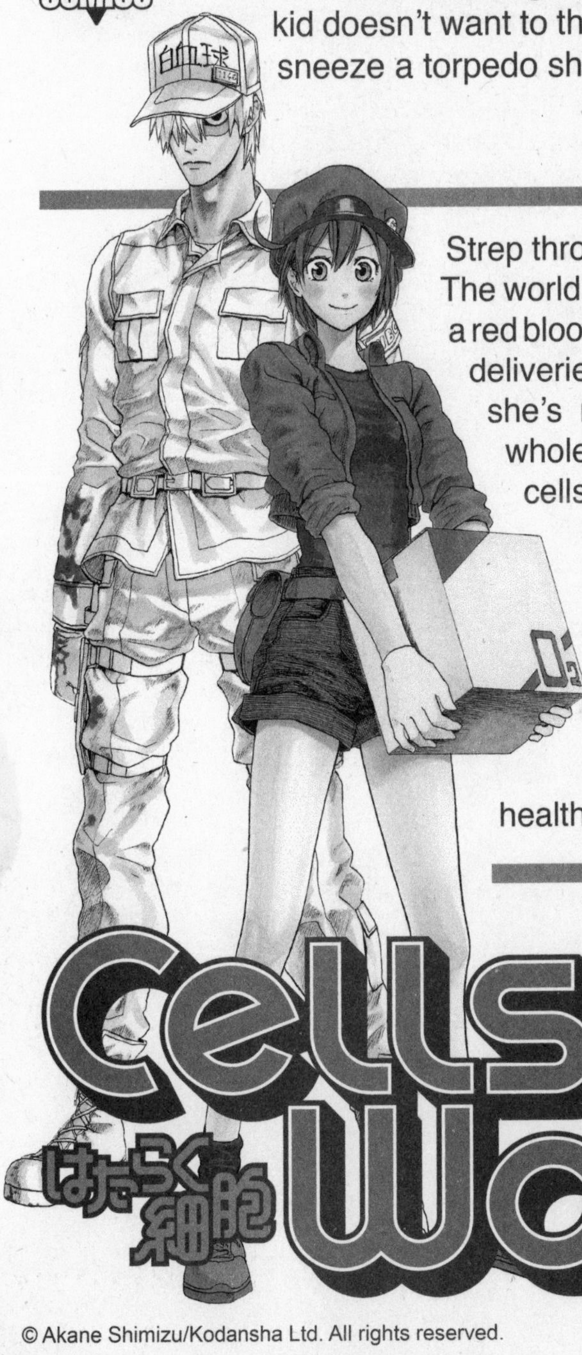

Strep throat! Hay fever! Influenza! The world is a dangerous place for a red blood cell just trying to get her deliveries finished. Fortunately, she's not alone...she's got a whole human body's worth of cells ready to help out! The mysterious white blood cells, the buff and brash killer T cells, even the cute little platelets—everyone's got to come together if they want to keep you healthy!

Cells at Work!

はたらく細胞

By Akane Shimizu

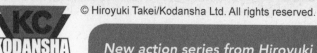

New action series from Hiroyuki Takei, creator of the classic shonen franchise Shaman King!

In medieval Japan, a bell hanging on the collar is a sign that a cat has a master. Norachiyo's bell hangs from his katana sheath, but he is nonetheless a stray — a ronin. This one-eyed cat samurai travels across a dishonest world, cutting through pretense and deception with his blade.

By

Hiroyuki Takei

Based on the critically acclaimed classic horror manga

The first new *Parasyte* manga in over 20 years!

NEO PARASYTE f

BY ASUMIKO NAKAMURA, EMA TOYAMA, MIKI RINNO, LALAKO KOJIMA, KAORI YUKI, BANKO KUZE, YUUKI OBATA, KASHIO, YUI KUROE, ASIA WATANABE, MIKIMAKI, HIKARU SURUGA, HAJIME SHINJO, RENJURO KINDAICHI, AND YURI NARUSHIMA

A collection of chilling new *Parasyte* stories from Japan's top shojo artists!

Parasites: shape-shifting aliens whose only purpose is to assimilate with and consume the human race... but do these monsters have a different side? A parasite becomes a prince to save his romance-obsessed female host from a dangerous stalker. Another hosts a cooking show, in which the real monsters are revealed. These and 13 more stories, from some of the greatest shojo manga artists alive today, together make up a chilling, funny, and entertaining tribute to one of manga's horror classics!

KC
KODANSHA
COMICS

Having lost his wife, high school teacher Kōhei Inuzuka is doing his best to raise his young daughter Tsumugi as a single father. He's pretty bad at cooking and doesn't have a huge appetite to begin with, but chance brings his little family together with one of his students, the lonely Kotori. The three of them are anything but comfortable in the kitchen, but the healing power of home cooking might just work on their grieving hearts.

"This season's number-one feel-good anime!" —Anime News Network

"A beautifully-drawn story about comfort food and family and grief. Recommended." —Otaku USA Magazine

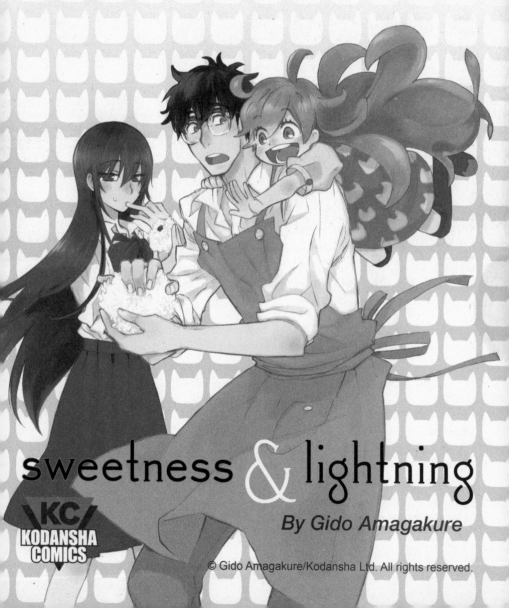

sweetness & lightning

By Gido Amagakure

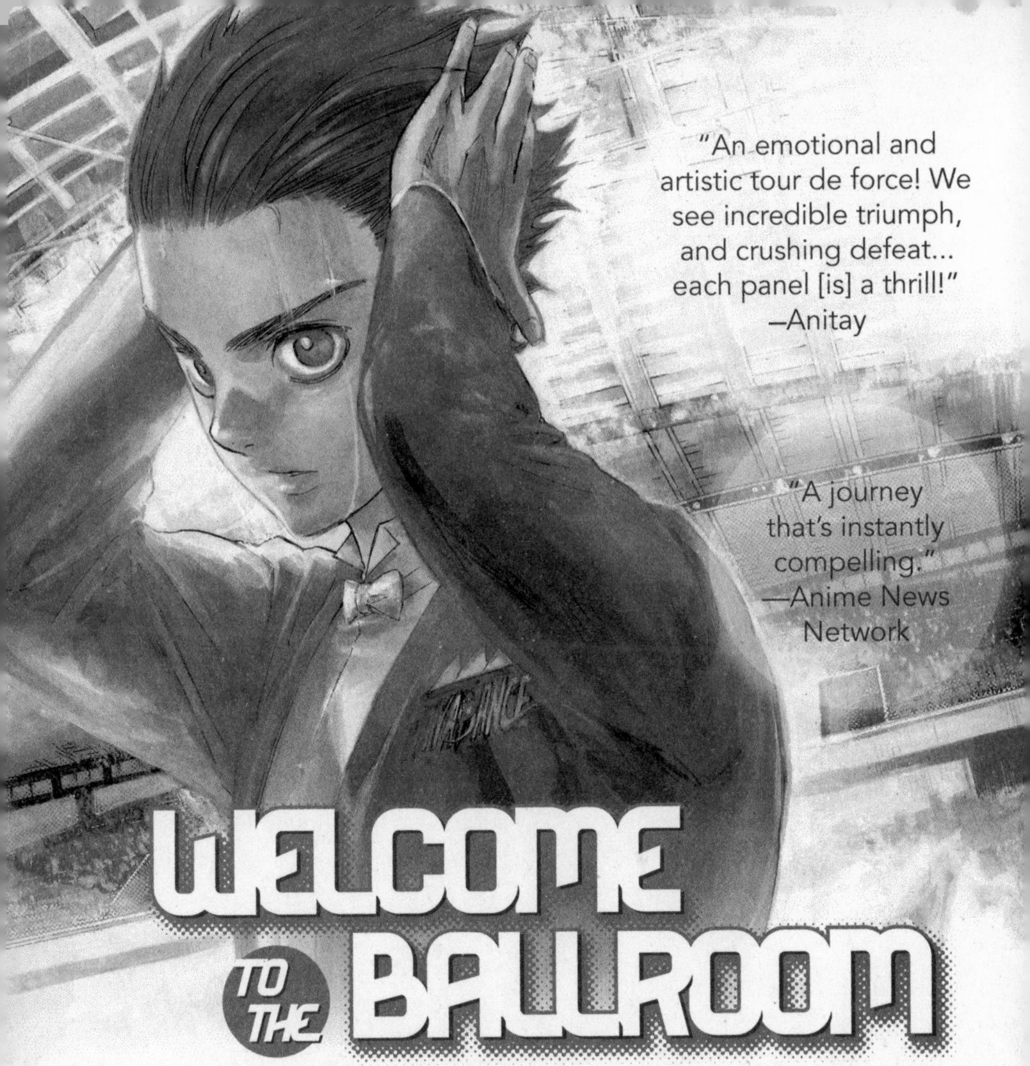

"An emotional and artistic tour de force! We see incredible triumph, and crushing defeat... each panel [is] a thrill!"
–Anitay

"A journey that's instantly compelling."
—Anime News Network

WELCOME TO THE BALLROOM

By Tomo Takeuchi

Feckless high school student Tatara Fujita wants to be good at something—anything. Unfortunately, he's about as average as a slouchy teen can be. The local bullies know this, and make it a habit to hit him up for cash, but all that changes when the debonair Kaname Sengoku sends them packing. Sengoku's not the neighborhood watch, though. He's a professional ballroom dancer. And once Tatara Fujita gets pulled into the world of ballroom, his life will never be the same.

KC KODANSHA COMICS

H·A·P·P·I·N·E·S·S

——ハピネス——

By Shuzo Oshimi

From the creator of _The Flowers of Evil_

Nothing interesting is happening in Makoto Ozaki's first year of high school. His life is a series of quiet humiliations: low-grade bullies, unreliable friends, and the constant frustration of his adolescent lust. But one night, a pale, thin girl knocks him to the ground in an alley and offers him a choice. Now everything is different. Daylight is searingly bright. Food tastes awful. And worse than anything is the terrible, consuming thirst...

Praise for Shuzo Oshimi's _The Flowers of Evil_

"A shockingly readable story that vividly—one might even say queasily—evokes the fear and confusion of discovering one's own sexuality. Recommended." —The Manga Critic

"A page-turning tale of sordid middle school blackmail." —Otaku USA Magazine

"A stunning new horror manga." —Third Eye Comics

KC
KODANSHA
COMICS

Japan's most powerful spirit medium delves into the ghost world's greatest mysteries!

Story by Kyo Shirodaira, famed author of mystery fiction and creator of *Spiral*, *Blast of Tempest*, and *The Record of a Fallen Vampire*.

Both touched by spirits called yôkai, Kotoko and Kurô have gained unique superhuman powers. But to gain her powers Kotoko has given up an eye and a leg, and Kurô's personal life is in shambles. So when Kotoko suggests they team up to deal with renegades from the spirit world, Kurô doesn't have many other choices, but Kotoko might just have a few ulterior motives...

IN/SPECTRE

STORY BY **KYO SHIRODAIRA**
ART BY **CHASHIBA KATASE**

That Time I Got Reincarnated as a Slime volume 2 is a work of fiction. Names, characters, places, and incidents are the products of the author's imagination or are used fictitiously. Any resemblance to actual events, locales, or persons, living or dead, is entirely coincidental.

A Kodansha Comics Trade Paperback Original.

Published in the United States by Kodansha Comics,
an imprint of Kodansha USA Publishing, LLC, New York.

Publication rights for this English edition arranged through Kodansha Ltd., Tokyo.

First published in Japan in 2016 by Kodansha Ltd., Tokyo, as *Tensei Shitara Suraimu Datta Ken* volume 2.

ISBN 978-1-63236-507-1

Printed in the United States of America.

www.kodanshacomics.com

9 8 7 6 5 4 3

Translation: Stephen Paul
Lettering: Evan Hayden
Editing: Ajani Oloye
Kodansha Comics edition cover design: Phil Balsman